A Comparative
Study of Romance

Studies in the Humanities
Literature—Politics—Society

Guy Mermier
General Editor

Vol. 46

PETER LANG
New York • Washington, D.C./Baltimore • Boston • Bern
Frankfurt am Main • Berlin • Brussels • Vienna • Canterbury

Frede Jensen

A Comparative
Study of Romance

PETER LANG
New York • Washington, D.C./Baltimore • Boston • Bern
Frankfurt am Main • Berlin • Brussels • Vienna • Canterbury

LIBRARY OF CONGRESS CATALOGING-IN-PUBLICATION DATA

Jensen, Frede.
A comparative study of romance / Frede Jensen.
p. cm. — (Studies in the humanities; vol. 46)
Includes bibliographical references and index.
1. Romance languages—Phonology. I. Title. II. Series: Studies
in the humanities (New York, N.Y.); vol. 46.
PC76.J46   440'.0415—dc21   98-48962
ISBN 0-8204-4253-4
ISSN 0742-6712

DIE DEUTSCHE BIBLIOTHEK-CIP-EINHEITSAUFNAHME

Jensen, Frede:
A comparative study of romance / Frede Jensen.
–New York; Washington, D.C./Baltimore; Boston; Bern;
Frankfurt am Main; Berlin; Brussels; Vienna; Canterbury: Lang.
(Studies in the humanities; Vol. 46)
ISBN 0-8204-4253-4

The paper in this book meets the guidelines for permanence and durability
of the Committee on Production Guidelines for Book Longevity
of the Council of Library Resources.

© 1999 Peter Lang Publishing, Inc., New York

Printed in the United States of America

CONTENTS

ACKNOWLEDGMENTS

I wish to thank the University of Colorado and specifically the Department of French and Italian for the financial assistance I have received. It gives me pleasure to acknowledge my indebtedness to my friend and former student Tobit Balsley for his help with the preparation of the word index. I wish to express my gratitude to Sandy Adler for the technical preparation of the manuscript.

Frede Jensen
Boulder, Colorado, September 1998

PREFACE

The present work falls into two parts. Part I consists of a fairly substantial introduction, serving the purpose of initiating the reader into the methods and goals of the philological discipline. Substantive sections of Part I focus on such topics as Vulgar Latin, the history of the discipline, the historical-comparative method, etymology, semantics and the earliest Romance texts.

Part II combines the sustained study of phonology in a philological perspective with a lexical dimension. The main objective is to provide the reader with insight into the workings of sound-laws and an understanding of the many factors that may interfere with regular developments: analogies of various kinds, learned Latinizing influence, borrowings from dialects or other languages.

For each sound change discussed, a concise and clearly formulated rule is offered, and each rule is illustrated by examples arranged in tables that allow for quick consultation. This is followed by a commentary which, first of all, discusses the development in more detail wherever called for. The cited examples are then examined, with due attention paid to such items as compliance with or deviation from the stated norm, prominent or unusual characteristics, borrowings and the lexical fragmentation.

Observations are based on the comparison of data drawn from a total of seven languages: Rumanian, Italian, Spanish, Portuguese, Catalan, Occitan (Provençal) and French. Words are not treated merely as elements in phonological equations, but are examined more globally wherever deemed appropriate and useful. This, however, is never allowed to distract from the main emphasis on phonology.

ABBREVIATIONS

AIS	:	K. Jaberg & J. Jud. *Sprach-und Sachatlas Italiens und der Südschweiz.* Zofingen, 1928–40
ALF	:	J. Gilliéron & E. Edmont. *Atlas linguistique de la France.* Paris, 1903–10
BDC	:	*Butlleti de Dialectologia Catalana*
Cat.	:	Catalan
CL	:	Classical Latin
DEI	:	C. Battisti & G. Alessio. *Dizionario etimologico italiano.* Firenze, 1950–57
E.	:	English
fem.	:	feminine
FEW	:	Wartburg, W. von. *Französisches etymologisches Wörterbuch.* Bonn-Leipzig-Berlin-Basel, 1928 ff
Fr.	:	French
Frk.	:	Frankish
G.	:	German
gen.	:	genitive
Gk.	:	Greek
Gmc	:	Germanic
inf.	:	infinitive
It.	:	Italian
Lat.	:	Latin
masc.	:	masculine
O	:	Old, as in OFr.: Old French
Occ.	:	Occitan
pers.	:	person
plur.	:	plural
Ptg.	:	Portuguese
REW	:	W. Meyer-Lübke. *Romanisches etymologisches Wörterbuch.* Heidelberg, 1935
RFE	:	*Revista de Filologia Española*

RLR	:	*Revue des Langues Romanes*
Rm.	:	Rumanian
RPh	:	*Romance Philology*
Sd.	:	Sardinian
Sp.	:	Spanish
VL	:	Vulgar Latin
Vox Rom.	:	*Vox Romanica*
ZRPh	:	*Zeitschrift für Romanische Philologie*

PHONETIC TRANSCRIPTIONS

Vowels

ę ǫ	:	open vowels, as *e* in Fr. *merci,* It. *merlo* and as *o* in Fr. *mort,* It. *morte*
ẹ ọ	:	close vowels, as *é* in Fr. *blé* and *e* in It. *vedo* and as *o* in Fr. *mot,* It. *voce*
ē ō	:	long vowels (with any vowel)
ĕ ŏ	:	short vowels (with any vowel)
ẽ õ	:	nasal vowels (with any vowel)
[ə]	:	weak *e,* Fr. *e féminin,* as *e* in Fr. *venir, devoir*
[ɛ] [ɔ]	:	same as ę ǫ
e o	:	same as ẹ ọ

Semi-Vowels

The sign ∩ placed under *i* and *u* indicates non-syllabic function. Occasionally, *y* and *w* are used for the same purpose.

i̭	:	as the initial *i* in It. *ieri,* as *i* in Fr. *pied,* Sp. *pie,* as *y* in E. *yes*
ṷ	:	as *u* in It. *uomo,* Sp. *hueso,* as *ou* in Fr. *oui,* as *w* in E. *wall*

Consonants

h	:	is not pronounced
ƀ	:	voiced bilabial fricative, as *b* in Sp. *haber* and *v* in Sp. *nieve*
[č]	:	= [tš]
đ	:	voiced interdental fricative, as *d* in Sp. *nada,* as *th* in E. *this*
ḍ	:	cacuminal *d* of Sardinian, as in Sd. *baḍḍe* (= It. *valle*)
[dž]	:	voiced prepalatal affricate, as *g* in It. *gente* and E. *gentle*
[ǧ]	:	= [dž]
g̶	:	voiced velar fricative, as *g* in Sp. *luego, hago*
[gʷ]	:	as *gu* in It. *guerra*
k', l', etc.	:	apostrophe marks palatalization of preceding consonant

k'	:	as *chi* in It. *chiave*, as *qui* in Sp. *quiero*
[*kʷ*]	:	as *qu* in It. *quello*, as *cu* in Sp. *cuatro*
l'	:	*l mouillé*, as *gli* in It. *figlio*, as *ll* in Sp. *caballo*
ñ	:	as *ñ* in Sp. *año*, as *gn* in It. *ogni*, Fr. *agneau*
[*ŋ*]	:	velar nasal, as *n* in It. *ancora*, E. *ink*
s	:	voiceless *s*, as *s* in It. *sera*, Fr. *sûr*
[*š*]	:	voiceless prepalatal fricative, as *ch* in Fr. *chanter*, Ptg. *chamar*, as *sh* in E. *shy*
z	:	voiced *s*, as *s* in Fr. *raison*, It. *chiesa*, E. *reason*
[*ž*]	:	voiced prepalatal fricative, as *j* in Fr. *jour*, as *g* in Fr. *genou*
[*θ*]	:	voiceless interdental fricative, as *c* in Sp. (Castilian) *cielo*, as *th* in E. *thin*
[*χ*]	:	voiceless velar fricative, as *j* in Sp. *ojo, caja*, as *ch* in G. *Nacht, Tochter*

Other Symbols

*	:	an asterisk introduces an undocumented, hypothetical form
[ ]	:	square brackets enclose phonetic transcriptions; they are used only with graphical signs that are foreign to the alphabet: [*tš*] but *ts;* they are not used with *i̯* or *u̯* or in combinations involving these diacritics nor with *ƀ, đ, ǥ d̦, n̦*
' '	:	single quotation marks are used with translations
>	:	becomes, is the source of
<	:	is derived from
=	:	is the same as, equals
p-	:	initial consonant (with any consonant)
-p-	:	intervocalic consonant (with any consonant)
-p	:	final consonant (with any consonant)
pr	:	marks a primary (Latin) cluster (with any group), as in *capra*

p'r	:	marks a secondary (Romance) cluster (with any group), as in *lĕpŏre > lep're*
ņ	:	unstable final *n* in Occitan
á	:	marks the stress when relevant to the discussion (with any vowel)
⌀	:	marks the disappearance of a sound

Phonetic Value of Certain Letters and Letter Combinations in Individual Romance Languages

Rumanian

e o	:	are always close
ă	:	= [ə], as in *roată, laudă,* close to the *e féminin* of French
î â	:	velar vowel between *i* and *u* in value, as in *înflă, câmp;* no exact equivalent in other Romance languages. Only *î* is used now; original distribution: *â* used internally, *î* in initial position and in *-rî* ending of verbs
ea oa	:	= *i̯a* and *u̯a,* as in *neagră, moară*
i, u	:	are not pronounced when final, as in *lupi, ochiu,* except where retained as support following mute and liquid cluster, as in *codri, templu*
c	:	= *k* before *a, o, u* or consonant, as in *cap, coamă, lăcustă, crede*
c	:	= [*tš*] before *e, i,* as in *vecin, măcelar*
ch	:	= *ki̯,* as in *chem*
g	:	= *g* before *a, o, u* or consonant, as in *găină, negoț, legumă, grîu*
g	:	= [*dž*] before *e, i,* as in *genuche, ginere*
gh	:	= *gi̯,* as in *ghindă*
ş	:	is voiceless
ţ	:	= [*š*], as in *uşă, cămaşă, şapte*
t	:	= *ts,* as in *Marţi, toţi, ţară*
z	:	= voiced *s,* as in *zbatere, dezlegà*

Italian

c	:	= *k* before *a, o, u* or consonant, as in *casa, colpo, cura, credere*
c	:	= [tš] or [š] before *e, i,* as in *cento, cima*
ch	:	= *k*, as in *chiaro, chiave*
g	:	= *g* before *a, o, u* or consonant, as in *gallo, gola, gusto, grande*
g	:	= [dž] before *e, i,* as in *gente, ginocchio*
gh	:	= *g*, as in *ghianda, ghiotto*
gli	:	= *l'*, as in *figlio, coniglio*
gn	:	= *ñ*, as in *bagno, vigna*
gu	:	= [gʷ], as in *guerra, guida, guancia*
qu	:	= [kʷ], as in *questo, quindici, quando*
s	:	mostly voiceless, occasionally voiced, as in *chiesa, francese, paese*

Spanish

e o	:	no distinction between open and close pronunciation
b d g	:	are occlusives when initial, fricatives (= ƀ đ ǥ) when intervocalic, as in *boca* vs. *lobo; dueño* vs. *vida; gota* vs. *seguro*
c	:	= *k* before *a, o, u* or consonant, as in *campo, comer, cura, creer*
c	:	= [θ] before *e, i* in Castilian (*s* in the dialects, *ts* in Old Spanish), as in *ceja, cinco*
ç	:	= *ts* in Old Spanish, as in *plaça, cabeça*
ch	:	= [tš], as in *chino, charla, chupar*
cu	:	= [kʷ] before *a*, as in *cuatro, cuando*
g	:	= *g* before *a, o, u* or consonant, as in *gallina, gordo, gustar, granja*
g	:	= [ž] before *e, i* in Old Spanish, = [χ] (jota) after 1500, as in *gente, gitano*
gu	:	= *g* or *ǥ* before *e, i,* as in *guerra, Miguel, seguir*

gu	:	= [gʷ] before *a*, as in *guardar, lengua*
j	:	= [χ], as in *jefe, jabón, jugo*
ll	:	= *l'*, as in *caballo, hallar*
qu	:	= *k* before *e, i*, as in *quedar, quince*
s	:	is always voiceless in the modern language, as in *sin, casa, muros*
x (OSp.)	:	= [š], as in OSp. *xabon, xugo*
z	:	= [θ] in Castilian, as in *zaguán, zorra*

Portuguese

ãe	:	= *ãi̯*, as in *cães*
am	:	*ã(m)*, as in *campo*; = *ãu̯* when final, as in OPtg. *cam*
an	:	= *ã(n)*, as in *andar, ante*
ão	:	*ãu̯*, as in *mão, pão, cão*
em	:	= *ẽ(m)*, as in *tempo*; = [ẽi̯] when final, as in *bem, quem*
õe	:	= *õi̯*, as in *razões*
om	:	= [ɔ̃], as in *bom*, OPtg. *razom*
ou	:	= *ǫ*, as in *touro, outro*
um	:	= *ũ*, as in *um, comum*
c	:	= *k* before *a, o, u* or consonant, as in *cabo, colar, custo, claro*
c	:	= *s* (*ts* in OPtg.) before *e, i*, as in *cego, cima*
ç	:	= *s*, as in *paço, oração*
ch	:	=[š], as in *chamar, cheirar, chumbo*
g	:	= *g* before *a, o, u* or consonant, as in *galo, gordo, gula, grão*
g	:	= [ž] ([dž] in OPtg.) before *e, i*, as in *gente, girar*
gu	:	= *g* before *e, i*, as in *guerra, guisa*
gu	:	= [gʷ] before *a*, as in *guardar, guarnecer*
l	:	= *ll* in E. *hill* (velar *l*) if final or in end-of-syllable position, as in *mal, caldo*; elsewhere, as in *lobo, gola*, = *l* of Fr. *loup*, Sp. *lobo*, It. *lupo*

lh	:	= *l'*, as in *palha, trabalho*
nh	:	= *ñ*, as in *banho, vinho*
qu	:	= *k* before *e, i*, as in *querer, quinto*
qu	:	= [*kʷ*] before *a*, as in *quatro, quando*
s	:	voiceless when initial or postconsonantal, as in *sim, farsa, observar*
s	:	= [*š*] when final or before a voiceless consonant, as in *homens, aspirar, as pedras*
s	:	= *z* (voiced *s*) when followed by a voiced consonant, as in *asno, os brasileiros*
x	:	= [*š*], as in *caixa, baixar;* less often = *s*, as in *exclusivo*
z	:	= voiced *s*, as in *fazer, cozer*

Catalan

The weak vowels *a* and *e* are reduced to [*∂*], and weak *o* tends toward *u* in pronunciation.

b d g	:	pronounced *ƀ, đ, ǥ* in intervocalic position, as in *nebot, madur, pregar*
c	:	= *k* before *a, o, u* or consonant, as in *cantar, coa, cup, créixer*
c	:	= *s* (OCat. *ts*) before *e, i*, as in *cel, ciutat*
ç	:	= *s*, as in *lliçó, llençol*
g	:	= *g* before *a, o, u* or consonant, as in *gall, gola, llegum, greu;* trend toward fricative pronunciation if intervocalic
g	:	= [*dž*] or [*ž*] before *e, i*, as in *gent, genoll*
gu	:	= *g* before *e, i*, as in *guerra, guiar*
gu	:	= [*gʷ*] before *a: guanyar, guarnir*
ix	:	see *x*
j	:	= [*dž*] or [*ž*], as in *joc, jutge*
l	:	= *l* in Ptg. *mal* and *ll* in E. *hill* (velar *l*) when final and in end-of-syllable position: *palma, moltons, hostal, cel,* elsewhere = *l* in It. *dolore*, Fr. *douleur*.
ll	:	= *l'*, as in *llebre, lluna, gallina, sella*

ny	:	= ñ, as in *any, senyor, muntanya*
qu	:	= *k* before *e, i*, as in *que, quinze*
qu	:	= [kʷ] before *a*, as in *quatre, quan*
s	:	= *z* (voiced *s*) intervocalically, as in *rosa, ase,* and before a voiced consonant, as in *esdevingué, esma;* it is voiceless elsewhere: *saber, escuma*
tg	:	= [dž], as in *viatge, jutge*
tx	:	= [tš], as in *casutxa, butxaca*
x, ix	:	= [š], as in *angoixa, deixar, dexelament*
z	:	= voiced *s*, as in *zona*

Occitan

c	:	= *k* before *a, o, u* or consonant, as in *cabra, cor, cura, creire*
c	:	= *ts* before *e, i*, as in *cel, cima*
ch	:	= [tš], as in *chantar, chap*
g	:	= *g* before *a, o, u* or consonant, as in *gabar, gostar, agulha, glai*
g	:	= [dž] before *e, i*, as in *genolh, gitar*
gu	:	= *g*, as in *guerra, guidar*
lh	:	= *l'*, as in *palha, olh*
nh	:	= ñ, as in *banh, franher*
qu	:	= *k*, as in *quan, quatre*

French

Vowels are nasalized when followed by a final nasal or by nasal plus consonant, as in *vin, vendre* vs. *pleine*

aim, ain	:	= [ɛ̃], as in *faim, pain*
am an	:	= [ã], as in *chambre, grand*
eim ein	:	= [ɛ̃], as in *Reims, plein*
em en	:	= [ã], as in *semble, souvent*
in	:	= [ɛ̃], as in *vin, raisin*

om on	:	= [ɔ̃], as in *nom, don*
un	:	= [œ̃], as in *un, brun*
c	:	= *k* before *a, o, u* or consonant, as in *cap, corps, curé, croire*
c	:	= *s* (*ts* in OFr.), as in *cerf, cent, cime*
ç	:	= *s*, as in *façon;* = *ts* in OFr., as in *ço*
ch	:	= [š] ([tš] in OFr.), as in *chanter, chef*
[ə]	:	= *e féminin*, as *e* in *venir, arbre*
eu œu	:	= [ø], as in *bœufs* or = [œ] as in *bœuf*
g	:	= *g* before *a, o, u* or consonant, as in *galet, goutte, légume, grand*
g	:	= [ž] ([dž] in OFr.), as in *gent, argile*
gn, ign, ingn	:	= *ñ*, as in *montagne, vigne*
gu	:	= *g*, as in *guerre*
h	:	Lat. *h*, as in *homme, herbe*, not pronounced, Gmc. *h*, as in *héron, haie*, pronounced until the seventeenth century
il ill	:	= *i̯* (*l'* in OFr.), as in *travail, travailler*
j	:	= [ž] ([dž] in OFr.), as in *jour, jeune*
œu	:	see *eu*
oi	:	= *u̯a* (*ói̯* in OFr.), as in *toile, moi*
ou	:	= *u*, as in *trouver*
qu	:	= *k*, as in *quand, quel*
s	:	voiceless, as in *soir, sage, verser, statue*
s	:	voiced when intervocalic or before a voiced consonant, as in *rose, braiser, svelte*
u	:	= [y], as in *mur, dur*
ue	:	= *u̯é*, as in OFr. *buef, uef, uevre*
z	:	= *ts*, as in OFr. *lez, braz*

PART I.

PROBLEMS, METHODS AND EARLY HISTORY

1. The number of Romance languages is traditionally set at ten: Rumanian, Dalmatian (extinct), Italian, Rhaeto-Romance (also known as Ladin), Sardinian, Occitan (or Provençal), French, Catalan, Spanish and Portuguese. Other divisions have been suggested; Franco-Provençal and Gascon are accorded language status by some scholars, and Italian is dialectally fragmented to the point where some linguists prefer to break it up into two or more separate linguistic zones. One such scheme is proposed by Togeby, who arrives at a list of fifteen languages by adding Franco-Provençal and Gascon, by splitting off Friulan as an independent type of Rhaeto-Romance and by dividing up the Italian domain into southern Italian, Tuscan and northern Italian (*Studia Neophilologica, 34* (1962), 319).

2. *Rumanian* is the only language of the Balkan-Romance group to have survived. Its history is quite complex. Modern Rumanian is derived from the Latin spoken in the Roman province of Dacia and is thus often referred to as Daco-Rumanian, but the earliest written text is from the sixteenth century, leaving a puzzling hiatus of some thirteen centuries during which time nothing is known about how or where a Romance linguistic tradition was kept alive in what is now Rumania. Traditionally, Rumanian is divided into four main dialects. *Daco-Rumanian (dacoromîn)* is the official language of Rumania and is also spoken in the former Soviet republic of Moldavia. The two are sometimes kept separate: *Muntenian* (or *Wallachian),* underlying the literary language, is based on the language of Bucharest, while *Moldavian,* which uses the Cyrillic alphabet, has managed to achieve some measure of linguistic independence for a variety of historico-political reasons. *Macedo-Rumanian* or *Arumanian (aromîn)* is spoken in northern Greece, parts of Albania and southwestern Yugoslavia. *Megleno-Rumanian* or *Meglenitic (meglenoromîn)* is spoken in the vicinity of the Greek city of Salonika. *Istro-Rumanian (istroromîn),* a dialect heavily influenced by Slavic, is spoken on the Istrian Peninsula not far from Rijeka by a couple of thousand speakers. Rumanian is spoken by some eighteen million people in Rumania, three million people in Moldavia and some 350,000 elsewhere. Demographic figures quoted here and in the following paragraphs are only approximations.

3. Many of the innovations that are characteristic of Rumanian are common to all four major dialect groups, and some of these features are of such great importance that they cannot have evolved separately in the scattered regions now occupied by these dialects. Most scholars seem to

agree that Proto-Rumanian must have developed in a relatively unified area where interdialectal communication was unhampered. Several arguments speak in favor of seeking the cradle of the Rumanian language South of the Danube: frequent correspondences with developments in Albanian, the Bulgarian aspect of the early Slavic elements in Rumanian, the absence of Germanic borrowings (Alexandru Philippide: *Originea Romînilor,* Iaşi, 1925–28; M. Friedwagner: "Über die Sprache und Heimat der Rumänen in ihrer Frühzeit," *ZRPh, 54* (1934), 641–715).

4. *Dalmatian,* which is now extinct, was spoken on the Adriatic coast and on the offshore islands, its most important centers being the town of Ragusa (now Dubrovnik) and the island of Veglia (now Krk). Structurally, it bridges the gap between Daco- and Italo-Romance in a number of ways. Two dialects are usually singled out: *Ragusan* and *Vegliote.* A strong Venetian influence in the region spelled the end of the Dalmatian language, unable to hold its own against a closely related and more prestigious dialect. Relatively independent of Venice, the town of Ragusa was, however, able to retain its language until the fifteenth century, while the last speaker of the Vegliote dialect, Antonio Udina called Burber, died in 1898.

5. Our knowledge of Dalmatian is rather limited; direct sources consist of documentary material from Dalmatian archives, specifically from Ragusa, and information gathered by the Italian scholar Bartoli through personal interrogation of the last speaker of Vegliote, who still knew the language at the end of the nineteenth century. The material collected by Bartoli, mostly in the form of narratives, was published in the book *Das Dalmatische* (Vienna, 1906). This, incidentally, ranks as an early example of the use in linguistics of a native informant. Indirect sources are the elements preserved in the toponymy and the material incorporated as substratum features in Venetian and Croatian. Bartoli considers Dalmatian to be related to the dialects of southern Italy. Though most scholars rally to this opinion, Clemente Merlo detects a closer affinity with the Rhaeto-Romance dialects to the North.

6. The term *Rhaeto-Romance* or *Ladin* designates a group of dialects spoken in certain Alpine regions of eastern Switzerland and northeastern Italy. The term Rhaetian, preferred in German scholarship (G. *Rätoromanisch,* Fr. *rhéto-roman),* is somewhat misleading since the eastern sections did not belong to the Roman province of Rhaetia, but to that of Noricum. Favored by Italian scholars is the word *ladino* representing a continuation of *latīnu.* Introduced by J. Th. Haller in 1832, this term has its own share of ambiguity since it also serves to designate the Judeo-Spanish dialects of

the Balkans. In recent years, the label *Alpine Romance* (G. *Alpen-romanisch)* has been suggested by Gamillscheg and Fr. Schürr.

7. The Rhaeto-Romance dialect group is divided into three major types spoken in certain western, central and eastern Alpine regions that are no longer geographically contiguous. The western group, located between Gotthard and Ortler in the Swiss *canton* of Graubünden (Fr. Grisons, It. Grigioni), is known as *Romantsch* (§32) or *Romantsch Grischun.* In 1938, Romantsch was declared the fourth national language of Switzerland. It counts a number of related dialects, foremost of which are *Surselvan* and *Sutselvan* and *Upper* and *Lower Engadine.* The central section, located in the valleys of the Italian Tirol in the area around Cortina d'Ampezzo and Bolzano, extends from Ortler to the Dolomites, the center being the Sella massif. Far more important is the dialect spoken in the eastern section. Named *Friulan* for the Italian province of Friul, it has as its major center the town of Udine, but in the nineteenth century, it was still spoken in the city of Trieste. The number of Rhaeto-Romance speakers is fairly limited: some 40,000 in Graubünden, some 12,000 in the Italian Tirol and some 400,000 in Friul.

8. The Rhaeto-Romance dialects do not have many shared features, and it is characteristic that the areas where they are spoken never formed a cohesive administrative unit. Ascoli, author of the first significant work on this dialect group (*Saggi ladini, Archivio glottologico italiano,* vol. I, 1873), and the Austrian scholar Theodor Gartner (*Rätoromanische Grammatik,* 1883) consider the three dialectal regions of Ladin to be remnants of an earlier linguistic unity, while Battisti and Salvioni voice opposition to the notion of a Ladin linguistic independence. Tagliavini, though recognizing the unity of the Rhaeto-Romance family, demonstrates its close links to the dialects of northern Italy. The Rhaeto-Romance dialect group is under constant pressure from German and Italian, which bodes ill for its long-term survival.

9. *Sardinian,* spoken only on the island of Sardinia by about a million people, has not developed a written language. In its linguistic development, it is the most conservative of all the Romance languages. It comprises three dialectal zones: *logudorese,* spoken in the center of the island (Logudoro), *campidanese,* spoken in the South (Campidano), and *gallurese* and *sassarese,* spoken in the North (Gallura and Sassari). *Logudorese* is the oldest and most authentic of the Sardinian dialects, its location in the center of the island having protected it to some extent against foreign encroachments. *Campidanese* is heavily influenced by southern Italian dialects, and *gallurese* and *sassarese* are the least "Sardinian" of the dialects, sharing many

characteristics with the Italian dialects of southern Corsica. *Nuorese* is a subvariety of *logudorese*. Four centuries of Spanish domination has left a certain impact on Sardinia. Alghero, a small town of some 25,000 inhabitants which for a time was annexed to Aragon, has still kept its Catalan dialect.

10. *Italian* is spoken on the Italian mainland, in Sicily, Sardinia and Corsica, in the Swiss *canton* of Ticino and a few other areas. Speakers of Italian number some sixty million in Italy and a quarter million in Switzerland. Italian unity was not achieved until 1870 while, prior to that date, the country was broken up into independent states and cities, which accounts for the profound dialectal fragmentation of the country. The northern Italian dialects comprise the *Gallo-Italic* group, *Venetian* and *Istrian*. The Gallo-Italic group, located North and West of the La Spezia-Rimini line, is made up of the dialects of Piemonte, Lombardy (including Ticino), Liguria and Emilia-Romagna. The term Gallo-Italic was coined by Biondelli (*Saggi sui dialetti gallo-italici,* Milano, 1853–56) and adopted by Ascoli. The Venetian dialects cover the provinces of Venice, Padua, Verona, Vicenza, etc. (for details, see Tagliavini, p. 341). Istrian dialects are spoken above all at Rovigno d'Istria. The central dialects comprise Tuscan and the dialects of le Marche, Umbria and Rome. Subdivisions of the important Tuscan group are the dialects of Florence, Siena, Pisa, Lucca, Pistoia and Arezzo, and Corsican is a Tuscan import. The Southern dialects are *abruzzese, pugliese, Neapolitan, calabrese* and *Sicilian.*

11. In a country where a number of regional standards are still in everyday use, and whose political unification is of a fairly recent date, selecting a form of Italian that was most appropriate for literary usage was the subject of a prolonged debate. As the medium of an important school of poetry in the thirteenth century, Sicilian acquires the status of a written language early on, but from the time of Dante, Petrarch and Boccaccio, the dialect of Florence came to be firmly established as the literary language.

12. *Occitan* or *Provençal* is spoken in the South of France in an area that comprises the Provence, Languedoc, Gascony, Auvergne and Limousin regions. Starting at the Gironde, the linguistic border separating Occitan from French runs North of the Massif Central and joins the Rhône river between Valence and Vienne. In the Middle Ages, when it was customary to designate a Romance language by means of the affirmative particle it made use of, Provençal was often referred to as *langue d'oc* as opposed to French, which was called *langue d'oïl* (Occ. *oc* and OFr. *oïl* = Fr. *oui).* Before the term Provençal came into use, other designations existed such as *lingua romana* (§69) and *limousin. Provensal* or *proensal,* an adjectival

derivation from *Provensa* or *Proensa* < *Provĩncia (Narbonensis),* is a misnomer since, strictly speaking, it refers only to the Provence area, and it is being increasingly replaced by the more accurate term Occitan. The dialectal subdivisions of Occitan comprise four major groups: *langue-docien, gascon, provençal* and *nord-occitan.* Of these, the *nord-occitan* group can further be divided into *limousin, auvergnat* and *vivaro-alpin,* the latter representing the dialects of the Dauphiné and the Haute-Provence area.

13. Documented early as a literary-administrative vehicle, Occitan flourished as the medium of the twelfth-thirteenth century troubadour poetry, but following the 1213 Albigensian crusade, French has ever increasingly replaced it as the official written language. Vigorous revival efforts pursued by the nineteenth-century Félibriges, a society founded on May 21, 1854 and counting such poets as Mistral, Aubanel and Roumanille, failed to create a universally accepted modern written language in spite of undeniable literary accomplishments. Very few native speakers of Occitan are left, and none of these is monolingual, which makes the long-term future of Occitan uncertain.

14. *French* has a significant diffusion, is spoken by some fifty-one million people in France, some four million Walloons in Belgium, over a million Swiss in the *Suisse romande* area, some six million Canadians, mostly living in the province of Québec, and many French speakers live in present or former colonies, such as Guadeloupe, Martinique, Haiti, Réunion, North Africa (Maghreb), etc. The dialectal situation prevalent in French today differs considerably from that of the Medieval period. Toward the end of the fifteenth century, *francien,* the dialect of Paris and the Ile-de-France region, gains supremacy over all other dialects as the sole literary medium, and with the Villers-Cotterets edict of 1539, it even replaces Latin as the official administrative language. It acquires a certain universality, playing a very important role as the leading international language of diplomacy for a long period of time. As a result of the ever-increasing role of *francien*, the spoken dialects are soon reduced to the status of *patois;* in fact, in a vast area surrounding Paris, the dialects have vanished. French is spoken not only in the North, but has also to a very large extent superseded the Occitan dialects of the South.

15. The northern dialects are *normand, picard* and *wallon,* the latter spoken in southern Belgium and adjacent regions in France. A variety of *normand,* known as *anglo-normand,* evolved in England after the Norman conquest in 1066 and remained alive for some three hundred years, exerting a considerable influence on the development of English. In the East, we

find the *champenois* and *lorrain* dialects while, in the Southwest, *poitevin, angevin* and *saintongeais* are spoken. The Walloon dialect has managed to remain relatively independent of Parisian influence, presumably because of its Belgian affiliation. The linguistic unification that characterizes the French domain is the result of a very high degree of political and cultural centralization. This contrasts sharply with the linguistic fragmentation of Italian. In the Middle Ages, *francien* was not the only literary medium in *langue d'oïl* territory; a written literature had developed in *wallon, picard, anglo-normand,* etc., but from the fifteenth century on, only Parisian French was used for writing purposes.

16. *Franco-Provençal*—the term was coined by Ascoli—designates a group of dialects spoken in an area of southeastern France (Dauphiné, Savoie), in the French-speaking region of Switzerland (Neuchâtel, Fribourg, Vaud) and in the Italian valley of Aosta. The old republic of Geneva abandoned its dialect, replacing it by French. Duraffour is of the opinion that these dialects are simply French, while Helmut Stimm takes them to be dialects that were originally French, but which later received an Occitan overlay. It is, however, not a recent mixture, and the group has its own historical independence.

17. *Catalan,* with some six million speakers, is the language of Catalonia as well as of a narrow coastal strip, encompassing the cities of Valencia and Alicante, which was seized from the Arabs and populated by Catalans. It is further spoken on the Balearic Islands and, across the Pyrenees, in the Roussillon region, which was annexed to France in 1659, and it is the official language of the tiny republic of Andorra. As an administrative language, it was brought to Sardinia, where it is still spoken in the town of Alghero. An important literary-administrative medium in the Middle Ages, it is now struggling for survival against the more prestigious Castilian. The language is fairly unified, but two major dialect groups are usually distinguished: eastern Catalan (with Barcelona) and western Catalan (with Lérida). Eastern Catalan is spoken in the ancient territory of the Marca Hispánica, founded by Charlemagne to protect his empire against the Arabs, while the western dialect has evolved in an area dominated by the diocese of Urgel. The river Llobregat forms the dividing line between the two groups.

18. *Spanish* is based on the Castilian dialect, hence the designation *lengua castellana* as the equivalent of *lengua española.* Originally the humble dialect of the Cantabrian tribesmen who had never surrendered to the Arabs, it spread southward with the *Reconquista,* which accounts for the fact that the dialectal differences on the Iberian Peninsula occur in an

East-West distribution and not in a North-South. The discovery of the New World and the important role Spain played in its colonization extended the domain of the Spanish language over a vast territory that far surpasses that of any other Romance idiom. It is the official language not only of Spain, but also of numerous republics in Central and South America and the Caribbean. Spanish is the native language of some 280 million people, of whom the largest number is to be found in Mexico. Millions of Hispanophones live in the USA; the figure is estimated at fourteen million, but could be much higher.

19. The most important dialect is *Castilian,* spoken in the center of the Peninsula, and which, as mentioned, has become the national language. *Leonese* extends between Castilian and the Galician-Portuguese dialectal area to the West; subvarieties are *Asturian* to the North and *mirandés* spoken at Miranda do Douro in the Tras-Os-Montes province of Portugal. *Aragonese* is located geographically between Castilian and Catalan. Propelled on a southward course with the *Reconquista,* Castilian replaced the Mozárabe dialects it came into contact with. The Romance-speaking people living under Arabic domination, but who were able to preserve their Christian religion, are referred to as *Mozárabes* < Arab. *mustarab* 'Arabicized'. Their numbers were particularly large in the southern part of the Peninsula. Most of them continued to speak Romance, but were probably bilingual, and it was through them that many Arabic elements came into the Hispanic lexicon. The only colonial dialect to have developed specific phonological characteristics is *Andalusian,* spoken in the South. Many early settlers in Latin America were from Andalusia, which accounts for the presence of Andalusian phonological features in the Spanish of the New World.

20. To this dialectal picture may be added *Judeo-Spanish,* the Romance language spoken by the Sephardic Jews settled in the Balkans and in Asia Minor, who were descendants of the Jews that were expelled from Spain in 1492. Completely cut off from contact with metropolitan Spanish, their language has preserved many archaic features: initial *f* is kept, [š] does not evolve to [χ] and the distinction between voiceless and voiced *s* is maintained. The number of Sephardic Jews has dwindled following Nazi persecutions: of the 53,000 registered in Salonika in 1940, only 1,800 were left in 1948, and of the 2,000 on the island of Corfu only 170. Many live in Morocco and in New York City. The total number of Sephardic Jews is estimated at some 200,000 speakers.

21. *Portuguese* is spoken in Portugal, including the Azores and the island of Madeira, in Galicia, in Brazil and in many former colonies in

Africa and elsewhere. There are some ten and a half million Portuguese speakers in Portugal, some 150 million in Brazil and several hundred thousand elsewhere. In addition, no other Romance language has given rise to such a large number of Creole formations as Portuguese: Indo-Portuguese Creole dialects in Goa, Sino-Portuguese dialects in Macao and other Creole varieties in Cape Verde and Guinea. The *Reconquista* feature characteristic of Spanish repeats itself for Portuguese, which means that the dialectal articulation is of scant importance. The subdivisions that are traditionally suggested are northern and southern Portuguese, the Portuguese spoken in the Azores and on the island of Madeira and Galician. The official language is based on the dialect of Lisbon. There is also a Judeo-Portuguese language, spoken by descendants of Jews who had been expelled from Portugal, and who had settled in the Netherlands, but their numbers are insignificant.

22. In its early stages, Galician is very close to northern Portuguese; the term that serves to designate this archaic period is Galician-Portuguese, and it is in this language that the early thirteenth-century troubadour-inspired poets expressed themselves. Historically, Portuguese is an extension of Galician, but a differentiation between the two languages began or intensified during the second half of the fourteenth century. The cradle of the Portuguese language is in the North and not in the center of the country, which was liberated much later from Moslem domination.

CLASSIFICATION OF THE ROMANCE LANGUAGES

23. A definitive linguistic classification of the Romance languages is not possible, as Schuchardt had noted as early as 1870 in a speech on the issue: "I wanted to talk about the classification of the Romance languages, and I have had to talk against it" (Schuchardt-Brevier, p. 166). Much ink has been spilled on discussions of this elusive problem. Generally speaking *Romania*, a linguistic term designating the Latin- or Romance-speaking world (§31), is divided up into three major areas: western Romance, eastern Romance and Sardinian, the first two of these comprising subdivisions as in the following presentation proposed by Lausberg (*Romanische Sprachwissenschaft*, Berlin, 1963, vol. I, 39), who bases his classification not on the modern national languages, but on the broader dialectal make-up of the Romance area:

I. Western Romance
  A. Gallo-Romance (Occitan, Franco-Provençal, French)
  B. Rhaeto-Romance
  C. Northern Italian
  D. Ibero-Romance (Catalan, Spanish, Portuguese)
II. Eastern Romance
  A. Central and southern Italian
  B. Dalmatian
  C. Rumanian
III. Sardinian

24. The division of the Romance languages into a western and an eastern group is already proposed by Diez, the dividing line between the two extending approximately from La Spezia to Rimini and thus cutting the linguistic map of Italy in two. The northern dialects are Gallo-Romance in nature and are thus aligned with the West, while the central-southern dialects, including the national language, belong to the eastern section.

25. The schematic division between East and West is based principally on a couple of linguistic criteria: the treatment of the intervocalic voiceless occlusives *p*, *t*, *k* and of final *s*. In the West, intervocalic *p*, *t*, *k* are voiced to *b*, *d*, *g* and may suffer further weakening, a process traditionally referred to as lenition, and final s is kept whereas, in the East, *p*, *t*, *k* are retained unchanged, and final *s* is dropped. For the lenition feature, see §261, and for final *s*, see §§356–357. The opposition between East and West as regards the treatment of final *s* is difficult to account for. Von Wartburg relates it to social differences in the pronunciation of Latin: the East, settled by the lower classes, drops *s*, while the West, Romanized by the bourgeoisie, retains it. This explanation has not met with general acceptance, however, and is specifically contradicted by the following considerations: in Pompeii, where popular graffiti abound, final *s* is stable, and Sardinia keeps *s*, although this remote island was mostly settled by humble shepherds. The treatment of final *s* was of the utmost importance for the declension system since, where *s* dropped, the formal difference between the singular and the plural was obliterated. Lat. *mūru–mūros*, continued regularly in Sp. *muro–muros*, would in Italian have evolved to *muro–*muro*. Italian solves the problem posed by this unacceptable morphological confusion by substituting the nominative plural *muri* < Lat. *mūrī* for the accusative. For the impact of the loss of *s* on the Italian conjugation system, see §357. Sardinian occupies an intermediate position between East and West: with the

East it retains the voiceless occlusives *p*, *t*, *k*, and with the West it keeps final *s*.

26. Diez, who does not include dialects in his scheme, distinguishes six Romance languages, which he divides into an eastern group (Italian and Wallachian, i.e., Rumanian), a western group (Portuguese and Spanish) and a northwestern section (French and Provençal). Dalmatian was unknown at the time. Meyer-Lübke draws up a list of nine: Rumanian, Dalmatian, Rhaeto-Romance, Italian, Sardinian, Provençal, French, Spanish and Portuguese. He accords independent status to Dalmatian, Sardinian and Rhaeto-Romance, but he does not include Franco-Provençal in his list. Like Diez, he still treats Catalan as dependent on Provençal. Tagliavini proposes a division in which Dalmatian bridges the gap between Balkan-Romance and Italo-Romance, and with Catalan playing a similar role between Gallo-Romance and Ibero-Romance. He does not suggest a complete *continuum*, however, inasmuch as no link is perceived between Italo-Romance and Gallo-Romance in the schematic chart he offers in his *Origini* (p. 298). The terms Balkan-Romance, Italo-Romance, Gallo-Romance and Ibero-Romance have great methodological value, but cannot be used without restrictions. Provençal, for example, is much closer to Catalan than it is to French, which could justify the creation of a separate Occitano-Romance label. Gascon forms a transition between French and Spanish, and it is particularly difficult to fit Sardinian into any classification scheme.

27. One of the most debated classification problems is that of establishing the linguistic position of Catalan, and at the same time it is, at least in an introductory volume, one of the most instructive. It was thought for a while that Catalan was an Occitan dialect brought to Spain in connection with the *Reconquista*. This theory, first formulated by Morel Fatio in 1888, was adopted by Meyer-Lübke as well as by Bourciez, who describes Catalan as "très voisin du provençal dont il n'est que le prolongement géographique" (*Eléments*, p. 288). In 1925, however, Meyer-Lübke recognized the independent status of Catalan. In his book *Das Katalanische. Seine Stellung zum Spanischen und Provenzalischen* (Heidelberg: Winter, 1925), he links Catalan to the Gallo-Romance sphere, while Menéndez Pidal (*Orígenes del español*, Madrid, 1926) defends its Ibero-Romance affiliation, as do also Saroïhandy, Morf and Amado Alonso. A. Griera (*Gramàtica historica del Català antic*, Barcelona, 1931, p. 3), like Bourciez, declares Catalan Gallo-Romance and a territorial continuation of Provençal, though containing a number of lexical items that separate it from Provençal. Another Catalan scholar, J. Corominas (*El que s'ha de saber de la llengua catalana*, Palma de Mallorca, 1954, p. 20), is likewise convinced that Cata-

lan is originally Gallo-Romance; it is Ibero-Romance only because of its geographical position, but its linguistic characteristics are Gallo-Romance in nature.

28. Meyer-Lübke ties Catalan to the Gallo-Romance domain on the basis of a series of phonological correspondences between Catalan and Provençal, which set the two apart from Spanish. Spanish diphthongizes tonic *ĕ* and *ŏ*, Catalan and Occitan do not: *sĕpte, mŏla* > Sp. *siete, muela* vs. Cat., Occ. *set, mola*. No diphthongization of these same vowels occurs in Spanish if they are followed by a palatal, while Catalan and Occitan display a conditioned diphthongization here: *pĕctu, fŏlia* > Sp. *pecho, hoja* vs. Cat. *pit, fulla* (with the vowels *i* and *u* stemming from a reduction of **iei* and **uei*) and Occ. *pieit, piech, fuelha, fuolha*. The final vowels *-o* and *-e* are kept in Spanish, but are eliminated in Catalan and Occitan: *caballu, parte* > Sp. *caballo, parte* vs. Cat. *cavall, part* and Occ. *caval, part*. Initial *f* is aspirated and subsequently dropped from pronunciation in Spanish, while Catalan and Occitan retain it: *formīca* > Sp. *hormiga* vs. Cat., Occ. *formiga*. The internal *cl* and *lị* clusters evolve via [*ž*] to [*χ*] in Spanish, but yield a palatal *l* in Catalan and Occitan: *vĕclu, palea* > Sp. *viejo, paja* vs. Cat. *vell, palla* and Occ. *v(i)elh, palha*. Conversely, there are a set of phonological developments which Catalan shares with Spanish, but which Occitan does not participate in. Spanish and Catalan palatalize *nn* to *n'*, while Occitan simplifies the geminate to *n*: *annu* > Sp. *año*, Cat. *any* vs. Occ. *an*. The diphthong *au* monophthongizes to *o* in Spanish and Catalan, but is retained in Occitan: *causa, auru* > Sp. *cosa, oro*, Cat. *cosa, or* vs. Occ. *cauza, aur*. The *ū* of Latin is retained as *u* in Spanish and Catalan, while Occitan fronts it to [*y*]: *mūru* > Sp. *muro*, Cat. *mur* vs. Occ. *mur* [*myr*]. In morphology, Occitan like Old French has a two-case declension system, Spanish and Catalan do not.

29. When defining the position of Catalan, Meyer-Lübke erred in not extending his comparisons to the Spanish dialects and to Galician and Portuguese. The diphthongization of tonic *ĕ* and *ŏ* before a palatal is not restricted to Catalan and Gallo-Romance, but occurs also in Leonese: *ŏcto* > *vuecho*; *nŏcte* > *nueche*; *ŏcŭlu* > *uueyo*, as well as in Aragonese: *pŏdiu* > *puio* (with *ui* from **uei*), and Aragonese drops final *e*: *mŏnte* > *mont*; *cŏrte* > *cort*. Even more enlightening is the fate of initial *f*, which is kept everywhere on the Iberian Peninsula except in Castilian. With his intervention in the debate, Menéndez Pidal has demonstrated the existence of a linguistic continuity extending from Catalonia via Aragón and León to Galicia and Portugal. Viewed in this light, Catalan is an Ibero-Romance language, which later develops close historical, cultural and linguistic ties

to Occitan, accounting for the numerous correspondences between the two languages. This is not to say, however, that Menéndez Pidal's intervention in the debate has effectively closed the chapter on the Gallo-Romance character of Catalan. In his study of the Romance lexicon (*Romanische Sprachgeographie*, München: C.H. Beck, pp. 201–205), Rohlfs culls an impressive word list showing that Catalan is far more closely related to Provençal than to Castilian in its vocabulary. He concludes from his examination that Catalan in its old (primitive) substance is essentially a *dépendance* of Provençal. A similar view is expressed by H. Kuen (*ZRPh, 66* (1950), 108ff.), who theorizes that Catalan formed a linguistic community with Provençal until the ninth century. This was followed by a period of relative independence, while Castilian influence is a more recent occurrence. Assuming the role of a *lengua-puente* bridging the gap between Ibero-Romance and Gallo-Romance, Catalan is defined by Amado Alonso as an *habla hispánica pirenaica* 'a Pyrenean Hispanic idiom' (A. Alonso: "La subagrupación románica del catalán," in *Estudos*, pp. 11–100).

30. Based on two important factors, the initial degree of romanization and the subsequent adherence to the Latin tradition, a new classification scheme is proposed by Amado Alonso. Italian, originally an eastern language, later finds itself aligned with the western group because of its strong attachment to the Latin tradition. Amado Alonso has thus constructed a *Romania continua* scheme, from which he excludes Rumanian because of its isolation and French because of the profound changes that have marked its evolution. Vidos, though expressing approval of the *Romania continua* concept, opposes the exclusion of Rumanian and French from it, suggesting instead a continuity that covers all areas of Romania. Dalmatian forms the transition between East and West, between Balkan-Romance and Italo-Romance, and Rhaeto-Romance is the link to Italo-Romance, whereupon the northern Italian dialects take us to Occitan, while Catalan bridges the gap between Occitan and Hispano-Romance. French need not be excluded in spite of its radical evolution, the transition from Occitan being assured by Franco-Provençal.

LATIN, ROMAN, ROMANIA

31. As a linguistic term, *Latin* refers originally to the dialect spoken only in the city of Rome, although formally it is derived from the name of the surrounding province *Latium*. Used as an ethnic term, it designates the *Latini*, the inhabitants of Latium. The language is mostly referred to as *latina lingua* 'Latin language', rarely as *romana lingua* 'Roman language'.

The adjective *romanus* 'Roman', drawn from the toponym *Roma* 'Rome', serves as a political designation in such expressions as *populus romanus* 'the Roman people' and *civis romanus* 'Roman citizen'. The inhabitants of Rome referred to themselves as *Romani* as opposed to the Latini at first, later also in opposition to other peoples of the empire (Etruscans, Greeks, etc.). With the edict of Caracalla in 212, which granted citizenship to all inhabitants of the Roman Empire, the term came to be applied to all the varied populations living within the confines of Roman political power. Linguistically, *Romani* denoted the speakers of Latin living within the Empire, and the Empire itself came to be known as *Romania*, modeled on such formations as *Gallia* 'Gaul' and *Graecia* 'Greece'. With the collapse of the Roman Empire, the word *Romania* was retained as a linguistic term, designating the linguistic and cultural unity of the Latin-speaking world. We may take note of the continuation of Lat. *romanus* in Balkan-Romance: Rumanians call themselves *Români*, and the terms designating their language are *limbă româna* or *limbă românească*.

32. A more popular adjective than *romanus* is the sporadically used *romanicus*, attested in Cato. It may perhaps be equated with 'in the Roman way', but examples are so few in number that the exact shade of meaning of this form escapes us. The corresponding adverb is *romanice*, which is chiefly encountered with verbs for 'to speak': *parabolare, fabulare, loquī*, the meaning being 'to speak in the vernacular, to speak Romance'. It is this adverb that is continued as *romantsch*, name of the Rhaeto-Romance dialect of the Swiss *canton* of Graubünden (§7), and other reflexes are OFr. *romanz* and Occ. *romans*. In a further semantic evolution, *romanz* came to designate any composition written in the vernacular as opposed to Latin. OFr. *romanz*, felt to be a noun in the nominative case, soon yielded an accusative *romant*, which was reduced to *roman* 'novel' in the sixteenth century. The earlier form *romant* is still seen in the designation *Suisse romande*, applied to the French-speaking area of Switzerland.

VULGAR LATIN

33. The Romance languages are descended from Vulgar Latin. They are not, however, as Vossler is quick to point out, daughters of Vulgar Latin, but are themselves Vulgar Latin. They are the Latin of today (K. Vossler: *Einführung ins Vulgärlatein*, München, 1954, p. 48). The word *Vulgar* is derived from the expression *sermo vulgaris* 'popular speech, the speech of the people'. Though traditionally accepted for lack of a more accurate label, the term is a misnomer inasmuch as it could be construed as referring solely

to the language of the lower classes when, in fact, it is the language spoken by all members of the Roman society. Many scholars explain the difference between Classical and Vulgar Latin in terms of an opposition between written and spoken (Meyer-Lübke, Bourciez, Menéndez Pidal, Vossler, etc.), while others propose a definition focusing on the social aspect of the problem, Vulgar Latin being conceived of as the language of the middle class, different not only from the refined language of the cultivated strata of society, but also from the coarse and careless speech of the lower classes (Grandgent). Vulgar Latin was never the homogeneous language it was thought to be by the Neogrammarians, but as long as the Roman Empire conserved its political and administrative centralizing role, it had a relative unity that cannot be denied. Inscriptions, which come from all corners of the empire, offer no documentation for specific regional developments. Inscriptions from Rome comprise examples of the addition of a prosthetic *i* before initial *s* plus consonant: *iscola < schŏla*, this in spite of the fact that Italian hardly uses this feature at all as opposed to conditions in Hispano- and Gallo-Romance (§257).

34. Vulgar Latin precedes Classical Latin in time, since the spoken language always develops earlier than the written; the literary language draws its nourishment from the spoken and could not have evolved without it. Classical Latin develops from the third century B.C. and reaches its culmination during the first century B.C. and the first century A.D., while Vulgar Latin lasts until approximately 600 A.D. Vulgar Latin is not to be considered inferior to the literary language; it is a living language open to innovations, while Classical Latin is congealed in its artificiality, remaining virtually unchanged throughout its history, aside from the fact that it absorbs a profound Hellenic influence.

35. Since Vulgar Latin is most accurately characterized as spoken Latin, it follows that our knowledge of a language spoken some two thousand years ago can only be imperfect. We are not in possession of a single text written exclusively and with a deliberate purpose in *sermo vulgaris*. There are various sources, however, that philologists can turn to for information about spoken Latin. In texts written by poorly educated people, many "vulgarisms" surface, either in the form of errors or as hyper-corrections, this latter term referring to corrections made on the basis of a false analogy in perfectly correct forms and constructions. The treatment of *h* provides an easy illustration of the two points raised here. One of the earliest sound changes suffered by Vulgar Latin was the fall of *h* from pro-nunciation. Consequently, uneducated writers would often drop *h* by mis-take, writing *ostis* for *hostis*; *abere* for *habere*; *ic* for *hic*, etc. Remembering

one's *h*'es thus became a sign of good education, and inexperienced writers would not infrequently add an *h* where none had ever been present in Latin. Examples of such hypercorrections are *homnis* for *omnis*; *hoctober* for *october*; *hinsidias* for *insidias*; *hornare* for *ornare*. Several Vulgar Latin features have survived in Romance and can thus be reconstructed.

36. Works by Latin grammarians censuring what they consider to be errors in usage or pronunciation are to be consulted with care, since they quite often establish arbitrary or faulty rules. Invaluable information is contained in the so-called *Appendix Probi*, a list of censured vulgarisms accompanied by the corresponding correct forms. The list, which dates from the third or fourth century A.D., derives its name from the fact that it was discovered in a copy of Probus' Latin Grammar. The author is an unknown schoolmaster, who has drawn up a list of 227 words which he considers wrong and then proceeds to correct. The method he uses is a simple "this not that": *vetulus non veclus*; *calida non calda*; *auris non oricla*; *vinea non vinia*. By warning against commonly made mistakes, the author informs us about the popular pronunciation of the time, and the fact that the censured forms are all continued in Romance confirms the validity of his observations.

37. Very primitive glossaries appear in Late Latin or early Romance, offering translations of words that had become obsolete and thus were no longer readily understood by the readers. Best known of the early Latin lexicographers is Isidore of Seville (ab. 570–636), whose work contains much information about popular and regional Latin. Most important to Romanists is the *Glossary of Reichenau*, which draws its name from the abbey where the manuscript was discovered. The glossary was probably composed in northern France in the eighth or ninth century. The first section explains difficult words and expressions from the Bible by proposing familiar terms for them, while the second part consists of an alphabetic glossary. Generally speaking, the words appearing in the translations are continued in Romance (French), while many of the glossed terms have disappeared. Following is a sampling of entries: *pulcra*: *bella* (cf. Fr. *belle*); *arena*: *sabulo* (cf. Fr. *sable*); *minatur*: *manatiat* (cf. OFr. *manatce*, Fr. *menace*); *concidit*: *taliavit* (cf. Fr. *tailla*, It. *tagliò*); *jecore*: *ficato* (cf. Sp. *hígado*, Fr. *foie*, It. *fegato*); *in ore*: *in bucca* (cf. Fr. *bouche*, It. *bocca*); *vespertiliones*: *calvas sorices* (cf. Fr. *chauves-souris*) and even *Gallia*: *Frantia*. The glossary reflects not so much Late Latin, but rather the very early beginnings of Romance. Glosses such as *uvas*: *racemos* and *liberos*: *infantes* reveal that the *Glossary of Reichenau* was destined for "French" readers. The word *uvas* never drops from Hispanic or Italian and thus

would be in no need of a gloss in those areas, while French replaces it by *raisins* < *racēmos*, and French alone uses a continuation of *infantes* > *enfants* as the basic word for 'children'. The *Glossary of Kassel* (from approximately the eleventh century) offers a Romance-German (Bavarian) word list. The following entry will suffice as a sampling: *figido: lepara* (cf. Fr. *foie*, G. *Leber*). A couple of glossaries were put together on the Iberian Peninsula: *las Glosas de San Millán* from the province of Logroño (tenth century) and *las Glosas de Silos* from Castile (eleventh century). Among the glosses recorded in these works, we find *repente: lueco* (cf. Sp. *luego*); *diversis: muitas* (cf. Aragonese *muitas*, Sp. *muchas*).

38. Private Latin inscriptions found, for example, on tombstones or scribbled on walls, are often the work of relatively uneducated people, unaccustomed to expressing themselves in writing. Extremely important are the graffiti preserved in Pompeii and Herculanum following the eruption of Vesuvius in 79 A.D. A special category is the *defixionum tabellae* or execration tablets, expressing curses directed against an enemy or perhaps a rival. The Latin inscriptions were collected by Mommsen in the monumental *Corpus Inscriptionum Latinarum* (*CIL*), published in Berlin in 1862ff. E. Diehl's *Vulgärlateinische Inschriften* (Bonn, 1910) contains an excellent anthology. The following inscription from Rome: *Deus magnu oclu abet* lit. 'God has a big eye', bears witness to various popular features: the loss of final *m* (*magnu oclu* for *magnum oculum*), the syncope of the posttonic penult (*oclu* for *oculum*) and the loss of Lat. *h* (*abet* for *habet*).

39. Even literary works may contain popular forms. In his comedies, Plautus makes use of words that are close to the spoken language, and Cicero's letters contain formulas that are characteristic of a conversational style. It is not CL *lac*, but a spontaneous *lacte* encountered in Plautus and Petronius that serves as the etymological base of Rm. *lapte*, It. *latte*, Sp. *leche*, Ptg. *leite*, Cat. *llet*, Fr. *lait* and Occ. *lach*. Intentional reproduction of nonstandard speech is above all practiced by Petronius, who imitates popular language in his *Satyricon*; particularly noteworthy is the *Coena Trimalchionis* episode, in which a *nouveau riche* makes ample use of popular and even plebeian forms. A specific Christian Latin developed in the early centuries of our era as a propaganda tool for the diffusion of the new religion. Writing in an atmosphere that was essentially popular, the Church Fathers soon realized that it was less important for them to write an impeccable Latin than to be understood by the people to whom they addressed their teachings. This attitude accounts for the presence of popular features in their writings as well as in the earliest Bible translations, the *Itala* and the *Vulgata*.

40. Authors of technical works, such as Cato, Columella, Varro and Paladius, often make use of popular words and expressions that are undocumented elsewhere. Noteworthy are a fourth-century veterinary handbook known as *Mulomedicina Chironis*, a cookbook by Apicius and the *Peregrinatio Aetheriae* (or *Aegeriae*) *ad Loca Sancta*, a narration of a journey to the Holy Land undertaken in the fourth century by a Spanish nun of a modest educational background. Histories and chronicles were composed from the sixth century, among them Gregory of Tours' *Historia Francorum*.

41. The comparative grammar of the Romance languages permits the reconstruction of many words that are not documented elsewhere. Such reconstructed items remain hypothetical, however, and are traditionally preceded by an asterisk. It is usually assumed that a reconstructed element must have been part of Latin if it is present in all or most Romance languages, provided we can be certain that it has not arisen independently in each language or through borrowing. A VL *pŏtēre* (cf. CL *posse*) can be reconstructed from It. *potere*, Rm. *puteà*, Sp., Ptg., Occ. *poder*, Fr. *pouvoir*. A comparison of It. *carognia*, Sp. *carroña*, Occ. *caronha* and Fr. *charogne* permits the reconstruction of a Vulgar Latin base *carōnia* 'carrion', derived from *caro, carōnis* 'flesh', since it does not seem at all plausible that each language could have created such a form independently. In all likelihood, Vulgar Latin must have known the verb *acūtiāre* 'to sharpen' since such a form can be reconstructed from half a dozen languages: It. *aguzzare*, Sp., Occ. *aguzar*, Ptg. *aguçar*, Cat. *aguar*, Fr. *aiguiser*. The sounds or sound combinations reconstructed for the source must evolve in accordance with the established norm in each language. Each case must be examined individually, and other factors supportive of the reconstruction must be assembled if possible: chronology, parallel developments, etc. In the case of *acūtiāre*, such a form could easily be derived from *acūtus*, past participle of the verb *acuĕre* 'to sharpen' (cf. the participle *oblītus* giving rise to the infinitive *oblītāre* 'to forget'), and there is documentation for the noun *acūtiātor* 'sharpener'. A reconstructed element can also be assigned to Vulgar Latin if it is shared by a geographically cohesive group of languages: a VL * *cominitiāre* can be extrapolated from It. *cominciare*, Occ. *comesar*, Cat. *comensar*, Fr. *commencer*.

42. Each individual language may create new words through derivational processes, and these words may be borrowed into other Romance languages, but such formations do not imply the existence of a direct Vulgar Latin source. French draws the verb *nettoyer* 'to clean' from the adjective *net* 'clean' (cf. *vert* 'green' and *verdoyer* 'to turn green'), but this

does not in any way allow us to postulate the existence in Vulgar Latin of a verb *nĭtidiāre*. What we have is a fairly late creation, which other Romance languages do not share; it is a French and not a Vulgar Latin derivation. Occitan makes ample use of abstract nouns in *-ansa* or *-ensa*: *remembransa, erransa, crezensa, cozensa*, but although the suffixes employed reflect Lat. *-antia* and *-entia*, most of the nouns formed in this manner are original Occitan creations that cannot be traced to Vulgar Latin. In Old Italian and Old Hispanic, the same abstract nouns are borrowings from Occitan; their appearance in Gallo-, Italo- and Hispano-Romance thus cannot serve as proof of a shared Latin source. French continues the Latin suffix *-bilis* in a number of adjectives, but this does not mean that all the words formed in this manner have Latin roots.

ROMANIZATION

43. Through an impressive series of military conquests, Latin gained recognition as the official language of a vast empire. Sicily became a Roman province in 240 B.C., Macedonia in 168 B.C., the Iberian Peninsula during the second century B.C., North Africa in 146 B.C., southern Gaul in 120 B.C., northern Gaul in 50 B.C., Noricum in 16 B.C. and Dacia in 106 A.D. The conquered areas were subjected to a Romanization process, which appears to have been swift and thorough at the official-administrative level, but which in the private sector was more gradual, though resulting eventually in the elimination of the primitive languages which Latin had come into contact with. This process was accelerated by such factors as administration, military service, commerce and education. In the year 212, the emperor Caracalla issued an edict declaring all free inhabitants of the Roman Empire citizens, and with the triumph of Christianity, the Church lent its strong support to the Latin language. Latin does not seem to have been forcibly imposed on the conquered peoples; it was its prestige as the vehicle of Roman culture and administration that assured it of its hegemony. Latin maintained a relative unity as long as the Empire was able to hold on to its centralizing role. Only relatively minor linguistic differences existed in the various regions occupied by the Romans: a few dialectalisms, a few regionalisms and some archaisms, but nothing that would amount to a beginning fragmentation.

44. While the influence of the languages of the conquered peoples on Latin is discussed elsewhere (§§45–51), it seems appropriate at this point to make mention of Gröber's attempt to explain the Romance diversity on the basis of the chronology of the Romanization process. Considering that

this process extended over some four hundred years, and on the assumption that Latin would have had to evolve considerably over such a large span of time, Gröber theorized that the Latin that was brought to Sicily in 240 B.C. must have been quite different from the Latin introduced in northern Gaul in 50 B.C. or in Dacia in 106 A.D. Consequently, a more archaic Latin must have been spoken in Sicily than in France and Rumania. While this observation has some merit, it should be kept in mind that the contact with Rome continued unabated after the initial conquest, and that any linguistic innovations occurring in Rome would automatically spread to the other areas of the Empire. Furthermore, the development which Latin underwent during that period was relatively minor. Generally speaking, it is only in the domain of vocabulary that examples can be found of innovations that did not spread throughout Romania.

SUBSTRATUM AND SUPERSTRATUM

45. As a direct consequence of the Roman expansion through military conquests, Latin came into contact with other languages. These are the substratum languages upon which Latin was superimposed. The Romanization process, which may be defined as the linguistic and spiritual assimilation of the conquered peoples, eventually resulted in the disappearance of the substratum languages, a fate which befell Oscan, Etruscan, Gaulish, Iberian, Ligurian, etc. We must bear in mind, however, that before these languages vanished completely from the scene, there must have existed a prolonged period of bilingualism. Gaulish, for example, was still spoken in the fourth century A.D. This period of interaction enabled the original languages to exert an influence, though usually fairly minimal and difficult to gauge, on those that replaced them, in this case Latin and Romance.

46. Latin was originally the modest dialect spoken by the founders of Rome. Of the Italic tribes that descended into the Italian Peninsula, the Latins settled in Latium along the Tiber river delta, while the Oscans established themselves in the southern and southeastern regions of the peninsula and the Umbrians in an area bordering on the northeastern edge of Latium. Oscan dialectal features are, in some instances, still traceable in Romance. One of the most conspicuous characteristics of Oscan speech habits is the use of intervocalic *f*, corresponding to *b* in Latin: Lat. *bubalu* (cf. Lat. *bŏve* 'ox') vs. Oscan *bufalu*, the latter continued in Italian as *bufalo*; Lat. *sibilāre* vs. Oscan *sifilare*, and hence It. *zufolare*, Fr. *siffler*; Lat. *scarabaeu* vs. Oscan **scarafaju*, continued as It. *scarafaggio*. Oscan relics are often continued in Italian dialects: corresponding to Lat. *october*, It. *ottobre*, Nea-

politan has *attrufë* and *ottrufë*, reflecting Oscan **úhtufri*. Another phonological trait characteristic of Oscan is the assimilation of *nd* to *nn*: Lat.
operandam vs. Oscan *upsannam*; Lat. *sacrandas* vs. Oscan *sakrannas*. This
same assimilation is widespread in northeastern Spain where Menéndez
Pidal (*Orígenes*, pp. 299–305) rates it as a feature imported by Roman
colonizers under the leadership of Sertorius, who established his administrative headquarters in *Huesca*, a place name which Menéndez Pidal draws
from *Osca*. This alleged Oscan substratal influence in Spain is upheld by
Vidos (pp. 215–216), but rejected vigorously by several scholars (Jungemann, Rohlfs, Corominas), and the proposed etymology of the toponym
Huesca is not at all certain.

47. The Etruscans dominated vast regions of the Italian Peninsula from
the seventh through the fifth century B.C. The name *Rome* is probably of
Etruscan origin (*Ruma*), as is also the name of the Tiber river (Lat. *Tiberis*),
and it seems likely that the Romans acquired their alphabet from the Greeks
through the Etruscans. Very little is known about the Etruscan language,
which is very different from Latin and may even have been non-Indo-
European. It is generally assumed that the use of *C* to represent both *C* and
G (cf. Lat. *Cnaeus*, which is pronounced with *g*) is attributable to Etruscan
influence, since the Etruscan language did not possess voiced occlusives.
The aspiration affecting the voiceless occlusives *p, t, k* in the dialects of
Tuscany, the so-called *gorgia toscana*, is often attributed to Etruscan
speech habits: *poho* for *poco*; *la hasa* for *la casa*; *miha* for *mica*. This is a
much debated problem and very difficult to settle since such claims are not
amenable to scientific proof. The fact that the aspiration does not affect
these consonants when they are followed by a palatal vowel seems to rule
out an ancient development.

48. The languages of the Ligurian peoples, who lived along the coast
in the general region where the modern city of Genoa is located, are virtually unknown. Meillet (*Esquisse d'une histoire de la langue latine*, 1931,
p. 80) assumes that such vocabulary items as *vinum* 'wine', *rosa* 'rose',
lilium 'lily', *ficus* 'fig' and *asinus* 'donkey' may have come into Latin from
these coastal areas. Greek influence was profound along the coast of
Campania and Apulia, a region which came to be known as *Graecia
magna*. Among early popular borrowings from Greek are *balneum* 'bath',
bracchium 'arm', *camera* 'room', *corōna* 'crown', *gubernāre* 'to govern'.
In addition, a number of learned words came into Latin from Greek:
bibliothēca 'library', *historia* 'history', *philosophia* 'philosophy', *poēma*
'poem', *poēta* 'poet', *schŏla* 'school', *theatrum* 'theater'.

49. France and most of northern Italy were inhabited by Celtic tribes prior to the Roman colonization. From Gaulish comes a certain number of lexical elements, such as *carru* 'carriage' > Rm., Occ. *car*, It., Sp., Ptg. *carro*, Fr. *char*; *cammīnu* or *camīnu* 'road' > It. *cammino*, Sp. *camino*, Fr. *chemin*; *bracas* 'trousers' > Sp., Ptg., Occ. *bragas*, Fr. *braies*; *cerevisia* 'beer' > Sp. *cerveza*, Ptg. *cerveja*, OFr. *cervoise*; *camīsia* 'shirt' > It. *camicia*, Sp., Ptg. *camisa*, Fr. *chemise*; *carrūca* 'plough' > Fr. *charrue*. These borrowings confirm the importance of the Celts as road-builders, and they reveal their cultural influence in many areas of everyday life. Gaulish influence on French toponymy is extensive: *Parisii* > *Paris*; *Lug(u)dunum* > *Lyon*; *Namnētes* > *Nantes*; *Rotomagus* > *Rouen*; *Arvernia* > *Auvergne*; *Catiliacum* > *Cadillac*. The change of Lat. *ū* to [y] in French and Occitan has often been ascribed to Gaulish substratal influence, but on purely chronological grounds this claim is not easy to defend (§149). Furthermore, [y] occurs where no Celts were ever settled.

50. In addition to Celtic, Hispanic also has a pre-Roman substratum that is still spoken today: Basque. The ancient Iberians, who probably came from North Africa, are believed by some scholars to be the ancestors of the Basques, but the relationship between these two peoples has not been fully elucidated. The Basques may descend from the Vascones, related to the Aquitani of southern France, but this does not in any way rule out the existence of an earlier Iberian substratum. Several lexical elements that are undocumented in Latin stem from a Basque or Iberian substratum, among them Sp. *izquierdo*, Ptg. *esquerdo*, Cat. *esquerre*, Gasc. *(es)querr* 'left' (cf. Basque *ezkerr*); Sp. *vega*, Ptg. *veiga* 'fertile river valley' < *vaika* (cf. Basque *i-bai* 'river'). For Basque loan-words in Hispanic, see J. Hubschmied: "Hispano-Baskisches," *BF, 14* (1953), 1–26. The phonological change of initial *f* to *h*, which subsequently drops, is characteristic of Spanish (Castilian) and ranks as an early development, which may be attributable to the influence of Iberian substratal dialects closely related to Basque. It is to be noted in this respect that *f* is lacking in the Basque phonological system, and that initial *f* undergoes the same change to *h* in Gascon which, like Castilian, is spoken in an area adjacent to the Basque domain.

51. The languages Latin came into contact with during its extraordinary expansion are often poorly known, the populations ethnically mixed and superimposed on earlier groups of people of a different linguistic and cultural background, and which have all vanished in the grey dawn of history. As a result, the problem of identifying substratal elements in Latin or Romance is a very complex one. Phonological influences are particularly

troublesome to establish, and the most disturbing fact is that, generally speaking, such claims can neither be proven nor disproven scientifically.

52. When the Roman Empire declined and eventually collapsed, Latin came into contact with the languages of the invaders, who were mostly speakers of Germanic dialects: Franks, Goths, Longobards, Burgundians, etc. These invaders, however, abandoned their own languages, adopting the culturally superior Latin, on which they exerted the influence of a super-stratum. In essence, we are dealing with the same process as that of a sub-stratum language: the superstratum survives only in a few relics, chiefly vocabulary items, following a period of bilingualism. Germanic influence on Popular Latin prior to the break-up of the Roman Empire is very minimal, but one such early borrowing is *sapōne* 'soap', which is mentioned by Pliny the Elder, and which is pan-Romance: Rm. *săpun*, It. *sapone*, Sp. *jabón*, Ptg. *sabāo*, Occ., Cat. *sabó*, Fr. *savon*. Germanic influence on a broad scale begins with the Germanic invasions and the collapse of the Empire at a point in time when Rumania had been effectively cut off from the Romance world. There are no Germanic borrowings in Rumanian and Sardinian. Germanic (Frankish) influence was particularly strong in northern Gaul, where it even extends to the name of the country: **Frankia > France*. It affects not only nouns, but also adjectives and verbs, which are much less prone to borrowing. Among military terms taken from Frankish are: **wardon >* OFr. *guarder > garder* 'to watch' and **helm >* Fr. *heaume* 'helmet', while **werra >* Fr. *guerre* 'war' may represent an earlier loan. Other borrowings are: **blank >* Fr. *blanc* 'white'; **brūn >* Fr. *brun* 'brown'; **gris >* Fr. *gris* 'grey'; **hatjan >* Fr. *haïr* 'to hate'; **kausjan >* Fr. *choisir* 'to choose'. With some of these borrowings, French also acquired a Germanic consonant, the aspirated *h*, which the other Romance idioms do not possess: **háigiro >* Fr. *héron* 'heron'; **hapja >* Fr. *hache* 'axe'. Longo-bardic influence was above all felt in Italian: **Longobardia >* It. *Lombardia* 'Lombardy'; **wangja >* It. *guancia* 'cheek' (cf. G. *Wange*); **balko > * It. *balcone* 'balcony'.

53. In addition to substratum and superstratum, the term adstratum is often used; it serves to designate languages that exist side by side and may therefore influence one another. This is the case with Basque, which continues to coexist with Spanish; Arabic and Hispanic were in contact for centuries, and Latin was an adstratum in Greece, when that country was occupied by the Romans. A precise distinction between these three features is not always possible (Tagliavini, p. 218). The Arabic legacy of vocabulary items is particularly strong in Hispanic as a result of several centuries of occupation; these loans, referring to practically all aspects of everyday life,

testify to a very close contact between the Arabs and the Christian population under their domination: *al-ka-di* > Sp. *alcalde* 'mayor'; *al-amir* > Sp. *almirante* 'admiral'; *rehén* > Sp. *rehén* 'hostage'; *al-kasr* > Sp. *alcázar* 'fortress'; *al-banni* > Sp. *albañil* 'mason'; *alhómbra* > Sp. *alfombra* 'rug; *al-máhzan* > Sp. *almacén* 'ware-house'. Many toponyms on the Iberian Peninsula are of Arabic origin: *Cáceres* < Arab. *kasr* 'fortress'; *Medina* < Arab. *madina* 'town'; *Guadalquivir* < Arab. *wadi-al-kabir* 'the big river'; *Gibraltar* < Arab. *ğabal-tariq* 'the mountain of Tarik'.

FROM UNITY TO DIVERSITY

54. From the relative unity of Vulgar Latin, ten Romance languages and numerous dialects are born. The questions that arise in this connection do not invite any easy answers. When did insignificant regional or dialectal differences take on the dimensions of a beginning fragmentation process? And under what circumstances and for what reasons was a differentiation developed and maintained? On the premise that the germ of a diversification was already inherent in the Romanization process itself, Krepinsky ("La naissance des langues romanes," *Romanica*, II, Prague, 1958) theorizes that the birth of each Romance language coincides with the moment of the Roman conquest, the chief agent in the differentiation being the contact of Latin with a substratum. This view overemphasizes the role of the substratum, and it disregards the unified character that Vulgar Latin was able to maintain for several centuries. As long as Rome exerted its centralizing role, the relations between the provinces and the capital remained strong, and Latin, in its capacity as the official language of culture, trade and administration, abided by the Roman norm, remaining fairly unified in all areas of the Empire. This linguistic stability was to change drastically with the collapse of the Roman Empire and the disintegration of the political-social organization that had held it together.

55. With the disappearance of the cultural unity, the factors of diversification grew in number and strength. Some of these have already been examined in our discussion of Vulgar Latin and the Romanization process: the substratum, superstratum and adstratum (§§45–53) and the chronological factor (§44), but other forces were at work as well. Dialectal differences often tend to appear if a language is spoken over a vast area. At the social level, linguistic differences must also have made themselves felt at a fairly early stage as evidenced in such rhetorical labels as *sermo urbanus, rusticus, plebeius, vulgaris* 'metropolitan-refined, rustic, plebeian, vulgar speech'. Yet these *sermos* are all part of the same language, the differences

being mostly confined to matters of style and tone. Administrative influences are discernible: isoglosses (boundary lines between particular linguistic features) are often shown to follow the borders of a political or ecclesiastical division. A well-known example is the presence of a Leonese dialect in the Miranda region of Portugal, which finds its explanation in the fact that Miranda belonged to the diocese of Astorga in León and not to that of the Portuguese city of Braga. The linguistic fragmentation of *Romania* is thus attributable to a number of factors, but the exact role of each single agent cannot be determined.

THE EARLIEST ROMANCE TEXTS

56. The use of Latin for writing purposes, unchallenged at first, lasted well into the medieval period and beyond, thus delaying the appearance of texts written in the vernacular. The earliest French text is the *Serments de Strasbourg*. Sworn near Strasbourg on February 14, 842, these oaths confirmed the alliance between Louis le Germanique and Charles le Chauve in their struggle against their brother Lothaire. Louis, who reigned over the eastern Franks in German-speaking territory, swore in Romance (French), thereby ascertaining that he would be understood by Charles' army of Gallo-Romance speakers, while conversely Charles swore in German. Referring to a well-known historical event, the earliest French text can thus be dated with great accuracy, but some doubt persists as to its exact linguistic affiliation, for while the dialect of the German oath is easily identifiable as Rhein-Frankish, that of the Romance oath has resisted a definitive localization. Gaston Paris identifies it as a northern dialect and more precisely as *picard*, many scholars (Koschwitz, Wallensköld, Ewert) consider the language a variety of *poitevin*, while still others remove the text from French proper, Castellani by taking it to be *aquitain* and hence Occitan, Schuchardt by describing it as Franco-Provençal. F. Lot (*Romania, 65* (1939), 145–163), Monteverdi (*Manuale di avviamento agli studi romanzi,* p. 153) and Tagliavini (p. 419) are probably closer to the truth when they suggest that the language of the *Serments* could be an artificial product, some sort of a *roman commun*, and thus not yet French, which it would be futile to attempt to localize.

57. The earliest literary French text is the *Séquence de Sainte Eulalie*, which was probably written toward the end of the ninth century. The manuscript, which is now kept at the library of Valenciennes, was discovered in the library of the Benedictine monastery of Saint-Amand. It seems likely that the *Séquence* was composed in northern France in a dialect close to

picard and *wallon*. A couple of other archaic texts, the *Passion* and the *Vie de Saint-Léger*, both written around the year 1000, are heavily influenced by Occitan. The *Vie de Saint-Alexis* was composed approximately in 1040 by an unknown Norman author. The date of composition of the *Chanson de Roland* is generally thought to be between 1060 and 1070; the oldest, assonanced version has survived in a manuscript from Oxford, displaying Anglo-Norman dialectal features, and the text is also preserved in a Venetian manuscript.

58. The Franco-Provençal dialects never attained literary status, but un-mistakable Franco-Provençal features are present in a document containing a list of vassals in the service of the Count of Forez. Dating from the middle of the thirteenth century, this list is preserved in an early fourteenth-century version.

59. Occitan forms occur sporadically in oaths of loyalty referring to the castle of Lautrec and composed in 985 and 989, as well as in other oaths from the year 1059. The earliest text written entirely in Occitan is a charter drawn up in Rodez in 1102 (C. Brunel: "Le plus ancien acte original en langue provençale," *Annales du Midi, 34* (1922), 249ff.). If we omit from consideration the mysterious eleventh-century *Alba bilingue*, written in a language that has not even been positively identified as Occitan, the earliest literary text is the *Boëci*, dating from the early eleventh century, and of which 257 verses have survived. Also dating from the eleventh century is the translation of chapters thirteen through seventeen of the gospel of Saint John, preserved in a manuscript kept in the British Museum. Another archaic Occitan text, composed toward the middle of the eleventh century, is the *Chanson de Sainte Foi d'Agen (Sancta Fides)*. Of only slight literary interest, but of great linguistic value, this text is preserved in a manuscript discovered at the University of Leiden in 1901 by the Portuguese philolo-gist Leite de Vasconcellos. Antoine Thomas published a critical edition in 1925. The earliest troubadour poet is Guillaume de Poitiers (Guilhem de Peitieus) (1071–1127). The Gascon dialect comes to light as a poetic medium in a stanza of Raimbaut de Vaqueiras' famous multilingual *descort*. In prose, it first appears in a document from 1179, issuing from the Order of the Templars in Montsaunès.

60. The earliest Catalan poets expressed themselves in Provençal: Guilhem de Berguedan, Guerau de Cabrera, Raimon Vidal de Besaudun, etc., and this practice lasted until the fifteenth century. As a result, the earli-est writings in Catalan are prose texts and not poetry as in most other areas of Romance. Catalan elements appear sporadically in public and private documents composed in Latin, while the first text to be written entirely in

Catalan is a fragment of a book of homilies from the church of Organyà dating from the end of the twelfth or the beginning of the thirteenth century. The artistic Catalan prose is created by Ramon Llull (1235–1315). The monarchs of the House of Aragón made use of Catalan as their official language, and many Latin juridical works were translated into Catalan.

61. Spanish is first documented in a few words and phrases in the *Glosas Emilianenses*, preserved in a manuscript from the monastery of San Millán de la Cogolla in the province of Logroño and dating from the middle of the tenth century. A work of a similar nature, the *Glosas Silenses*, contained in a manuscript from the monastery of Santo Domingo de Silos in Castile, dates from roughly the same period. A document consisting of a brief list of expenses, dating from about 980, is kept in the archives of the cathedral of León. The existence of an ancient poetry in the early vernacular came to light with the discovery of final stanzas in Romance, called *haraǧat* or *kharǧe*, serving to mark the conclusion of poems written in Arabic or in Hebrew. These poems, known as *muwaššahās*, are written in Arabic or Hebrew characters and are composed as early as the eleventh-twelfth century. Spanish epic poetry begins with the *Cantar de mio Cid*, written about 1140 and preserved in a single manuscript copied in 1307 by a certain Pedro Abad. The manuscript was first discovered in 1779. *Los siete Infantes de Lara* is an anonymous work dating back to the second half of the twelfth century. The earliest Spanish poet whose name is known to us is Gonzalo de Berceo, who was active during the first half of the thirteenth century. He is the author of three saint's lives, three poems dedicated to the Virgin and three poems on religious topics.

62. In Portugal, the language of the early lyrical poetry of troubadour inspiration is Galician-Portuguese. Even poets from other regions of the Peninsula, including King Alfonso X, made use of Galician-Portuguese as their lyrical medium. Documents written entirely in the vernacular appear at the end of the twelfth century, the earliest being Elvira Sanchiz' testament from 1193.

63. Scholars seem mostly inclined to reject the claim made by Marchot to the effect that the Romance portion of the *Glossary of Kassel* constitutes the earliest text in the western Ladin dialect. The first document that is undeniably Ladin is a fragment of a twelfth-century sermon. No old texts have survived in the central Rhaeto-Romance dialects, while eastern Ladin or Friulan has an uninterrupted literary tradition and is documented in many medieval texts. The earliest specimen is a Cividale register dating from between 1284 and 1304. Of great philological interest are the fourteenth-century Friulan grammatical fragments and translation exercises, edited by

Schiaffini (*Frammenti grammaticali latino-friulani del secolo XIV*, Udine, 1921). The earliest poem appears to be the obscure *Piruç myó doç inculurit*, found scribbled on the back of a legal document issued at Cividale on April 14, 1380.

64. Ancient documents written in Sardinian are fairly abundant; they are all official pieces of no literary value, but of great linguistic interest, some of them dating back to the eleventh and twelfth centuries. They confirm the creation on the island of a vernacular based on the Logudorese dialect. It is assumed that this development may have been accelerated by the isolation of Sardinia, which led to a weakening of the Latin culture and the subsequent use of an island dialect in the composition of official documents. Many so-called *condaghi*, collections of juridical documents that mostly bear on ecclesiastical matters, have survived. Among the most important are the *condaghi* of San Pietro di Silki (a monastery in the vicinity of Sassari), San Nicola di Trullas, containing documents from 1113 to the middle of the thirteenth century, and S. Maria di Bonàrcado, which contains material from the twelfth and thirteenth centuries. The so-called *Carte d'Arborea*, demonstrating the existence of a poetic literature in Sardinian prior to the Sicilian School, have been proven to be a hoax.

65. The earliest manifestation of Italian is usually held to be the *Placito capuano* of 960. There exists, however, an earlier document, the so-called *Indovinello veronese* which, though carrying unmistakable Venetian features, may be composed in what is still to be considered Vulgar Latin or Semi-Vulgar Latin, antedating Italian. Truly "vulgar" is the formula of swearing contained in the *Placito capuano*; the text itself is in Latin, but the witnesses swear in the vernacular. Dating from March 960, the manuscript is kept in the archives of Montecassino. The formulas preserved in documents from Sessa Aurunca (963) and Teano (963) are of a very similar format. From the eleventh century comes the *Formula di confessione umbra*. An ancient inscription from the cathedral of Ferrara, which has not survived in its primitive version, is thought by some scholars to have been originally made in 1135 or between that date and the year 1200. If this dating is correct, it would make the Ferrara inscription not only one of the earliest documents of Italian, but also the oldest example of verse. There is always the lingering suspicion, however, that a document which no longer exists in its original version might have been amended or falsified. An archaic text, known as the *Ritmo bellunese*, dates from 1193. Other twelfth-century texts are twenty-two Gallo-Italic sermons, the *Ritmo di S. Alessio*, the *Ritmo cassinese* and a Judeo-Italian elegy.

66. Raimbaut de Vaqueiras' multilingual *descort* contains a stanza in Italian, and the same troubadour is the author of a bilingual *Contrasto* exchanged between a Provençal troubadour and a Genovese lady. This poem may have been composed toward the end of the twelfth century. A literary medium was forming in various regions of northern Italy with Bonvesin da Riva, Uguccione da Lodi, Gerardo Patecchio, etc., in Umbria with S. Francesco, and above all at Frederick II's court at Palermo, where the first true school of poetry saw the light under the leadership of Giacomo da Lentini. Following these initial attempts, the Italian literary language eventually evolved in Tuscany, based on the Florentine dialect and with the great writers Dante, Petrarch and Boccacio as models.

67. There are very scant traces of Dalmatian in a tenth-century testament, and some vernacular expressions are found in an inventory drawn up in Ragusa in 1280. The earliest entirely Dalmatian text is a letter written in 1397 by a certain Francesco di Fanfona from Zara to his father.

68. Cut off from the Neolatin world, Rumanian evolved in an atmosphere of Byzantine and Slavic culture, with Greek and Old Church Slavonic serving as the official administrative and ecclesiastical languages. Official and private documents do not appear until the second half of the fourteenth century; they are written in Middle Bulgarian, but they do contain a few Rumanian toponyms and names of persons. Some Rumanian lexical items appear in the fifteenth and the early sixteenth century. The earliest texts written entirely in Rumanian are an oath of homage sworn on September 16, 1485 at Colomea by Stefan the Great to King Casimir IV of Poland and a letter addressed in 1521 by Neacşu di Câmpulung to the judge Hans Benkner in Braşov. The letter is written in the Cyrillic alphabet, which was very generally used in Rumania until the middle of the nineteenth century. Four manuscripts from the second half of the sixteenth century offer the first religious texts written in Rumanian. Rumanian lacks a medieval literature.

EARLY HISTORY OF ROMANCE STUDIES

69. From a purely chronological point of view, François Raynouard (1761–1836) is fully deserving of the title of father of Romance linguistics, which Diez bestows upon him. His work on the French Academy dictionary, published in 1798, had convinced him that in order to study the French lexicon, it was necessary to examine the earlier stages of the language. Focusing his research on Old Provençal, he published an anthology of texts, *Choix de poésies originales des troubadours* (Paris, 1816–1821),

accompanied by a grammar of Provençal entitled *Grammaire de la langue romane*, the first grammar of an old Romance language, and he compiled a six-volume dictionary, *Lexique roman ou dictionnaire de la langue des troubadours* (Paris, 1838–1844), which still remains an indispensable tool for Provençalists, and which has since been reprinted (Heidelberg: Winter, 1929ff.). Raynouard expresses the erroneous belief that the Romance languages are not descended directly from Latin, but from a *lingua romana* issued from the popular language spoken from the seventh through the ninth century, and which he identifies with the language of the troubadours. Provençal is thus assigned the important position of an intermediary between Latin and the remaining Romance languages, the latter becoming Neoprovençal rather than Neolatin.

70. Although Raynouard thus takes his place as an important pioneering figure, he cannot be called the true founder of Comparative Romance philology. For one thing, he mostly devotes his study to only one Romance language, and furthermore, the work that was to provide the impetus for comparative language studies in the Romance field and elsewhere, Franz Bopp's *Über das Conjugationssystem der Sanskritsprache, in Vergleichung mit jenem der griechischen, lateinischen, persischen und germanischen Sprachen* (Frankfurt, 1816), was published the same year as Raynouard's *Grammaire*. With this work, Bopp (1791–1867) inaugurated the comparative method. Primarily concerned with tracing the unity of the Indo-European languages rather than with accounting for their ulterior developments, he pursues this interest in his later work, *Vergleichende Grammatik des Sanskrit, Send, Griechischen, Litauischen, Gotischen und Deutschen* (1833–1852). The pioneer in language history is the German scholar Jakob Grimm (1785–1863) who, in his *Deutsche Grammatik* (1819), demonstrates that sound changes are not arbitrary, but obey definite laws, as had already been established by the Danish philologist Rasmus Rask (1787–1832). The title of Grimm's work needs some clarification: the term *Deutsch* is used with the meaning of Germanic, and the word *Grammatik* does not carry the basic sense of a normative grammar prescribing correct usage, but represents historical grammar. The name of the new discipline, *Romanische Sprachwissenschaft*, was coined in 1863 by the German provençalist K.A. Mahn (1802–1887).

71. The true founder of the Romance discipline is Friedrich Diez (1794–1876) who, in the spiritual climate surrounding German romanticism, composes his three-volume *Grammatik* der romanischen Sprachen (Bonn, 1836–1843), in which he applies the comparative and historical methods inaugurated by Bopp and Grimm. This is followed up by the publi-

cation in 1853 of his *Etymologisches Wörterbuch der romanischen Sprachen*, which remains a fundamental work. The first two volumes of his *Grammatik*, dealing with phonology and morphology, are now only of historical interest, while the third volume, devoted to syntax, has kept its intrinsic value. Influenced by Grimm, Diez came into language study via literature, his first work focusing on the *Altspanische Romanzen* (Frankfurt, 1818). During a famous visit he paid to Goethe in Jena in 1818, the German poet drew Diez's attention to Raynouard's Provençal studies. This led to the publication in Zwickau in 1826 of *Die Poesie der Troubadours* and in 1829 of *Leben und Werke der Troubadours*. In his *Grammatik*, Diez discards Raynouard's erroneous theory concerning the position of Provençal, then proceeds to demonstrate the relationship between Latin and Romance, and he correctly derives the Romance languages not from Classical Latin, but from the spoken popular language. He compares six Romance languages: two in the East, Italian and Wallachian (i.e., Rumanian), two in the southwest, Spanish and Portuguese, and two in the northeast, Provençal and French. He bases these divisions on two criteria: the grammatical characteristics and the literary importance. Only quite exceptionally does he include dialectal material.

72. A new era begins with the inclusion of dialectology as a branch of Romance studies. The undisputed master in this field is the Italian G.I. Ascoli (1829–1907), who is the first to have established truly scientific principles for the study of Romance dialects. In 1873, he founded the *Archivio glottologico italiano*. Volume 8 (1882–1885) of this journal contains his important study of Italian dialects entitled *Italia dialettale*, and in the opening volume (1873) of the same journal he published his fundamental *Saggi ladini*, a rigorous study of Rhaeto-Romance, a dialectal group which, until then, had been only poorly and incompletely known. In volume 3 (1875 or 1878) of the journal, Ascoli identifies and describes another Romance dialect group, Franco-Provençal, placed geographically and linguistically between French and Provençal (§16). With his dialectal studies, Ascoli stresses the importance of observing and investigating the living, spoken languages, and he is the first scholar to provide a scientific basis for the study of substratum influence on language development (§§45–51).

73. Toward the middle of the past century, the natural sciences began to exert a powerful influence on the Romance discipline, which came under the sway of positivist and naturalist thought. August Schleicher (1821–1868) considered languages to be natural organisms which are born, develop, age and die in accordance with fixed laws that are independent of

the speakers (*Die Darwinsche Theorie und die Sprachwissenschaft*, Weimar, 1863). This concept is reflected in the titles of a couple of important works of the period: *La vie des mots* (Paris, 1887) by Arsène Darmesteter (1846–1888) and *The Life and Growth of Language* (London, 1875) by the American linguist William Dwight Whitney (1827–1894). Among the earliest critics of this trend is Gaston Paris (1839–1903), who rightly observes that languages do not depend in their evolution on their organic structure, but on the people who speak them, which is to say on purely external and historical causes.

74. By emphasizing the phonetic element of language, Schleicher reduced the phonemes to purely physiological products evolving according to fixed laws, while Diez viewed language above all as a psychological phenomenon. It is from the conflict between these two concepts that a new linguistic school arose, whose goal was to reconcile the opposing views. The new school was headed by a group of German Indo-Europeanists from the University of Leipzig, referred to jokingly by F. Zarncke as *Junggrammatiker* 'Neogrammarians'. The most prominent members of the group, Leskien (1840–1916), Osthoff (1847–1909) and Brugmann (1849–1919), declare their fundamental methodological principle to be the *Ausnahmslosigkeit* of sound-laws, which is to say the idea that sound-laws admit of no exceptions, yet at the same time they attach great importance to analogy: to the notion of sound-laws that are blindly followed they add the principle of analogy as a human or psychological factor. If there are cases where the sound-laws do not seem to function properly, it must be attributable to the influence of forms which are already present in the language and thus capable of exerting analogical or paradigmatic pressure. In Italian, for example, Lat. *ŏ* diphthongizes to *uo* only if it is stressed and free: *nuoto, nuoti, nuota, nuotano*, not if it is pretonic, but the *uo* diphthong is extended analogically to *nuotiamo, nuotate, nuotare*. One would expect the Neogrammarians to give preference to analogy over the purely mechanical sound-laws, but the fact of the matter is that they have recourse to analogy only as a last resort. They have exaggerated the material aspect of language at the expense of the psychological, yet theirs has been a lasting contribution to the linguistic discipline: they have introduced, developed and refined the historical-comparative method, they have gathered and interpreted an astounding amount of data, and they have emphasized the need for studying the modern idioms since these alone can give us insight into the workings of language.

75. Wilhelm Meyer-Lübke (1861–1936) is in Bartoli's words the "prince" of Romance philology; he is also one of the most fervent disciples

of the *Junggrammatiker*. His monumental *Grammatik der romanischen Sprachen* (4 vols., Leipzig, 1890–1902) marks a distinct advancement over Diez's *Grammatik*, specifically as regards the wealth and variety of the material discussed. Unlike Diez, he does not limit his treatment to the literary languages, but he also extends his probings to the dialects. He shows unswerving adherence to the Neogrammarian doctrine in all of his major works: his *Italienische Grammatik* (Leipzig, 1890), his *Einführung in das Studium der romanischen Sprachwissenschaft* (Heidelberg, 1901), which is still very useful, his *Historische Grammatik der französischen Sprache* (Heidelberg, 1909–1921), his fundamental and indispensable *Romanisches etymologisches Wörterbuch* or *REW* (Heidelberg, 1911–1920, revised ed., 1935), his *Das Katalanische* (Heidelberg, 1925) and, of course, the already mentioned *Grammatik*. Although Meyer-Lübke declares himself averse to theoretical discussions, he is always open to new ideas. He is attracted to the geographical method as well as to the *Wörter und Sachen* doctrine.

76. Among other scholars devoted to Neogrammarian principles, we may mention Adolf Tobler (1835–1910), known for his pioneering work in Old French syntax (*Vermischte Beiträge zur französischen Grammatik*, 5 vols., Leipzig: Hirzel, 1906–1921) and for his thorough investigation of the Old French lexicon (Tobler-Lommatzsch: *Altfranzösisches Wörterbuch*, Berlin, 1925ff.), and the French etymologist Antoine Thomas (1851–1935), whose *Essais de philologie française* (1897), *Mélanges d'étymologie française* (1902) and *Nouveaux essais de philologie française* (1904) bear witness to his firm belief in the rigid Neogrammarian concept of sound-laws.

77. Opposition to the Neogrammarian principles comes from many quarters. Scholars are quick to take issue with the notion of sound-laws that are blindly followed as if they were natural laws. Most prominent among the adversaries of the Neogrammarian doctrine is Hugo Schuchardt (1842–1927) who, in his opuscule *Über die Lautgesetze. Gegen die Junggrammatiker* (Berlin, 1885), argues against universally applied language norms and calls into question the very notion of uniform dialects spoken over the same area and during a specific time limit. Instead, he claims, there exist individual speech forms influencing one another reciprocally, a linguistic mixture which admits of no fixed boundaries and of no chronological divisions. This mixture, this infinite linguistic variety, is tied to the human factor (age, sex, social status, level of culture, etc., of the speakers). In a period of systematization, Schuchardt proposes an atomizing view; disregarding vast syntheses, he turns his attention to the nuance. In his view,

each word finds itself in a specific environment, which rules out generalizations. L'abbé Rousselot (1846–1920), author of a dialect study entitled *Modifications phonétiques du langage étudiées dans le patois d'une famille de Cellefrouin* (Charente) (Paris, 1891), demonstrates that uniformity of speech does not even exist within a single family, and Louis Gauchat (1866–1942) reaches a similar conclusion concerning the speech habits of the inhabitants of a small village. Yet in spite of these various arguments, the principle of the regularity of phonological correspondences remains fundamental in linguistics.

78. Schleicher depicts the distribution of the Indo-European languages graphically in the form of a family tree, with branches springing out from the main trunk, and these in turn producing new branches and so on. This simplistic and overly mechanical diagram of language genealogy focuses on the erroneous idea of languages as separate entities, detachable at some point in time from the trunk in a mother-daughter relationship, while linguistic evolution is a *continuum* without any sudden breaks (§33). It is not surprising therefore that the family-tree diagram was soon challenged. A methodological innovation is the so-called wave theory, proposed by Johannes Schmidt (1843–1901), in terms of which linguistic changes spread like waves originating in different centers, the waves of innovations crossing each others' paths in an unpredictable pattern.

79. Initiated by the Indo-Europeanist Rudolf Meringer (1859–1931), the word and thing method (*Wörter und Sachen*) is an approach to vocabulary study, which couples the history of the words with that of the objects they designate. The history of language thus becomes the history of culture. Dealing chiefly, though not exclusively, with the things of material civilization, the *Wörter und Sachen* approach has close ties to ethnology. Among the founders of this methodological innovation one may also count Gottfried Baist and Schuchardt, and the label *Wörter und Sachen* itself is drawn from a remark made by Jakob Grimm. It is Max Leopold Wagner (1880–1962) who composes the most significant work resulting from the new methodology: *Das ländliche Leben Sardiniens im Spiegel der Sprache* (Heidelberg, 1921).

80. By linguistic geography (G. *Sprachgeographie*) is meant the cartographical representation of linguistic phenomena. Generally speaking, the method focuses on the spoken dialects and not on the standard written languages. Drawing on the Neogrammarian concept of uniform dialect areas for his inspiration, the German linguist Georg Wenker (1852–1911) engaged in the task of marking the boundaries of the German dialects on a geographical map. His work, which remained unfinished, was flawed by the

inadequacy of the questionnaire used and by an unreliable method of administering it. The result turned out to be the opposite of what he had set out to demonstrate: he discovered that dialect boundaries are irregular, and that it is impossible to trace clear lines of demarcation or isoglosses. Gustav Weigand (1860–1930) conducted similar investigations in Rumania, but the first truly modern linguistic atlas is the *Atlas linguistique de la France* (*ALF*) executed by the Swiss scholar Jules Gilliéron (1854–1926), professor of French dialectology in Paris, in collaboration with Edmond Edmont. The questionnaire put together by the team contained some 2,000 entries, mostly isolated words, but also a few sentences. The field work was carried out in 639 localities, excluding all major cities and the bilingual areas such as the Basque country and Brittany, but including the French-speaking regions of Belgium and Switzerland and the Piemonte province of Italy. The gathering of the material was done entirely by Edmont, a store-keeper from the Artois region, who had received no scientific training, but who was reputed to have a fine ear, and who had already demonstrated his unusual gift for collecting dialectal data in his *Lexique Saint-polois* (Saint-Pol, 1897), a study of the dialect of Saint-Pol-sur-Ternoise (Pas-de-Calais). The collected material was published by Gilliéron in the form of a ten-volume atlas containing 1920 maps, on which the 639 localities are marked by a number.

81. Gilliéron's methodology soon found followers in the entire Romance area and beyond. The masterpiece of the genre was produced by two Swiss scholars, Karl Jaberg (1877–1958) and Jakob Jud (1882–1952) who, from 1928 to 1940, published an eight-volume linguistic atlas of Italy and southern Switzerland, *Sprach- und Sachatlas Italiens und der Südschweiz*, accompanied by two ethnographical volumes by P. Scheuermeier: *Bauernwerk in Italien und rätoromanischen Schweiz*. In this case, the material was not gathered by an amateur, but by three of the most prominent scholars in the Italian field, P. Scheuermeier, Gerhard Rohlfs and Max Leopold Wagner. The preoccupation with *Wörter und Sachen* principles is evident from the title as well as from P. Scheuermeier's companion volumes and the specific interests of the researchers. The work combines carefully documented considerations of geographical distribution with a thorough historical and comparative study in the traditional vein. Far from sharing Gilliéron's antagonistic attitude, the two Swiss scholars have shown through their work that the historical and the geographical methods are complementary.

82. Linguistic maps offer visible proof that words travel, and they provide information about the itineraries they follow in their migrations. Paris

is a powerful center of linguistic innovations, and most of the words created in the metropolis migrate to the provinces, following important arteries of communication, such as rivers or rail lines. The Rhone valley is strongly influenced by Parisian speech despite its distance from the capital, while peripheral rural areas are more resistant to innovations. The word *blaireau* 'badger', first documented in the late fourteenth century, is gradually crowding out *tais, taisson* (cf. It. *tasso*, Sp. *tejón* < Gmc. **thahs*), but the *ALF* maps show that this latter word family still survives in the South, in Burgundy and Lorraine as well as in the Walloon dialect. In the same areas, *banc de menuisier* 'carpenter's bench' has not yet been replaced by *établi*. Differences in dialectal structure between French and Italian are vividly illustrated through the cartographical method, as shown here with the words for 'apron'. Fr. *tablier*, a Parisian creation drawn from *table* 'table', is steadily pushing back the zones of regional forms (*devantier, fald-*, etc.), while It. *grembiale*, a derivation from Lat. *gremium* 'bosom', has no comparable power of diffusion, leaving the dialectal forms pretty much intact: *fald-* in Piemonte, *scossal*, from Langobard **skauz*, in Lombardy, *zinale* or *sinale*, derived from Lat. *sīnus* 'chest' and 'fold', in Rome, Latium, Apulia, southern Marche, and derivations from *(a)vanti* 'in front, before' or a *mant-* root in the South. The French dialects are receding as the language of Paris extends its domain while, in Italian, the dialects are strongly entrenched.

83. The geographical method may shed light on linguistic conflicts, un-covering reasons for the disappearance of certain vocabulary items. Gillié-ron demonstrates that words may disappear if, through regular devel-opment, they lose a considerable portion of their phonological substance, thus becoming phonetically mutilated (*mutilés phonétiques* in Gilliéron's terminology). In his *Généalogie des mots qui désignent l'abeille d'après l'Atlas linguistique de la France* (Paris, 1918), Gilliéron cites the fate of Lat. *apis— apem* 'bee' in French as an example. Reduced through regular phonological attrition to *ef, ep, es, e*, the reflexes have become so phoneti-cally weak that therapeutic devices, another Gilliéronian term, are needed to cure the ailing word, hence its replacement in various zones by *mouche à miel, abeille, avette, mouchette, essaim*, etc.

84. Homonymy is of particular importance in Gilliéron's discussion of language change. The demise of the *apis—apem* reflex in northern France may have been precipitated by the homonymy of *és* 'bee' with *wés* 'wasp', which creates an intolerable entomological confusion. In Gascon, where final *ll* becomes *t*, *gallu* 'rooster' would evolve to **gat*, but this slot is already filled by *gat* 'cat' < *cattu* (cf. It. *gatto*, Sp., Ptg. *gato*, Occ. *cat, gat*, Fr. *chat*). As a result, **gat* 'rooster' disappears, while the more widely

established *gat* 'cat' is retained. The cartographical representation shows **gat* 'rooster' to have been replaced by *azā* (cf. Fr. *faisan* 'pheasant') and by the humorous *bigey* (cf. Fr. *vicaire* 'vicar') in Gascon. Lat. *mŭlgĕre* 'to milk' would have evolved to **moldre* and **moudre* in French, thus creating an intolerable clash with *moudre* 'to grind' from Lat. *mŏlĕre*. Peasants cannot have the same word for 'to milk' and 'to grind', and this explains why French turns to *traire* 'to milk' from VL *tragĕre*, lit. 'to pull' in order to establish a linguistic differentiation between the two activities. Much attention is focused on contamination and popular etymology as agents of change, forces which are not easily kept apart. The form *mouche-ep* 'bee', encountered in certain French dialects, may have acquired its *p* from a contamination with *avispa* 'wasp', and Fr. *fumier* < OFr. *femier* < **fĭmariu* may have rounded its pretonic vowel through the influence of the verb *fumer* 'to smoke'.

85. In sharp contrast to the Neogrammarian doctrine that sound-laws apply to all words that are similarly constituted, Gilliéron affirms that each word has its own history. This ties in with Vossler's belief that linguistic innovations come from the individual, and Schuchardt had already voiced a similar skepticism concerning the principle of phonological generalizations. It would be a mistake to assume, however, that the historical-comparative method would not be capable of determining whether a given Romance word is a reflex of Latin or an independent creation. The Romance words for 'fish' are all derived from Lat. *pĭsce*: It. *pesce*, Sp. *pez*, Ptg. *peixe*, Cat. *peix*, Occ. *peis*, Rm. *peşte*, with the exception of the French form *poisson*, which could be derived from Lat. **pĭsciōne*, but the fact that Old French has *peis, pois* < *pĭsce* (cf. OFr. *porpois* 'porpoise', *craspois* 'whale') proves that *poisson* is an independent French formation, which does not date back to Latin. This is also confirmed by the geographical method, which reveals the survival of *pois* in peripheral zones of French dialects.

86. A linguistic atlas such as the *ALF* or the *AIS* has perforce certain inevitable flaws, which the authors are perfectly aware of. It examines only selected points of a dialectal area, it is not based on spontaneous discourse, but on solicited answers, it does not provide a general picture of the dialect, but gives only the speech pattern of a single individual at a particular moment of his life, and it cannot offer a historical perspective.

87. Neolinguistics or areal linguistics (It. *linguistica spaziale*), founded by Matteo Bartoli (1873–1946), represents a combination of Neogrammarian doctrine and Gilliéron's geographical principles. With the aid of the geographical method, Bartoli establishes five areal norms based on the

position of the word in space. These norms are designed to contribute to a better understanding of chronological relationships between linguistic phenomena. If of two chronological phases, one is largely confined to outlying or inaccessible areas, it can usually be considered the older form. Lat. *domus* 'house', *janua* 'door', *magnus* 'great, big,' have survived in Sardinian: *domo, giànna, mannu,* while other areas mostly continue the synonyms *casa, pŏrta, grandis* (cf. It. *casa, porta, grande* and Sp. *casa, puerta, grande*). If one phase is documented in lateral areas and the other in the central zones, the former is usually older. Lat. *fĕrvĕre* or *fĕrvēre* 'to boil' is kept in lateral areas (Hispanic and Rumanian): Ptg. *ferver,* Sp. *hervir,* Rm. *fierbe,* while central areas (Catalan, Gallo-Romance, Italian, Rhaeto-Romance) have adopted the more recent *bŭllīre* 'to boil': Cat. *bullir,* Occ. *bolhir* or *bolir,* Fr. *bouillir,* Rhaeto-Romance *bòli,* It. *bollire.* Lateral areas continue Lat. *arēna* 'sand': dial. Rm. *arină,* Sp. *arena,* Ptg. *areia,* while the central zones have reflexes of Lat. *sabŭlu* 'sand': Fr. *sable,* It. *sabbia.* The more widely diffused phase is normally the older: Lat. *frater* 'brother' is continued in Fr. *frère,* Occ. *fraire,* Rm., OIt. *frate,* Sd. *fradi,* while the more recent *germanu* is limited to Hispanic: Sp. *hermano,* Ptg. *irmão.* It may happen, however, that the older form is preserved in isolated or peripheral areas, while the more recent formation commands a more extensive spread; this is the case with Lat. *densu* 'thick' > Rm. *des* vs. Lat. *spĭssu* 'thick' > It. *spesso,* Sp. *espeso,* Ptg. *espesso,* Occ. *espes,* Fr. *épais,* and with Lat. *lĭngŭla* 'spoon' > Rm. *lingură* vs. Lat. *cŏchleariu* 'spoon' > It. *cucchiaio,* Sp. *cuchara,* Fr. *cuiller.* Territories that were Romanized late tend to preserve an earlier phase: Lat. *avŭncŭlu* 'oncle' > Fr. *oncle* vs. Lat. *thius* 'uncle' > It. *zio.* If of two words one is discontinued, it is usually the older form that is lost: Lat. *ignis* 'fire' is older than *fŏcus* which, alone, survives: It. *fuoco,* Sp. *fuego,* Ptg. *fogo,* Fr. *feu.*

88. It will be noted that some of the areal norms already form part of Gilliéron's geographical approach (cf. the presence of *apis—apem* in lateral areas of French), and that none is entirely free of exceptions and contradictions. Bartoli's areal norms serve merely as a rigid classification scheme, paying little or no attention to other linguistic factors. The validity of some of the examples from which the norms are inferred is often quite relative. Lat. *ĕqua* 'mare', as an older form, is kept in lateral areas: Sp. *yégua,* Ptg. *égua,* Rm. *iapă* , while the central regions continue the more recent *caballa*: It. *cavalla,* Occ. *cavala.* This scheme omits from consideration the fact that *ĕqua* was commonly used in the Gallo-Romance area: Occ. *ega* and OFr. *ive,* and that OFr. *ive* was still alive in the fourteenth century.

89. Onomasiology is a discipline which studies the nomenclature applied to a given object, animal, plant or concept; it is either limited to a single linguistic area, or it may be comparative in scope. In its methodology, it is closely linked to linguistic geography and has above all affinities with the *Wörter und Sachen* movement. Like *Wörter und Sachen*, it focuses on the semantic aspect, and like *Wörter und Sachen* and linguistic geography, it zeroes in on the creative forces in the popular language. The discipline is initiated by the Swiss scholar Ernst Tappolet (1870–1939), who studies the kinship terms in Romance: *Die romanischen Verwandtschaftsnamen mit besonderer Berücksichtigung der französischen und italienischen Mundarten. Ein Beitrag zur vergleichenden Lexicologie* (Strasbourg, 1895). He still refers to his work as "comparative lexicology," while the term onomasiology makes its first appearance in 1902 with a work on the Romance names for the parts of the body by the Austrian scholar Adolf Zauner (1870–1943): *Die romanischen Namen der Körperteile. Eine onomasiologische Studie* (Erlangen, 1902). Another pioneering work is *I nomi romanzi delle stagioni e dei mesi* (Torino, 1904) by Clemente Merlo (1879–1960). Etymological research is no longer limited to phonology; it is, whenever possible, the entire story of a word, its biography, that is examined. The creative force of the popular language is evident in such formations as *saute-mottes*, name given in French to the wagtail. This same bird is known in Spanish as *pajarita de las nieves, nevatilla* or *nevereta*; the naming follows from the observation that the bird, migrating to Spain from the North, is a harbinger of the snowy season (cf. Sp. *nieve* 'snow').

90. A vehement opposition to Neogrammarian rigidity is already voiced by Gilliéron, but it is Karl Vossler's idealistic and esthetic school which initiates a true battle against linguistic positivism. Inspired by Benedetto Croce, who views language as a perpetual creation, thus emphasizing its esthetic, artistic and expressive functions, Karl Vossler applies Crocean linguistic thought to the Romance field with his work *Positivismus und Idealismus in der Sprachwissenschaft* (Heidelberg: Winter, 1904), which may be considered the manifesto of the idealistic school. Among the pioneers of idealistic linguistic thought is W. von Humboldt (1767–1835), who regards language as a product of the human spirit. Language, he maintains, does not reproduce things as they are in reality, but as the speaker imagines them to be. This personal vision of reality is the "innere Sprachform" or internal linguistic form, while the external form is the phonetic and grammatical constitution of the language. Positivism signals to Vossler a mere gathering of linguistic materials as an end in itself, while idealism aims at

determining the causes of linguistic change. Vossler is not opposed to thorough documentation; where he differs from positivism is in attitude. Central to his thought is the consideration of language as an expression of the human spirit. The spirit is the only true cause of linguistic change, and every linguistic expression has a purely individual character, becoming generalized only when accepted by other speakers. Linguistic changes are of an esthetic nature and are not based on modifications in human psychology.

91. Vossler is not solely a theoretician of idealistic thought in matters of language, he has also put his principles into practice in his book *Frankreichs Kultur im Spiegel seiner Sprachentwicklung* (Heidelberg, 1913), which later appeared in a revised edition: *Frankreichs Kultur und Sprache. Geschichte der französischen Schriftsprache von den Anfängen bis zur Gegenwart* (1929). His aim is to uncover the close links that exist between the evolution of the French language and that of the political and literary life in France. Speech, in other words, is a mirror of cultural phenomena. A precise example may serve as an illustration. There is general consensus that a commercial mentality develops in France in the fourteenth and fifteenth centuries, and Vossler relates this cultural development to the fact that the partitive article, still rare in the thirteenth century, comes to be very widely used at the end of the medieval period. The partitive article becomes firmly established in the language as the product of a strong materialistic spirit, which considers everything divisible. This new spirit needs the partitive article as an indispensable tool for its calculations. The flaws of this reasoning are quite obvious. The partitive article was more commonly used in Old Italian than it is now, leading one to draw the absurd conclusion that Italians are less materialistic now than in the past. And how does one explain that the British and the Americans, whose materialistic spirit is highly developed, never created a partitive article in their language? Vossler further errs in considering the French partitive article a sudden creation in the fourteenth century when, as a matter of fact, this grammatical tool evolved very gradually over a prolonged period of gestation. To many scholars, specifically those of a positivist bent, intuition is an unacceptable method of linguistic study.

92. The concept of language as a manifestation of national peculiarity (G. *Eigenart*) derives from the idealistic method, but where Vossler makes the spirit and the culture the starting-point for his linguistic observations, this method moves in the opposite direction: from the language it draws conclusions about the cultural conditions of a nation. Attempts to establish a *Wesenskunde* 'knowledge of the essence or the character of a nation' from

the observation of the language it uses for communication purposes are bound to fail, however, since a nation is never homogeneous, and since many often opposing factors are involved in the formation of the language. The method is totally lacking in scientific foundation.

93. The Swiss scholar Ferdinand de Saussure (1857–1913) has exerted a decisive influence on modern linguistic thought. Considering human speech to be a product of society, he emphasizes the role of language as a means of communication. His theory of language is expressed in his *Cours de linguistique générale* (published posthumously in Paris-Lausanne in 1916, third ed., 1931). From 1906 to 1911, Saussure taught three courses in general linguistics, but he never felt obliged to publish his material. The *Cours* was compiled from lecture notes taken by two of his students, Charles Bally (1865–1947) and Albert Sechehaye (1880–1946). The most revolutionary of Saussure's linguistic theories is the distinction he establishes between *langue* (E. *language*, Sp. *lengua*) and *parole* (E. speech, Sp. *lenguaje*). *Langue* is a social institution; it represents the lexical and grammatical system and has a virtual existence in the minds of the members of the linguistic community. Without the existence of such a group, 'language' would not be possible. *Parole* is the individual speech act, the concrete realization. 'Language' is imposed on the speaker, who can neither create it nor modify it, while 'speech' is free of restraints. It follows that all linguistic changes originate in 'speech'; they become part of 'language' if they are generally accepted by the linguistic community.

94. From sociology, Saussure also draws the distinction between static, descriptive, synchronic linguistics on one hand, historical, evolutional, diachronic linguistics on the other. Synchronic language study focuses on the state of the language at the present time or at a given point in the past without any preoccupation with what has gone before or what will follow, while diachronic linguistics focuses on the history of the various elements of the language. Both pursuits are valid, but Saussure gives precedence to synchrony, since it is the only reality the individual speaker is familiar with; to the individual speaker the evolution of linguistic facts through time does not exist. The distinction between synchronic and diachronic considerations is essentially identifiable with the distinction between *langue* and *parole*. In Saussure's scheme, the synchronic and diachronic methods are kept separate while, with the historical-comparative and the geographical methods, they are correlated.

95. In Saussure's terminology, language consists of signs. By the word *sign* is meant the bond that exists between the value at the phonic-acoustic level, which Saussure terms *signifiant* (E. *signifier*), and the value at the

logical-psychological level, referred to by Saussure as *signifié* (E. *signified*). The link between *signifiant* and *signifié* is very close; the *signifiant* of, for example, *fleur* is its phonological constitution, a combination of certain consonants and a vowel, while the *signifié* is the concept of 'flower'. The principal characteristic of the linguistic sign is its arbitrariness; there is no logically justified connection between a word and the thing or notion it serves to address. The linguistic sign is, however, constant and cannot in any way be altered by the individual speaker without causing chaos. Yet there is one group of words that seems to contradict the arbitrariness that is characteristic of the *signifiant–signifié* relationship, namely onomatopoeics. While the phonological constitution of Fr. *vache* is completely arbitrary as a designation for the animal, the same cannot be said about Fr. *coucou*, a noun which obviously imitates the cry of the bird. Saussure observes that not all onomatopoeics are logically motivated. Fr. *fouet* 'whip' is felt as an onomatopoeic, but the *signifiant* has evolved regularly from *fagus* 'beech tree' > OFr. *fou* with an added suffix. *Fouet* has become an onomatopoeic, and contrasting with this example, there are also occurrences of original onomatopoeics that have completely lost their sound-imitating property, as seen in §111.

THE HISTORICAL-COMPARATIVE METHOD

96. Comparative Romance philology focuses on what the Neolatin languages have in common; it examines the *romanité*, the Romance character, they share. It does not normally concern itself with features that belong to a single language, as for example the changes Spanish undergoes as it is extended to Latin America. The dividing line between Romance and single-language development is, however, not always sharply drawn.

97. It is in the area of Romance that the comparative method becomes truly historical since this is the only language family whose ancestor, Latin, is known. A comparison of the Germanic, Slavic or Indo-European language families establishes an affinity within each of these groups, but the exact historical source remains undocumented and can only be hypothetically reconstructed. It is true, of course, that even here the correspondences that can be established are not accidental, but display a regular pattern, yet they remain correspondences only whereas, in the Romance field, we are dealing with a scientific reality. We are able to follow the historical evolution of Latin and Romance over a period of more than two thousand years.

98. The workings of the historical-comparative method are best explained on the basis of a few examples. A comparison of It. *otto*, Sp. *ocho*, Rm. *opt* and Fr. *huit* reveals the existence of a certain affinity between these forms, which are all derived from a single source, Lat *ŏcto*. Not only do we know this because the Romance languages have evolved from Latin, but we can prove it scientifically by extending our examination to other lexical items displaying the *ct* nexus in Latin: *nŏcte* > It. *notte*, Sp. *noche*, Rm. *noapte*, Fr. *nuit*; *factu* > It. *fatto*, Sp. *hecho*, Rm. *fapt*, Fr. *fait*; *lacte* > It. *latte*, Sp. *leche*, Rm. *lapte*, Fr. *lait*. It immediately becomes clear that we are not confronted with random changes in these words, that a rigorous pattern can be observed for the development of the *ct* cluster in Romance: Lat. *ct* becomes *tt* in Italian, [*tš*] spelled *ch* in Spanish, *pt* in Rumanian and *i̯t* in French. This happens not only in the case of *ŏcto*, but occurs very generally wherever the *ct* cluster is found in words of the core vocabulary (§309). To the Neogrammarians, this phonological change has the rigor of a sound-law; it is a solidly established norm.

99. The words designating the ear in the Romance languages may give an idea of some of the complexities involved in applying the comparative method to a language family. A comparison of It. *orecchio*, Sp. *oreja*, Ptg. *orelha*, Fr. *oreille* and Rm. *ureche* immediately confirms a great similarity between these forms, yet it is obvious that they cannot be drawn from CL *auris*. Latin further has a diminutive *aurĭcŭla*, and it is this form that accounts for the ending present in the Romance words. The *c'l* cluster gives a lengthened *ki̯* in Italian (*cchi*), [*χ*] in Spanish (*j*), a palatal *l* in Portuguese (*lh*) and Old French, *ki̯* in Rumanian (*ch* or *chi*) and *i̯* in French (*ill* or *il*), as demonstrated by the reflexes of *ŏcŭlu*: It. *occhio*, Sp. *ojo*, Ptg. *olho*, Fr. *œil*, Rm. *ochiu*. The pretonic *au* of CL *aurĭcŭla* would be acceptable as the source of *o* in Italian, Spanish and French (§189), as a comparison with other words containing a pretonic *au* will confirm: *laudāre* > It. *lodare*, Sp. *loar*, OFr. *loer*, Fr. *louer*; *pausāre* > It. *posare*, Sp. *posar*, Fr. *poser*, but there are problems with Portuguese and Rumanian which, for the words cited here, have Ptg. *louvar* and *pousar* and Rm. *lăudà*. *Pausāre* is not continued in Rumanian, but *audīre* > Rm. *auzì* may serve as an additional example. Portuguese thus continues pretonic *au* as *ou*, while Rumanian offers *au* or *ău* as a reflex, but in the word under discussion, Portuguese has *o* and Rumanian *u*. These vowels normally reflect a Latin *o*, and since the Italian, Spanish and French developments could similarly continue the vowel *o* (§187), the comparative method would yield *oricla* as the source. The existence of such a form is confirmed by the *Appendix Probi* entry *auris non oricla*, which suggests that the popular pronunciation of CL

aurĭcŭla was *oricla*. This popular form is also found in Plautus, Cicero and Pliny. The syncope of *-cŭl-* to *c'l* is amply documented in the *Appendix Probi*: *speculum non speclum, articulus non articlus, oculus non oclus.* Only Occ. *aurelha* represents a direct continuation of *aurĭcŭla*; it is a learned form.

100. The Neogrammarians were firm believers in the principle of *Ausnahmslosigkeit*, which is to say that they were convinced that sound-laws suffer no exceptions other than those determined by analogical pressures (§§101–104). If irregularities do occur, it may simply be that our methods of analysis are still insufficiently refined. New discoveries are made from time to time, which would tend to support this optimistic view. Stressed free *a* evolves regularly to *e* in French (§152): *mare > mer; sāle > sel*, but a fairly common variant development to *ie*: *navigāre >* OFr. *nagier; carrĭcāre >* OFr. *chargier; capra >* OFr. *chievre; laxāre >* OFr. *laissier; cane > chien* (§171), remained unaccounted for until the German scholar Karl Bartsch (1832–1888) discovered that *ie* was the regular outcome whenever the Latin stressed free *a* was preceded by a palatal, a rule that has come to be known as Bartsch's Law. An excessively rigid formulation of sound-laws, equated with laws of nature, soon led to criticism of the Neogrammarian principles, but there can be no denying that the achievements brought about by this school have led to a more accurate knowledge of the processes of phonological change.

ANALOGY

101. A large number of exceptions that do exist to established phonological norms are explained by the Neogrammarians through the workings of the principle of analogy. In its traditional use, analogy may be defined as a force of attraction: one word is influenced formally by another, either because they both belong to the same semantic sphere, or because they are part of a paradigm, such as verb forms, word derivations or suffixal formations. CL *lĕvis* 'light, easy' and CL *gravis* 'heavy, severe' are continued in Vulgar Latin as *lĕvis* and **grĕvis*, the tonic vowel of *gravis* having been replaced analogically by that of its antonym *lĕvis*. Generally speaking, the Romance forms are derived from VL **grĕve*: It. *greve*, Rm., Cat. *greu*, Occ. *gr(i)eu*, Fr. *grief*, OSp. *grieve*, while Sp., Ptg., Fr. *grave* is a learned form.

102. Verb paradigms offer the greatest potential for analogical change, since a vocalic alternation or apophony evolves in many verbs due to a differing stress pattern. Stressed free close *o* becomes *eu* in French, while the same vowel yields *ou* in pretonic position: *cōlat >* OFr. *keule* vs. *cōlāre >*

couler; *plōrat* > *pleure* vs. *plōrāre* > OFr. *plourer*. For the open *o*, the alternation is similarly between a tonic *eu* and a pretonic *ou*: **mŏrit* > *meurt* vs. **mŏrīre* > *mourir*. Analogical changes are sudden and do not display the pattern of predictability that is characteristic of sound-laws; in *couler*, the pretonic vowel has been generalized in the paradigm, in *pleurer* the tonic, while no analogical leveling has taken place in the case of *meurt–mourir*, but the reasons for this diversity escape us.

103. In word derivations, the tonic vowel of the root word is often kept even though a change in stress would call for a different outcome: It. *tela* < *tēla* is responsible for the retention of *e* in *telaio* < *tēlāriu*, where one would have expected the pretonic *e* to close to *i* (cf. *sēcūru* > It. *sicuro* and see §185), and the same observations apply to It. *fedele* < *fĭdēle*, influenced by *fede* < *fĭde*. OFr. *pelu* < *pĭlūtu* yields to *poilu*, obtained analogically from *poil* < *pĭlu*, whereby the [ə]/*oi* apophony, with [ə] reflecting the pretonic outcome, *oi* the tonic, is leveled out. The suffixes -*īcŭlum* and -*ĭcŭlum* are often confused: Lat. *lentĭcŭla* should have evolved to **lentecchia* in Italian, but instead we find *lenticchia*.

104. Far-reaching external analogies take place in the morphological systems. The Italian *passato remoto* form *mossi* cannot be derived from Lat. *movi*; it is obtained analogically from another category of *passati remoti*, the *s* perfects: *scrīpsī* > It. *scrissi*; *dīxī* > It. *dissi*. Paradigmatic pressure exerted by *scrivere – scrissi* yields a *muovere – mossi* correspondence. In Old French, the *passé simple* form *misdrent* < *mīsĕrunt* with *d* inserted as a glide between voiced *s* and *r*, is a rare form, which is mostly replaced by OFr. *mistrent*, analogical from perfects displaying the insertion of a *t* between a voiceless *s* and *r* as in *dīxĕrunt* > OFr. *distrent* and *traxĕrunt* > OFr. *traistrent*. Both *misdrent* and *mistrent* eventually give way to *mirent*, analogical from Fr. *firent* < *fēcĕrunt* and Fr. *virent* < *vīderunt*.

POPULAR WORDS AND LEARNED WORDS

105. Popular words (G. *Erbwörter*) are words which have always remained in the oral tradition from one generation to the next, and which have consequently undergone all the regular phonological changes that are applicable to them. Learned words or Latinisms (G. *Buchwörter*), on the other hand, are not part of an uninterrupted transmission process. Used in a learned context, these words were taken over from Latin whenever the need arose for new lexical items. As a result, they remain very close to the Latin base. Normal phonological changes may be seen in *ŏcŭlu* > It. *occhio*, Fr. *œil*, while the corresponding adjective, Fr. *oculaire*, It. *oculare*, is a

Latinism that has undergone only minimal changes from its Latin source *ŏcŭlāre*. The many translations from Latin into French that were undertaken in the late Middle Ages necessitated the creation of several abstract nouns. These often replaced earlier forms deemed unworthy of appearing in philosophical or religious works: *maturité* replaces OFr. *meüreté*, *calvitie* takes the place of OFr. *chauvece*, and *surdité* is substituted for OFr. *sourdece*. This practice singularly weakens the formal links that usually tie adjective and noun together: *maturité* and *calvitie* are far removed formally from *mûr* and *chauve*, and in the case of *cécité* the old adjective *cieu* 'blind' < *caecu* that it refers to has long ago been replaced by *aveugle*.

106. The identification of a word as learned can only be made on the basis of a phonological analysis, demonstrating that the word has not evolved in conformity with prevailing sound-laws. Common use is not a valid criterion; a Frenchman would not consider *nation* learned, yet a comparison of *natiōne* > Fr. *nation* with the popularly developed *ratiōne* > Fr. *raison* and *satiōne* > Fr. *saison* clearly reveals that it has not been popularly transmitted. Several words are semi-learned; they have come into the language early enough to participate in certain changes, but these popularly obtained elements coexist with learned features. Lat. *saecŭlu* evolves to *siècle* in French, showing popular diphthongization of the stressed vowel, but learned retention of the *c'l* cluster. Since the identification of learned words follows from phonological criteria and not from frequency of use, it is obvious that the learned character of a word is most readily singled out in French which, of all the Romance languages, has undergone the most profound sound changes. It is far more difficult to establish a distinction between learned and popular treatment in a language like Italian, which has remained very conservative in its evolution. In many instances, a Latin word is continued in Romance both in a popular development and as a Latinism. Such double forms, termed *doublets* in French and *allòtropi* in Italian, are for the above-mentioned reasons particularly common or most easily identifiable in French: *hŏspĭtāle* > *hostel* > *hôtel* 'hotel' and *hôpital* 'hospital'; *fragĭle* > *frêle* 'frail' and *fragile* 'fragile'; *redēmptiōne* > *rançon* 'ransom' and *rédemption* 'redemption'; *fabrica* > *forge* 'smithy' and *fabrique* 'factory'; *pēnsare* > *peser* 'to weigh' and *penser* 'to think'; *sacramentu* > *serment* 'oath' and *sacrement* 'sacrament'; *separare*, VL *seperare* > *sevrer* 'to wean' and *séparer* 'to separate'. Italian examples are: *vĭtiu* > *vezzo* 'habit, trick' and *vizio* 'vice'; *pēnsāre* > *pesare* 'to weigh' and *pensare* 'to think', while Spanish offers: *pēnsāre* > *pesar* 'to weigh' and *pensar* 'to think'; *artĭcŭlu* > *artejo* 'knuckle' and *artículo* 'article, articulation'; *fĭngĕre*, *fĭngīre > *heñir* 'to knead' and

fingir 'to feign, to simulate'; *cŏllŏcāre > colgar* 'to hang' and *colocar* 'to place, to put'. A Portuguese example is: *artĭcŭlu > artelho* 'ankle' and *artigo* 'article'.

BORROWINGS OR LOANWORDS

107. Borrowings constitute another source of irregular phonological development. The term *borrowing* or *loanword* (G. *Lehnwort*, Fr. *mot d'emprunt*, Sp. *préstamo*), though universally recognized, is infelicitous inasmuch as borrowing usually implies a restitution and thus could be taken to mean that the language which "lends" a lexical item is itself, at least temporarily, deprived of it. In many instances, words have not come in directly from Latin, but are borrowed from another Romance language (or from another language group). It. *mangiare* cannot be explained as a reflex of Lat. *manducare*, but is borrowed from OFr. *mangier*, where the voicing and subsequent palatalization of intervocalic *k* to [*dž*] represents a normal development. Fr. *abeille* does not reflect Lat. *apĭcŭla* directly, but must have come into the language via Occitan, which voices intervocalic *p* to *b*, whereas French has the labio-dental fricative *v* (cf. *sapēre* > Occ. *saber* vs. Fr. *savoir*). Sp. *batalla* cannot be drawn from VL **battalia*, since the *lị* combination gives [χ] in Spanish and not a palatal *l* (cf. *fīliu* > Sp. *hijo*); it must be a borrowing from Gallo-Romance, where a palatal *l* represents the regular outcome of the *lị* group. The *-āta* suffix is continued as *-ée* in French and as *-ada* in Occitan; the form *-ade*, encountered in some French words, reveals Occitan influence: Fr. *croisade* (cf. Fr. *croisée*), *ballade*.

ETYMOLOGY

108. Etymology may be defined in its most abstract sense as the discipline that studies the origin of words. It investigates the relations that link one word to another which precedes it in time, and from which it is derived. Coined by the Stoics, the term is drawn from the Greek adjective *étymos* 'true, authentic', and etymology is thus in its literal sense a quest for the truth. To the Ancients, the goal of the etymological discipline was to trace a word back to its origin, to unravel its "true" or "correct" meaning and, in so doing, to achieve a better understanding of the world, governed by complex relations which the discovery of a primitive linguistic stage was supposed to be able to elucidate. It goes without saying that the terms "true" or "correct" do not in any way reflect an attempt to prescribe correct usage of a given word in the modern language. It is not the purpose of

etymology to bring about a return to primitive semantic values whose existence the average speaker is not even aware of. The primitive sense of OFr. *navré* is 'wounded' while, in the modern language, the word is used solely as a formula of regret, carrying the figurative meaning of 'very sorry'. Derived from Old Norse **nafra* 'to wound', the verb *nafrer* and the variant *navrer* are first documented in the eleventh and twelfth centuries, and this word family keeps its primitive values until the seventeenth while, in the modern language, the original sense is irretrievably lost.

109. Of fundamental importance to any study of etymology is the notion of motivation, which is to say the relation that exists between form and meaning, between the word and the thing or concept it serves to designate, in Ferdinand de Saussure's terminology between the *signifiant* ('signifier', i.e., the word) and the *signifié* ('signified', i.e., the thing or concept). The link between word and thing can be either arbitrary or motivated. In a diachronic perspective, most words are motivated. Sp. *gallo* is motivated historically since it can be traced to Lat. *gallu,* but at the synchronic level, Sp. *gallo* is entirely arbitrary. There is no reason other than historical why this particular combination of sounds should be the only one capable of designating this particular bird in Spanish.

110. Some vocabulary items may be said to be at least relatively motivated; they are motivated in their morphological structure either through compounding or through derivation. Fr. *vingt* is unmotivated, while Fr. *dix-neuf* is motivated, as is also the Rumanian word for 'twenty' *douăzeci* lit. 'two tens', since we recognize how these words are formed. In French, *poire* is unmotivated, while the derivation *poirier* is transparent, for we know that French forms names of fruit trees through suffixation with *-ier.* Words may, however, lose their motivation through regular linguistic change. Thus Fr. *berger* 'shepherd' is unmotivated whereas the earlier form *berbicarius,* documented in the ninth-century *Glossary of Reichenau,* is still clearly related to *berbice* 'sheep', being as transparent in its formation as are *vaccarius* 'cowherd', drawn from *vacca* 'cow', and *bovarius* 'cowherd', based on *bove* 'ox'.

111. Onomatopoeics are words which are created through a deliberate attempt to imitate natural sounds (§95). Fr. *coucou* draws its phonological configuration from an imitation of the cry of the bird. Corominas considers Sp. *chupar* 'to suck' to be imitative of the noise produced by the lips when sucking. It. *lupo* instead of a regularly developed **lopo* from Lat. *lŭpu* (cf. Sp., Ptg. *lobo,* Cat. *llop,* Occ. *lop)* is considered by Rohlfs (§71) to be an onomatopoeic creation, with the vowel *u* intuitively felt as better able than *o* to render the howling of the wolf, but it could simply be a dialectal

variant, which has come into the standard language from regions where the wolf was commonly found. Yet even lexical items created through the direct imitation of a natural sound are subject to linguistic change, which may result in the obscuration and eventual demise of their onomatopoeic quality. Thus Lat. *pipione* or **pibione,* which may well be an onomatopoeic creation, rendering the chirping of the young bird, evolves to *pigeon* in French, which is void of any sound-imitating property. To Antoine Thomas, all onomatopoeic etymologies are provisional only, destined to disappear as soon as the true etymology has been established.

112. Modern etymology is, as already mentioned (§§96–100), a product of the historical-comparative method developed in the early nineteenth century for the Indo-European language family. The Romance language family is privileged in having a known ancestor, which is well documented, and this raises the question as to how far back etymological investigations should be pursued in the Romance field. Italian scholars distinguish between an *etimologia prossima,* which stops at Latin, and an *etimologia remota,* which takes the quest for origins all the way back to Indo-European. It is the *etimologia prossima* approach that is used in most Romance scholarship.

113. To Diez, an etymological problem is solved if a basic form can be found in Latin from which the Romance reflexes can be derived in accordance with phonological norms. An etymology thus becomes a succinct phonological formula, as exemplified here by Lat. *pacare:* It. *pagare,* Sp., Ptg. *pagar,* Occ. *pagar, payar,* Fr. *payer.* Although the change in meaning from 'to pacify' to 'to pay' is briefly mentioned the semantic aspect of the etymology is not central to Diez's concerns, as is true very generally of Neogrammarian methodology. Meyer-Lübke uses similar phonological formulas, but they represent a wider spread, including dialectal variants. Important derivations are discussed, and bibliographical references to treatments of problem areas are given.

114. With Schuchardt, etymology becomes word biography, an in-depth history of a given word in its totality of sounds and meanings. Dialectal variants are quoted, as are also all documented phases the word has undergone, and great importance is attached to the date of its earliest appearance (G. *Erstbeleg*). In a significant departure from Neogrammarian practice, Schuchardt places major emphasis on semantics. His etymological sketches focus on the relationship between the word and the thing or concept it serves to designate (*Wörter und Sachen*), the diffusion of the word in time and space is shown (linguistic geography), and its interaction

with other words of the same associative field, whether relating to form or to meaning, is examined (*Wortfeld*).

115. The insipid or unimaginative line, to use von Wartburg's phrase, which simply connects the point of departure with the outcome of an etymological equation, is no longer sufficient. The discipline must also provide a detailed discussion of the two-thousand-year history of the word. It is not only the birth, but also, and to an even greater extent, the life of the word that is of interest to the etymologist. This does not at all mean that phonology is no longer of any value; quite to the contrary, the two methods, phonology and word history, are complementary to one another, but are usually kept separate in modern research. Baldinger distinguishes between *étymologie-origine* and *étymologie-histoire du mot*, Guiraud between *étymologie phono-historique* and *étymologie lexico-historique*. Putting this relationship into its proper perspective, the Russian scholar Abaev declares that an etymological investigation is only half done if it is limited to phonology; it is worthless if it does not at all take phonology into account.

116. A true word history begins with the *Wörter und Sachen* approach. The quest for the phonological source of a word must go hand in hand with an investigation of the cultural and linguistic life of the given area. The technical knowledge which word historians must acquire is stupendous. The article on Fr. *charrue* 'plough' < *carrūca* reflects technical advances in construction involving terminologies and descriptions that are often difficult to cope with for the non-specialist. The word makes its first appearance in the Frankish *Lex Salica*, which leads one to believe that the Franks introduced the new plough, but this is refuted on the basis of archeological and historical evidence showing the Franks to have been primarily engaged in the raising of livestock rather than in the growing of crops. The investigation of *realia* is not undertaken lightly. Jaberg-Jud's linguistic atlas of Italy and southern Switzerland has two companion volumes by Scheuermeier on rural life in those regions, and von Wartburg does not hesitate to affirm that he would never have been able to finish his *magnum opus*, the twenty-five volume French etymological dictionary, if he had not been raised in the country and been familiar with agricultural pursuits from his childhood.

117. The interdependence of the *Wörter und Sachen* oriented approach and the historical-comparative method may be illustrated by the following example. As the designation for 'liver', Classical Latin has *jĕcur*, while the Romance words: It. *fegato*, Sp. *hígado*, Ptg. *fégado*, Cat., Occ. *fetge*, Fr. *foie*, Rm. *ficat*, can be traced phonologically to Lat. *ficatum* (*FEW* III 490–493). The problem posed by this disparity was not solved until the cultural

aspect of the *Sache,* of the thing designated by the word, had been clarified. The Greeks used to fatten geese and pigs with a diet of figs in order to obtain a larger and tastier liver, and they called this liver *hēpar sykōtón,* from Gk. *sykon* 'fig'. The Romans, who imported this culinary art from Greece, rendered *sykōtón* by *ficatum* 'liver of an animal fattened with figs', from Lat. *fīcus* 'fig'. This new formation completely replaces CL *jĕcur.* The etymological probing has thus far focused solely on the semantic aspect, on the *Sache.* Von Wartburg then proceeds to discuss the various phonological changes which Lat. *ficatum* has suffered in Romance: 1) an alternation between *fe-* and *fi-* (It. *fegato* vs. Sp. *hígado),* 2) a shift in stress *(ficátum* vs. *fícatum),* 3) a metathesis of *c-t* to *t-c,* 4) a suffixal change *(-atum, -acum* replaced by *-itum* and *-icum).* The source of these multiple changes has been the object of much scholarly debate which, for obvious reasons of space, von Wartburg refrains from covering in detail, but a number of bibliographical references are offered, specifically for changes 3 and 4, which occur only sporadically and are thus of minor importance. More attention is paid to the *fe-/fi-* alternation and to the stress pattern, including a detailed geographical distribution of these various forms. Lat. *ficātum* is continued in Rm. *ficat,* Dalm. (Vegl.) *feguat,* in Rhaeto-Romance, Venetian and southern Sardinian. Outside of this archaic linguistic zone, the stress has shifted to the initial syllable under Greek influence, as seen from Hispanic, Gallo-Romance and most Italian reflexes. Cat., Occ. *fetge* goes back to a metathesized **feticu* which, in addition, displays a suffixal change or perhaps rather a weakening of the posttonic vowel (cf. *monichus* for *monachus*), and a few Italian dialectal forms can be drawn from the same source.

118. In his book *Gli arabismi nelle lingue neolatine,* Pellegrini offers an eloquent example of the close links that exist between word history and culture. It. *facchino* 'porter' is drawn from Arabic *faqih,* designating an expert in customs matters, a person who held an important function during the period of intense commercial exchange between the Arabs and the powerful Italian maritime republics. With the decline of this trade and with the waning of Arabic influence in Italy, the term suffered a severe erosion in value, coming to designate the humble tasks of the modern-day Italian *facchino,* carrying baggage in transportation terminals.

119. The *Wörter und Sachen* methodology adds a structural orientation to etymological speculation. An etymological investigation no longer focuses on the observation of an isolated change, but rather on the perception of a general and systematic evolution. Each word forms part of a system in relation to shape and meaning, and the change of one member of

the unit will automatically lead to a reshuffling of the whole. The designations for 'thigh' and 'hip' in Latin and Romance offer a classical example of this approach. Lat. *fĕmur* 'thigh' drops, presumably as a result of homonymy with *fĭmus* 'dung', and in its stead French has *cuisse,* a reflex of Lat. *cŏxa* 'hip'. This semantic change, in turn, brings on the need for a new designation for 'hip'. The system recovers its equilibrium through the borrowing of Gmc. **hanka* > Fr. *hanche* 'hip'. Corresponding to Lat. *cŏxa—fĕmur,* French thus has *hanche—cuisse,* and Italian similarly has *anca—coscia.*

120. To a positivist like Antoine Thomas, etymology is a science, but in certain respects it may also be termed an art. Just like a poet, an etymologist is a word seeker, both must establish a harmony between form and meaning, both are engaged in a pursuit that is creative and imaginative. An etymologist is expected to have sudden flashes of intuition which unexpectedly put him on the track of a stubbornly elusive etymology. It goes without saying, however, that an etymological source gained by intuition is unacceptable unless it is found to be in accordance with sound- laws and causes no semantic difficulties. The quest for the etymology of Fr. *mauvais* may serve as an illustration. Schuchardt (*ZRPh, 14* (1891), 181–183 and *30* (1907), 320–328) proposes as the source **malifatiu* 'who has an unhappy fate', composed of *mălum* 'bad' and *fătum* 'fate' and with *Bonifatius,* preserved as the proper noun *Boniface* in French, serving as the model. The suggested etymology was later documented in an inscription from the year 23 A.D., which means that the asterisk can now be removed, and Schuchardt was able to convincingly refute objections raised against his suggested etymology both on phonological and semantic grounds. He shows that we do not have to do with an isolated occurrence of the voicing of intervocalic *f* to *v,* citing such cases as *raphănu* > Fr. *rave* and the proper noun *Stĕphanu* > OFr. *Estievne* > *Etienne.* The composite nature of *malifatiu* accounts for the prolonged retention of the weak vowel *i* needed for the voicing of *f,* and at the semantic level Schuchardt explains that it is quite common for words meaning 'unhappy, miserable' to come to render the notion of 'evil'. A parallel example is OFr. *mescheant* 'whom misfortune befalls, miserable' > *méchant* 'evil'.

121. For a large segment of the vocabulary, however, the etymological source is very straightforward and irrefutable, yet even here the etymologist must beware of pitfalls. Fr. *fesser* 'to spank', first documented in 1489, can without the slightest phonological or semantic difficulty be derived from *fesse* 'buttocks', the literal meaning of the verb being 'to strike on the buttocks', and a Frenchman will immediately establish this connection be-

tween verb and noun. However, certain dialects, among them *normand,* have a variant *fessier,* which proves that the stem of the verb must have ended in a palatal. The verb thus is not derived from *fesse* 'buttocks', but from another *fesse* 'rod or stick cut from a tree or bush' < Lat. *fascia* 'tie' and which has since disappeared. It follows that the true meaning is not 'to strike on the buttocks', but 'to strike with a rod or a stick'; the verb is formed in the same manner as *fouetter* 'to whip' is drawn from *fouet* 'whip'. While this example vividly illustrates the need for the etymologist to harbor a healthy skepticism toward the results obtained by his predecessors, the French scholar Meillet vastly exaggerates the importance of this attitude when he proclaims that as many as ninety out of one hundred etymologies are either false or doubtful.

122. Etymology is a complex discipline with multiple applications and therefore open to influences often of massive proportions from the various fields it is connected with. It is particularly in the area of technical-cultural investigations that the discipline is in danger of bursting at the seams, unless great care is taken to safeguard the purely linguistic element present in all etymological research. The powerful cultural-technical component inherent in word history pursuits may turn the etymological discipline into a mere by-product of the history of culture, making it exclusively tributary to culturally slanted investigations, which would mean a formidable threat to its status as a separate branch of knowledge. Word history pursuits must be undertaken as linguistic research on a cultural basis.

Semantics

123. Semantics is the study of word-meanings; the name of the discipline was first introduced by Bréal in 1883. As a linguistic term, meaning may be defined as the reciprocal and reversible relationship that exists between sound and sense. This definition is already implicit in Saussure's theory of the *signifiant* and the *signifié,* and the same scholar likens the close relationship between sound and meaning to the recto and verso of a page: you cannot cut one without cutting the other. Yet in spite of this close interrelationship, in spite of the preference accorded to the thing over the word by many scholars, semantics was slow in forming as a separate division of the linguistic discipline, although it was already treated as such by K. Ch. Reisig in his 1839 *Vorlesungen über lateinische Sprachwissenschaft.* This may be linked to the fact that principles governing the development of meaning are very difficult to establish and to systematize.

124. Changes of meaning may be caused by factors of a linguistic, historical, social or psychological nature. Through a process of contiguity, referred to by Bréal as "contagion," the meaning of one word may be transferred to another simply because the two terms very often appear together. One of the most striking examples of this phenomenon is the French negation system. Fr. *pas* lit. 'step' becomes a negation when combined with *ne*. Lat. *fŏcum* 'fireplace' comes to mean 'fire' in the combination *fŏcum ĭncĕndĕre* 'to light the fireplace' > 'to light the fire', and it completely replaces CL *ignis* 'fire'. The thing may change while the designation remains the same. The word *papier* 'paper' is still used in French although nobody writes on papyrus any more, nor does anybody write with a goose quill (Lat. *plūma*), but here too, the word is continued (Fr. *plume*) in spite of important material changes. It may also happen that the name changes, while the thing remains essentially unaltered: Lat. *habēnae* 'reins' collides phonologically with *avēna* 'oats' and is replaced by *rĕtĭna* > It. *redini*, Sp. *rienda*, Fr. *rêne*. In other instances, both name and function of a tool suffer little change: Lat. *martĕllu* 'hammer' > It. *martello*, Sp. *martillo*, Ptg. *martelo*, Fr. *marteau*. A material modification may have lexical consequences: when Fr. *poudre* < Lat. *pŭlvĕre* takes on the meaning of 'gunpowder', it is replaced in its basic acceptation of 'dust' by *poussière*.

125. A socially determined change affects the French word *pendant* which, from its use in the legal language as the equivalent of E. *pending*, comes to serve as a very common preposition with the value of 'during'. Psychological causes of change focus on the affective aspect of words. A basic term often yields to a more expressive word. This is the case with Lat. *cutis* 'skin', which is replaced by *pĕllis* 'hide, skin' > It. *pelle*, Sp. *piel*, Ptg. *pele*, Fr. *peau*. It is not uncommon for words that are normally used about animals to be applied to humans. Lat. *ŭmĕrus* 'shoulder' is continued in Rm. *umar*, Sp. *hombro*, Ptg. *ombro*, but is replaced elsewhere by *spatŭla*, which originally meant 'shoulder blade (of pig)'. Romance reflexes of this word, carrying the meaning of 'shoulder', are It. *spalla*, Sp. *espalda*, Cat. *espattla*, Occ. *espatla*, *espala* and Fr. *épaule*. *Camba*, a word of Greek origin whose primitive value is 'knee joint (of horse)', is continued with the value of 'leg' in It. *gamba*, Occ., Cat. *camba*, Fr. *jambe*, while CL *crus* 'leg' is completely abandoned.

126. A taboo ban may be imposed on certain words. The devil is often referred to in Old French simply as *aversier* 'adversary' or 'enemy'. *Mŭstēla*, the Latin name for 'weasel', has left few reflexes in Romance: OFr. *mosteile*, the Spanish diminutives *mustelilla* and *mostalilla*, Occ. *mostela*, Cat. *mostella* (*REW* 5778). French has replaced it by a hypo-

coristic *belette,* a diminutive of *bel* 'beautiful' (cf. G. *Schöntierlein* lit. 'beautiful little animal'), Portuguese has *doninha* lit. 'little woman', Spanish *comadreja,* derived from *comadre* 'godmother'. The Old Spanish word for the fox, *rabosa,* may find its explanation in folklore. To avoid the ill omen associated with the fox, Spanish peasants would make it a habit not to mention the animal by name (OSp. *gulpeja),* referring to it simply as *la del gran rabo* 'the one with the large tail'. Words may develop a pejorative sense. Fr. *bougre* 'Bulgarian' is used in the Middle Ages with the meaning of 'heretic' because the Bulgarians belonged to the Eastern Church, and the word eventually evolved into a term of abuse. Conversely, there are also instances of ameliorative developments. Lat. *mandūcāre* 'to chew' is continued in Fr. *manger* 'to eat', and Fr. *blâmer* 'to blame' has evolved historically from Lat. *blasphēmāre* 'to revile, to insult'.

127. Semantic changes may be divided into three categories, depending on whether the new sense is quantitatively larger or smaller than or the same as the old one. This scheme is noted for its simplicity, but if all changes fit into this rigid classification, it is simply because the third group is some kind of catch-all that takes in everything that does not belong to the other two. Another drawback is that this arrangement tells us nothing about the semantic processes involved in the changes. An extension of meaning often occurs in connection with a transition from technical to everyday usage. Fr. *arriver* is historically a marine term evolving from VL **adrīpāre,* which is derived from the noun *rīpa* 'bank, shore'. As a technical term used by sailors, it meant 'to go ashore', but it subsequently came into common use with the extended value of 'to arrive'. The origin of Fr. *panier* is Lat. *panāriu,* made up of the noun *pāne* 'bread' and the *-āriu* suffix. The primitive value of *panier* is thus 'bread-basket', but the word soon takes on the broader meaning of 'basket'. Restriction of meaning is a more common process than extension. OFr. *viande* < Lat. *vivenda* is used with the general meaning of 'food, provisions', then narrows its sense to 'meat' in the sixteenth century. A restriction of meaning occurs when a word of the common lexicon comes into technical use: CL *trahĕre* > VL **tragĕre* lit. 'to pull' is continued in French as *traire,* an agricultural term meaning 'to milk' (§244). Lat. *pŏnĕre* 'to place, to put' is continued in Sp. *poner* with its primitive value kept intact, while its French reflex *pondre* has adopted the highly specialized meaning of 'to lay an egg'. Fr. *noyer* 'to drown' reflects Lat. *nĕcāre* 'to kill'. The third category is composed of transfers of meaning involving no quantitative element; an example is Fr. *langue* 'tongue', which comes to be used with the value of 'language'.

128. A formal similarity between two words which are otherwise unrelated can lead to a semantic change. This feature is usually referred to as popular etymology. The earlier meaning of Fr. *souffreteux* is 'needy, destitute', its source being a suffixal derivation from the past participle *suffractu* of the Old French verb *soufraindre* 'to be in need, to be destitute' < *sŭffrangĕre* for CL *sŭffrĭngĕre*. When, with the loss of the noun *soufraite* 'scarcity, dearth, deprivation' and the verb *soufraindre,* the adjective *souffreteux* finds itself isolated in the system, French speakers associate it with the verb *souffrir* 'to suffer', and as a result the meaning of the adjective has changed to 'sickly, suffering'. This new semantic value is first documented in the early decades of the nineteenth century.

PART II.

PHONOLOGY

THE LATIN VOCALIC SYSTEM

129. The vocalic system of Classical Latin is based on quantity, which is to say that a vowel may be either long or short. Length is a phonemic feature in the classical language as shown by the following examples of word pairs, which differ from one another solely on the basis of the vocalic quantity: *pŏpŭlus* 'people' vs. *pōpŭlus'* 'poplar'; *mălum* 'evil' vs. *mālum* 'apple'; *ŏs* 'bone' vs. *ōs* 'mouth'; *vĕnit* 'he comes' vs. *vēnit* 'he came'. The Classical Latin vocalic system consists of five long and five short vowels and three diphthongs:

Vowels

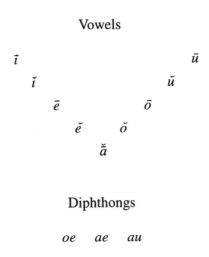

Diphthongs

oe   ae   au

130. In the spoken language, the long vowels began to acquire a close quality, while the short vowels tended to be pronounced more open. As a result of these trends, the quantity system eventually collapsed and was replaced in Vulgar Latin by a system built on quality, by which is meant on differing degrees of opening. A vowel thus is no longer short or long, but open or close. This change was accomplished approximately by the third century A.D. The Vulgar Latin vocalic system was never totally unified, but there is one scheme which underlies all the written Romance languages with the exception of Rumanian, and which for pedagogical purposes is conveniently labeled the Vulgar Latin system, although it is also quite often referred to more precisely as the Italic quality system. It consists of seven vowels: a palatal or front vowel series representing three degrees of opening: a close *i,* a mid *ẹ* and an open *ę* and paralleling that a velar or back vowel series: a close *u,* a mid *ọ* and an open *ǫ*, plus the vowel *a* which is isolated in the system. The Vulgar Latin system derives as follows from the Classical scheme:

Classical Latin	ī	ĭ	ē	ĕ	ū	ŭ	ō	ŏ	ā	ă
			\/				\/			\/
Vulgar Latin	i		ẹ	ę	u		ọ		ǫ	a

Of the Classical Latin diphthongs, *oe* merges with *ẹ* and *ae* with *ę*, while the diphthong *au* is still retained, although there are early occurrences of the change of *au* to *ō* in popular lexical items such as CL *cauda* > VL *cōda* 'tail'; CL *aurĭcŭla* > VL *oricla* 'ear'. Cases of *e* for *ĭ* are encountered in inscriptions prior to the third century A.D.: *menus* for *mĭnus; accepere* for *accĭpere,* and the change of *ŭ* to *o* is documented in the *Appendix Probi: columna non colomna.*

131. As mentioned, Vulgar Latin had no unified vocalic system. Sardinian vocalism flows from an archaic system, which differs from the Italic model in its treatment of both the palatal and the velar vowels:

Classical Latin	ī	ĭ	ē	ĕ	ū	ŭ	ō	ŏ	ā	ă
		\/		\/		\/		\/		\/
Sardinian	i		e		u		o		a	

The regular development of *ĭ* to *i* and of *ŭ* to *u* in Sardinian is illustrated in the following examples: *pĭra > pira; nĭve > nie; pĭce > pighe; nŭce > nughe; bŭcca > bukka; fŭrca > furca.* The archaic system is also retained in certain dialects of the continental *Mezzogiorno,* especially in South Lucanian.

132. Balkan Romance and East Lucanian have adopted a compromise system between the Italic and the archaic or Sardinian scheme; the palatal vowels follow the Italic model, whereas the velar series is treated as in the archaic system:

Classical Latin	ī	ĭ	ē	ĕ	ū	ŭ	ō	ŏ	ā	ă
		\/		\/		\/		\/		\/
Rumanian	i		ẹ		ę	u		ǫ		a

The Rumanian developments are illustrated in the following examples: *fīlu > fir; vĭrĭde > vẹrde; lĭgnu > lẹmn; crēdo > crẹd; *mĕle > miere; lūna > lună; mūru > mur; crŭce > cruce; fŭrca > furcă; sōle > soare; mŏla > moară; lātus > lat; mắre > mare.*

THE SYLLABLE

133. A syllable is said to be *free* or *open* if it ends in a vowel; it is *blocked* if it ends in a consonant. A single consonant goes with the following vowel, which leaves the syllable open as in *a-ma-re, fa-cĕ-re*. If two consonants are present, the first one goes with the preceding vowel, thus blocking the syllable: *par-te, gŭt-ta, per-do*. However, the combination of occlusive and liquid is not split up, but goes jointly with the following vowel, leaving the preceding syllable free: *pĕ-tra, te-nĕ-bras, a-prī-le*. We may assume that the nature of the syllable was of no importance in the archaic stages of Romance since this is still the case in Hispanic, Occitan, Sardinian and Rumanian, while Italian and French have innovated, restricting the diphthongization of tonic vowels to the free position: Lat. *sĕpte* gives It. *sette* and Fr. *sept* as opposed to Sp. *siete,* and Lat. *pŏrta* evolves to It. *porta* and Fr. *porte* vs. Sp. *puerta*.

THE ACCENT

134. Concurrently with the loss of vocalic quantity, the Latin accent becomes, like the English or Romance, one of intensity. Aside from proclitics, i.e., words that are not independently stressed, such as articles, certain pronouns, etc., each word has a tonic or stressed syllable which is given prominence over adjacent syllables, and Latin further possesses a strong secondary stress, which falls on the initial syllable. Unstressed or weak syllables are those that receive neither the main nor the secondary stress. This information is important since vowels depend in their evolution on the place they assume in relation to the stress. The word

$$dŏr\text{-}mi\text{-}tō\text{-}ri\text{-}um$$
$$1 \quad 2 \quad 3 \quad 4 \quad 5$$

consisting of a total of five syllables, may serve as an illustration of the stress pattern in Latin. The main stress is on 3, which contains the *tonic* or *stressed vowel,* and the secondary stress falls on 1. While, strictly speaking, the pretonic portion of a word is the segment that precedes the stress, the term *pretonic* is used here as the equivalent of *initial,* referring only to the vowel of the opening syllable. Lodged between the initial and the main stress, 2 finds itself in the weak intertonic position which is referred to by French philologists as *contrefinale,* a term which follows from the observation that the fate of the *intertonic vowel* matches that of the *final.* The posttonic segment of the word similarly contains two vowels, of which 4 is referred to simply as the *posttonic non-final vowel* or as the *weak penult,* while 5 is the *final vowel.* It matters little whether the final vowel is actually the last pronounced sound of a given word as in *fīlia,* or whether it is followed by a consonant as in *fīlias,* since both cases conform to the definition of the final vowel as the vowel contained in the final syllable.

135. A Latin word is said to be *oxytone* if the last syllable (*ultima*) is stressed; it is *paroxytone* if the stress falls on the next-to-last syllable (*paenultima*), and it is *proparoxytone* if it is the third syllable from the end (*antepaenultima*) that carries the stress. The oxytone category is made up solely of monosyllables: *rēm, plūs, hīc, vas,* since Latin never stresses the final syllable of a word. Most Latin words are paroxytones; this category is made up of all two-syllable words: *pŏrta, rŏta, plēnu,* as well as of all words of more than two syllables in which length is present in the penult. The penult is said to be long by nature if it contains a long vowel: *habēre, marītu, latrōne;* it is long by position if it contains a short vowel in a blocked syllable, in which case it is the consonantal component that displays the length feature: *arĭsta, genĭsta.* Proparoxytone stress obtains when the penult consists of a short vowel in an open syllable: *pĕrdĕre, spĕcŭlum, cathĕdra.* For this last word, see further §137.

136. The stress in Vulgar Latin and Romance usually falls on the same syllable as in Classical Latin: CL *matúrum* > Rm. *matúr,* It. *matúro,* Sp., Ptg. *madúro,* Occ., Cat. *madúr,* OFr. *mëúr,* Fr. *mûr;* CL *marítum* > It. *maríto,* Sd. *marídu,* Sp., Ptg. *marído,* Occ., Cat. *marít,* Fr. *marí.* However, a few changes do occur in Vulgar Latin and Romance.

137. The combination of an occlusive (*p, t, k, b, d, g*) and the liquid *r,* traditionally referred to as *muta cum liquida,* attracts the stress to the immediately preceding vowel, whereby length by position is created: CL *cáthĕdra* > VL *cathédra* > Sp. *cadera,* OFr. *chaiere;* CL *tónĭtru* > VL *tonítru* > Occ. *toneire,* OFr. *toneire, tonoire;* CL *cólŭbra* > VL **cōlóbra* > OSp. **culuebra,* Sp. *culebra,* OFr. *coluevre,* Fr. *couleuvre;* CL *ténĕbras* > VL *tĕnébras* > Sp. *tinieblas.* As a result of this change, it becomes possible to formulate a very simple rule concerning proparoxytone stress in Vulgar Latin: it obtains only where the penult is a short vowel followed by a single consonant.

138. A shift in stress of great phonological significance occurs in proparoxytones where a short *i* or a short *e* is followed immediately by *ĕ* or *ŏ.* Not only does the stress shift to the more open vowel, but at the same time the now unstressed hiatus vowel loses its syllabic value, becoming a semi-vowel, which is referred to as *yod* from the letter *j* of the German

alphabet: CL *mŭlíĕrem* > VL *muliére* > Sp. *mujer,* Ptg. *mulher,* Occ. *molher,* OFr. *moillier;* CL *fīlíŏlum* > VL *fīliólu* > It. *figliuolo,* Sp. *hijuelo,* OFr. *filluel,* Fr. *filleul;* CL *Pŭtéŏli* > VL *Pŭtióli* > It. *Pozzuoli;* CL *lĭntéŏlum* > VL *lĭntiólo* > It. *lenzuolo,* Sp. *lenzuelo,* Fr. *linceul.* The loss of syllabic value suffered by the hiatus vowel is already noted in the *Appendix Probi: vinea non vinia; calceus non calcius; linteum non lintium.* In the word *pariĕtem,* the hiatus *i* is absorbed by the preceding consonant as a result of the shift in stress: CL *paríĕtem* > VL *pariéte, paréte* > Rm. *pắrete,* It. *parete,* Sp. *pared,* Ptg. *parede,* Cat., Occ. *paret,* Fr. *paroi,* but before falling, the yod closes *ę* to *ẹ.*

139. The third person plural perfect adopts an unstressed *-ĕrunt* ending as opposed to the stressed *-ērunt* of the classical language. Characteristic of the popular, spoken language, this accentual change has resulted from a strong paradigmatic pressure exerted by other stem-stressed perfect forms. VL *díxĕrunt,* obtained from an alignment with the stress of the first and third person singular *díxi* and *díxit,* is continued as It. *dissero,* OFr. *distrent,* and VL *fécĕrunt,* similarly influenced by *fécī* and *fécit,* yields It. *fecero,* OFr. *fisdrent, fistrent,* Fr. *firent.* Other examples of this development are VL *míserunt* > It. *misero,* OFr. *misdrent, mistrent,* Fr. *mirent;* VL *fúĕrunt* > It. *furono,* Fr. *furent.* Some of the quoted forms are of analogical origin.

140. When CL *báttuo* is reduced to VL **batto,* the infinitive *battúĕre* evolves to **báttĕre* under the analogical influence of such paradigms as *mítto –míttĕre.* The loss of the semi-vowel *ụ* following a geminate or a consonant cluster is a common phonological development in the popular language: CL *quattuor* > VL *quattor;* CL *februariu* > VL *febrariu;* CL *mortuum* > VL *mortu.*

141. Compound verbs consisting of prefix and stem were stressed on the prefix in the classical language, and this accentuation often resulted in a weakening of the stem vowel: *placet* and *dísplĭcet; tĕnet* and *cóntĭnet.* A process known as recomposition took place in Vulgar Latin, with the stress shifting back to the stem vowel, and in most instances this was accompanied by the restoration of the original vowel of the uncompounded form: CL *dísplĭcet* > VL *displácet* > It. *dispiace,* OFr. *desplaist,* Fr. *déplaît;* CL *cóntĭnet* > VL *conténet* > It., Sp. *contiene,* Fr. *contient.* If, however, the verb was no longer felt as compounded, no restoration occurred. This is the case with *cóllocat* < *con-locat,* where an early assimilation had made the presence of the prefix *con-* less transparent: *cóllocat* > It. *corica,* Sp. *cuelga,* OFr. *colche,* Fr. *couche.* The shift of the stress back to the stem was not always accompanied by a restoration of the primitive vowel: CL *récĭpit,*

a compound of *capĕre*, becomes VL *recípit* > It. *riceve*, OFr. *receit*, Fr. *reçoit*.

THE LATIN CONSONANTS

142. Latin has a fairly simplified consonantal system compared to that of Indo-European:

		Labials		Labio-Velars		Dentals		Palatals	Velars		Latyngeals
		Voiced	Voiceless	Voiced	Voiceless	Voiced	Voiceless	Voiced	Voiced	Voiceless	Voiceless
Occlusives	Oral	*b*	*p*	*gʷ*	*kʷ*	*d*	*t*		*g*	*k*	
	Nasal	*m*				*n*			*η*		
Constrictives				*f*	*u̯*	*r* *l*	*s*	*i̯*			*h*

Latin has no palatals aside from the semi-vowel *i̯*, it lacks a voiced *s* and a labiodental *v*, but it has geminates or double consonants (cf. *annus* 'year' vs. *ānus* 'old woman'). The graphical representation presents few problems. The letter *C*, derived from the Greek letter *gamma*, serves originally to denote the voiced velar *g*. This has left traces in the standard abbreviations *C.* for *Gaius* and *Cn.* for *Gnaeus* and has caused some confusion in inscriptions (*pagatus* for *pacatus* and *dicitus* for *digitus*). Under the influence of Etruscan, which does not have voiced occlusives, *C* later comes to represent the voiceless velar *k*, and a new letter *G* is formed in the third century B.C. through a simple modification of *C*. The *k* sound is not marked uniformly; it is represented by *c* before front vowels and *a*, while *q*, which is usually combined with *u*, serves to mark the labiovelar [*kʷ*]. In the archaic language, *k* may have represented the norm before the vowel *a*, but the only trace of this graphical practice is the word *kalendae*. The semi-vowels *i̯* and *u̯* were not distinguished graphically from the corresponding vowels: *u* represents *u* and *v*, and *i* stands for *i* and *j*. The graphical distinction between *u* and *v* and between *i* and *j* was first established by Pierre La Ramée (1515–1572), hence the term *lettres ramistes* applied to *j* and *v*. The letters *z* and *y* were added in the first century B.C. to facilitate the graphical representation of Greek borrowings.

143. Early Vulgar Latin changes in the consonantal system are as follows. In Vulgar Latin, *b* and *u̯* merge into the bilabial fricative *ƀ*, pro-

nounced like intervocalic *b* or *v* in Spanish and Catalan. This *ƀ* is ultimately resolved as a labiodental *v* in most areas of Romance. Before a velar vowel, *ƀ* tends to drop in Vulgar Latin, and the *Appendix Probi* warns repeatedly against this popular pronunciation: *rivus non rius; pavor non paor.* The labiovelar [*kʷ*] is reduced early to *k* under the same conditions, as shown in several *Appendix Probi* entries: *equs non ecus; coqus non cocus,* and by extension from there *cocīna* for *coquīna.* Inscriptions testify to the early assibilation of *i̯, di̯, gi̯,* and *ti̯: oze* for *hŏdie; zavolus* for *diabolus; ampitza-tru* for *amphiteatrum. H,* considered a mere aspiration by Latin grammarians, drops very early: *omo* for *homo; nil* for *nihil.* Greek aspirated occlusives are usually rendered by the corresponding simple occlusives; cf. *Appendix Probi: cochlearium non cocliarium; cithara non citera.* In words borrowed after *ph* had become *f* in Greek, *f* is considered the correct pronunciation in Vulgar Latin; cf. *Appendix Probi: amfora non ampora.* Expressive gemination is a fairly common feature in the popular language: *tōttus* for *tōtus.* The assimilation of *rs* to *ss* occurs early: *dossum* for *dorsum* and cf. *Appendix Probi: persica non pessica.* There is ample documentation for the early reduction of *ns* to *s;* cf. *Appendix Probi: mensa non mesa.* The unfamiliar *t'l* cluster is changed to *cl;* cf. *Appendix Probi: vetulus non veclus.* In words other than monosyllables, final *m* tended to drop already in archaic Latin.

144. The governing principle in the area of consonantal change is the position which the consonant occupies within a given word. It is of importance to know whether a consonant is word-initial (*t-* in *tĕrra*) or syllable-initial following a consonant (*t-* in *mŏnte*), intervocalic (*-t-* in *vīta*) or final (*-t* in *caput*), and whether it is simple (*-p-* in *cūpa*) or appears in clusters (*-pp-* in *cŭppa, pl-* in *plēnu, -rt-* in *parte*). The place of the consonant in relation to stress does not appear to have had any very significant role to play, this in spite of the occasional recourse by scholars to this principle in order to account for heterogeneous developments, such as for example the hesitation in Spanish between the weakening of intervocalic *d* to a fricative *đ* or its total elimination (§266) or the continuation in Italian of intervocalic *x* (*cs*) as either *ss* or [*šš*] (§311).

SPONTANEOUS AND CONDITIONED SOUND CHANGES

145. A distinction is made between spontaneous and conditioned sound changes. A spontaneous change is one which takes place very generally, and which does not require the presence of specific conditions, beyond certain very broad features relating to stress or to the nature of the syllable,

in order to take effect. The change of *a* to *e* in *mare* > Fr. *mer* is a spontaneous development which occurs quite regularly provided the vowel is tonic and free, but no other conditions have to be met for this change to take place. The diphthongization process affects only stressed vowels, and in French and Italian these vowels must further appear in a free syllable: *pĕtra* > It. *pietra,* Sp. *piedra,* Fr. *pierre.* No such restriction applies to Spanish: *sĕpte* > *siete; pŏrta* > *puerta.* Conditioned changes, on the other hand, are caused by specific factors which interfere with regular developments. The tonic vowel *ī* is regularly kept as *i* in French: *fīlu* > *fil,* but the presence of a final nasal consonant will nasalize *i* to [*ẽ*]: *vīnu* > *vin* [*vẽ*]. A palatal or a final *u̯* may cause a conditioned diphthongization of stressed *ĕ* or *ŏ* in Occitan: *lĕctu* > *lieit; lĕve* > *lieu.* Conversely, the presence of a palatal prevents these same vowels from diphthongizing in Spanish: *fŏlia* > *hoja; nŏcte* > *noche.* A final *u* causes the closure of *ǫ* to *ọ* in Portuguese: *pŏrcu* > *pọrco.* The diphthong *ie* is reduced to *e* in Italian if it is preceded by an occlusive plus *r* cluster: *brĕve* > *brieve* > *breve; praeda* > *prieda* > *preda.* Consonants are similarly subject to conditioned changes. In Rumanian, initial *t* is usually kept intact: *tāle* > *tare; tauru* > *taur,* but it assibilates to *ts,* spelled *ţ,* before *i* from Lat *ī* or before *ie* from Lat. *ĕ: sŭbtīle* > *subţire; tĕrra* > *ţară* (§227).

VOWELS

I. TONIC VOWELS

Spontaneous Developments

146. CL ī > VL *i*

    i: Rm., It., Sp., Ptg., Cat., Occ., Fr.

Latin
Free: *fīlu, vīta*
Blocked: *scrīptu, fīlia, frīgĭdu, *frĭgĭdu*

Rm.	It.	Sp.	Ptg.	Cat.	Occ.	OFr.	Fr.
fir	*filo*	*hilo*	*fio*	*fil*	*fil*	[1]	*fil*
vită̆	*vita*	*vida*	*vida*	*vida*	*vida*	*vidhe*	*vie*
	scritto	*escrito*	*escrito*	*escrit*	*escrit*	*escrit*	*écrit*
fie	*figlia*	*hija*	*filha*	*filla*	*filha*	*fille*	
		frío	*frio*				
	freddo			*fred*	*freit, freg*	*freit*	*froid*

Commentary
  The long *i* of Classical Latin becomes *i* in Vulgar Latin and remains unchanged everywhere.

  Ptg. *fio*: with the regular loss of intervocalic *l* in Portuguese (§270), *i* combines with the final vowel to form the diphthong [*iw*]. The diphthong arises through a simple coalescence of two contiguous elements.
  OFr. *vidhe*: for *dh* as a graph for the voiced dental fricative *đ*, see §267.
  Rm. *scris*: the Rumanian past participle *scris* does not represent a continuation of the Classical Latin form, but is based on a hypothetical *scrīpsu drawn from an alignment with the perfect *scrīpsī*. To many Latin perfects in -*si* corresponds a past participle in -*su*: *rīsī—rīsu; clausī—clausu; rasī—rasu*, etc., and *scrīpsu is obtained analogically from such cases.

Lat. *fīlia*: counting three syllables in the classical language, *filia* becomes dissyllabic in Vulgar Latin when *i* loses its vocalic quality, merging with *l* into a palatal *l* which forms a blocked syllable, as may be seen from the retention of *a* in *palea* > Fr. *paille* vs. the change of free *a* to *e* in *mare* > *mer* (§152).

Rm. *fie*: Rumanian has adopted a diminutive formation *fiică* as its basic term for 'daughter', but *fie,* showing the regular absorption of *l* into a following yod (§326), is documented for the Arumanian dialect (cf. *fŏlia* > Rm. *foaie*).

Lat. *frīgĭdu* and **frĭgĭdu*: outside of the Hispanic area, the Romance developments presuppose the existence of a VL **frĭgĭdu* with a short *i* (§147), perhaps obtained via a formal analogy with *rĭgĭdu*. The Spanish reflexes are quite complex and somewhat difficult to sort out. CL *frīgĭdu* would presumably move via a hypothetical **friyio* to *frio,* paralleling the development of other adjectives presenting an unstressed *-ĭdu* ending: *lĭmpĭdu* > *limpio*. What appears to have been overlooked is the fact that a VL **frĭgĭdu* would yield the same result through the regular yod-caused inflection of *ę* as in the case of *limpio* (§161), which in turn means that the conjectural **frĭgĭdu* would fit all Romance reflexes. The form *fridus,* encountered in Pompeii, is the likely source of the Old Spanish variant *frido* since, in accordance with a rule formulated by Meyer-Lübke (*Grammaire* I 382), intervocalic *d* is kept when following the stressed vowel (§266). To complicate matters further, however, there is also documentation for an Old Spanish form *fredo* (Menéndez Pidal: *Orígenes,* p. 270; *REW* 3512), which leads one to suspect that *frido* could simply be a Latinizing, literary form (Corominas II 959–960; Menéndez Pidal §11.c; García de Diego, p. 97). Ptg. *frio* could relate to either *frio* or *frido* of Spanish, since intervocalic *d* drops more generally here.

147. CL *ĭ, ē* > VL *ę*

ę:	Rm., It., Ptg., Occ.
e (mid):	Sp.
ę or *ę:*	Cat.
ei, oi, [*wa*]/² *ę*:	Fr.

---

²A slash serves to separate free-syllable treatment (left) from blocked (right).

Latin
Free: *tēla, sǐte, nǐve*
Blocked: *spǐssu, stēlla, vǐr(i)de*

Rm.	It.	Sp.	Ptg.	Cat.	Occ.	OFr.	Fr.
teară	*tẹla*	*tela*	*teia*	*tela*	*tẹla*	*teile*	*toile*
sẹte	*sẹte*	*sed*	*sede*	*set*	*sẹt*	*seif*	*soif*
nea	*nẹve*	*nieve*	*nẹve*	*néu*	*nẹu,*	*neif,*	
					nẹu	*noif*	
	spẹsso	*espeso*	*espẹsso*	*espes*	*espẹs*	*espes*	*épais*
stea	*stẹlla*	*estrella*	*estrẹla*	*estrella*	*est ẹla*	*esteile*	*étoile*
vẹrde	*vẹrde*	*verde*	*vẹrde*	*vert*	*vẹrt*		*vert*

Commentary

Rumanian, Italian, Portuguese and Occitan keep the close *e* of Vulgar Latin, while Spanish *e* is of a half-open or mid quality. Catalan hesitates between a dialectally determined open or close *e*. French has [*wa*], but in a few words also [*ɛ*] in a free syllable vs. [*ɛ*] in blocked position.

No opposition exists in Spanish between a close and an open *e*, since the stressed short *e* never gives *ẹ*, but diphthongizes to *ie* both in the free and the blocked syllable (§148). The degree of opening, in other words, is not phonemic in Spanish, and the same holds true of the vowel *o* (§150).

The development of the close *e* of Vulgar Latin in Catalan is particularly complex, providing one of the main criteria supportive of the division of Catalan dialects into an eastern and a western group. Basically, *ẹ* is retained in the western dialects, while the eastern group modifies the sound which, in the central regions, opens all the way to *ẹ*. For a detailed description of the dialectal outcomes of VL *ẹ* in Catalan, see Badía Margarit §49 and B. Moll §§39–41. French is the only language which diphthongizes the close vowels *ẹ* and *ọ*. The nature of the syllable is important here: diphthongization occurs only in the free syllable in French. Free *ẹ* first changes to *ei*, which is subsequently rounded to *oi*. In the thirteenth century, a tendency to eliminate falling diphthongs in French leads to the change of *ói* to [*wɛ*] which, in the course of the sixteenth century, evolves to [*wa*], but this pronunciation is not officially recognized until the very end of the eighteenth century. In a few words, the evolution leads from [*wɛ*] to [*ɛ*]: *crēta* > *craie;* VL *tonǐtru* > OFr. *toneire* > Fr. *tonnerre*. The change to [*ɛ*] may have penetrated into *francien* from northern or western dialects

(Rheinfelder I 21; Lausberg §170), but it also affects the imperfect ending: *debē(b)at > deveit > devoit > devait,* which can hardly be considered dialectal. In a blocked position the vowel, which may have had a close quality in the early stages of the language, soon opens to ę.

Rm. *teară:* for the conditioned break-up of tonic ẹ into *ea* in Rumanian under the influence of final *a* or *e,* see §159, and see also Rothe §16; Tiktin §50; Nandris, pp. 17, 210–213.

Ptg. *teia:* when tonic ẹ comes into contact with a final *a* or *o* through the loss of an intervocalic consonant, a yod is inserted: *vēna > veia; crēdo > creio; aliēnu > alheio; plēnu > cheio* (Williams §§35.7, 48.2.A). Where the final vowel is *o,* the insertion of yod as a glide prevents the formation of an [*ew*] diphthong.

Rm. *sete:* the breaking of stressed ẹ into a diphthong in Rumanian is subject to some fluctuation; Nandris (p. 60), who makes mention of a *siete* pronunciation for this word, refers to this feature as a popular diphthongization, thereby emphasizing its lack of consistency (Lausberg §197).

OFr. *seif,* Fr. *soif:* the *f* is very difficult to account for as a purely phonological development. It seems likelier that it was obtained analogically from the declension, with *seif* paralleling the nominative *seis* or *seiz < sĭtis* in the same manner as the accusative *neif < nĭve* corresponds to the nominative *neis* < VL **nĭvis* (Rheinfelder I 293).

Rm. *nea:* intervocalic *v* drops regularly (§264), and *a* represents a morphological adjustment (Nandris, p. 12).

Sp. *nieve,* Ptg. *nęve,* Cat. *néu,* Occ. *nęu:* these forms are reflexes of a variant **nęve,* showing the regular development of *ĕ* to *ie* in Spanish and to an open *e* in Portuguese (§148), while Occitan hesitates between ę and ẹ. Cat. *néu* evolves regularly from **nęve,* with ę closing to ẹ and with vocalization of final *v.* The labiodental *v* may be responsible for this regional opening of the classical *nĭve* to **nĕve* (Lausberg §238). There are also occurrences of *nęve* and *nieve* in Italian dialects (Rohlfs §51), and this wide spread of the open-vowel feature points to the coexistence in Vulgar Latin of *nęve* and **nęve.* The regular vocalization of final *v* in Catalan and Occitan (§363) leads to the creation in these languages of an [ɛw] or [ew] diphthong through coalescence.

OFr. *neif, noif:* this word disappears in the fourteenth century, replaced by *neige,* which is drawn from the verb *neiger. Noif* had ceased to be perceived as related to the verb, as one may infer from the common Old French locution *noif negiee* '(white like) freshly fallen snow'. The Classical Latin verb *ninguĕre* is not continued anywhere; it is replaced by a pop.

*nĭvĭcāre > It. *nevicare,* OFr. *negier,* Fr. *neiger,* while Sp., Ptg., Cat., Occ. *nevar* reflects a **nĭvāre* base.

OFr. *espes:* as far as it can at all be ascertained, *espes* may originally have had a close *e* in conformity with its Vulgar Latin source, but this *ẹ* soon opened to *ę* in blocked position. Lausberg (§169) dates this opening to the twelfth-thirteenth century. Such changes can only be inferred from a close scrutiny of *e* in rhyme position.

Rm. *stea:* when following the stressed vowel, double *l* drops before a weak *a* (Nandris, p. 139; Rothe §98; Tiktin §161.1; Lausberg §498). This development is accompanied by a shift in stress to the vowel *a*; cf. *maxĭlla* > Rm. *măseá.*

Sp., Cat. *estrella,* Ptg. *estrela:* Hispanic reveals some involvement with *astru,* which accounts for the added *r*. Cat. *estrella* may be a borrowing from Castilian, while *estela* is archaic and dialectal.

OFr. *esteile,* Fr. *étoile:* since this word displays free-syllable treatment of its tonic vowel, the etymon must be a conjectural **stēla,* showing early degemination. The same source is required for the Catalan variant *estela.*

Lat. *vĭr(ĭ)de:* an early loss of the weak, posttonic *ĭ* makes this a bona fide example of a blocked tonic *ę*.

148. CL *ĕ* > VL *ę*

ie:	Rm., Sp.
ie/ę:	It., Fr.
ę:	Ptg., Occ.
ẹ or *ę*:	Cat.

Latin

Free: *mĕle, pĕtra, mĕtu*; blocked: *sĕpte, fĕrru*

Rm.	It.	Sp.	Ptg.	Cat.	Occ.	OFr.	Fr.
miere	miele	miel	męl	męl	męl		miel
piatră	pietra	piedra	pędra	pędra	peira		pierre
		miedo	mędo		męt		
şapte	sette	siete	sęte	sęt	sęt	set	sept
fier	fęrro	hierro	fęrro	ferr,	fęr,	fer	
				ferro	fęrre		

Commentary

Portuguese and Occitan retain the open *e* of Vulgar Latin, while Rumanian and Spanish show diphthongization to *ie*. Italian and French diphthongize *ę* to *ie* in a free syllable only, while *ę* is retained when blocked. There are, however, many cases of non-diphthongization in a free syllable in Italian. This feature is not solely relegated to dialects, but occurs also in the written language itself, which has both *miele* and *mele,* for example. Many of the non-diphthongized words are learned (Rohlfs §85). Conditions in Catalan are quite difficult to plot. Fouché (*Phonétique historique,* pp. 28–29) affirms that VL *ę* retains its open quality in the western dialects, closes to *ẹ* in the central regions and evolves to a double *ę* in Balearic. Badía Margarit (§48, I) and B. Moll (§35) draw up a more unified picture of the Catalan developments, asserting that the fundamental change throughout the Catalan-speaking area is the closure of *ę* to *ẹ,* but this conclusion is reached at the cost of an impressive list of conditioned developments. Among specific consonants or consonant clusters that are instrumental in the retention of the open quality of *e* are *rr: fęrru > fęrro, l: caelu > cęl, r* and a non-labial consonant: *hībęrnu > hivęrn,* final *ų* < *-ti̯-, -d-* or *-c- + i, e: prętiu > pręu; pęde > pęu; dęce > dęu, n'r: tęnęru > tęndre.*

Rm. *miere,* It. *miele,* Fr. *miel:* the source is not CL *mĕl,* but an analogical accusative **mĕle,* aligned with such neuter accusative forms as *sale* and *mare.* For a similar development see **cŏre* (§151). This substitution gives rise to an open syllable, in which diphthongization can take place, and it accounts for the final *e* of Rumanian and Italian. There are several instances in French of free-syllable treatment of the vowel in monosyllables, even though they end in a consonant: *quĭd >* Fr. *quoi; trans >* Fr. *très* (Rheinfelder I 69). Strictly speaking then, CL *mĕl* would be acceptable as etymon for French, but the Rumanian and Italian developments with their final *e* speak clearly in favor of **mĕle,* and furthermore *l* has received intervocalic treatment in Rumanian (§270).

Cat. *męl:* final *l* is the conditioning factor in the retention of the open *e.*

Rm. *piatră,* Cat. *pedra:* a change of *ie* to *ia* is noted for Rumanian with final *a* acting as the conditioning factor. The vowel quality of Cat. *pedra* is quite fluctuating in the dialects.

Occ. *pęira:* the yod in the Occitan reflex represents the regular outcome of *t* in the *tr* cluster, and the same development obtains for *dr: patre >* Occ. *paire; crēdĕre >* Occ. *creire* (§§290, 293). The short *e* evolves regularly to *ę,* while the diphthong is obtained through the coalescence of this vowel with the *i* that evolves from the dental. The word displays a diphthong, but no diphthongization is involved.

Ptg. *mẹdo*: Portuguese is subject to a process of umlaut or vowel inflection or *Fernharmonisierung*: if the final vowel of the Latin etymon is *-ŭ*, the tonic vowels *ẹ* and *ǫ* are closed to *e* and *o*: *pŏrcŭ > pǫrco* vs. *pŏrcos > pǫrcos* (Lausberg §195; Huber §85.2; Williams §34.8, and see §§158, 207).

Rm. *şapte*: the final *e* is instrumental in changing *ie* to *ia* (cf. *piatră*), whereupon the yod is absorbed into *s*, the outcome being *ş*, the standard graphical representation for [*š*] (Lausberg §§197, 214).

Cat. *sẹt*: *pt* does not cause retention of the open vowel. Badía Margarit (§48, I) sees in this development an attempt to avoid homonymy with *sẹt* 'thirst' < *sĭte*, while B. Moll (§35) explains it as resulting from an analogy with the numeral *dẹu* 'ten' < *dĕce*, but the two numerals are too far apart from one another to allow for any such case of serialization to take place.

Fr. *sept*: the reintroduction of *p* is purely graphical, but compare OFr. *setembre > septembre*, where the restored *p* has found its way back into the pronunciation.

Ptg. *fẹrro*: it is not immediately clear why vowel inflection has not taken hold here (cf. *mẹdo*). Lausberg (§274) explains that the umlaut feature does not affect the neuter nouns in *-ŭm*: *fẹrro, cǫllo*, but it is hard to see how a declension feature, eradicated already in Vulgar Latin, could have influenced the pronunciation in this manner. The retention of an open vowel quality in these words may be linked to the nature of the following consonant, *r* and *l* being known to exert an opening influence on the preceding vowel.

OCat. *ferr*, Cat. *ferro*, Occ. *ferre, fer*, Fr. *fer*: Old Catalan has *ferr*, but a supporting vowel, which can be either *e* or *o*, depending on the dialects, is added in the modern language. In Occitan, double *r* may be retained, in which case a supporting vowel is needed, or it may simplify as in French.

149. CL *ū* > VL *u*

> *u*:   Rm., It., Sp., Ptg., Cat.
> [*y*]:   Occ., Fr.

Latin
Free: *mūru*
Blocked: *fŭste*

Rm.	It.	Sp.	Ptg.	Cat.	Occ.	OFr.	Fr.
muro	*muro*	*muro*	*mur*	*mur*			*mur*
fuşte	*fusto*	*fuste*	*fuste*	*fust*	*fust*	*fust*	*fût*

Commentary

The *u* of Vulgar Latin is retained in Rumanian, Italian, Spanish, Portuguese and Catalan, but fronted to [y] in Occitan and French. The change of *u* to [y] in Gallo-Romance is very difficult to date, since it involves no change in graphical representation. Nothing permits us to attribute this fronting of *u* to a Celtic substratum. The lack of any assibilation of *k* before *u* as in *cūra* > Fr. *cure* (cf. *cēra* > *cire*) points to a relatively late sound change, occurring at a point in time when Gaulish had long ago ceased to be spoken.

Rm. *fuşte*: the *st* cluster is usually kept intact in Rumanian: *cŏsta* > *coastă*, but it palatalizes to *şt* if followed by a front vowel: **accu-istī* > *aceşti* (Rothe §85, and see §304).

It. *fusto*: the change of the final vowel to *o* represents a morphological adjustment.

150. CL *ŭ, ō* > VL *ǫ*

ǫ:	It., Ptg., Cat., Occ.
o (mid):	Sp.
eu/ou:	Fr.
ŭ > u:	Rm.
ō > o:	Rm.

Latin

Free: *gŭla, hōra, flōre*
Blocked: *bŭcca, sŭrdu*

Rm.	It.	Sp.	Ptg.	Cat.	Occ.	OFr.	Fr.
gură	*gǫla*	*gola*	*gola*	*gola*	*gǫla*		*gueule*
oră	*ǫra*	*hora*	*hǫra*	*hora*	*ǫra*		*heure*
floare	*fiǫre*	*flor*	*flor, frol*	*flor*	*flǫr*		*fleur*

Rm.	It.	Sp.	Ptg.	Cat.	Occ.	OFr.	Fr.
bucă	*boçcca*	*boca*	*boçca*	*boçca*	*boçca*	*boche*	*bouche*
surd	*soçrdo*	*sordo*	*surdo*	*soçrt*	*soçrt*	*sort*	*sourd*

Commentary

The close *o* of Vulgar Latin remains unchanged in Italian, Portuguese, Catalan and Occitan. The half-open pronunciation of *o* in Spanish parallels that of *e* (§147). With the passage of the short *o* to *ue*, the degree of opening ceases to play a phonemic role. In French, the nature of the syllable determines the fate of *o̦*: it diphthongizes to *eu* in an open syllable and evolves to *ou* when blocked. In the old language, an *o* spelling predominates, while *ou* appears in the thirteenth century. The change to *eu* in free position represents a dissimilation feature, paralleling the evolution of *ei* to *oi*. Monophthongization of *eu* to [æ] occurs in the thirteenth century. Although *o̦* and *ǫ* both evolve to *eu* in French in a free syllable, they do not follow identical paths in their development. The open *o* moves via *ue* to *eu* as in *bŏve* > *buef* > *bœuf*, whereas *o̦* is represented graphically by *o, u* or *ou* in its intermediate stages: *flōre* > *flor, flur, flour* > *fleur*. A few words show the irregular development of tonic free *o̦* to *ou* in French instead of *eu*: *amōre* > *amour*; *spōnsa* > *épouse* (§268).

The Rumanian development is based on a different vocalic system, in which *ŭ* merges with *ū* and *ō* with *ŏ*, as seen in §132. Lat. *ŭ* is continued regularly as *u*: *lŭpu* > *lup*; *fŭrca* > *furcă*. Rumanian thus does not have the change of *ŭ* to *o̦*, which is characteristic of the Italic system, but it does participate in the opening of *ĭ* to *ę* (§147). This would indicate that the opening in the front-vowel system must have taken place earlier than for the velar group. This latter change was apparently interrupted when Rumanian became separated from the other Romance-speaking regions. Tonic *ō* and *ŏ* of Latin merge into *o* in Rumanian: *nōdu* > *nod*; *tōtu* > *tot*; *fŏrmōsu* > *frumos*; *fŏcu* > *foc*; *lŏcu* > *loc*. The degree of opening is not phonemic; the pronunciation is described by Nandris (p. 32) as mid, by Lausberg (§176) as close.

Ptg. *gola*: the retention of intervocalic *l* is irregular.

Fr. *gueule*: the first *u* is a mere spelling device, serving to indicate the velar quality of *g*.

Rm. *oră, floare*: the break-up of *o* into *oa* in Rumanian is a conditioned change triggered by the presence of a final *a* or a final *e* in the Latin etymon. It follows from this observation that *flōre* > *floare* is phonological, while *hōra* > *oră* may be learned; the popular pronunciation is *oară* (Rothe §6).

Cat. *hora, flor*: the *o* of *hora* is pronounced open, while the degree of opening of the *o* of *flor* is somewhat fluctuating in the dialects (B. Moll §62).

Ptg. *surdo*, Fr. *sourd*: the continuation of *ŭ* as *u* in Portuguese is learned, and the final *d* of French *sourd* is a case of Latinizing spelling.

151. CL *ŏ* > VL *ǫ*

o:	Rm.
uo/ǫ:	It.
ue:	Sp.
ǫ:	Ptg., Cat., Occ.
eu/ǫ:	Fr.

Latin
Free: *nŏve, *cŏre, *ŏvu*
Blocked: *pŏrta, pŏrcu*

Rm.	**It.**	**Sp.**	**Ptg.**	**Cat.**	**Occ.**	**OFr.**	**Fr.**
nouă	*nǫve*	*nueve*	*nǫve*	*nǫu*	*nǫu*	*nuef*	*neuf*
	cuore	*cuer*	*cor*	*cǫr*	*cǫr*	*cuer*	*cœur*
		(old)	(old)				
ou	*uovo*	*huevo*	*ǫvo*	*ǫu*	*ǫu,*	*uef*	*œuf*
					uǫu,		
					uęu		
poartă	*porta*	*puerta*	*pǫrta*	*pǫrta*	*pǫrta*		*porte*
porc	*pǫrco*	*puerco*	*pǫrco*	*pǫrc*	*pǫrc*		*porc*

Commentary

In Rumanian, *ŏ* and *ō* both give *o* (§150). Portuguese, Catalan and Occitan keep the open *o* unchanged. In Italian and French, where the structure of the syllable is of importance, the open *o* is retained only in the blocked syllable, but is subject to diphthongization when free. Italian has *uo*, but with not infrequent occurrences of non-diphthongization, paralleling the development of *ę* (§148). Many of the non-diphthongized words are of a learned nature: *modo, tono, popolo, cronaca, rosa,* and *ǫ* is common in many dialects (Rohlfs §§ 106–107). In Old French, the diphthong *uo* is rare and archaic or dialectal; it soon dissimilates to *ue*, which is the standard medieval form. Monophthongization to [*œ*] sets in during the latter half of the thirteenth century, at which point the outcome of *ǫ* merges with that of *ọ*. The spelling reflects this change, *ue* being replaced by *eu*, except where *ue* is preceded by *c* or *g*: *cueille, orgueil* (Rheinfelder I 28). The present-day distinction between [*œ*] and [*ø*] is based on structure: *bœuf* vs. *bœufs*, with closure occurring if the vowel is the last pronounced sound. The change to *ou* in *rŏta* > Fr. *roue* is unexplained. Spanish diphthongizes *ǫ* to *ue* in both free and blocked position with, just as in French, *uo* representing a rare archaic or dialectal stage in the evolution (García de Diego, pp. 60–61).

Rm. *nouă*: *u* evolves as a glide between *o* < *oa* and final *e*, and in the process the final vowel is changed to *ă* (Rothe §62; Nandris, p. 67).

It. *nǫve*: Old Italian had a regularly developed *nuove* (Rohlfs §106). The modern form is extremely difficult to account for, since cardinals are firmly entrenched in the core vocabulary and thus can be considered neither learned nor borrowed. Nor does the importance of numerals allow for proclitic use, and homonymy with *nuove* 'new' is hardly a sufficient reason for this development.

Cat., Occ. *nǫu*: final *v* vocalizes to *u̯* in Catalan and Occitan (§363), thus giving rise to the formation of a diphthong through a process of coalescence.

Lat. **cŏre*: the Latin genitive is *cordis,* but Vulgar Latin drops the *cord-* stem, creating instead a popular **cŏre –*cŏris* declension, which is obtained analogically from neuters such as *mare–maris.* The addition of *e* creates an open syllable; for details, see *mĕle* (§148).

OSp. *cuer,* OPtg. *cǫr*: Old Spanish has *cuer,* encountered in the *Cid,* Berceo, *Libro de Alexandre* and other thirteenth-century texts, and Old Portuguese has *cǫr.* These regularly developed forms soon yield to Sp. *corazón,* Ptg. *coração,* reflexes of an augmentative **coratiōne.* Sp. *corazón* makes its debut around the year 1100. Diez attributes its creation to a desire to avoid homonymy with *cuero* 'hide', but this explanation would not apply to conditions in Old Portuguese, where *cor* and *coiro* were not easily confused (Corominas II 192).

Lat. **ŏvu*: the Romance forms provide proof that CL *ōvu* had been replaced by a form with open *o* in the popular language. For the opening influence of *v*, see Lat. *nĭve* (§147), and see §181.

Rm. *ou*: intervocalic *v* drops, and the final vowel becomes *u̯*, forming a diphthong with the stressed vowel.

Sp. *huevo*: if the *ue* diphthong constitutes the opening element of a word, it is regularly preceded by an *h* graph: *hueso* < *ŏssu; huérfano* < *ŏrphănu*.

Occ. *ǫu, uǫu, uęu*: while Occitan does not have spontaneous diphthongization, *ŏ* may diphthongize provided certain factors are present, among them a final *u̯*, as is the case here. This diphthongization is optional only, and if it occurs, it may take the form of either *uo* or *ue*, perhaps in a dialectically determined distribution (Anglade, pp. 72–76). The vowel *ĕ* is subject to the same type of conditioned diphthongization (§162).

Fr. *porc*: the loss of *c* from pronunciation follows from *porcus, porcos* > *pors*, where *c* regularly drops between two consonants (§347).

152. CL *ā, ă* > VL *a*

> *a*:   Rm., It., Sp., Ptg., Cat., Occ.
> *e/a*:   Fr.

Latin
Free: *mare, sale, latus*
Blocked: *caballu, cal(i)du*

Rm.	It.	Sp.	Ptg.	Cat.	Occ.	OFr.	Fr.
mare	*mare*	*mar*	*mar*	*mar*	*mar*		*mer*
sare	*sale*	*sal*	*sal*	*sal*	*sal*		*sel*
lat	*lato*	*lado,*	*lado,*		*latz*	*lez*	*lez, les*
		lados	*lados*				
		(old)	(old)				
cal	*cavallo*	*caballo*	*cavalo*	*cavall*	*caval*		*cheval*
cald	*caldo*	*caldo*	*caldo*		*calt,*	*chalt*	*chaud*
	caut						

Commentary
The tonic *a* is kept practically everywhere, the sole exception being the change to *e* in free position in French. This treatment of *a* constitutes the most important vocalic difference between French on one hand, Occitan and Franco-Provençal on the other. The *ę* that evolves from *a* is at first kept separate from the *ę* that comes from *ĕ*: *pert* < *paret* vs. *pert* < *pĕrdit*, but

the two soon merge. Lausberg (§174) theorizes that the ę that comes from tonic free *a* may originally have had length as a distinctive feature. Generally speaking, French words that show retention of *a* in the free, stressed position are either learned or borrowed: *cas, pape, avare, croisade, façade, camarade* (Rheinfelder I 31–32).

Rm. *lat*, It. *lato*, OSp., OPtg. *lados*: while the loss of final *s* is a regular feature of Rumanian and Italian (§357), retention is the norm in Hispanic, where final *s* assumes important morphological functions. It specifically serves to mark plurality as in *muros* vs. *muro*, and this very easily explains why its presence in the singular noun *lados* soon comes to be felt as a morphological anomaly. Through the removal of *s* from the singular, the unusual *lados–lados* scheme is made to conform to the standard plural formation in the language. The loss of *s*, in other words, does not follow from the workings of sound-laws, but is caused by paradigmatic pressure. A sing. *lados* is contained in the locution *al lados de* 'next to, beside', encountered in a 1225 document from Burgos.

Fr. *lez*: this word, spelled *lez, les* or *lès*, has survived only in toponyms: *Plessis-lez-Tours, Villeneuve-les-Avignon,* where it carries the meaning of 'next to, beside'.

Lat. *caballu*: the phonological development of this word is regular, showing retention of double *l* in Italian, change to a palatal *l* in Spanish and Catalan and simplification to *l* elsewhere. In Rumanian, where intervocalic *b* drops (§263), whereupon the two *a*'s are contracted, *caballu* is regularly reduced to *cal*. VL *caballu* replaces CL *ĕquus* as the standard term for 'horse' in Romance. For the survival of the fem. *ĕqua* 'mare', see §336.

Lat. *cal(i)du*: with the early loss of the weak posttonic *i*, the initial syllable counts as blocked.

Sp., Ptg. *caldo*: the old adjective *caldo* was soon lost in Hispanic, but the form survived as a noun meaning 'broth'. In its basic acceptation, *caldo* was replaced by Sp. *caliente*, Ptg. *quente*, Cat. *calent*, drawn from the present participle *calĕnte* of the verb *calēre* 'to be hot'. The Portuguese form follows regularly from *caente*, with the traditional loss of intervocalic *l* (§270) and with absorption of *a* in hiatus (§190). Sp., Ptg. *cálido* is a *cultismo* (Corominas I 759–760). The formal resemblance between *caldo* and E. *cold*, G. *kalt* is merely accidental; the Germanic forms are related to Lat. *gĕlu* 'frost'.

Occ. *calt, caut*, Fr. *chaud*: for the vocalization in Gallo-Romance of *l* before a consonant, see §282. The final *d* of Fr. *chaud* is a case of learned spelling.

153. CL *oe* > VL *ę*

ę:	Rm., It., Ptg., Occ.
e (mid):	Sp.
ę or *ę*:	Cat.
ei, oi [*wa*]/	
no blocked examples:	Fr.

Latin
poena, foenu

It.	Sp.	Ptg.	Cat.	Occ.	OFr.	Fr.
pęna	*pena*	*pęna*	*pena*	*pęna*		*peine*
fięno	*heno*	*fęno*		*fęn,*	*fein,*	*foin*
				fę	*fain*	

Commentary

The diphthongs *oe, ae* and *au* appear in a free position only. The diphthong *oe* merges with close *e* in Vulgar Latin, and this vowel is kept in Rumanian, Italian, Portuguese and Occitan; Catalan hesitates between *ę* and *ę*, while Spanish has a mid quality *e*. French diphthongizes the close *e* in a free syllable. The *ae* diphthong evolves to an open *e*, but a certain amount of confusion between the two diphthongs may lead to regional differences for certain words. Examples of reflexes of Lat. *oe* in Rumanian and Catalan are virtually non-existent; the proposed rules are inferred from CL *ĭ, ē* (§147).

Ptg. *pena*: the retention of intervocalic *n* points to a borrowing from Spanish or to learned treatment (§272).

Fr. *peine*: the presence of a nasal usually prevents tonic *ę* from moving beyond the *ei* stage (§179).

Lat. *foenu*: Latin has both *foenu* and *fēnu*, and *foenu* could actually be a later creation; the *REW* (3247) has *fēnum*.

It. *fięno*: the *ie* diphthong reflects a dialectal (Oscan) **faenu*, but it could also be drawn from a hypothetical **flēnu*, obtained from the diminutive *foenulu* through a metathesis of *l*. Initial *fl-* gives *fi̯-*, whereupon the rare *ie* merges with the common *ię* diphthong (cf. *plēnu > pięno > pięno*). Support for this latter explanation comes from the existence in *abruzzese* of *flene* and in southern *calabrese* of *frenu* (Rohlfs §51).

Ptg. *feno*, Occ. *fęn, fę*: since vowel closure would automatically follow from inflection in Portuguese (§§148, 158) and from the presence of a final, unstable nasal in Occitan (§178), it cannot be determined whether these forms are reflexes of *foenu* or *faenu*. Ptg. *feno* is a regressive form, replacing OPtg. *feo* or *feio;* the *n* may have been reintroduced very quickly in an effort to avoid a homonymic clash with *feo, feio* 'ugly' < *foedu* (Williams §78.7.b). Final *n* becomes unstable in Occitan (§368), which is to say that it may or may not be pronounced: *manu > man, ma; vīnu > vin, vi; plēnu > plęn, plę,* and it closes open vowels: *bĕne > bęn, bę; bŏnu > bǫn, bǫ.*

Fr. *foin*: the *francien* development *fein, fain* was still in existence in the sixteenth century, while *foin* may have come in from western or southwestern dialects (Rheinfelder I 83). The presence of a nasal normally prevents the change of *ei* to *oi*, as seen under *peine* above.

154. CL *ae* > VL *ę*

ie:	Rm., Sp.	
ie/		
no blocked examples:	It., Fr.	
ę:	Ptg., Occ.	
ẹ:	Cat.	

Latin
praeda, caecu, laetu

Rm.	It.	Sp.	Ptg.	Cat.	Occ.	OFr.	Fr.
pradă	*pręda*	*prea* (old)		*presa*	*pręza, pręa*	*preie*	*proie*
	cieco	*ciego*	*cęgo*	*cęc*	*cęc*	*cieu*	
	lieto	*ledo*	*lędo*		*lęt*	*lié*	*lie*

Commentary
The diphthong *ae* merges with the open *e* in Vulgar Latin, though not without sporadic occurrences of close vowel quality in some regions. The open *e* is kept in Portuguese and Occitan, is closed to *ę* in Catalan, while diphthongization to *ie* is the norm elsewhere. Structuralists believe that *ae* evolved into a lengthened short *e,* and that this feature eventually led to the collapse of the quantity system, since length and openness do not go

together. The occasional change of *ę* to *ẹ* is seen by the same scholars as attempts to overcome this difficulty (Lausberg §242). The variant **prēda* may be analogical from *prē(n)sa* (*REW* 6714).

It. *pręda*, Rm. *pradă*: the *ie* diphthong is reduced to *ę* in Italian when following an occlusive plus *r* cluster: *praeda > prieda > preda*, and Rumanian *pradă* similarly follows from an earlier *priadă* (§172).

OSp. *prea*, Occ. *prẹza, prẹa*, OFr. *preie*, Fr. *proie:* these forms are all derived from VL **prẹda* with a close *e*.

Ptg. *cẹgo*: one would have expected a close *e* in Portuguese because of the inflection feature, while *ę* is regularly kept in the feminine: *caeca > cẹga*, and in the plural: *caecos > cẹgos* and *caecas > cẹgas*. The open vowel was then transferred from here to the masculine singular. The opposite leveling, favoring the close *e* of the masculine, may be seen in *lẹdo– lẹda < laetu–laeta* and *grẹgo–grẹga < graecu–graeca* (Williams §126.9).

OFr. *cieu*: French retains final *u*, when it stands in direct contact with the *ie* diphthong, which is the case here after the loss of *c* before a velar vowel (§210). Another example of this development is *Dĕu > Dieu*. OFr. *cieu* disappears in the sixteenth century and is replaced by *orb < orbu*, lit. 'deprived' and often found combined with *luminibus* 'lights', i.e., 'deprived of eye-sight'. *Orb* is still the standard term for 'blind' in Rumanian, while, in Gallo-Romance, this lexical item has been replaced by reflexes of **ab oculis* lit. 'without eyes': Occ. *avogol*, Fr. *aveugle*.

Sp. *ledo*: this rare and poetic word is probably a borrowing from Galician-Portuguese poetry, where *ledo* is frequently found. In a genuinely Spanish evolution, the word would have displayed a *ie* diphthong. For Ptg. *lẹdo*, see Ptg. *cẹgo* above.

OFr. *lié*: this adjective has survived only in the locution *faire chère lie*, in which *chère* itself (< *cara*) is archaic for *visage*. The fem. *lie* is a *picard* form, which has replaced the regular *liee* (*FEW* V 130). The noun *liesse*, from OFr. *leesse < laetitia*, is influenced by the adjective.

155. CL *au* > VL *au*

au:	Rm., Occ.
ǫ:	It., Cat., Fr.
o (mid):	Sp.
ou [*ọ*]:	Ptg.

Latin
auru, paucu, pauper

Rm.	It.	Sp.	Ptg.	Cat.	Occ.	OFr.	Fr.
aur	ǫro	oro	ouro	or	aur		or
	pǫco	poco	pouco	poc	pauc	pou	peu
	pǫvero	pobre	pǫbre	pǫbre	paubre	povre	pauvre

Commentary

Rumanian and Occitan keep *au* unchanged, and Portuguese has *ou* pronounced as a close *o*. In Italian, Catalan and French, *au* evolves to an open *o*, while Spanish has a mid quality *o*. In modern French, the open *o* remains before *r*: *auru* > *or*, it closes to *ǫ* before *v* and before a voiced *s*: *pauperu* > *pauvre; causa* > *chose*, and it becomes *ou* [*u*] in hiatus position: *laudat* > *loe* > *loue*.

The monophthongization of *au* to *o* cannot be dated back to the Vulgar Latin period, since Occitan and Rumanian keep *au* intact, and since, in Portuguese, the outcome of *au* differs from that of *o*. Furthermore, it is the primitive *au* which permits palatalization of *k* and *g* in Fr. *chose* < *causa* and *joie* < *gaudia*. Because this palatalization occurs before *a*, but not before a velar vowel, it must have taken place before the change of *au* to *o*. In Spanish and Portuguese, Lat. *au* prevents lenition (weakening of intervocalic consonants), since it does not create a truly intervocalic position: Sp. *poco*, Ptg. *pouco* (§261). Cases of an early change of *au* to *o* in Vulgar Latin are extremely rare and probably of dialectal (Umbrian) origin: CL *cauda* > VL *cōda* > Rm. *coadă*, It. *cǫda*, OSp., OPtg., Cat., Occ. *coa*, Fr. *queue;* CL *fauces* > VL *fǫces* > It. *fǫci*. Monophthongization of *au*, occurring only very sporadically in the Vulgar Latin period, represents an early, popular trend. The emperor Claudius referred to himself as *Clodius* in order to please the people, and the *Appendix Probi* censures the use of the diminutive *oricla* for CL *auris: auris non oricla*. On the other hand, new instances of *au* come about through the vocalization of *v* before a consonant: **avica* > *auca* > It., Cat. *ǫca*, Occ. *auca*, OFr. *oe*, Fr. *oie* (with *i* obtained analogically from *oisel* < *aucĕllu*); *cantāvit* > **cantaut* > It. *cantò*, Sp. *cantó*, and of *b* before *l* in *parabola* > **paraula* > Fr. *parole*. The open *o* that arises in Italian, Spanish and French is prevented chronologically from participating in the developments which the primitive *ǫ* undergoes. In Portuguese, *ou* remains the standard graph, although the pronunciation is a close *o*, except in northern dialects, which still have [*ow*].

OFr. *pou,* Fr. *peu*: the *c* of *paucu* drops before *u,* and the final vowel is kept in direct contact with the tonic *o* from *au* (§210). The change of *pou* to *peu* is difficult to account for, *peu* being mostly explained as a *picard* form (Rheinfelder I 128, 272). The *picard* dialect has *peu, bleu* and *treu* for *francien pou, blou* and *trou.*

It. *pǫvero*: the change of *p* to *v* points to a borrowing from French. The final *o* of *pǫvero* represents a morphological adjustment to the category of gender-distinguishing adjectives, which have an *o* ending in the masculine: *bello, buono, chiaro,* etc. Italian is not alone in making this morphological change; Occitan has a distinct feminine form *paubra.*

Sp. *pobre,* Ptg. *pǫbre*: since *au* functions as a barrier to intervocalic voicing, and since Portuguese does not display an *ou* vocalism here, the etymology cannot be CL *pauper,* but a pop. **pōpĕre* (Menéndez Pidal §47.3; Williams §33.4.D), unless *pobre* is simply a borrowing from French (Lausberg §243, n. 3) or obtained through a close association with *nǫbre* (Huber §82.a Anm. 1). García de Diego (pp. 78–79) sees no need for positing a **pōpĕre* base, considering the non-voicing rule less than absolute. It is difficult to see, with Corominas (IV 584–585), why *au* would prevent voicing of *t* and *c,* but not of *p,* the more so as this rule seems based on a single example. Corominas further explains that the *u* of *ou* is absorbed by the labial, yet Portuguese has such forms as *soube* and *ouve.* **Pōpĕre* is rejected as the source on the grounds that Ptg. *pobre* has an open *o.* There is documentation, however, for the opening influence of labials: *nōbĭle* > Ptg. *nǫbre*; CL *colŭber* > VL **colǫbra.* It does not seem convincing that *pobre* could be a foreign import, since the word is squarely rooted in the core vocabulary. It is to be noted, however, that *pauper* is not continued in Rumanian.

Fr. *pauvre*: *au* is a learned spelling.

Conditioned Developments

156. Vowels in Hiatus
    A certain trend is noted toward a closer vowel quality in hiatus position. In Lat. *dĭe,* this closure takes place across the board: Rm. *zi,* It. *dì,* Sp. *día,* Ptg., Cat. *dia,* Occ., OFr. *di,* while in *vĭa,* French has resisted this trend: *vĭa* > *vẹa* > OFr. *veie* > *voie,* as opposed to *via* in the other languages. An example of *ę* closing to *ẹ* may be seen in the possessive *mĕa* > **mēa* > OFr. *meie, moie,* while Italian displays a more drastic change from *ę* to *i*: *mĕa* > *mia; mĕu* > *mio.* However, since the masc. plur. *mĕī* is continued in Italian as *miei,* It. *mia* and *mio* are perhaps more convincingly

explained as having arisen through the reduction of a regularly obtained, though undocumented triphthong: *mĕa* > **miea* > *mia* and *mĕu* > **mieo* > *mio,* but a similar explanation would, of course, not apply to Occ. *mia,* where no diphthongization could occur. The vowel *ǫ* is closed to *u* in *tŭa* > It. *tua* and *tŭo* > It. *tuo,* while Occitan hesitates between *toa* and *tua.* Most likely, however, the Italian forms may stem from a dissimilated VL **tǫu* > **tuoo* > *tuo* where, once again, the diphthong is recorded only in the masc. plur. **tŏi* > *tuoi* (Rohlfs §§71, 110, 427). The change of *o* to *u* in hiatus is also encountered in Catalan: *sŭa* > *sua; dŭas* > *dues.*

Commentary

It *dì,* Occ., OFr. *di,* Fr. *di*: this noun has survived in the names of the days of the week, where it is found combined with the genitive case of the name of a Pagan divinity as in *Jŏvis die* lit. 'the day of Jupiter'. The reflex of *die* appears in post-position in Italian and French: *Jŏvis die* > It. *giovedì,* OFr. *juesdi,* Fr. *jeudi,* while pre-position is the norm in Occitan: *dijous,* and is found sporadically in certain dialects of northern France. Spanish and Rumanian drop the *die* element altogether: Sp. *jueves,* Rm. *joi,* and an alternate Occitan form is *jous.* In Portuguese, a strong Church influence did away with these Pagan terms altogether, replacing them by *segunda-feira* 'Monday', *terça-feira* 'Tuesday', *quarta-feira* 'Wednesday', *quinta-feira* 'Thursday', and *sexta-feira* 'Friday' (Rohlfs: *Estudios,* pp. 161–164). The genitive *s* of Lat. *Martis, Jŏvis, Vĕneris* has spread analogically to the forms *lūnae* and *Mercŭrii* that have no etymological *s*: *lūnae die* > Sp. *lunes,* OFr. *lunsdi; Mercŭrii die* > Sp. *miércoles,* OFr. *mercresdi.* As the basic word for 'day', *di* has been replaced in Italian and French and mostly also in Occitan by reflexes of the adjective *diŭrnu*: It. *giorno,* Occ., OFr. *jorn,* Fr. *jour.* The loss of *n* in French occurs phonologically in the plural, where it stands between two consonants: *diŭrnos* > *jorz,* and hence a new singular *jor, jour* (§347).

Sp. *día,* Ptg., Occ. *dia*: the fifth declension of Latin was attracted to the first. Classical Latin had such variants as *materies* and *materia, luxuries* and *luxuria,* and this led to the creation of an analogical **dia* from CL *dĭes.* It is this form which is continued in Hispanic, and which is also encountered in Occitan, where it displays a fluctuating gender. As a feminine noun, it is mostly restricted to the fixed locutions *tota dia* and *una dia* (Jensen: *Provençal Philology,* p. 195).

It. *mia, mio,* Occ. *tua, toa,* etc.: for the complex developments that take place in the Romance possessives, purely phonological explanations are not always possible.

Lat. *cŭī*: metaphony or umlaut rather than hiatus position accounts for the change of the *-ŭī* sequence to *-ui* (§161).

157. Paragogical *e*

A final *e* is often added to monosyllabic nouns in Vulgar Latin, and this *e* is retained in Rumanian and Italian: CL *sal* > VL **sale* > Rm. *sare*, It. *sale;* CL *mĕl* > VL **mĕle* > Rm. *miere*, It. *miele;* CL *fĕl* > VL **fĕle* > Rm. *fiere*, It. *fiele;* CL *cŏr* > VL **cŏre* > It. *cuore*. This feature is treated here because of the impact it exerts on the tonic vowel. The addition of a final *e* creates open-syllable conditions allowing for the change of *a* to *e* and for the diphthongization of *ĕ* and *ŏ* in French: *sel, miel, fiel,* OFr. *cuer* > *cœur.* Since this extension is limited to the noun category, there can be no doubt, however, that the addition of a final *e* is a morphological rather than a phonological feature. **Cŏre*–gen. **cŏris* has adopted the flexional scheme of *mare*–gen. *maris.*

158. Vowel Inflection in Portuguese

The tonic vowel may be influenced by a sound with which it is not even in direct contact. Lausberg (§193) uses the term *Fernharmonisierung* for this feature, which is particularly widespread in Sardinian and Rumanian. It is also a common process in Portuguese, where the final *u* of Latin closes the tonic open vowels *ę* and *ǫ* to *ẹ* and *ọ* (§207), as opposed to the retention of the open quality of the vowel, where this condition is not present:

pŏrcu > pǫrco	*mŏrtu > mǫrto*
pŏrcos > pǫrcos	*mŏrtos > mǫrtos*
pŏrca > pǫrca	*mŏrta > mǫrta*
pŏrcas > pǫrcas	*mŏrtas > mǫrtas*

The close vowels *ẹ* and *ọ* are unaffected by the inflection feature:

qu(i)ētu > quẹdo	*tōtu > tọdo*
qu(i)ētos > quẹdos	*tōtos > tọdos*
qu(i)ēta > quẹda	*tōta > tọda*
qu(i)ētas > quẹdas	*tōtas > tọdas*

But the coexistence of such forms as *mǫrto–mǫrtos* and *tọdo–tọdos* inevitably led to some confusion, noticeable above all in the reflexes of the suffix *-ōsu*, which regularly evolves to *-ǫso* in the masc. sing., but shows analogical forms elsewhere: *-ǫsos, -ǫsa, -ǫsas.*

159. Vowel Inflection in Rumanian

Rumanian has a very complex vowel inflection system resulting from the conditioned diphthongization of stressed *e* and *o* under the influence of an *a, ă* or *e* in the following syllable which, in by far most instances, means that the conditioning factor is the final vowel. This entire process has still not been fully elucidated, and there is some disagreement among scholars as to whether the agents are *a, ă* and *e* (Densuşianu) or *ă* and *e* (Iordan). This is essentially a chronological problem, depending on whether final *a* was still intact when the diphthongization occurred, or whether it had already become *ă*. Rosetti retains only *a* and *e* as agents in the diphthongization process, and there is even some doubt about the role of *e*. The feature does appear to be fairly old, since it is shared by all the dialects.

Rumanian retains tonic *ǫ* (< Lat. *ō, ŏ*) if the final vowel is *ŭ, o* or *i*: *pŏrcu > porc; lŏcu > loc; -ōsu > -os; ŏcto > opt; -ōsī > -oşi; nostrī > noştri*. If the final vowel is *a (ă)* or *e*, tonic *ǫ* breaks into *oa*: *sōle > soare; rŏta > roată; mŏla > moară; -ōsa > -oasă; -ōsae > -oase; nostrae > noaştre*. The close *e* that comes from Lat. *ē, ĭ* is kept before final *ŭ, o* or *i*: *dirēctu > drept; dirēctī > drepţi; nĭgru > negru; crēsco > cresc*, but if the final vowel is *a (ă)* or *e, ę* diphthongizes to *ea*: *dirēcta > dreaptă; nĭgra > neagră; lĭgat > leagă*. At times, the modern language changes *ea* back to *e: vĭdet > veade > vede*. The open *e* evolving from Lat. *ĕ* or *ae* diphthongizes regularly to *ie: fĕrru > fier; pĕctu > piept*, but before a final *a (ă)* or *e*, this diphthong opens to *ia*, perhaps via an intermediate stage **iea* (Nandris, p. 71): *hĕrba > *iearbă > iarbă; ĕqua > iapă; pĕtra > piatră*. If the final vowel is *e*, Rumanian often reverts to *ie: pĕtrae > piatre > pietre; pĕrdit > piarde > pierde*. It seems likely that a feature of vowel harmony or assimilation is involved in this regressive process. For further details, one may consult Nandris, pp. 17, 35, 70–71, 74–75, 210–213; Lausberg §197; Rothe §16; Tiktin §50.

160. Vowel Inflection in Sardinian

In Sardinian, *e* (< Lat. *ē, ĕ*) and *o* (< Lat. *ō, ŏ*) have a close pronunciation before final *i* or *u*, but are pronounced open if the final syllable contains *e, o* or *a*. A close *e* is seen in: *gĕneru > ghęneru; cĕntu > kęntu; caelu > kęlu; vēnī > vęni*, a close *o* in: *lŏco > lǫku; sŏcru > sǫkru; nōbis > nǫis*, while an open *e* is found in: *sĕpte > sętte; catēna > katęna*, and an open *o* in: *ŏcto > ǫtto; nŏve > nǫve; sōle > sǫle*.

161. Metaphony, Umlaut, Vowel Harmony

Metaphony is basically an assimilation feature, which may also be referred to as vowel harmony. The final long *i* and the yod are the chief agents in this process. Final long *i* works in conjunction with the hiatus position to change *-ŭī* to *-ui* instead of the expected *-ǫi*: Lat. *cŭī* > It., Occ., OFr. *cui;* Lat. *fŭī* > It., OSp., Ptg., Occ., OFr. *fui,* Sp. *fuí.* The final long *ī* is active in closing the stem vowel of Spanish perfects from *e* to *i* or from *o* to *u* as in: *fēci* > *hice;* *vēnī* > *vine;* *pŏtuī* > *pude;* *pŏsuī* > *puse* (Menén-dez Pidal §§11.2.d, 120.3; García de Diego, pp. 198, 247). The yod, which comes about through the early loss of a *d,* closes the preceding vowel in Spanish, again from *e* to *i* or from *o* to *u*: *lĭmpĭdu* > *limpio; tĕpĭdu* > *tibio; tŭrbĭdu* > *turbio,* and so do a few clusters of consonant and yod: *navĭgiu* > *navío; vĭndēmia* > *vendimia; sēpia* > *jibia.* Catalan similarly has *sēpia* > *sípia; cērĕu* > *ciri.*

162. Conditioned Diphthongization in Occitan and French

Occitan does not have any spontaneous diphthongizations, but the open vowels *ĕ* and *ŏ* are subject to diphthongization provided specific conditions are present. The elements capable of acting as agents in this process are chiefly a final long *i,* a palatal (yod, *c, g*) and a final *u̯,* obtained from *v* in final position, less commonly a velar *c* (Anglade, pp. 63–65, 72–76). The diphthongization is optional only, originally perhaps in accordance with geographical criteria; *ĕ* gives *ie,* while *ŏ* moves to either *uo* or *ue.*

mĕī > *mei, miei*	*pŏtuī* > *poc, puoc, puec*
hĕrī > *er, ier*	*nŏcte* > *noit, nuoit, nueit,*
vendĕdī > *vendei, vendiei*	*noch, nuoch, nuech*
lĕctu > *leit, lieit*	*hŏdie* > *oi, uoi, uei*
vĕtŭlu > *vĕclu* > *velh, vielh*	*ŏcŭlu* > *olh, uolh, uelh*
mĕlius > *melz, mielz*	*fŏlia* > *folha, fuolha, fuelha*
lĕve > *leu, lieu*	*fŏcu* > *foc, fuoc, fuec*
mĕu > *meu, mieu*	*lŏcu* > *loc, luoc, luec*
CL *ĕgo* > VL *eo* > *eu, ieu*	**ŏvu* > *ou, uou, ueu*

In French, where the spontaneous diphthongization is restricted to the open syllable, a conditioned diphthongization occurs automatically when blocked *ĕ* or *ŏ* is followed by a palatal. The diphthongs *ie* < *ĕ* and *ue* < *ŏ* subsequently merge with the palatal into the triphthongs **iei* and **uei* (via an earlier *uoi*), whereupon this conjectural stage is reduced to *i* and *ui*:

lĕctu > **lieit* > *lit*   *nŏcte* > **nuoit* > **nueit* > *nuit*
pĕctus > **pieiz* > *piz* > *pis*   *cŏxa* > **cuoisse* > **cueisse* > *cuisse*
ĕxĭt > **ieist* > OFr. *ist*   **pŏssio* > **puois* > **pueis* > *puis*

163. Conditioned Diphthongization or Vowel Inflection in Catalan

A tonic *ĕ* followed by a yod evolves to *i* in Catalan: *lĕctu* > *llit; profĕctu* > *profit; sĕx* > *sis; ĕxit* > *ix; vĕnio* > *vinc.* This extreme vowel closure is explained by some scholars as having resulted from a diphthongization of *ĕ,* leading to the creation of an undocumented triphthong **iei,* which is subsequently reduced to *i.* The diphthongization theory gains support from a certain parallelism with conditions in Occitan, yet there are also major differences between the two languages. The diphthong is retained in Occitan, but reduced in Catalan, and the diphthongization is triggered solely by palatals in Catalan, and infrequently by a final long *i: hĕrī* > OCat. *i, ir,* Mod.Cat. *ahir,* while other agents are involved in the Occitan development, notably the velar element wau. This is not without casting some doubt on the validity of the diphthongization theory, leading some scholars to maintain instead that the *i* is obtained from a yod-caused inflection of the open *e.* That this closure affects *ę* rather than *ẹ* does not appear to be an obstacle: the yod, which has a very close pronunciation, tends to affect the vowels that are most different from it in articulation, as may be seen from parallel developments in Spanish (Menéndez Pidal, pp. 47–50; Badía Margarit §§48, II–III, 51, II–III; B. Moll §§36, 55; P. Fouché: "La diphtongaison en catalan"; *BDC, 13* (1925), 1–46). In his description of the Catalan diphthongization, Badía Margarit focuses his attention on a comparison between Catalan and Occitan, but the Catalan development would seem to have a closer parallel in French: both languages display a reduction to *i,* and the conditioning factors are practically identical.

The treatment of *ŏ* + yod parallels that of *ĕ* + yod. The open *o* evolves to *u* or *ui* through inflection or via a diphthongization to **uei* (or an earlier **uoi*) and a subsequent reduction of the triphthong to *ui* or *u: cŏctu* > *cuit; ŏcŭlu* > *ull; fŏlia* > *fulla; lŏnge* > *lluny; *plŏia* > *pluja; pŏdiu* > *puig.* The unusual reduction of *ui* to *i,* which occurs in *nŏcte* > OCat. *nuit* > Mod. Cat. *nit,* is explained variously as resulting from a shift in stress (Badía Margarit §51, III) or, less convincingly, obtained through an analogy with its antonym *dia* (B. Moll §55; Fouché: *Phonétique historique,* p. 225).

164. Conditioned Non-Diphthongization in Spanish

In Spanish, tonic *ĕ* and *ŏ* diphthongize, regardless of the nature of the syllable, but the close vowels are not subject to this change. If palatals prevent the open vowels from diphthongizing, we may assume that they exert a closing influence on the stressed vowel. In fact, Portuguese often has a close vowel here, as in *fŏlia > fŏlha; ŏcŭlu > ǫlho; tĕrtiu > tęrço.* The following examples may serve to illustrate the non-diphthongization feature in Spanish:

lĕctu > lecho	*fŏlia > hoja*
pĕctu > pecho	*ŏcŭlu > ojo*
sĕx > seis	*hŏdie > hoy*
matĕria > madera	*nŏcte > noche*
profĕctu > provecho	**cŏxu > cojo*

An important exception is *vĕtulu > vĕclu > viejo* which, though very much part of the core vocabulary, undergoes a vowel change that points to dialectal influence. Many dialects have a diphthong here: Aragonese *viello,* Leonese and *asturiano vieyo.* Or could it be that the [χ] that comes from *cl* blocks diphthongization of *ŏ,* but not of *ĕ?* The word *espejo* would not invalidate such a theory, since Latin has both *spĕculum* and *spēculum.*

While the palatal *l* that comes from *l* + yod, and which evolves to [χ], prevents diphthongization, this is not the case with the palatal *l* that derives from *ll,* and which does not participate in the change to [χ]. The double *l* becomes a palatal group only after the diphthongization has taken place, and after the earlier palatal *l* had moved on to [χ]. The *ie* diphthong is reduced to *i* when preceding this secondarily obtained palatal: *castĕllu > castiello > castillo* (§173).

165. Vowel Closure Caused by Palatals or Palatal Groups in Spanish and Portuguese

The *-ŭlt-* sequence becomes palatal in Hispanic, causing the closure of *ǫ* to *u.* In Spanish, *l* is palatalized in this cluster, then changes to yod, whereupon it evolves to *ch* [tš], while Old Portuguese has *it,* which is later reduced to *t* (Menéndez Pidal §47.2.c; García de Diego, p. 119; Williams §38.5): CL *auscŭltat > VL ascǫltat > Sp. escucha, OPtg. ascuita, Ptg. escuta* vs. It. *ascolta,* Cat., Occ. *escolta,* Occ. *escouta,* OFr. *escoute,* Fr. *écoute;* CL *mŭltu > VL mǫlto > Sp. mucho, Ptg. muito* vs. It. *molto,* Cat. *molt,* Occ., OFr. *molt, mout.* Rm. *ascultă* obtains its *u* regularly in accordance with §150.

The *-ŭct-* combination receives a treatment similar to that of *-ŭlt-* in Hispanic, showing the same intermediate stages: *lŭcta* > Sp. *lucha,* OPtg. *luita,* Ptg. *luta; trŭcta* > Sp. *trucha,* OPtg. *truita,* Ptg. *truta.*

Commentary

CL *auscŭltat,* VL *ascoltat*: for the dissimilation process that reduces *au* to *a* when followed by a stressed *ŭ,* see §192. The unusual *as-* of Vulgar Latin is retained only in Rumanian, Italian and Old Portuguese, having yielded elsewhere to pressure from the prefix *ex-.*

Ptg. *muito*: the existence of an apocopated *mui* (cf. Sp. *muy*) prevented the *i* from falling in this word. Apocopated forms are rare in Portuguese because of the relative strength of unaccented vowels; the few cases that do exist are mostly attributable to Spanish influence (Williams §107). The change to [*tš*] in Spanish does not take place if *t* becomes final through apocopation: OSp. *muyt'* > Sp. *muy.* There are sporadic occurrences in Portuguese of nasalization caused by a preceding nasal consonant; *muito,* with its nasal diphthong, is an example, as is also *mãe* < *madre* (§§224, 229).

Lat. *lŭcta, lŭctare*: the exact quantity of Lat. *u* in this word is unknown (*FEW* V 438–440; Bloch-Wartburg, pp. 377–378; Corominas III, 706–707). The hesitation in quantity focuses chiefly on Gallo-Romance. The normal development of the verb *lŭctāre* (CL *lŭctārī*) is represented by OFr. *loitier,* while the variant *luitier* > *lutter* reflects a *lūctāre* base. Rheinfelder (I 99) believes the modern form to have come in from eastern dialects, but Occitan similarly has both *lochar* and *luchar.* For Hispanic, both *ŭ* and *ū* are acceptable, since *o̜* closes to *u* in this sound sequence, and in Rumanian, which has *luptă* here, *ŭ* and *ū* regularly merge in *u* (§132). The hesitation in Gallo-Romance could perhaps be indicative of an incipient palatalization move. Italian has settled for the short *u,* but the form *lo̜tta* has a surprising open *o,* which could represent nothing more than an alternation with the close *o* of the pretonic syllable in *lo̜ttare,* or it could be dialectal (Rohlfs §69).

It. *tro̜ta,* Fr. *truite*: once again, the vowel quantity in the *-ŭct-* sequence is indecisive. It. *tro̜ta,* with its open *o* and irregular also in that *ct* has simplified to *t* instead of assimilating to *tt* (cf. *factu* > *fatto*), is dialectal from the Romagna province (Rohlfs §69), while Fr. *truite* is unexplained. The form *troite,* which one would have expected, is documented in the *normand* dialect. Fr. *truite* requires an etymon in *ū* or *o̜* (§162), while *o̜* would be unacceptable. Occitan has a regular *tro̜cha* and a form *truita,* paralleling the French development.

166. Inflection of Tonic *a* in Hispanic

Menéndez Pidal (§8bis.a–d) distinguishes between four categories of yods in Spanish: the first yod is derived from *ti̯* and *ki̯*, the second from *li̯*, *c'l*, *g'l*, and *t'l*, the third from *gi̯*, *di̯*, *bi̯* and *vi̯*, the fourth from *ct*, *cs*, *ri̯*, *si̯*, *pi̯* or from mere vocalic contiguity as in *cantavi* > *cantai* and *laicu* > *lego*. It is only the most persistent yod, the one of the fourth group, which is capable of inflecting the vowel *a*. Menéndez Pidal proposes the following stages in this evolution: *ai̯* > *ei̯* > *ee* > *e;* there are cases of *ai* in tenth-century Leonese documents, *ei* is the stage reached by Portuguese, Galician and Leonese, while Spanish has *e*, Catalan *e* or *ei* (for cases of *ai* in Catalan, see below): *lacte* > Sp. *leche,* Ptg. *leite,* Cat. *llet; factu* > Sp. *hecho,* Ptg. *feito,* Cat. *fet; fraxĭnu* > Sp. *fresno,* Ptg. *freixo,* Cat. *freixe; arĕa* > Sp., Cat. *era,* Ptg. *eira; basiu* > Sp. *beso,* Ptg. *beijo,* Cat. *bes; laicu* > Sp. *lego,* Ptg. *leigo,* Cat. *llec.* By way of comparison, the following examples may serve as a sampling of the yods that leave *a* uninflected in Hispanic: *mĭnācia* > Sp. *amenaza,* Ptg. *ameaça,* Cat. *menassa; palea* > Sp. *paja,* Ptg. *palha,* Cat. *palla; arānea* > Sp. *araña,* Ptg. *aranha,* Cat. *aranya; stagnu* > Sp. *estaño,* Ptg. *estanho,* Cat. *estany; radiu* > Sp., Ptg. *rayo,* Cat. *raig; labiu* > Sp., *labio,* Ptg. *lábio,* Cat. *llavi.*

A fair amount of fluctuation between *a* and *e* is noted for Catalan in cases where tonic *a* is followed by a palatal [š] spelled *ix* and obtained from *cs* or *si̯*: **bassiat* > *baixa; capsa* > *caixa; fascia* > *faixa; ascia* > *aixa* vs. **grasseu* > *greix; capsu* > *queix.* B. Moll (§52) adopts Fouché's explanation (*Phonétique historique,* p. 36) in terms of which *a* evolves to *e* with final *ix,* but remains *a* with internal *ix,* yet in §51 he gives both *feixa* < *fascia* and *feix* < *fasce,* and the rule is contradicted by *freixe* < *fraxĭnu* and *madeixa* < *mataxa.* Grammont (*RLR 62,* 487) seeks the conditioning factor in the nature of the final vowel: *a* is kept if the final vowel is *a,* while it drops elsewhere, and we thus get *queix* vs. *caixa* and *feix* vs. *faixa.* This theory is accepted by Corominas, but even with this explanation there are problems: *madeixa* < *mataxa,* and we are left with many deviations that can only be accounted for through paradigmatic pressure: *deixa* < *laxat* is analogical from *deix* < *laxo,* and *baix* < **bassiu* draws its *a* from *baixa* < **bassiat.*

167. Vowel Closure Caused by Palatal *n* in Italian and Hispanic

The palatal *n* and, specifically for Italian, *n* + palatal combinations close a preceding tonic *ǫ* to *u* in Italian and Hispanic, while Gallo-Romance usually remains unaffected by this development: Lat. *pŭgnu* > It. *pugno,* Sp. *puño,* Ptg. *punho,* Cat. *puny* vs. Occ. *ponh, punh,* Fr. *poing;* Lat. *ŭngula*

> It. *unghia* (rarely *ugna*), Sp. *uña*, Ptg. *unha*, Cat. *ungla* vs. Occ. *ongla*, Fr. *ongle*.

Additional Italian examples of *n* + palatal are: *giungere* < *jŭngĕre; giunto* < *jŭnctu; punto* < *pŭnctu*, while an exception to the rule may be seen in *vergogna* < *verecŭndia*, but this word is probably a borrowing from Occitan. Also in Italian, *n* + *c* or *g* closes *ę* to *i*: *vĭncĕre* > It. *vincere; fĭngĕre* > It. *fingere*, but *ę* usually resists this trend when a palatal *n* follows: *lĭgnu* > It. *legno*, Sp. *leño*, Ptg. *lenho; sĭgnu/sĭgna* > It. *segno*, Sp. *seña*, Ptg. *senha*. In Catalan, *nc* and *ng* close a preceding tonic *ǫ* to *u*: *jŭnctu* > *junt; jŭngĕre* > *júnyer*, and the same clusters may close *ę* to *i*: *cĭncta* > *cinta; cĭngula* > *cingla* (B. Moll §45).

Commentary

Occ. *punh*: this variant offers an instance of closure in the Gallo-Romance area.

Lat. *lĭgnu, sĭgnu*: these neuter nouns may be continued either via the singular (*lĭgnu* > Sp. *leño*) or via the plural (*lĭgna* > Sp. *leña*, Cat. *llenya*, OFr. *leigne*). In French, *sĭgnu* is continued as OFr. *sein* > *seing*, while *signe* is learned, and Occitan has the parallel developments *senh* and *signe*.

168. Vowel Closure with Palatal *l*

The palatal *l* may cause the closure of *e* to *i*, but a somewhat fluctuating outcome may perhaps signal an uncertain vowel quantity in popular Latin. Hispanic does not inflect, but there are occurrences in Italian and Gallo-Romance:

Latin
*cĭliu, cĭlia, *tĭliu, *tĭlia*

Rm.	It.	Sp.	Ptg.	Cat.	Occ.	OFr.	Fr.
	ciglio				cilh, celh		cil
		ceja	celha	cella	cilha, celha		
teiu	tiglio	teja			telh	til	

Commentary
Occ. *cilh, celh, cilha, celha*: Occitan forms a transitional area, having both inflected and non-inflected reflexes. For the continuation of neuter nouns in Vulgar Latin and Romance, see §167.
Ptg. *tília* is learned; OFr. *til* is continued in *tilleul.*

169. Early Metaphony with the *sti* Cluster

Latin
bēstia, ōstiu, bīstia, ūstiu

Rm.	It.	Sp.	Ptg.	Occ.	OFr.	Fr.
	biscia	*bicha*	*bicha*	*bestia*	*bisse*	*biche*
uşă	*uscio*	*uço*		*uis*	*uis*	*huis*
		(old)				

Commentary
Lat. *bīstia*: Hispanic and Occ. *bestia* is learned. OFr. *bisse* represents the phonological outcome of *bīstia* (cf. *angŭstia > angoisse*), while Fr. *biche* is *normand* or *picard*. Fr. *bête* is somewhat obscure, although a form **besta* is easily derived from a documented diminutive *bestula*. Hispanic mostly has a masculine form: Sp., Ptg. *bicho,* derived from a VL *bēstiu* for CL *bēstia,* and comparable to the form *bescio,* cited for Italian by Rohlfs (§292). Corominas (I 580–582) theorizes that *bicho* came into Spanish from Portuguese, presumably because of its late appearance in Castilian. While *bestia* is the word for 'animal' in a broad acceptation, the Romance reflexes have narrowed down the meaning in various ways. It. *biscia* denotes an evil animal, the snake, and so does Hispanic *bicha,* while the masculine *bicho* 'small animal, worm, insect' appears to be a euphemism, being more or less the equivalent of Fr. *bestiole*. Fr. *biche* denotes a common species, the deer, a meaning it may have acquired from the language of hunters.
Rm. *uşă*: the Rumanian reflex is drawn from a form **ūstia,* which has adopted the feminine gender via the neuter plural.
OSp. *uço*: the *sti* cluster regularly gives *ç* in Spanish, while the alternate form *uzo* contains an imperfect archaic graph (Corominas V 726).
Fr. *huis*: the unetymological *h* may originally have served the purpose of stressing the vocalic quality of *u,* since *u* and *v* were not kept separate graphically. Von Wartburg (*FEW* VII 437–440) suggests that OFr. *huis* may have denoted a smaller, inner door, while *porte* was the outer door of

the main entrance way. This explanation is contradicted by the following passage from the *Queste del Saint Graal*: *si vient au mestre huis dou palés* (8.26–27) 'and he gets to the main door of the palace'. *Porte* quickly becomes the preferred term, leading to the virtual elimination of *huis*, which has survived only in the locution *à huis clos* and in the derivation *huissier.*

170. Palatals Form Blocked Syllable in French

> *palea > paille*
> *consĭliu > conseil*
> *rŭbeu > rouge*
> *genŭcŭlu >* OFr. *genouil*
> *vōce >* OFr. *voiz*

Commentary
The above examples show blocked-syllable treatment of the tonic vowel. It is to be noted that *il* or *ill* represents the standard graph for *l mouillé; paille* thus has *a*, not *e* (cf. *mare > mer*), and *conseil* has *ę̧*, with the *ei* diphthong arising from a coalescence of *e* with the *i̯* obtained from a late reduction of palatal *l* and not from a diphthongization.

rouge: the palatal [*dž*] requires a supporting vowel.
genouil: the palatal *l* is still in evidence in the verb *s'agenouiller;* the modern form *genou* is drawn from the plural *genouz < genŭcŭlos* through the elimination of the plural marker *z*.
voiz: the final *-ce* releases a yod, which forms a diphthong by coalescence with *o*.

171. Palatal and Tonic Free *a* and *ę* in French
Two tonic vowels, *a* and *ę*, are directly influenced by a preceding palatal, provided they appear in a free syllable:

CL *caput* > VL *capu* > OFr. *chief* > *chef*	*cēra > cire*
caru > OFr. *chier* > *cher*	*cēpa > cive*
capra > OFr. *chievre* > *chèvre*	*placēre > plaisir*

Commentary
Lat. *k* is palatalized to [*tš*] before *a* in a process that further involves the release of a yod in front of *e*, the regular outcome of tonic free *a*: *caru >*

chier. This rule is known as Bartsch's Law in honor of the German scholar, who first plotted its workings. The affricate [*tš*] is later reduced to [*š*], and the yod is absorbed into the palatal: *chier > cher.* Even where the yod is distinctly pronounced, as in *laissier < laxāre* and *traitier < tractāre,* it is removed analogically through paradigmatic pressure: the unusual *-ier* infinitive is made to conform to the *-er* group. It is only where a nasalization takes place that the *ie* spelling is preserved: *cane > chien.*

Standing before a stressed free *ẹ, k* evolves to *ts,* and this change is again accompanied by the release of a yod toward the regular outcome of the tonic vowel, in this instance the diphthong *ei,* whereupon the resulting triphthong **iei* is resolved as *i: cēra > *cieire > cire,* and *ts* is reduced to *s.* Since *k* is intervocalic in *placēre, ts* voices to *dz,* which is subsequently reduced to a voiced *s,* and an additional yod is released toward the pretonic *a.*

Fr. *cendre < cĭnĕre:* a change of *ẹ* to *i* does not occur here, because an early loss of the weak *ĕ* had created a blocked syllable.

OFr. *receit,* Fr. *reçoit < VL recĭpit:* morphological pressure may be adduced to explain this exception to the rule. It does not seem possible to date the rule back to a point in time when *ĭ* had not yet merged with *ē.* It is probably a mere coincidence that there are no occurrences of this palatalization feature with *ĭ.*

172. Reduction of the Diphthong *ie* to *ẹ* in Italian and Rumanian
In the same manner as OFr. *chief* is reduced to *chef,* the initial element of the Italian diphthong *ie* is absorbed into an immediately preceding palatal [*tš*] or [*dž*]. Phonologically, this occurs even where *i* continues to appear in spelling, as in *cielo* [*tšɛlo*]. Other examples are: *gĕlu > *gielo > gelo; gĕmĕre > *giemere > gemere,* and compare Fr. *gel.* Italian shares this feature with Rumanian: Rm. *cer < caelu; ger < gĕlu; geme < gĕmĕre.* In Rumanian, the yod of the *ia* diphthong may be absorbed by *s* and *t,* giving rise to the sounds [*š*] and *ts* spelled *ş* and *ţ* respectively: *sĕpte > *siapte > şapte; tĕrra > *tiară > ţară.*

Italian also reduces the *ie* diphthong to *ẹ* when it is preceded by an occlusive plus *r* cluster: *praeda > prieda > preda; *prĕco > priego > prego; brĕve > brieve > breve; crĕpat > criepa > crepa; praebyter > priete > prete,* and once again, Rumanian shows a similar development: *praeda > priadă > pradă* (with the inflection of *ie* to *ia* caused by the final *a*), while the change of *ie* to *ẹ* in French is merely an isolated regressive feature, or a less firmly established incipient move, encountered in *brĕve*

> OFr. *brief* > *bref* (but cf. *brièvement)* as well as in Frk. **treuwa* > OFr. *trieve* > *trève.* In verb forms, there is further the possibility that the pre-tonic vowel may be extended to the stem-stressed forms. *Criepa,* for example, may have reverted to *crepa* through the additional influence of *crepare* < *crĕpāre,* and OIt. *niega–negare* is replaced by a *nega–negare* paradigm.

Commentary

It. *prete,* Fr. *prêtre*: Ecclesiastical Lat. *presbyter* is continued in the nominative form as OFr. *prestre,* Fr. *prêtre,* while It. *prete* (*DEI* IV 3073–3074) flows from a variant *praebiter,* documented in Latin inscriptions, but it displays a series of irregular features in its evolution. The lack of a diphthong is normal following a cluster with *r,* or it may be indicative of proclitic treatment of the word as a title. The loss of intervocalic *b* is obscure; Wiese (§79) suggests that *b* may have dropped between two *e*'s as in *bere* < *bĭbĕre* while Rohlfs (§215), more convincingly, obtains *bere* from the same type of dissimilation that yields the imperfect ending *-ea* from *-ēbam* in the verbs *habēbam, debēbam.* This explanation, however, does not apply to *praebiter,* which must have been proclitically shortened in its Italian evolution. Final *r* may have dropped through dissimilation (cf. *frater* > *frate)* or as part of a more general phonological process (Meyer-Lübke, p. 116; Wiese §98; Rohlfs §307). OIt. *preite* is an obscure variant. *Prete* offers an instance of the continuation of the nominative singular case in Italian; other occurrences are *uomo* < *hŏmo; ladro* < *latro; sarto* < *sartor; moglie* < *mŭlier* (Rohlfs §344; Wiese §107.1; Meyer-Lübke, pp. 129–130).

Frk. **treuwa,* OFr. *trieve,* Fr. *trève*: Frk. **treuwa* (*FEW* XVII 361) is superior to the form **triuwa* suggested by Corominas (V 618), since the French forms and Occ. *trẹva* require an etymon in *ẹ.* Goth. **trĭggwa* is the source of Sp. *tregua,* Ptg. *trégua,* while It. *tregua* and the Occitan variant *trẹga* may stem from a mixed Gothic-Frankish source, heavily influenced by Frankish phonology as seen from the Old Italian variants *triegua, treva* and *trieva* (Corominas V 618; Gamillscheg: *Rom. Germ.* I 369).

173. Reduction of the Diphthong *ie* to *i* in Spanish

The diphthong *ie* is in some instances reduced to *i* in Spanish. This occurs with the greatest frequency in connection with the palatalization of *ll* as in *castĕllu* > OSp. *castiello* > *castillo; scūtĕlla* > OSp. *escudiella* > *escudilla; sĕlla* > OSp. *siella* > *silla.* Double *l* acquires a palatal pronunciation only after the diphthongization has taken place, and *e* is then absorbed into *i.* The modern forms become generalized in fourteenth-century texts, but the phonological change is documented in non-literary texts as early as the tenth century (Menéndez Pidal §10.2; García de Diego, p. 59). When standing before a consonant, *s* acquires a palatal value which may cause a similar reduction of *ie* to *i*: *věspěra* > OSp. *viéspera* > *víspera; věspa* > OSp. *aviespa* > *avispa; měspĭlu* > OSp. *niéspero* > *níspero*, although with some cases of retention: *fěsta* > *fiesta; sěxta* > *sesta* > *siesta*.

Triphthong reduction occurs commonly before a final *o* or *a*: *měu* > OSp. *mieo* > *mío; jūdaeu* > OSp. *judieo* > *judío; jūdaea* > OSp. *judiea* > *judía; Děus* > old and dial. *Dieos* > *Dios*.

Commentary

Sp. *avispa*: the addition of an initial *a* is attributable to the influence of *abeja*, an explanation which finds further support in the existence of a variant *abispa*. Portuguese similarly has *bespa* as a collateral form of the regular *vespa*.

Sp. *níspero*: borrowed from Greek, CL *měspĭlu* undergoes certain phonological changes that have not all been convincingly elucidated. Foreign origin would seem to be the main factor in the replacement of initial *m* by *n* rather than a consonantal dissimilation. Corominas (IV 229–230) gives the direct source as VL *něspĭru*, in which he detects the influence of Lat. *pĭru* 'pear'. Old French has *mesle* and *nesple,* while the modern form *nèfle* goes back to *měsfīla* (*FEW* VI 44–47).

Sp. *siesta*: this noun is drawn from the ordinal *sěxta*, appearing in the combination *hōra sěxta* 'sixth hour'. Portuguese has an independently developed *sesta*, while It. *siesta* and Fr. *sieste* are borrowed from Spanish. Characteristic of the Spanish development is the reduction of *cs* (spelled *x*) to *s* before a consonant: *sěxta* > *sesta* > *siesta* (Menéndez Pidal §51.3); cf. *děxtru* > *destro* > *diestro*. This must be an early development, since *ě* could not have diphthongized before a palatal (§164).

174. The *-ariu* Suffix

Latin

-āriu

Rm.	It.	Sp.	Ptg.	Cat.	Occ.	Fr.
-áriu	*-aio,*	*-ero*	*-eiro*	*-er*	*-ier*	*-ier*
	-aro					

Commentary

This extremely common suffix contains a palatal *rį* combination which, in most areas, lets the palatal element slip through, releasing it in front, with Lat. *-āriu* evolving to *-airo* and hence Sp. *-ero*, Ptg. *-eiro*: *caballariu* > Sp. *caballero*, Ptg. *caval(h)eiro; fŭrnariu* > Sp. *hornero*, Ptg. *forneiro; fĕrrariu* > Sp. *herrero*, Ptg. *ferreiro*. Characteristically, Italian reduces *rį* to *į*, with *-aio* thus representing the phonological outcome: *notariu* > *notaio; fŭrnariu* > *fornaio; floraria* > *fioraia*, but *-aro* is common in both southern and northern dialects: *notaro, furnaru*, and the written language has both *marinaio* and *marinaro, porcaio* and *porcaro*, etc. (Rohlfs §1072). Occ. *-ier*: *cavalier, fornier, ferrier*, is identical with and perhaps borrowed from the French form. Fr. *-ier* is difficult to account for phonologically, since one would have expected **-air* (cf. *variu* > *vair*). Lausberg (§207) obtains it from a palatal dissimilation in cases where *-ariu* is preceded by a palatal, as in *vĭridiariu* > **viridiaru* > *vergier*, while Rheinfelder (I 107), in the wake of Antoine Thomas' findings, suggests that *-ariu* was changed to *-ęro* under the influence of an umlauted Frankish **-(h)āri*. It. *-iere*, as in *cavaliere*, is borrowed from French.

175. Influence of Velar *l*

It is probably a velar *l* as in E. *hill* that stands before a consonant in Latin and in the early stages of Romance. This velar *l* vocalizes to a non-syllabic *ų* very generally in French and, in more restricted fashion, in Occitan and Hispanic, never in Italian and Rumanian. Retention of *l* is the norm in Catalan, where vocalization is limited to a few dialectal occurrences (B. Moll §164). While the overall treatment of *l* is discussed elsewhere, it will suffice at this point to mention that, with but one exception, the *ų* that comes from *l* influences the tonic vowel merely by coalescing with it. Generally speaking, the resulting diphthong then monophthongizes.

In Hispanic, only the vowel *a* is affected, and this secondarily obtained diphthong evolves like the primitive *au* (§155) to *o* in Spanish and to *ou* in Portuguese. In Portuguese, however, the pronunciation is now *ǫ*, although the graph *ou* remains intact:

> *alteru* > Sp. *otro*, Ptg. *outro*
> *saltu* > Sp. *soto*, Ptg. *souto*
> *falce* > Sp. *hoz*, Ptg. *fouce*
> *calce* > Sp. *coz*, Ptg. *couce*

In Occitan, the diphthongs obtained through coalescence of the vowel with *u̯* remain, but the vocalization of *l* is optional only and occurs only with certain consonants (§282):

> *altu* > *alt, aut*
> *falsu* > *fals, faus*
> *dŭlce* > *dols, dous*
> *mŭltu* > *molt, mout*
> *ĭllos* > *els, eus*

In French, the velar *l* changes to *u̯* after the vowels *a, ǫ, o̧, ę̆* and *ę,* but it disappears after *u* and *i*. The diphthongs created through this process remain at first: *au, ǫu, ọu* and *ęu* (*ę̆ + l* is treated separately), then monophthongize to [*o*], [*u*] and [*ø*], approximately in the thirteenth century:

> *caballos* > *chevaus*
> *alba* > *aube*
> *altu* > *haut*
> *cŏl(a)phu* > *coup*
> *dŭlce* > *douz*
> *capĭllos* > *cheveus*

The short *e* breaks into *ea* when followed by a velar *l,* and *a* soon attracts the stress: *-ęls* > *-eals* > *-eaus,* yielding the triphthong [*əaw*], which subsequently evolves via [*əo*] to [*o*]:

> *bĕllos* > *beals* > *beaux*
> *pĕlles* > *peals* > *peaux*
> *castĕllos* > *chasteals* > *châteaux*
> *pŏrcĕllos* > *porceals* > *pourceaux*

Commentary

The *picard* and *champenois* dialects have *-iau* instead of *-eau*: *biaux, chastiaus*. A vestige of this dialectal development may be seen in the word *fabliau,* designating a literary genre cultivated above all in northern France.

A triphthong arises in *caelos* > *cieus* > *cieux* because of the open syllable; the diphthong *ie* suffers no influence from *u̯* beyond coalescence and subsequent rounding.

176. Vocalic Changes Caused by Final *u* in French and Occitan

Final *u* is retained as *u̯* in Old French and Occitan if it finds itself in direct contact with tonic *ĕ*: *Dĕu* > Fr. *Dieu*, Occ. *Deu, Dieu*. With *ie*, this *u̯* forms the triphthong *-ieu* [jɛw] which in French is rounded to [jø]. It is perhaps with *Dieu, mieu* as a model that Occitan tends to enlarge the combination *-iu* to *-ieu*: *rīvu* > *riu* > *rieu;* *vīvit* > *viu* > *vieu*. For final *u̯* as an agent in the conditioned diphthongization of *ĕ* and *ŏ* in Occitan, see §162.

177. Influence of *r*

The open quality of *r* causes some fluctuation in French between *er* and *ar*. This occurs in a few loan-words from Germanic: Frk. **garba* > *jarbe, gerbe;* Dutch *bolwerk* > *boulevard,* but may also affect words of Latin origin: *lacrĭma* > *lairme* > *lerme* and *larme; carne* > *charn* > *char* and *chair* (for the loss of *n,* see *jorz* §156).

178. Closing Influence of Nasals

The influence which a nasal consonant may exert on the preceding tonic vowel is of a dual nature: the nasal may cause a closure of the vowel, or it may nasalize it.

Latin inscriptions demonstrate that a trend toward vowel closure before a nasal existed already in the first and second century: *punere* for *ponere; frunte* for *fronte*. The Romance language that has continued this trend most persistently is Rumanian: *plēnu* > *plin; dĕnte* > *dinte; tĕmpus* > *timp; nōmen* > *nume; bŏnu* > *bun; mŏnte* > *munte,* but it is also a fairly common feature of Italian and Spanish. Italian closes *ǫ* to *o* before a blocked nasal, which is to say a nasal plus consonant combination: *mŏnte* > *monte; pŏnte* > *ponte; cŏm(ĭ)te* > *conte; in abscŏndit* > *nasconde*. The open *e,* on the other hand, is closed to *e* only between *m* and a blocked nasal: *-mĕnte* > *-mente; -mĕntu* > *-mento; mĕntit* > *mente* vs. *dĕnte* > *dẹnte; sĕmper* > *sẹmpre* (Rohlfs §§110,88; Lausberg §232). In Spanish, where the closure of *ǫ* to *o* may interfere with diphthongization, this development is more difficult to plot than in Italian. *Pŏnte* > *puente; frŏnte* > *fruente* > *frente; cŏmpŭtat* > *cuenta* show regular diphthongization of open *o,* while *mŏnte* had closed to *monte* too early for participation in this feature. The *-ŏnd-* sequence is subject to a fair amount of fluctuation: *abscŏndo* is continued in the old language as *escuendo* and *escondo, respŏndo* as *respuendo* and *respondo. Cŏmĭte* evolved to *conde,* but with not infrequent occurrences of *cuende* in the medieval language, and *homĭne* similarly fluctuates between *hombre* and *huembre,* which proves that the two developments involved here, diphthongization and vowel closure, must have taken place at approximately the same time. There is no need, with García de Diego (p. 60), to suggest that the non-diphthongized vowels are reflexes of *u* (*ascundo, respundo*); a closure to *ọ* would be sufficient (Menéndez Pidal §13.4). Admittedly, *u* is encountered in an early inscription from Spain: *muntanus,* but *u* is pretonic here. As a title, *conde* could presumably be proclitic; cf. *don* vs. *dueño.*

In Occitan, where nasalization is not very firmly entrenched, *ẹ* and *ọ* close to *ẹ* and *ọ,* not only before a final, unstable nasal: *bĕne > bẹn, bẹ; bŏnu > bọn, bọ,* but before *n* and *m* very generally: *tĕmpus > tẹms; vĕntu > vẹn; cŏmes > cọms; hŏmo > ọm.* The closure of *ọ* to *ọ* before a blocked nasal is also a common feature of Catalan: *cŏmparat* or **cŏmperat > cọmpra; mŏnte > mọnt.* The variant *munt* of this last word may be attributed to the frequent proclitic use of the word in toponyms or to the pretonic *o* in *montanea > muntanya.* A different phonological outcome is the change of *a* to *â in* Rumanian before a nasal (except before *nn* and *mn*): *lana > lână; campu > câmp.* Placed before a nasal, *e* likewise evolves to *â: fēnu > fân; vĕntu > vânt.*

179. Nasalization in French

In French, any vowel followed by *m* or *n* was originally nasalized, but with an intervocalic nasal consonant this feature was slow in establishing itself and was soon abandoned. In essence then, nasalized vowels are found only in two positions: before a final (or free) nasal consonant and before a blocked nasal consonant. The term *final nasal* refers not only to cases such as *rĕm* and *non,* but also to consonants appearing in the secondarily obtained final position caused by the loss of a final vowel as in *amo, pane, vinu.* The precarious nasality brought about by nasal consonants in intervocalic position makes the term *final nasal* more useful than *free nasal.* The blocked nasal is the nasal followed by a consonant, as in *vĕndĕre.* In Old French, the nasal resonance of the vowel did not immediately lead to the complete obliteration of the nasal consonant. A nasal resonance is not readily combined with a very close vowel quality; nasalization, in other words, tends to be accompanied by an opening of the vowel, resulting in the following developments:

Final Nasal

VL	*i*	*ẹ*	*ę*	*u*	*ọ*	*ǫ*	*a*
Fr.	*in* [ɛ̃]	*eim, ein* [ɛ̃]	*ien* [jɛ̃]	*un* [œ̃]	*on, om* [ɔ̃]		*ain, aim* [ɛ̃]

Blocked Nasal

VL	*i*	*ẹ*	*ę*	*u*	*ọ*	*ǫ*	*a*
Fr.	*in* [ɛ̃]	*en, em, an* [ã]	*ę*	*un* [œ̃]	*on, om* [ɔ̃]		*an, am* [ã]

Final Nasal	**Blocked Nasal**
vīnu > vin	*quīnque >* VL *cīnque > cinq*
pīnu > pin	*fǐnděre > fendre*
sǐnu > sein	*sǔbǐnde > souvent*
plēnu > plein	*věntu > vent*
běne > bien	*pěnděre > pendre*
rěm > rien	*ǔmbra > ombre*
ūnu > un	*ǔnda > onde*
dōnu > don	*mǒnte > mont*
latrōne > larron	*pǒnte > pont*
bǒnu > bon	*tǒnděre > tondre*
hǒmo > on	*cantat > chante*
fame > faim	*grande > grant*
pane > pain	*cambiat > change*

Commentary

While, originally, all tonic vowels are nasalized when they stand before a final or blocked nasal consonant, only the open qualities remain. The nasalized *i* moves from [ĩ] via [ẽ] to [ɛ̃]: *vīnu >* [vĩ] > [vẽ] > [vɛ̃], the nasal [ẽ] opens to [ã]: *lǐngua > langue,* but the open quality of the nasalized [ɔ̃] is disputed. Nasalization also occurred in intervocalic, non-final position, at least in the form of an inceptive move, which was never carried through, or which was soon abandoned, but which, in many instances, has left its mark on the pronunciation. When the vowel *ọ* nasalizes in *pōma,* it acquires an open quality, while the *mm* spelling is introduced as a result of the dual function of the nasal consonant: it imparts a nasal resonance to the vowel, but is still pronounced as a consonant: [pɔ̃mə]. When denasalization takes place, the open vowel quality remains: *pomme* [pɔm]. Another example of this feature is *fēmĭna* > [fẽmə] > [fãmə] > *femme* [fam].

Nasalization represents a conservative force, which often interferes with spontaneous vocalic changes. It prevents the *ei* diphthong from moving on to *oi*: *plēnu* > *plein* vs. *hēre* > *heir* > *hoir,* it does not allow for any diphthongization of *ǫ*: *dōnu* > *don* vs. *flōre* > *fleur,* and it quickly puts an end to the incipient diphthongization of *ǫ,* documented only for a few words in the medieval language: *bǒnu* > *buen; cǒmes* > *cuens,* the possessives *tuen, suen* < **tǒum, *sǒum.* If we assume that the change from a tonic free *a* to *e* (§152) passed through a diphthongal state **ae* or **ai,* the change of *-ane* to *-ain* as in *pain* < *pane* may be attributable to the delaying force of nasals (Ineichen, p. 30). In a total of three words: *foin* < *foenu* (§153); *avoine* < *avēna* and *moins* < *mǐnus, ei* does move on to *oi* in spite of the presence of a nasal. *Foin* and *avoine,* both designating agricultural products, are easily explained as dialectalisms imported from eastern regions, but a word like *moins* cannot convincingly be considered a borrowing. The bilabial *m* may have caused the rounding of *ei* to *oi* in this instance.

Nasals which originally occur in a free position, as in *cǐnĕre, tĕnĕru, camĕra, cǒmǐte, nŭmĕru,* become blocked as a result of weak-vowel loss and are thus able to permanently nasalize the preceding vowel: *cendre, tendre, chambre, comte, nombre.* In *fēmĭna* and *hǒmǐne,* the early loss of the weak posttonic vowel leads to the emergence of a double nasal, which allows for nasalization, but prevents diphthongization of the tonic vowel. When the nasal is degeminated, denasalization follows.

Palatal *n* is retained in intervocalic position: *montanea* > *montagne.* Nasalization occurs if it is final or blocked, and in addition, the palatal element is resolved as *i̯* which forms a diphthong with the preceding vowel: *testĭmōniu* > *tesmoin* > *témoin; jūniu* > *juin; plangĕre* > *plaindre.* Deviations from these rules are caused by analogy or by graphical influence: *testĭmōniāre* > OFr. *tesmognier* becomes *témoigner* by analogy with *témoin,* while spelling leads to the wrong interpretation of the name *Montaigne* and is responsible for the not infrequent erroneous pronunciation of *oignon* < *ŭniōne* with a [wa] diphthong.

180. Nasalization in Portuguese

Tonic vowels are nasalized when followed by a nasal in blocked position, but the nasal consonant is in some instances still pronounced, chiefly before *d, t, b, p, g* and *k* (Williams §95.1): *campu* > *campo* [kãmpu]; *tĕmpus* > *tempo* [tẽmpu]; *ŭnda* > *onda; quīnque* > VL *cinque* >

cinco; lŏngu > longo. When intervocalic, the nasal consonant imparts nasal resonance to the preceding vowel, and this resonance is kept if it occurs in the final syllable, either as a diphthong: *bĕne > bem [bēj]*, or as a vowel: *bŏnu > bom [bõ]; ūna > um [ũ].* Nasal diphthongs arise from the combinations *-anu, -ane, -one* which all flow together in *-am*, probably toward the end of the fifteenth century while, prior to that date, *-am* and *-om* were still differentiated: *pane > pam* vs. **coratiōne > coraçom* (Huber §96.1). The *-am* spelling comes to represent *-ão*, into which Lat. *-anu, -ane* and *-one* had all merged, and it is soon replaced graphically by it: *manu > mão; pane > pão; ratiōne > razão*. Rhyme position offers proof of this phonological merger. In the plural, the individuality of these suffixes is kept: *manos > mãos; panes > pães; ratiōnes > razões.*

In the free, non-final position, the nasal consonant nasalizes the vowel and then falls, whereupon the nasal resonance is dropped: *bŏna > bõa > boa; lūna > lũa > lua; persōna > pessoa.* It is not easy to establish a chronology here, since omission of the tilde, a common feature of the early poetry, could be attributed either to a loss of nasal resonance or to scribal carelessness. In the medieval manuscripts, nasality is marked in a variety of ways: *mĩ, min, mim* and probably also *mi; coraçon, coraçom, coraçam, coração.* If the tonic and the final vowel are identical, they merge following the loss of the intervocalic nasal consonant, and the nasal resonance remains (Williams §78.2): *lana > lãa > lã; germāna > irmãa > irmã; bŏnu > bõo > bom; ūnu > ũu > um.* The close vowel *i* was nasalized, but the nasal resonance was soon dropped, and *n* was palatalized: *vīnu > vĩo > vinho; pīnu > pinho; farīna > farinha.* For the difficulty of adding a nasal resonance to the close vowel *i*, see Fr. *vin* (§179).

Commentary

VL *cinque*, Ptg. *cinco*: VL *cinque* is obtained by dissimilation. In its final vowel Ptg., Sp. *cinco* has undergone the influence of Ptg. *quatro*, Sp. *cuatro*, the two numerals often being mentioned together. This is a case of serialization.

Retention of the suffix *-ano* in Portuguese is characteristic of learned words: *humano, americano, italiano,* and of borrowings from Spanish: OPtg. *castelhão*, replaced by *castelhano.*

Ptg. *uma*: the feminine *uma* is drawn analogically from the masc. *um.* Phonologically, Lat. *ūna* is continued in the old language as *ũa*, which one would then have expected to denasalize to **ua.* A variant *unha* is encountered in northern dialects.

181. Influence of Labials

Vulgar Latin shows sporadic occurrences of the opening of *ọ* to *ǫ* through the influence of *v* or *b*. CL *ōvu* is replaced by VL **ŏvu* as shown by the Romance reflexes (§151). In an early change, CL *colŭbra* evolves to *colǫbra*. The *Appendix Probi* censures this open pronunciation: *coluber non colober,* but is unsuccessful in weeding out this popular form, whose open *o* is the source of the *ue* diphthong of Old Spanish and Old French: OSp. *culuebra > culebra;* OFr. *coluevre > couleuvre.* OFr. *juevne, juene* shows Fr. *jeune* to be the reflex of a conjectural **jŏvene* for CL *jŭvene.* A similar opening of *ẹ* to *ę* under the influence of *v* occurs in Hispanic, in certain Italian dialects and in Occitan for CL *nĭve* as seen in §147.

In Romance, the presence of a labial may occasionally lead to the retention of the rounded stage in the vocalic evolution. Lat. *lŭpa* evolves to *louve* in French, but the word does not participate in the further change of *ou* to *eu,* and OFr. *double < dŭplu* is similarly arrested at the *ou* stage, while the labials play a more active role in actually rounding OFr. *veve < vĭdua* to *veuve.* Ptg. *fome* and Rm. *foame* presuppose the rounding of CL *fame* (cf. It. *fame,* Occ. *fam,* Fr. *faim*) to **fome,* obtained through the influence of the surrounding labials (Huber §83). Some scholars attribute this change to the influence of the verb *come* (Williams §33.6.B), but the need for a similar etymon for the Rumanian form makes a phonological explanation preferable. The change of *e* to *ă* following a labial is a common feature of Rumanian; it occurs when the final syllable carries a velar vowel: *pĭru > păr; pĭlu > păr; mēlu > măr,* whereas *e* remains before the vowels *e* and *i,* which accounts for the retention of *e* in the plural forms of these same words: *peri* and *meri.* Preceded by a labial, the *ea* diphthong is reduced to *a,* probably via an assimilation, but this seems mostly restricted to popular speech: CL *mēnsa >* VL *mēsa > *measă > *măasă > masă; vēra > vară; pĭra > pară; fēta > fată.*

Commentary

Ptg. *cobra:* through the regular loss of intervocalic *l* in Portuguese (§270), VL **colǫbra* evolves to *coovra,* which is replaced by a regressive or Latinizing *cobra.*

Sp. *joven:* Sp. *joven* is not a regularly developed descendant of Lat. *jŭvene,* but a learned form which, aside from a few sporadic occurrences, does not come into general use prior to the seventeenth century, and the same is essentially true of Ptg. *joven* (Corominas III 529–530). The basic word for 'young' in Castilian and Portuguese is *mozo,* of disputed origin and probably related to the equally problematic *mocho* (cf. OSp. *mochacho*, Sp. *muchacho*).

II. Pretonic Vowels

182. Cases of Pretonic Vowel Elimination in Vulgar Latin

Vowels which do not receive the main stress are not pronounced as distinctly as the tonic vowels and are therefore prone to reductions. This may even affect the secondarily stressed pretonic vowel, which may drop in Vulgar Latin in certain hiatus positions or in specific vowel combinations. Two identical short vowels merge into the corresponding long vowel, when they come into direct contact with one another through the loss of *h*: CL *cŏhŏrte* > VL *cōrte;* CL *prĕhĕndĕre* > VL *prēndĕre*, and the *iē* combination may in some instances be contracted to *ē*: CL *quiētu* > VL *quētu*.

Latin
cŏhŏrte, VL *cōrte*, *quiētu*, VL *quētu*

Rm.	**It.**	**Sp.**	**Ptg.**	**Cat.**	**Occ.**	**OFr.**	**Fr.**
curte	cọrte	corte	cọrte	cort	cọrt	cọrt	cour
cet	chẹto	quedo	quẹdo	quet	quẹt, quẹt	quei	coi

Commentary

OFr. *cọrt*, Fr. *cour*, Rm. *curte*: the Old French form *cort* or *court* still exists in the sixteenth century and is the source of E. *court*. Final *t* usually persists when following a consonant (cf. *parte* > *part*), but falls early after a vowel (cf. *parēte* > *paroi*). Bloch-Wartburg (p. 164) attributes the modern spelling to the influence of *curia*, which may also be responsible for the Rumanian outcome with its irregular tonic vowel.

Occ. *quẹt*, *quẹt*: besides the regularly developed *quẹt*, Levy also cites the variant *quẹt*, which probably draws its open vowel from an analogy with learned words in -*ẹt*, such as *secrẹt* < *secrētu* and *decrẹt* < *decrētu* (Anglade, p. 57).

Fr. *coi*: this adjective has hardly survived outside of the locution *se tenir coi*, and the learned *quiet* is no longer in common use.

183. The Pretonic Vowel System of Vulgar Latin

The initial or pretonic vowels receive secondary stress in Latin. The differences in quality, which is to say in degree of openness, are less important here than for the tonic vowels, hence the establishment of the following simplified system, which favors the close vowel quality:

CL	ī	ĭ ē ĕ	ū	ŭ ō ŏ	ā ă	au
	|	∨	|	∨	∨	|
VL	i	ẹ	u	ọ	a	au

Vulgar Latin retains the extreme close vowels *i* and *u*, the vowel *a* and the diphthong *au* just as in the tonic vocalic system, but it does not maintain any distinction between a close and an open *e* or between a close and an open *o*. The pretonic position automatically leads to the closure of the open vowels, and this trend may in many areas of Romance carry an even greater force, leading to the closure of *e* to *i* and of *o* to *u*, whether as a regular or as a sporadic feature. In pretonic position, the diphthongs *oe* and *ae* are continued as ẹ in Vulgar Latin.

Spontaneous Developments

184. Pretonic *i*: CL ī > VL *i*

i: Rm., It., Sp., Ptg., Cat., Occ., Fr.

Latin
Free: *fīlāre, hībĕrnu, -a*
Blocked: *vīllānu*

Rm.	**It.**	**Sp.**	**Ptg.**	**Cat.**	**Occ.**	**Fr.**
	filare	*hilar*	*fiar*	*filar*	*filar*	*filer*
iarnă	*inverno*	*invierno*	*inverno*	*ivern*	*ivern,*	*hiver*
					invern,	
					uvern	
	villano	*villano*	*villão*	*vilá*	*vilá*	*villain*

Commentary
The pretonic long *i* of Classical Latin is retained as *i* in Vulgar Latin, and it is kept throughout.

Lat. *hībĕrnu*: the noun *hiems* 'winter' of Classical Latin is not continued anywhere. The adjective *hībĕrnu*, which has taken its place, derives its masculine gender from an underlying *tĕmpus* 'season'. A feminine *iarnă* has evolved in Rumanian, its gender having been determined by the feminine noun *satiōne* (cf. Fr. *saison*). With the meaning of 'season', *tĕmpus* is present in Fr. *printemps* < *prīmu tĕmpus* lit. 'first season'.

Rm. *iarnă*: the evolution of *hībĕrna* to *iarnă* shows the regular loss of intervocalic *b* (§263), whereupon the pretonic *i* is absorbed into the yod of the *ia* diphthong, with which it has come into direct contact. The retention of pretonic *i* may be seen in *mīrāre* > *miră; frīctūra* > *friptură*.

It., Ptg. *inverno*, Sp. *invierno*, Occ. *invern*: the unetymological *n* present in these forms reveals some involvement with the prefix *in-*. French is unaffected by this process, while Occitan is subject to some hesitation. Spanish has an archaic and popular variant *ivierno*, encountered in the *Cid* and commonly used by Berceo.

Occ. *uvern*: this variant owes its existence to the rounding influence of labiodental *v* (cf. **in devināre* > It. *indovinare*).

OFr. *ivern*, Fr. *hiver*: the loss of *n* originates in the plural, where the nasal drops between the consonants *r* and *s*, changing the latter to *z* [*ts*]: *hībĕrnos* > OFr. *iverz; diŭrnos* > OFr. *jorz*. The *h* of Modern French is mere learned spelling.

185. Pretonic *ẹ:* CL *ĭ, ē, ĕ* > VL *ẹ*

ẹ:	Rm., Sp., Ptg., Cat., Occ.
i:	It.
ə/[ɛ]:	Fr.

Latin
Free: *mĭnūtu, sēcūru, nĕpōte*
Blocked: *cĭrcāre, sĕptĭmāna, vĭrtūte*

Rm.	It.	Sp.	Ptg.	Cat.	Occ.	OFr.	Fr.
mărunt	*minuto*	*menudo*	*miudo*	*menut*	*menut*		*menu*
	sicuro	*seguro*	*seguro*	*segur*	*segur*	*sëur*	*sûr*
nepot	*nipote*				*nebot*	*nevout*	*neveu*

Rm.	It.	Sp.	Ptg.	Cat.	Occ.	OFr.	Fr.
cercà	*cercare*	*cercar*	*cercar*	*cercar*	*cercar*	*cerchier*	*chercher*
săptă-	*setti-*	*se-*	*semana*	*set-*	*semana,*		
mână	*mana*	*mana*		*mana*	*setmana*		*semaine*
vărtute	*virtù*	*virtud*	*virtude*		*vertut*		*vertu*

Commentary

In pretonic position, CL *ĭ*, *ē* and *ĕ* merge into a close *e*, which is generally retained in Rumanian, Hispanic and Occitan, while Italian shows a closure of *ẹ* to *i*. French has [ə] if the syllable is free, [ɛ] if it is blocked.

The treatment of pretonic *e* is somewhat lacking in uniformity in Rumanian. The closure of *e* to *i* is not too uncommon: *pĕtiŏlu > picior; mĭsĕllu > mişel*, and is above all characteristic of the Moldavian dialects. The change of pretonic *e* to *ă* is particularly widespread, occurring specifically when a labial consonant precedes, but also with *r* (Lausberg §262), and the lists proposed by Densuşianu and Nandris (Nandris, p. 24) are even more comprehensive, pointing to what appears to be a very general feature in the language: *vĕt(e)rānu > bătrân; pĕccātu > păcat; mēnsūra > măsură; rēsīna > răşină*. It is *e*, however, which represents the norm: *dēsĕrtu > deşert; nĕgōtiu > negoţ; lēgūmen > legumă*.

The norm in Italian is for pretonic *e* to close to *i*: *mēnsūra > misura; mĕliōre > migliore; gĕnŭcŭlu > ginocchio; fĕnĕstra > finestra; mĭnōre > minore*. This change affects the prefixes *de-, re-, ĭn-*, which evolve to *di-, ri-, in-* as in *difendere, ritornare, incontrare;* the preposition *de*, being unstressed, becomes *di*, and the proclitic (weak) pronouns *mē, tē, sē* change to *mi, ti, si*. Yet retention of *ẹ* is a common feature in Italian. It is encountered in learned or dialectal or borrowed words: *segreto, questione, estate, delicato, regalo*, but far more importantly, *e* is often kept through the analogical influence of the stressed *e* of the root word: *fedele* follows from *fede; telaio* from *tela; pesante* from *peso; peggiore* from *peggio; gentile* from *gente*, etc. Furthermore, in verb paradigms the stem-stressed forms in *e* prevent a closure to *i* in the pretonic position: *cercare, pesare, fermare* are modeled on *cerca, pesa, ferma*, etc. (Rohlfs §130). Lausberg (§255) distinguishes between *i* in the free position and *e* in the blocked: *nipote* vs. *cercare*. While this view may have some statistical merit, it does not seem to reflect any basic division in the language. In the absence of any rigorously observed rules, it seems safer to state that Italian is characterized by a very prominent trend toward a closure of pretonic *ẹ* to *i*, but that analogies of various kinds constitute a powerful disturbance in the regular course of this development (Rohlfs §130; Meyer-Lübke, pp. 61–62).

In French, the pretonic *ę* evolves to a weak [ə] in a free syllable: *mĭnāre* > *mener;* *dēbēre* > *devoir;* *vĕnīre* > *venir,* while [ɛ] is the norm if the syllable is blocked: *fĭrmāre* > *fermer;* *sĕrvīre* > *servir.*

Rm. *mărunt:* a spread of the nasality feature leads to the creation of **menūto* which is resolved as **menuntu,* whereupon *n—n* is dissimilated to *r—n* (cf. *genunchiu* §237).

Ptg. *miudo:* the closure to *i* is caused by the hiatus position; cf. *creātu* > *criado* (Williams §41.15). The syllabic value of *i* is lost in *miudo.*

OFr. *sëur,* Fr. *sûr:* when pretonic *e* comes into direct contact with the stressed vowel, as it does here through the regular loss of *c* before a velar vowel, it is absorbed.

Rm. *nepot,* It. *nipote,* Fr. *nièce:* since *o* is not broken into *oa* in Rumanian (cf. *sōle* > *soare*), the etymology cannot be *nĕpōte,* but a conjectural **nĕpōtu,* showing a declensional change. Rumanian has a fem. *nepoată,* which could hardly have been kept phonologically distinct from the reflex which one would regularly expect from *nĕpōte.* It. *nipote* serves both as a masculine and a feminine noun, while Lat. *nĕptia* 'niece' is continued in Fr. *nièce,* in Rhaeto-Romance and in several Italian dialects.

Hispanic abandons Lat. *nĕpōte* altogether, turning instead to Lat. *consobrīnu* which, in aphaeretic form, yields Sp. *sobrino,* Ptg. *sobrinho,* with *sobrina* and *sobrinha* as the corresponding feminine forms (*REW* 2165; Corominas V 280–281).

OFr. *cerchier,* Fr. *chercher:* *k* evolves to *s* before *e* and to [š] before *a,* but in Modern French, the *s* –[š] sequence that is regularly obtained for this word has been assimilated to [š] – [š]. E. *search* is clearly borrowed from the earlier, phonological stage in the development.

It. *settimana:* the closure of pretonic *e* to *i* was prevented from taking place in this word because of its obvious tie to the numeral *sette.* Occitan has *setmana* and *semana,* and a dental is also present in earlier stages of French and Spanish.

It. *virtù,* Sp. *virtud,* Ptg. *virtude:* the Hispanic forms show learned treatment of the pretonic *ĭ* while, in Italian, *i* could be either phonological or a Latinism. Old Portuguese has a popularly developed *vertude.*

186. Pretonic *u:* CL *ū* > VL *u*

u: Rm., It., Sp., Ptg., Cat.
[y]:   Occ., Fr.

Latin
Free: *mūtāre*
Blocked: *pūrgāre*

Rm.	It.	Sp.	Ptg.	Cat.	Occ.	OFr.	Fr.
mutà	mutare	mudar	mudar		mudar		muer
	purgare	purgar	porgar	purgar	purgar	purgier	purger

Commentary

VL *u* is kept unchanged, except in the Gallo-Romance area, where the vowel is fronted to [y], though without any change in spelling. Lausberg (§254) maintains that pretonic *ū* had merged with *ǫ* < CL *ŭ, ō, ŏ* in French. Not only would such a rule break the parallelism with the front vowel development, but it would also necessitate considering a great many seemingly popular words as learned: *unir, curé, putain*, or, in the case of verbs, as obtained via an analogy with the stem-stressed forms: *muer, purger, user, juger*. In several words, the quantity of Lat. *u* was unknown: Fr. *oignon* reflects *ŭniōne* (Rheinfelder §284), while Occitan has both *onhon* and *unhon*, and Fr. *foison* comes from VL *fŭsiōne*, which acquires its short *u* from an analogy with the verb *fŭndĕre*. Since Fr. *froment* has parallels in OIt. *formento*, OSp. *hormiento* and Occ. *fromen, formen*, this combined evidence provides very strong proof that CL *frūmĕntu* was superseded by a Vulgar Latin form in *ŭ*.

Cat. *porgar*: the Catalan form reflects a variant *pŭrgāre* with a short *u*, and a similar form is found in the Aragonese dialect.

187. Pretonic *ǫ*: CL *ŭ, ō, ŏ* > VL *ǫ*

> *u*:   Rm.
> *ǫ*:   It., Sp.
> *o* [*u*]:   Ptg.
> *ǫ* or *ou*:   Occ., Cat.
> *ǫ* or *ou*:   Fr.

Latin
Free: *cŏrōna, dŏlōre*
Blocked: *pŏrtāre, tŏrmentu*

Rm.	It.	Sp.	Ptg.	Cat.	Occ.	Fr.
coroană, cunună	corona	corona	coroa, corõa (old)	corona	corona	cou- ronne
duroare	dolore	dolor	dor, door (old)	dolor	dolor	douleur
purtà	portare	portar	portar	portar	portar	porter
	tor- mento	tor- mento	tor- mento		tormen	tour- ment

Commentary

Rumanian has *u* while, generally speaking, the pretonic *ǫ* is kept unchanged in Italian, Spanish and Catalan and to some extent also in Occitan. Portuguese favors an [u] pronunciation, even though the spelling is mostly left intact (Williams §43.1; Huber §126). As one might expect, however, a fluctuating graphical representation is characteristic of Old Portuguese: *molher* and *mulher; pojar* and *pujar; fogir* and *fugir*, etc., and similarly for the proclitics *o* and *u; os* and *us;* and also *com* and *cum* (Huber §126). Occitan is subject to the same graphical fluctuation: *cobrir* and *cubrir; sofrir* and *sufrir; morir* and *murir; tormen* and *turmen* (Anglade, p. 107), which proves that a close pronunciation was widespread. In Catalan, occurrences of *u* are quite common, specifically in eastern dialects. In French, the situation is quite complex. First of all, there is no unified outcome, since some words have *ou* (*tourment*) and others *ǫ* (*dormir*) in no predictable pattern. Most of the occurrences of *ǫ* can be explained as resulting from the analogical influence of stem-stressed forms or of the root word: *dormir* from *dort; mortel* from *mort*. Secondly, the earlier graph *o* is very generally replaced by *ou: sŭbĭnde* > OFr. *sovent* > *souvent; mŏvēre* > OFr. *moveir* > *mouvoir; nŏvĕllu* > OFr. *novel* > *nouvel; cōlāre* > OFr. *coler* > *couler*, but in a few, mostly learned words, *o* was restored both in spelling and pronunciation: *sōlĭcŭlu* > OFr. *souleil* > *soleil; *rosāta* > OFr. *rousee* > *rosée*. There are sporadic occurrences of *u* in Spanish: *jŏcāre* > *jugar; lŏcāle* > *lugar*. Italian is thus the language which most consistently resists the trend toward a closure of pretonic *ǫ* to *u*, which is all the more striking as it moves further than the other languages in its acceptance of pretonic *i* for VL *ę*.

Rm. *coroană*: the retention of pretonic *o* in this word is a learned feature; cf. *romānu*, which should evolve to *rumîn*, but which in the modern language is continued in the Latinizing form *romîn*. As the reflex of Lat. *corōna*, Meyer-Lübke (*REW* 2245) lists *cunună*, which shows the regular development of pretonic *o* to *u*. In Rumanian, an *n—n* sequence is often dissimilated to *r—n* (cf. *canūtu* > **canuntu* > *cărunt*), but the opposite feature, an assimilation of *r—n* to *n—n*, is also encountered: *serēnu* > *senin; farīna* > ORm. *fănină*. For this last word, Modern Rumanian has *făină*, which may have resulted from the elimination of the first *n* through dissimilation. In the word *cunună*, the closure of the tonic vowel to *u* under the influence of the following nasal has occurred too early for the break of *o* to *oa* to take place; a similar development may be seen in *bĕne* > *bine; bŏna* > *bună; pŏnte* > *punte*, etc.

OPtg. *corōa*, Ptg. *coroa*: the intervocalic *n* gives rise to a nasal resonance, which disappears in the fifteenth century: *bŏna* > *bōa* > *boa* (§272).

Rm. *duroare*: this form exists only in the Arumanian dialect.

OPtg. *door*, Ptg. *dor*: pretonic *o* is absorbed in hiatus with a tonic *o*: *dŏlōre* > OPtg. *door* > *dor*.

188. Pretonic *a*: CL *ā*, *ă* > VL *a*

      ă or *a:* Rm.
          a: It., Sp., Ptg., Cat., Occ., Fr.

Latin
Free: *habēre, matūru*
Blocked: *carbōne*

Rm.	It.	Sp.	Ptg.	Cat.	Occ.	OFr.	Fr.
aveà	*avere*	*haber*	*haver*	*aver*	*aver*	*aveir*	*avoir*
matur	*maturo*	*maduro*	*maduro*	*madur*	*madur*	*meür*	*mûr*
cărbune	*carbone*	*carbón*	*carvão*	*carbó*	*carbon̦*		*charbon*

Commentary
Generally speaking, pretonic *a*, whether free or blocked, remains unchanged in Romance. In Rumanian, however, it suffers a weakening to *ă*, and it is only in the absolute initial position that *a* is retained unaltered:

barbātu > *bărbat; gallīna* > *găină; camĭsia* > *cămaşa;* vs. *amāru* > *amar; ariēte* > *arete; argĕntu* > *argint.*

Rm. *matur:* the retention of *a* here may be a learned feature; the Moldavian dialect has *mătur.*

OFr. *mëur,* Fr. *mûr:* the hiatus *a* is weakened to *e* [ə] and then absorbed into the tonic vowel; cf. *pavōre* > *paour* > *poour* > *peur;* *habūtu > *au > *eu* > [y]. In this last word, *e* remains in spelling only.

189. Pretonic *au:* CL *au* > VL *au*

ău or *au:*	Rm.
u or *o:*	It.
o:	Sp., Cat., Fr.
ou [o]:	Ptg.
au:	Occ.

Latin
audīre, laudāre

Rm.	It.	Sp.	Ptg.	Cat.	Occ.	OFr.	Fr.
auzì	*udire*	*oír*	*ouvir*	*oir*	*auzir*	*oïr*	
lăudà	*lodare*	*loar*	*louvar*	*lloar*	*lauzar*	*loer*	*louer*

Commentary

Pretonic *au* evolves to *ău* or *au* in Rumanian, while Italian mostly has *u,* though with some occurrences of *o.* Spanish and French have *o,* and the same is generally true of Catalan, although here the eastern dialects favor a close pronunciation *u.* Portuguese has *ou,* pronounced [o], while Occitan retains *au* unaltered.

Paralleling the development of pretonic *a* (§188), Rumanian has *au* in absolute initial position and *ău* elsewhere: *audīre* > *auzì* vs. *laudāre* > *lăudà.* Considering the preservation of pretonic *au* or *ău* in the quoted examples analogical from the stem-stressed forms of the paradigms, and taking *aurar* < *aurāriu* to be dependent on *aur* in its vocalism, Rothe (§38) concludes that the outcome of pretonic *au* is *u,* but his only example: *aurĭcŭla* > *ureche,* is highly suspect since the *Appendix Probi* entry: *auris non oricla,* shows that the etymon has a pretonic *o* and not *au.* Italian mostly has *u: raubāre* > *rubare; aucĕllu* > *uccello; aucīdĕre* > *uccidere*

(Rohlfs §134; Meyer-Lübke, p. 173), but *o* occurs in *laudare* > *lodare*. While *lodare* could conceivably have obtained its *o* from the stem-stressed forms *lodo, lodi, loda,* no such leveling has occurred with *udire—odo*. *Rubare* is of Germanic extraction, which may perhaps explain the generalization of *u* in this verb. A conditioned development in French closes *o* to [*u*] in hiatus.

Ptg. *ouvir*: following the loss of intervocalic *d* (§266), *v* is inserted as a hiatus-separating device; cf. *laudare* > *louvar* (Huber §295). The same feature is encountered in French: *paradīsu* > *parëis* > *parevis* > *parvis,* and perhaps also *pŏtēre* > *poeir* > *pooir* > *pouvoir,* unless this word owes its modern shape to a formal analogy with *mouvoir*.

OFr. *oïr*: the singular of the present indicative of this verb consists of monosyllables: *oi, oz, ot*. This deficiency in phonetic substance, combined with the vexing homonymy of *ot* < *audit* 'he hears' and *ot* < *habuit* 'he had', leads to the elimination of the verb *oïr*. It is replaced by *entendre,* whose primitive meaning 'to pay attention to' and hence 'to understand' is still present in the locutions *bien entendu* and *s'entendre avec*. Relics of *oïr* are *inoui, par ouir dire* > *par oui-dire* and the noun *l'ouïe*. Bloch-Wartburg (p. 452) dates the elimination of *ouïr* to the seventeenth century.

CL *aurĭcŭla,* VL *oricla*: the *Appendix Probi* contains the entry *auris non oricla* (§99). An intolerable homonymy between *auris* 'ear' and *oris* 'mouth' arose with the change of tonic *au* to *o*. It is in an effort to remedy this situation that Vulgar Latin replaced CL *auris* by the diminutive formation *oricla,* displaying an early change of pretonic *au* to *o*. This early vocalic change is further corroborated by some of the Romance forms: Rm. *ureche,* It. *orecchio* and Ptg. *orelha*. Rumanian has *u* and not *au,* Italian has *o* and not *u,* while Portuguese has *o* and not *ou*. Since Spanish, Catalan and French treat pretonic *au* and *o* alike, it cannot be determined whether Sp. *oreja,* Cat. *orella* and Fr. *oreille* continue *aurĭcŭla* or *oricla*. The only problematic form is Occ. *aurelha* which, in all likelihood, is learned. The final *o* of It. *orecchio* reflects a morphological adjustment (Rohlfs §384).

Conditioned Developments

190. Hiatus Position
  The hiatus position may be primary: *crĕātu* > Sp., Ptg. *criado,* or it may be secondarily obtained through the loss of an intervocalic consonant. This latter development happens with particular frequency in Portuguese and French, since intervocalic consonants are most prone to elimination in these

languages. Identical vowels coalesce, with the pretonic vowel being absorbed into the tonic: *dŏlōre* > OPtg. *door* > *dor; cŏlōre* > OPtg. *coor* > *cor;* VL *cŏlŏbra* > OPtg. *coovra* > *cobra; vĭdēre* > OSp., OPtg. *veer* > Sp., Ptg. *ver; *crēdēre* > OPtg. *creer* > *crer.* This contraction is not entirely predictable, however. At times, the hiatus is tolerated: *crēdēre* > Sp. *creer; laud-* + *-ōre* > Sp. *loor,* or a hiatus-separating device is used: *laud-* + *-ōre* > Ptg. *louvor.* In French, the hiatus vowel is weakened to [ə] and then absorbed: *sēcūru* > *sëur* > *sûr; vĭdēre* > *veeir* > *veoir* > *voir; matūru* > *mëur* > *mûr.* In some instances, the spelling reveals an assimilation stage prior to the coalescence: *aetatĭcu* > *eage* > *aage* > *âge; pavōre* > *paour* > *poour* > *peeur* > *peur.* In Portuguese, a similar assimilation stage may be posited for *calĕnte* > OPtg. *caente* > *queente* > *quente* (§152), and, also in Portuguese, *palŭmbu* moves via *paombo* and *poombo* to *pọmbo,* with the closure of the vowel to *ọ* caused by the following blocked nasal (Williams §40,11,A). Closure of *e* to *i* in hiatus is encountered in *creātu* > Sp., Ptg. *criado.* If *i* and *u* come into direct contact with the stressed vowel, they tend to lose their syllabic value: *leōne* > Fr. *lion; mūtāre* > Fr. *muer; jōcāre* > Fr. *jouer; vīvenda* > Fr. *viande; monēta* > Ptg. *moeda.*

191. Assimilation

The assimilation of the pretonic vowel to the tonic is a sporadic, non-predictable feature which, for some words, may date back to Vulgar Latin, judging from its spread to all or most Romance languages. Individual languages or dialects may, of course, resist this development, which does not have the force of a sound-law.

Latin
bĭlancia, VL *balancia, sĭlvatĭcu,* VL *salvatĭcu, trĭpaliu,* VL *trapaliu*

Rm.	It.	Sp.	Ptg.	Cat.	Occ.	Fr.
	bilancia	*balanza*	*balança*	*balança*	*balansa*	*balance*
	selvatico,		*selvagem,*	*selvatge*		
	selvaggio		*selvatico*			
sălbatic	*salvatico*	*salvaje*	*salvagem*		*salvatge*	*sauvage*
				treball	*trebalh*	
	travaglio	*trabajo*	*trabalho*		*trabalh*	*travail*

Commentary

It. *bilancia*: Italian is alone in continuing the non-dissimilated *bǐlancia*.

Lat. *sǐlvatǐcu*: this adjective is made up of the noun *sǐlva* 'forest' and the *-aticu* suffix. The phonological development of this suffix in French is quite complex, involving the change of *i* to *i̯*, the voicing of *t* to *d* and the assibilation of the secondarily obtained *di̯* cluster to [*dž*] and [*ž*] (§352): *-atǐcu* > **-adio* > *-age* (Rheinfelder I 270). It. *-aggio,* Sp. *-aje* and Ptg. *-agem* are not native, but derived from French (Rohlfs §1060; García de Diego, p. 271).

It. *travaglio*: since Italian keeps intervocalic *p* intact (cf. *sapēre* > It. *sapere), travaglio* is clearly a borrowing, and it must have come from French, since this is the only language where *v* is justified (cf. *sapēre* > Fr. *savoir).* The basic word for 'work' in Italian is *lavoro,* while *travaglio* is a literary term emphasizing the connotation of 'strenuous effort' and, figuratively, that of 'anguish, pain, suffering'.

Cat. *treball,* Occ. *trebalh*: Cat. *treball* and the Occitan variant *trebalh* reflect Lat. *trǐpāliu* or *trēpāliu,* while the remaining forms are drawn from an assimilated **trapāliu.*

192. Dissimilation

Dissimilation, likewise a sporadic feature, represents the opposite trend from assimilation, a desire for differentiating two identical sounds, in this particular instance for keeping the pretonic vowel formally distinct from the tonic.

Latin
vīcīnu, VL **vēcīnu, dīvīnu,* VL *devīnu*

Rm.	It.	Sp.	Ptg.	Cat.	Occ.	OFr.	Fr.
vecin	*vicino*	*vecino*	*vizinho, vezinho* (old)	*veí*	*vezin*	*veisin*	*voisin*
	divino	*divino*	*divino, devino* (old)	*diví*	*devin*		*divin, devin*

Commentary

It. *vicino*, Ptg. *vizinho*: It. *vicino* can reflect either *vīcīnu* or *vēcīnu*, since pretonic *e* is regularly continued as *i* in Italian (§185). Ptg. *vizinho* contains a purely orthographic *i*, which is pronounced [ə] (Williams §110.1). The same observations apply to It., Ptg. *divino*, while Sp. *divino* is learned.

Fr. *divin, devin*: the adjective *divin* of Modern French is learned, while the popularly developed *devin* is still used as a noun. Other examples of dissimilation are Fr. *Noël < natāle* vs. Occ. *Nadal*, and Sp. *hermoso*, OPtg. *fermoso* vs. Ptg. *formoso < formōsu*. The verb *natāre* is continued as Sp., Ptg., Cat., Occ. *nadar,* while Italian has *nuotare*, drawn from a dissimilated **nŏtare* and with the diphthong traceable to the stem-stressed forms of the verb. OFr. *noer*, which likewise goes back to **nŏtāre*, soon found itself on a collision course with OFr. *noer*, Fr. *nouer* from *nōdāre*. It was replaced by *nager,* representing the popular reflex of *navĭgāre*, which is continued in a learned development as *naviguer* and also *naviger*, this latter form still encountered in the eighteenth century. The *o—o* sequence was often subject to dissimilation: *rŏtŭndu >* Sp. *redondo;* *sŭbdiŭrnāre >* Fr. *séjourner; sŏrōre >* OFr. *serour.*

Dissimilation causes the reduction of pretonic *au* to *a,* when the tonic syllable contains the vowel *ŭ*:

Latin

augŭstu, VL *agosto, auscultāre*, VL *ascoltare, augŭriu*, VL **agŭriu*, VL **agūru*

Rm.	It.	Sp.	Ptg.	Cat.	Occ.	OFr.	Fr.
august	*agosto*	*agosto*	*agosto*	*agost, ahost* (old)	*agost, aost, avost*	*aost*	*août*
ascultà	*ascol- tare*	*escuchar*	*escutar, ascuitar* (old)	*escol- tar*	*escol- tar*	*escol- ter*	*écou- ter*
	augurio	*agüero*	*agoiro*		*agur, aür*	*eur*	*heur*

Commentary
Rm. *august*: is learned.

Occ. *agost, aost, avost*: Occitan may keep intervocalic *g* before a velar vowel, or it may drop it, in which case a *v* may be inserted in order to separate the hiatus (Anglade, p. 173). For this role of *v*, see §189.

Fr. *août*: the graph does not fully account for the reduction of VL *agosto* to [*u*] or [*ut*], Intervocalic *g* is eliminated before a velar vowel, *a* is absorbed in hiatus with the stressed vowel (§190), *s* drops before *t*, and final *t* usually ceases to be pronounced, although it may be retained here to preserve some phonetic substance.

VL *ascoltare*: the reflexes of *ascoltare* are discussed in §165.

It. *augurio*: this form is entirely learned and can thus be disregarded for comparative purposes.

Ptg. *agoiro*, Sp. *agüero*: in both languages, the *ri̯* cluster lets the palatal element slip through. In Spanish, the resulting *oi̯* diphthong is subsequently palatalized to *ui̯*, and both *agoiro* and *agüiro* are encountered in the *Fuero Juzgo*. The rare *ui* is soon attracted to the very common *ue* diphthong, which gives us the modern form.

Occ. *agur, aür*: these forms, which reflect a hypothetical **agūru* base, in which the yod has dropped after closing the tonic vowel to *u*, display the retention or the loss of *g*, as seen above.

Fr. *(h)eur*: like the Occitan reflexes, Fr. *(h)eur* is drawn from **agūru*, which should have evolved to **ur*, and there is documentation for a dialectal *bonür* (*FEW* I 175). The vowel *eu* and the unetymological *h* are attributable to the analogical influence of *heure* < *hōra*. A close association exists between *augurium* and *hōra* inasmuch as being born under a good omen is the same as being born at a propitious moment. Thus, the Cid is often referred to as *el que en buen ora naçió* (*Cid*, v. 2016) 'he who was born at a propitious moment'. Fr. *(h)eur* has survived only in the combinations *bonheur* and *malheur.*

193. Inflection in the Spanish Pretonic Vowel
In Spanish, the Romance yod that arises through the diphthongization of tonic *ě* causes the closure of pretonic *ę* to *i*: *těněbras* > *tinieblas; sēměnte* > *simiente; děcěmber* > *diciembre; fěněstra* > OSp. *finiestra;* Basque *ezkerr* > *izquierdo; *seněxtru* > **seněstru* > *siniestro*. A Latin yod may cause the same inflection: *prehensiōne* > VL *presione* > *prisión*, even though the yod may later disappear: *rēniōne* > *riñón*. Inflection occurs with verbs in *-ir* whenever a Romance yod is present: *fěrvěnte* > *hirviente;*

sĕntīvit > *sintió;* *mētīvit > *midió,* but *e* is kept if this condition is not met. The result is an alternation in these verbs between *e* and *i* in the pretonic syllable: *sentir, sentimos, sentiria* vs. *sintió, sintieron, sintiera, sintiese.* The word *setiembre* < *sĕptĕmber* is irregular (cf. *diciembre*), while *trescientos* keeps its *e* because of the numeral *tres* (Menéndez Pidal §18.2; García de Diego, pp. 170–171). A [*w*] in the tonic syllable closes *e* to *i* in *aequāle* > *equal* > *igual.*

Commentary

Lat. *sĭnĭstru,* **senĕxtru:* the word for 'left' in Latin is *sĭnĭstru,* but a variant **senĕxtru,* analogical from *dĕxtru* 'right', must have coexisted with the classical form, since the *ie* diphthong of Spanish would otherwise be unexplained: Sp. *diestro* < *dĕxtru* and *siniestro* < **senĕxtru.* Both of these forms presuppose a fairly early reduction of the *cstr* (*xtr*) cluster to *str* since the presence of a palatal would have prevented a diphthong from forming (§164). Other Romance forms are: OIt. *sinestro,* OPtg. *seestro, sestro,* Occ., OFr. *senestre.* Closely tied to the vocabulary of divination, *sinistru* soon came to acquire unfavorable connotations (cf. Fr. *sinistre*). Retained in Italian, it was mostly replaced elsewhere; Rumanian has *stâng* < *stancu,* lit. 'tired' (*REW* 8225), French *gauche* from the verb *gauchir* 'to go astray', evolving from an obscure Germanic source, a possible cross of *wenkjan and *walkan (*FEW* XV 555–560), while Hispanic draws on Basque for a replacement.

Sp. *izquierdo,* Ptg. *esquerdo:* the source of the Hispanic forms is Basque *ezkerr,* as first suggested by Mahn and Diez. The word is of pre-Romance Iberian stock and may have spread from the Basque region, probably during the Visigothic era, since it must have been introduced into Spanish at a time when the diphthongization of *ę* to *ie* was still operative. Basque *esku* means 'hand', and the *-err* suffix may perhaps evoke such connotations as 'smaller, weaker'. The primitive *rr* cluster encountered in pre-Romance words evolves to *rd* (Meyer-Lübke: *Das Katalanische,* 1925, pp. 65–67; Rohlfs: *Le Gascon* §384; Corominas III 469). Catalan has *esquerre,* Occitan both *senestre* and *esquer.*

194. Closure of Pretonic *o* to *u* in Hispanic and Occitan
    This inflection is more frequent than that of *e* to *i,* and its causes are more complex. A Romance yod exerts the same closing influence here as with *e: coopĕrtu* > Sp. *cubierto; dŭcĕntos* > OSp. *ducientos* and *dozientos,* and an *o—u* alternation is characteristic of *-ir* verbs in Spanish: *dormīmus* > *dormimos* vs. *dormiamus* > *durmamos; dormīvit* > *durmió.* Palatal

consonants are responsible for the vowel closure in *cŏgnātu* > Sp. *cuñado;* *mŭliére* > Sp. *mujer; cŏchleāre* > OSp. *cuchar* > *cuchara,* while a [*w*] in the tonic syllable accounts for the pretonic *u* in Sp. *culebra* < *culuebra* < *cŏlŏbra.* Other occurrences of *u* may stem from a general trend toward a close pronunciation in the pretonic syllable: *lŏcāle* > Sp., Ptg. *lugar;* *jŏcāre* > OSp. *jogar* > *jugar; rŭgītu* > OSp. *roido,* Sp. *ruido,* Ptg. *ruído.* In Portuguese, pretonic *o* becomes *u,* although graphically *o* is kept. The spelling *u* occurs only very sporadically before palatals and in a few words revealing Spanish or Latin influence: *mulher, cunhado.* It is found more frequently in Catalan with palatals: *mŭliĕre* > *muller; mŏlliāre* > *mullar* (cf. Sp. *mojar,* Ptg. *molhar*); *cŏchlearia* > *cullera* (cf. Ptg. *colher*). The graphical fluctuation in Occitan between pretonic *o* and pretonic *u* is a very general feature which is not tied to the nature of the following consonants: *mŏrīre* > *morir* and *murir,* etc. See §178 for further details and examples.

Commentary

   Lat. *cŏchleāre,* OSp. *cuchar,* Sp. *cuchara*: the change of pretonic *o* to *u* is easily accounted for through the influence of the palatal cluster that follows, and the only phonological difficulty thus centers around the treatment of the unusual *kli̯* cluster. The palatal *l* does not move to [*χ*], but to a voiceless *ch* [*tš*] when following a consonant: *cĭngŭla* > OSp. *cinlla* > *cincha* (Corominas II 267–268; *REW* 2012). The consonant that precedes the palatal *l* does not have to be voiceless (Menéndez Pidal §53.6).

   Sp. *lugar*: Lat. *lŏcu* is continued as Rm. *loc,* It. *luogo,* Cat. *lloc,* Occ. *lǫc, luec,* Fr. *lieu,* but OSp. *luego* and Ptg. *logo* have survived only as adverbs meaning 'immediately, at once'. As nouns, they have been replaced by reflexes of *lŏcāle* > Sp., Ptg. *lugar,* in both languages with the dissimilation of the *l—l* sequence to *l—r.* This change may have originated from a desire to keep the noun distinct from the adverb.

   OSp. *roido,* Sp. *ruido*: the etymon of OSp. *roido* is *rŭgītu* with a short *u* and a tonic long *i,* but the modern form *ruido* and Ptg. *ruído* suggest that the length of the pretonic vowel was uncertain, and a long *u* is also required for OFr. *ruit,* Fr. *rut.* The uncertainty extends to the participial ending, since the preservation of *t* in French rules out *-ītu* as the source. We may assume therefore that *rŭgīre* coexisted with *rŭgĕre* and hence *rŭgītu* with *rŭgĭtu.* The posttonic *ĭ* of *rŭgĭtu* drops, yielding a *g't* cluster, which evolves to *i̯t* (cf. **frĭgĭdu* > OFr. *freit*). The loss of the weak vowel took place early, judging from the fact that no proparoxytone vowel support ever developed in this word (cf. the variant *fricda* for **frĭgĭda*).

195. Pretonic Vowel and yod Release

A yod attracted from the following syllable combines with the pretonic vowel in French: *ratiōne* > *raison; potiōne* > *poison; lĭcēre*> *leisir* > *loisir; placēre* > *plaisir*. In Spanish, pretonic *a* changes to *e* when followed by an attracted yod: *maxĭlla* > *mejilla; basiāre* > *besar; lactūca* > *lechuga*. Portuguese derives *ai* or *ei* from the combination of *a* and a palatal: **bassiāre* > *baixar; basiāre* > *beijar; fragrāre* > *flagrare* > *cheirar; lactūca* > *leituga*, and Catalan has *e*: *basiāre* > *besar; lactūca* > *lletuga; *taxōne* > *teixó*.

196. Palatal and Pretonic Free *a* in French

In French, pretonic *a* becomes [ə] in a free position when preceded by a palatal: *caballu* > *cheval; capĭllos* > *cheveux*. The blocked *a* is not affected: *carbōne* > *charbon*.

197. Initial *ja-* and *ju-*

Vulgar Latin tends to alter initial *ja-* to *je-* and initial *ju-* to *je-* or *ji-*. The change of *ja-* to *je-* is, generally speaking, reflected in Romance, although there are occurrences of the retention of *a*: CL *januariu* > VL *jĕnuariu* > It. *gennaio*, Sp. *enero*, Cat. *gener*, OFr. *jenvier*, but the Portuguese reflex is *janeiro*, the form *janer* is encountered in a twelfth-century Aragonese document, and Occitan has both *genier* and *janier*. Fr. *janvier* contains a Latinizing graph, or it may testify to a widespread confusion between *en* and *an*, which had come to be pronounced alike in French. Lat. *jūnĭperu* underwent a change to **jenĭperu* and hence It. *ginepro*, Sp. *enebro*, Cat. *ginebre*, Occ. *genebre*, OFr. *geneivre*, while Sp., Ptg. *junípero* is learned. The popular development in Portuguese is unclear; the fall of intervocalic *n* yields a form **jēebro* or **jīebro*, which is ultimately resolved as OPtg. *jimbro*, Ptg. *zimbro*. The modern French form *genièvre*, first documented in the sixteenth century, reflects a suffixal change to *-ǫpru*, or *genevrier—genièvre* may have been modeled on *levrier—lièvre* (*FEW* V 76).

198. Nasalization in French and Portuguese

In French, nasalization takes place before a blocked nasal, i.e., a nasal followed by a consonant. Pretonic *i* moves via [ĩ] and [ẽ] to [ɛ̃], spelled *in* or *im*, and pretonic *e* gives [ã], spelled *en* or *em*: *prīmu tĕmpus* > OFr. *printens* > *printemps; intrāre* > *entrer; sĭmŭlāre* > *sembler*. Pretonic *ū* is nasalized to [œ̃], rendered graphically by *un* or *um*: *lūnae die* > VL **lūnis die* > OFr. *lunsdi* > *lundi*, while pretonic *o* nasalizes to [ɔ̃], spelled *on* or *om: compŭtāre > conter; cŭmŭlāre > combler; montanea > montagne.* The nasalized *a* [*ā*] is spelled *an* or *am: cantare > chanter; sanĭtāte > santé; camerāta > chambrée.* The double *n* graph in *sŏnāre > sonner* points to an inceptive nasalization with an intervocalic nasal consonant, but this development was soon abandoned (§179).

In Portuguese, nasalization likewise occurs before a blocked nasal, but the difference is that the nasal consonant is still pronounced: *sentīre > sentir* [*sēntir*]; *volŭntāte > vontade* [*võntadə*]; *cantāre > cantar* [*kãntar*]. Here, too, nasalization caused by intervocalic nasal consonants was abandoned: *tĕnēre >* OPtg. *tēer > ter; manēre >* OPtg. *māer, maer.*

199. Influence of Velar *l* in French

The velar *l*, which stands before a consonant, vocalizes to *u̯*, whereupon *u̯* combines with the pretonic vowel: *falcōne > faucon; collocāre >* OFr. *colchier > coucher; *bĕllĭtāte >* OFr. *belté.* The modern form *beauté* is influenced by the adjective *beaus < bĕllos,* since the breaking of *ĕ* to *ea* occurs only in the tonic position (§175).

200. Influence of Labials

A labial consonant, most frequently *m*, but others as well, may cause rounding of the preceding pretonic vowel. It is mostly the vowel *e* that is affected by this sporadic feature: *demandāre >* It. *domandare; de mane >* It. *domani; sĕptĭmāna >* OPtg. *somana; remanēre >* OSp. *romaner; dēbēre >* It. *dovere; *in devināre >* It. *indovinare; epīscŏpu >* Sp. *obispo; gemĕllos >* Fr. *jumeaux.* It. *uscire* cannot be accounted for phonologically as a reflex of Lat. *exīre;* it is obtained from an analogy with the noun *uscio* 'door'; Old Italian has both *escire* and *oscire.*

201. Loss of Pretonic Vowel

The pretonic vowel has fallen in *quĭrītāre* and, in most areas, also in *dīrēctu.*

Latin
quĭrītāre, dīrēctu

Rm.	It.	Sp.	Ptg.	Cat.	Occ.	OFr.	Fr.
	gridare	*gritar, cridar* (old)	*gritar*	*cridar*	*cridar*		*crier*

Rm.	It.	Sp.	Ptg.	Cat.	Occ.	OFr.	Fr.
drept	dritto, diritto	derecho	direito	dret	dreit, drech	dreit	droit

Commentary

CL *quĭrĭtāre* becomes **crītāre* in Vulgar Latin. Italian, Spanish and Portuguese show voicing of initial *cr* to *gr,* while Gallo-Romance and Catalan retain *cr,* and in Old Italian there is documentation for a variant *cridare.* The voicing of intervocalic *t* in Italian points to influence of northern, Gallo-Romance dialects, while the *t* encountered in Hispanic makes **crīttāre* a likelier source than **crītāre* in that region, yet the two etyma must have coexisted since *cridar* is documented for Old Spanish.

CL *dīrēctu:* the classical form is found coexisting with VL *dērēctu* in many manuscripts. All Romance reflexes can be derived from *dērēctu* with the exception of It. *dritto* and *diritto,* which require a metathesized **dērīctu* from CL *dīrēctu* as their source. French and Occitan can go back to either form. If *dīrēctu* is kept as etymon, it is the Spanish development that becomes irregular. Sp. *derecho* can then be accounted for as having suffered the influence of the prefix *de-,* and the same may be true of Ptg. *direito,* since pretonic *i* may represent an [ə] sound (cf. Ptg. *vizinho* §192).

202. Aphaeresis

By aphaeresis is understood the loss of a sound or a group of sounds at the beginning of a word. The loss of initial *a* or *o* is a sporadic feature, which often results from a false interpretation of *l'a-* and *l'o-* as the definite article, leading to the deglutination of the vowel. Lat. *acūcŭla* may serve as an illustration of this development. The word is continued in Occitan as *agulha,* whereupon the combination *l'agulha* is wrongly interpreted as *la gulha.* When *hŏspĭtāle* becomes *ospedale* in Italian, Old Italian resolves *l'ospedale* as *lo spedale.* Another example of aphaeresis is *occasiōne* > It. *cagione,* Ptg. *cajom.* The Greek borrowing *apothēca* suffers the loss of the initial *a:* It. *bottega,* Sp., Ptg. *bodega,* Cat. *botiga,* Occ. *botica, botiga,* Fr. *boutique.* Aphaeresis is not limited to the article deglutination feature, but is encountered with other vowels as well: *epĭscŏpu* > It. *vescovo,* Cat., Occ. *bisbe;* **inŏdiu* > OPtg. *enojo* > *nojo;* *aestĭmāre* > OIt. *estimare* > *stimare;* *autŭmnu* > VL **atomno* > Rm. *toamnă* (with a change in gender); *agnĕllu* > Rm. *miel.* The prefix *con-* is dropped by aphaeresis as Lat. *consobrīnu* evolves to Sp. *sobrino,* Ptg. *sobrinho.*

Fr. *aiguille*: the development of Fr. *aiguille* presents a couple of problems; *-uille* for *-ulle* may have originated from a misinterpretation of the graph *ill* for palatal *l*, while the initial portion of the word may have undergone the analogical influence of the adjective *aigu*. *Aigu* < *acūtu* is itself, however, quite obscure in its evolution, since the intervocalic *c* should have dropped before a velar vowel (cf. *sēcūru* > OFr. *sëur* > *sûr*).

apothēca: the unaspirated Greek *p* is pronounced voiced in the Romance derivations (Rheinfelder I 147). The tonic vowel of this Greek word is rendered by *e* in Italian and Hispanic, while the Gallo-Romance and Catalan reflexes have *i*. It. *bottega* may have obtained its geminate *t* through the influence of *botte* (Rohlfs §228). The retention of *t* in Gallo-Romance is irregular, whereas Hispanic shows the normal lenition feature.

203. Influence of Prefixes

Common prefixes may play a role in reshaping the pretonic vowel. The relatively infrequent *abs-, as-, obs-* openings are quite often replaced by *es-* from Lat. *ex-*: VL *ascoltāre* > Sp. *escuchar,* Ptg. *escutar,* Cat., Occ. *escoltar,* Fr. *écouter* vs. It. *ascoltare,* OSp. *ascuchar,* OPtg. *ascuitar.* Lat. *abscondĕre* is continued as Sp., Ptg. *esconder* and Cat. *escondir,* and Old French has *esconser,* built on the Latin past participle *absconsu.* Lat. *obscūru* evolves to Ptg., OSp. *escuro,* while Modern Spanish reverts to a Latinizing *oscuro.* The continuation of Lat. *rŏtŭndu* as Sp., Ptg. *redondo,* OIt. *ritondo,* Cat. *redó,* Occ. *redon* may be attributed to the influence of the prefix *re-* in the view of some scholars, while others consider these forms obtained through dissimilation. The prefix *in-* has left its mark on *exagiu* > Sp. *ensayo,* Ptg. *ensaio* vs. It. *saggio,* Occ., Fr. *essai,* and on *hībĕrnu* > It., Ptg. *inverno,* Sp. *invierno,* Occ. *invern* vs. Cat. *hivern,* Occ. *ivern,* Fr. *hiver.*

III. *Final Vowels*

204. Two Extremes: the Italian and the Gallo-Romance Developments

Final vowels are retained in Italian while, by and large, they are eliminated in French, Occitan, and Catalan. Portuguese and Spanish take up an intermediate position between these two extremes, which means that rules are quite difficult to establish for the Hispanic area. In Rumanian, final *o* and *u* drop, while final *i* is reduced to a barely audible whisper. Because of its greater strength, the vowel *a* has resisted elimination in final position, surviving either in full or weakened form.

Spontaneous Developments

205. Final *i* : CL *ī* > VL *i*

$$\begin{aligned} \varnothing&: \text{Rm., Cat., Occ., Fr.} \\ i&: \text{It.} \\ e \text{ or } \varnothing&: \text{Sp., Ptg.} \end{aligned}$$

Latin
fēcī, vīgĭntī

It.	Sp.	Ptg.	Cat.	Occ.	OFr.	Fr.
feci	*hice*	*fiz*	*fiu*	*fis*		*fis*
venti	*veinte,*	*vinte*	*vint*	*vint*	*vint*	*vingt*
	veínte					
	(old)					

Commentary

Final long *i* is kept in Italian, changes to *e* in Spanish and Portuguese, but drops in Catalan, Occitan and French and is practically eliminated in Rumanian.

In Spanish, all front vowels are reduced to *e* in final position, but *ī* must have been kept differentiated from the other front vowels for quite some time since it alone was able to cause inflection of tonic *e* and *o*: *fēcī > hice; vēnī > vine; pōtuī > pude; habuī > hube,* and relics such as *esti, esi* and first-person perfects *pude, presi,* etc., were able to survive for a while (Menéndez Pidal §28.1; García de Diego, pp. 74–75). In Portuguese, the regular outcome of final *ī* is likewise *e: habuī > houve; amastī*

> *amaste,* but this change does not come about until the fourteenth century. In the medieval period, the first-person singular strong and the second-person singular weak perfects all end in *i: ouvi, pudi, quigi, tivi, amasti, partisti,* and so do the singular imperatives: *pidi, servi.* A non-syllabic final *i̯* is the norm in hiatus in Portuguese: *amāvi* > *amai* > *amei; fuī* > *fui.* Final *ī* drops in Portuguese after *c* and *s: fēcī* > *fiz; pŏsuī* > *pus,* and in direct contact with a tonic *ī: vīdī* > *vii* > *vi* (Williams §47; Huber §§152–154). In Rumanian, final *i* is reduced to a voiceless, non-syllabic whisper, serving merely to soften the preceding consonant: *domĭnī* > *domni; dŏrmīs* > *dormi.* It preserves its syllabic value and is fully pronounced when functioning as a supporting vowel with *muta cum liquida* consonant groups: *socerī* > *socri* (§209).

Lat. *fēcī:* the long *i* causes inflection or umlaut of tonic *e* in Hispanic and Gallo-Romance: Sp. *hice,* Ptg. *fiz,* Cat. *fiu,* Occ., Fr. *fis.*

Lat. *vīgĭntī:* the stress pattern of Lat. *vīgĭntī* is somewhat uncertain in the spoken language (Väänänen §267). Stressed on the long *i* of the initial syllable, the word is resolved as *vīntī,* while a form stressed on the short *i* would evolve to **venti.* Most scholars usually propose **ventī* as the source of Cat., Occ., OFr. *vint,* Fr. *vingt,* OPtg. *viinti, viinte,* Ptg. *vinte,* given the fact that a final long *i* acts as an inflectional agent on tonic *e,* changing it to *i* in these languages (Badía Margarit §46, VI; B. Moll §45; Roncaglia, p. 51; Bourciez: *Phonétique* §55, Rem. II; Williams §35.4). Many Italian dialects have *vint* or *vinti,* but standard Italian has a non-inflected *venti.* This form, however, could, as Jud suggests, have been obtained analogically from *trenta* (Rohlfs §§49, 974). Unlike Portuguese, which shows a reduction of *viinte* to *vinte,* OSp. *viinte,* which is likewise obtained through inflection, dissimilates the *ii* sequence to *ei,* and once this is achieved, the stress shifts to the more open of the two vowels, yielding Mod. Sp. *veinte* (García de Diego, pp. 175, 215). Rumanian does not continue Lat. *vīgĭntī* at all, replacing it by *douăzeci* lit. 'two tens', and similarly for the other multiples of ten: *treizeci* 'thirty', *patruzeci* 'forty', etc.

206. Final *e:* CL *ĭ, ē, ĕ, ae* > VL *e*

e:	Rm., It.
e or *∅:*	Sp., Ptg.
∅:	Cat., Occ., Fr.

132 *A Comparative Study of Romance*

Latin
vĕnĭt, lēvāre, dĕntēs, stellae

Rm.	It.	Sp.	Ptg.	Cat.	Occ.	OFr.	Fr.
vine	viene	viene	vem	ve	veṇ		vient
luà	levare	llevar	levar	llevar	levar		lever
dinţi	denti	dientes	dentes	dents	dens	denz	dents
stele	stelle						

Commentary

The norm calls for retention of final *e* in Rumanian and Italian as opposed to elimination in Catalan, Occitan and French. For Hispanic, the fate of final *e* is very complex. In Spanish, *e* drops when following the consonants *t, d, n, l, r, s* or *c: tĕnēte > tened; mĕrcēde > merced; pane > pan; sale > sal; mare > mar; mēnse > VL mese > mes; lūce > luz*, but various morphological pressures are often seen to perturb the workings of this rule. While the noun is *sal*, the verb form *sale* is analogical from *sales, salen*. Paradigmatic pressure often leads to the reintroduction of an *e* that had fallen earlier: OSp. *quier < quaerit* becomes *quiere* due to the analogical influence of *quieres* and *quieren*. In the noun and adjective declension, similar adjustments are made. Many consonant clusters were tolerated in final position in the old language, but toward the end of the medieval period, *e* was often restored: *pŏnte > OSp. puent; dŭlce > OSp. dulz; parte > OSp. part; nŏcte > OSp. noch* are replaced by Sp. *puente, dulce, parte, noche*, obtained from the plural forms *puentes, dulces, partes, noches*, for while *puent* was tolerated in Old Spanish, **puents < pŏntes* was not. Palatal *l* was depalatalized when final: *pĕlle > piel; mĭlle > mil; ĭlle > él; valle > val*. Final *e* was quite consistently kept in Spanish as a supporting vowel following an occlusive plus liquid combination: *patre > padre; lĕpŏre > liebre; nōbĭle > noble* (Menéndez Pidal §§28, 63; García de Diego, pp. 71–72). Conditions in Portuguese are equally complex. Final *e* falls when preceded by *l, n, r, s* or *c: male > mal; valet > val; bĕne > bem; partīre > partir; amōre > amor; mēnse > VL mese > mes; prehensit > VL presit > pres; vĭce > vez; facit > faz*. Portuguese is more conservative than Spanish, as seen from its retention of final *e* after *t: vērĭtāte > Ptg. verdade* vs. Sp. *verdad; bŏnĭtāte > Ptg. bondade* vs. Sp. *bondad; sĭtim > Ptg. sede* vs. Sp. ___ Final *e* is consistently kept after labials: *dēbet > deve; capit > cabe; *fome > fome*. Following geminates or consonant clusters, *e* is kept: *ĭlle > ele* (cf. Sp. *él); pĕlle > pele* (cf. Sp. *piel); tŭrre > torre;*

děnte > *dente; carne* > *carne.* It is absorbed in hiatus with tonic *e* or *i: fīde* > *fee* > *fé; pěde* > *pee* > *pé; cīvīles* > *civis.* In hiatus with *a*, *o* or *u*, it becomes a non-syllabic *i̯: vadit* > *vai; quāles* > *quais; sōles* > *sois,* and this yod may form part of a nasal diphthong: *canes* > *cães; ratiōnes* > *razões* (Huber §§149–151; Williams §46).

Rm. *vine:* for the change of tonic *ẹ* or *ẹ* to *i* when a nasal follows, see §178, and see Rothe §13.

It. *denti,* Rm. *dinţi:* common in medieval Italian texts are such plural formations as *i dente,* displaying the regular retention of final *e.* The modern plural *i denti* follows from an analogy with the plural of the masculine declension in *-o: muri, galli, lupi.* Rumanian obtains its plural in the same manner; the final stem consonant *t* becomes *ţ* [*ts*] before *i.*

207. Final *o:* CL *ū, ŭ, ō, ŏ* > VL *o*

> ∅: Rm., Cat., Occ., Fr.
>
> *o:* It., Sp.
>
> *o* [*u*]: Ptg.

Latin
cantō, caballu

Rm.	It.	Sp.	Ptg.	Cat.	Occ.	OFr.	Fr.
cânt	*canto*	*canto*	*canto*	*cant*	*can,* *cant*	*chant*	*chante*
cal	*cavallo*	*caballo*	*cavalo*	*cavall*	*caval*		*cheval*

Commentary
In Rumanian, final velar vowels merge in *u* (Lausberg §274) and are eliminated. Elsewhere, the velar vowels in final position flow together in a single quality *o*, which is retained in Italian and Spanish. In Portuguese, *o* is kept in spelling only, while the pronunciation has closed to [*u*]. It seems plausible that the *o* graph may reflect the medieval pronunciation. In Rumanian, Catalan, Occitan and French, final velar vowels are dropped. While final *u* and *o* have merged in Romance, the vowel inflection feature of Portuguese offers proof that a differentiation did exist initially and was able to survive for some time, at least in certain regions. Final *u* inflects

tonic ρ to ρ, a capacity which final *o* does not have: *pŏrcu* > Ptg. *porco* vs. *pŏrcos* > Ptg. *porcos* (§§148, 158).

Occ. *can, cant*: when the cluster *nt* becomes final, it is reduced to a stable *n*; the variant *cant* owes the retention of *t* to the analogical influence of *cantas, canta, cantam*, etc.

OFr. *chant*, Fr. *chante*: in Old French, the first person singular of the present tense is characterized by the lack of any ending, since final *o* regularly drops. The *-e* is obtained analogically from verbs such as *semble* < *sĭmŭlo* and *tremble* < *trĕmŭlo*, where it functions as a supporting vowel.

Sp. *apóstol*: *apóstol* is probably not a religious provençalism; the apocope or elimination of the final part of a word, as in Sp. *santo* > *san*, may have arisen from the frequent use of the word as a title followed immediately by a name: *apóstol santi Yague* (*Cid*, v. 1690b).

208. Final *a*: CL *ā, ă* > VL *a*

> ă: Rm.
> a: It., Sp., Ptg., Cat., Occ.
> *e* [ə]: Fr.

Latin
lūna, cantat, laudat

Rm.	It.	Sp.	Ptg.	Cat.	Occ.	OFr.	Fr.
lună	*luna*	*luna*	*lua*	*lluna*	*luna*		*lune*
cântă	*canta*	*canta*	*canta*	*canta*	*canta*		*chante*
lăudă	*loda*	*loa*	*louva*	*lloa*	*lauza*	*loe*	*loue*

Commentary
Final *a* is kept in Italian, Spanish, Portuguese, Catalan and Occitan, while it is weakened to [ə] in French and also in Rumanian where this sound is represented graphically by *ă*.

Conditioned Developments

209. Supporting Vowels
A supporting vowel is needed in French following certain consonant clusters, foremost among them the occlusive and liquid combination, but also *mn, nt* and affricates arising from labial and *i̯* groupings. The sup-

porting vowel is always a weak *e* [ə]: *alteru > altre > autre; fēbre > fièvre; patre > père; sŏmnu > somme; rŭbeu > rouge; sīmiu > singe; vĕndunt > vendent,* and also *extraneu > estrange,* where *n* is followed by [*dž*]. Furthermore, a supporting vowel develops in words with proparoxytone stress: *tĕpĭdu > tiède; jŭvĕne > *jŏvene > juevne > jeune; cŭbĭtu >* OFr. *cote, code > coude; fraxinu >* OFr. *fraisne > frêne.*

A supporting vowel *e* is encountered in Occitan following consonant clusters that are essentially the same as in French, although a few differences are noted here. Most widespread is the use of vocalic support with *muta cum liquida,* the occlusive plus liquid combination: *acre > agre; dŭplu > doble; fratre > fraire; saecŭlu > segle; *sĕquĕre > segre.* When double *r* becomes final, it may simplify as in French: *tŭrre >* Occ., OFr. *tor,* Fr. *tour; fĕrru >* Occ., Fr. *fer,* but Occitan may keep the geminate unchanged, in which case a supporting vowel is added: *torre, ferre.* A striking difference exists in the treatment of palatal plus *r* groups, for here Occitan inserts the vocalic support between the two consonants while French, as usual, adds the *e* at the end: *mĕlior >* Occ. *mélher,* OFr. *mieldre; pĕior >* Occ. *péier,* Fr. *pire; sĕnior >* Occ. *sénher,* OFr. *sendra* (Fr. *sire* comes from **sĕior*). Some clusters may or may not need a support: *rŭbeu > rog, roge; *hĕlmu > elm, elme.* The retention of final *o* in the verbal ending *-ŭnt* is probably morphologically determined; *o* coexists with *e* here: *vendŭnt > vendon, venden.* A supporting vowel is present in the reflexes of Latin proparoxytones: *asĭnu > asne; cŏmĭte > comte; hŏmĭne > omne, ome.*

Catalan similarly has a supporting *e* following the *muta cum liquida* grouping and the *rr* cluster: *pătre > pare; lātro > lladre; nostru > nostre; fĕrru > ferre; tŭrre > torre,* and a final *e* serves as support for words that had proparoxytone stress in Latin: *hŏspĭte > hoste; salice > salze; die sabbati > dissabte; mĕdĭcu > metge.* The Latin verbal endings *-ent* and *-unt* are continued as *-en: dēbent > deuen; dīcunt > diuen.* Characteristic of Catalan is the occasional appearance of *o* as support vowel, mostly as an assimilation feature in words that have a tonic *o: rŏtŭlu > rotllo; pŏrtĭcu > porxo,* but the use of *o* may also be morphologically determined as in the case of for example **mŏnĭchu > monjo,* where *o* reflects a desire to keep the masculine differentiated from the feminine *monja.* Also linked to morphology is the retention of final *o* in plural nouns or adjectives whose stem ends in a sibilant or in *s* + consonant: *bracchiu > braç* and *bracchios > braços; triste > trist* and *tristos > tristos.* The *-as* ending is weakened to *-es: casas > cases; cordas > cordes; cantas > cantes.* Written documentation for this change dates back as far as the end of the tenth century.

Rumanian retains final *i* and *u* after *muta cum liquida*, and final *o* is kept as *u* in the same position; in its supporting role final *i* is fully pronounced and is not reduced to a whisper: *sŏc(e)rī* > *socri; sŏc(e)ru* > *socru; ambulo* > *umblu*. Final *u* remains as support vowel for the enclitic article *-l*: *dŏmĭnu īllu* > *domnul*.

210. Retention of Final *u* and *i* in Hiatus

If final *u* is in direct contact with tonic *ĕ*, it is kept in French, Occitan and Catalan, but loses its syllabic value: *dĕu* > Fr. *Dieu*, Occ. *Deu, Dieu*, Cat. *Déu*. Occitan has [ɛw] or [jɛw], Cat. [ɛw], while French moves via [jɛw] to [jø]: *Matthaeu* > Fr. *Mathieu; mĕu* > Occ. *meu, mieu*, Cat. *meu*. In hiatus position, final *i* similarly combines with the tonic vowel into a diphthong or a triphthong: *mĕ ī* > Occ. *mei, miei*, It. *miei; perdĕdī* > Occ. *perdei, perdiei; cantāvī* > VL *cantai* > It. *cantai*. Rumanian likewise retains final *i* and *u* in non-syllabic function when they appear in hiatus position with the stressed vowel: *Dŏmĭne Dĕus* > *Dumnezeu; *ŏvu* > *ou; nŏvi* > *noi*.

211. Final *i* in Italian

While *e* is the regular outcome of final *e* in Italian, there are not infrequent occurrences of *i* replacing an earlier, phonological stage: *dĕcem* > OIt. *diece* > *dieci; hŏdie* > OIt. *ogge* > *oggi*. It seems very likely that *dieci* is obtained by analogy with *venti*, while *oggi* may have been modeled on *ieri* < *hĕrĭ*. In a more general evolution, however, final *i* seems to have become some sort of an adverbial marker: *ab ante* > OIt. *avante* > *avanti; dē māne* > OIt. *domane* > *domani; tarde* > *tardi* (Rohlfs §142). This parallels conditions in French, where *s* had come to play a similar role because of the frequency of Latin adverbs in *s* (*mĕlius, pĕius*, etc.).

The origin of the Italian second-person singular present-tense ending *-i* has been the subject of much debate. It does not seem possible to draw it phonologically from the *-as* and *-es* endings: *cantas* > **cantes* > *canti; dēbes* > *devi; vendĭs* > *vendi*, an explanation proposed by Meyer-Lübke (p. 56) and still upheld by Lausberg (§§280, 542). Rohlfs (§142) suggests more convincingly that *i* may have spread analogically from the *-īre* conjugation, where a final *ī* is present: *sentīs* > *senti*. The loss of final *s* is standard in Italian, except in monosyllables, where it evolves to a nonsyllabic *i̯*: *nōs* > *noi; vōs* > *voi; cras* > OIt. *crai* (§357). Similarly, Latin nominative plural nouns in *-es* do not develop an *i* ending phonologically in Italian (§206); they align themselves with the far more common masculine declension in -*o,* whose plural formation has an -*i* ending in Latin (*mūrī, gallī,* etc.). It. *uomini* is obtained from an analogical nominative, regardless of whether or not a form **hŏmĭnī* actually existed in the popular language; it corresponds to the Old French nominative plural *ome* (Rohlfs §§364–365). The two cases discussed here of final *i* involving verb and noun endings thus represent morphological adjustments rather than phonological developments.

212. Analogical and Conditioned Final Vowel Developments in Rumanian
    The problems discussed in the preceding paragraph pertaining to Italian noun and verb morphology have their parallel in Rumanian, where the same analogical leveling processes may be observed. The -*i* plurals of the masculine declension in -*o* (*mūrī, gallī,* etc.) spread analogically to the Latin masculine plurals in -*es*: *dentes* is replaced by **denti,* giving *dinţi,* and the second-pers. sing. verbal endings -*as,* -*ēs,* -*ĭs,* and -*īs* all flow together in -*i*: *cantas* > *cânti; tacēs* > *taci; vendis* > *vinzi; dormīs* > *dormi.* Rumanian changes final *a* to *e* when a palatal precedes: *fŏlia* > *foaie; *plŏja* > *ploaie; aranea* > *rǎie.* When *u* is inserted as a hiatus-separating device between tonic *o* and final *e,* the latter is weakened to *ǎ*: *nŏve* > *nouǎ; *doe* > *douǎ* (Rothe §§62, 177).

IV. *POSTTONIC NON-FINAL VOWELS*

213. The Posttonic Penult in Proparoxytones
Proparoxytone stress had disappeared in many words already in Vulgar Latin through the fall of the weak, posttonic penult. This seems chiefly to have occurred where liquid consonants were present or between *s* and *t*: CL *ŏcŭlu* > VL *oclu;* CL *spĕculu* > VL *speclu;* CL *calĭdu* > VL *caldu;* CL *sŏlĭdu* > VL *soldu;* CL *colaphu* > VL *colpu;* CL *pŏsĭtu* > VL *postu.* In hiatus position, posttonic *i* tends to lose its syllabic value: CL *fīliu* > VL *filiu;* CL *vīnea* > VL *vinia,* while *u* is subject to elimination: CL *battuo* > VL **batto;* CL *quattuor* > VL *quattor;* CL *mŏrtuus* > VL *mŏrtus.* These developments contribute to a reduction in the number of proparoxytones in Vulgar Latin. The posttonic penults that do remain suffer further eliminations in Romance, even in Italian, which usually retains weak vowels: *lĕpŏre* > *lepre* (cf. Rm. *iepure*); *persĭca* > *pesca* (cf. Rm. *piersică,* Sp. *pérsico,* Ptg. *pêssego*). Some of the proparoxytones retained in Italian are learned: *tegola* (cf. pop. It. *tegghia*), *regola, isola* (cf. *Ischia* < **iscla* < **isla* < *īnsŭla*), *larice,* but many are popularly developed. Rumanian is also quite conservative in its treatment of proparoxytones.

214. The Penult in Italian, Portuguese and Spanish
Closure of *e* to *i* in the penult is a characteristic feature of Italian: *fraxĭnu* > *frassino; tĕpĭdu* > *tiepido; *hŏmĭnī* > *uomini; līmĭte* > *limite,* and it is encountered in Portuguese as well: *dĕcĭmu* > *dizimo; *dŭbĭta* > *dúvida.* In Spanish, posttonic *i* is fairly rare. It is encountered in continuations of the *-ĭdu* suffix where, following the elimination of *d, i* comes to form a diphthong with the final vowel: *līmpĭdu* > *limpio; sūcĭdu* > *sucio; tĕpidu* > *tibio.* The outcome of the *-ĭcu* suffix contains a vocalic *i* or *e*: *pĕrsĭcu* > OSp. *pérsigo, présego; afrĭcu* > *ábrego; pertĭca* > *pértiga,* or the vowel may drop; *pĕrsĭcu* > OSp. *piesco, prisco.* The penult vowel *e* is kept in *hŏspĭte* > *huésped* and in a few learned words: *ordĭne* > *orden.* In Hispanic, the posttonic penults *e* and *i* mostly fell, specifically when preceded by a liquid or a nasal: *alĭquod* > Sp., Ptg. *algo; gallicu* > Sp., Ptg. *galgo; līmĭte* > Sp., Ptg. *linde; anĭma* > Sp., Ptg. *alma;* (*die*) *dŏmĭnĭcu* > Sp., Ptg. *domingo.* Hispanic usually drops the weak penult *o*: *cŏmpŭtat* > Sp. *cuenta,* Ptg. *conta,* though with rare cases of retention: *arbŏre* > Sp. *árbol,* Ptg. *árvore.* There are occurrences in Italian of the rounding of *e* to *o* in the penult, specifically before *l*: *flēbĭle* > It. *fievole* (cf. Occ. *frevol*): *dēbĭle* > It. *debole; mespĭlu* > It. *nespolo* (cf. Occ. *nespola*). The only

vowel that is firmly entrenched in the penult in Italian and Hispanic is *a*: *orphănu* > It. *orfano,* Sp. *huérfano; sabăna* > Sp. *sábana; anăte* > Sp. *ánade.* Its elimination in *colaphu* dates back to Vulgar Latin. The vowel *a* may even replace other penult vowels. The change to *a* seems to occur with the greatest frequency when the penult vowel is in contact with *n* or *r,* but is not restricted to this environment: *jŭvĕne* > It. *giovane; cophĭnu* > It. *cofano,* Sp. *cuévano; pampĭnu* > It. *pampano,* Sp. *pámpano,* Ptg. *pâmpano; syndĭcu* > It. *sindaco; chronĭca* > It. *cronaca; Bergŏmu* > It. *Bergamo; aurĭfex* > It. *orafo; passĕre* > Sp. *pájaro,* Ptg. *pássaro; camĕra* > Sp. *cámara,* Ptg. *câmara.* Retention of the penult at the expense of the final vowel, a prominent feature of Occitan and Catalan, is also attested for Portuguese and Spanish. In Portuguese, words formed with the *-bĭle* suffix drop the final vowel while keeping the penult: *amabĭle* > *amável; dūrabĭle* > *durável; mŏbĭle* > *móvel,* and Spanish offers *arbŏre* > *árbol; carcĕre* > *cárcel.* Sp. *ángel* < *angĕlu* may be an ecclesiastical provençalism.

215. The Penult in Gallo-Romance and Catalan
    In French, all penult vowels are dropped: *jŭvĕne* > **jŏvĕne* > OFr. *juevne* > *jeune; dēbĭta* > OFr. *dete* > *dette; camĕra* > *chambre,* including *a*: *Stēphănu* > OFr. *Estievne* > *Etienne; balsamu* > *baume,* but the propa-roxytone stress requires a supporting vowel: *tĕpĭdu* > *tiède; cŭbĭtu* > *coude; asĭnu* > OFr. *asne* > *âne; jeune, Etienne, baume.* Occitan shares these features with French. It drops its weak penults: *dŏmĭna* > *domna; anĭma* > *arma; subĭto* > *sobde, sopte; medicu* > *metge; *viatĭcu* > *viatge,* including the vowel *a*: *sabbatu* > *sabde, sapte; balsamu* > *balme, basme,* although there are a few occurrences of the weakening of *a* to *e*: *Rhŏdănu* > *Rozen, Rozer; *cassanu* > *casse, casser,* and it develops a supporting vowel: *asĭnu* > *asne; sobde, sabde, metge.* In spite of this parallelism, the two languages differ significantly in their treatment of the posttonic vowels. While, in French, the penult vowel is consistently dropped, Occitan quite often retains the penult at the expense of the final vowel: *fraxinu* > *fraisse, fraisser; *cassănu* > *casse, casser; pŏpŭlu* > *pobol; apŏstŏlu* > *apostol.* This feature acquires morphological significance since it gives rise to an unstressed *-er* infinitive ending: *plangĕre* > Occ. *planher* vs. Fr. *plaindre; fingĕre* > Occ. *fenher* vs. Fr. *feindre; vĭncĕre* > Occ. *venser* vs. Fr. *vaincre.*
    Catalan changes posttonic *a* to *e,* but unlike Spanish, it tends to avoid retention of the proparoxytone stress through the elimination of the final vowel: *orphănu* > *orfe; asparăgu* > *espàrec; raphănu* > *rave; anăte* > *ànec* (cf. Sp. *huérfano, espárrago, rábano, ánade*). The other posttonic vowels usually disappear: *pĭpĕre* > *pebre; lĭttĕra* > *lletra; cŏmĭte* > *comte;*

arbŏre > *arbre; lĕpŏre* > *llebre.* The vowel *e* is kept before *n*: *asĭnu* > *ase; cŏphĭnu* > *cove; fraxĭnu* > *freixe; homĭne* > *home; ordĭne* > *orde,* unless these are cases of vowel support with proparoxytone stress. Like Occitan, Catalan has an unstressed -*er* infinitive ending: **conōscĕre* > *conéixer; crēscĕre* > *créixer; *nascĕre* > *néixer; vĭncĕre* > *véncer.* Retention of *e* also occurs in certain suffixes: *persĭcu* > *préssec; Domĭnĭcu* > *Domènec; rapĭdu* > *ràbeu,* and *o* is kept in the -*ŭlu,* -*ŏlu* endings: *apostŏlu* > *apòstol; tĭtŭlu* > *titol.*

216. The Penult in Rumanian

Rumanian weakens the penult vowel *a* to *ă,* while *o* and *u* merge into *u*: *comparat* > *compără; lĕpore* > *iepure; mascŭlu* > *mascur.* Lat. *arbŏre* or **arburu* yields an older form *arbur(e),* which soon suffers a learned restitution of *o,* being replaced by *arbor(e)* (Nandris, p. 37; Rothe §56). A suffixal change may hold the clue to the continuation of *pŏpŭlu* as *popor* instead of **popur.* The penult vowel *e* is usually kept: *pŭlĭce* > *purece; fŏrfĭce* > *foarfece,* but the change of *e* to *i* is a common occurrence although it does not seem to obey any fixed rules. The dual outcome of VL *salvatĭcu*: *sălbatic* and an older variant *sălbatec,* may have resulted from a suffixal change. The closure of *e* to *i,* which is often attributed to the position before *n,* is a process that lacks a definite pattern: *margine* > *margine* vs. *pĕctĭne* > *pieptene* and a variant *pieptine.* More consistent is the change of *e* to *ă* when following a labial consonant: *sēmĭnat* > *seamănă; frĕmĭtu* > *freamăt.* This change does not take place, however, if the final syllable ends in a long *i*: **hŏmĭnī* > *oameni.*

The most conspicuous aspect of penult vowel treatment in Rumanian is beyond any doubt its lack of homogeneity. The same vowel may either be retained or fall in identical environments: *ŭngŭla* > *unghie* vs. *lĭngŭla* > *lingură; salĭce* > *salce* vs. *pūlĭce* > *purece; cŏllŏcāre* > *culcà* vs. *incaballĭcāre* > *încălecà; dŏmĭnī* > *domni* vs. **hŏmĭnī* > *oameni.* Such divergencies can only be accounted for on the basis of chronological and regional evidence: early or late syncopes, learned influence that may vary from one word or from one region to the next, etc. The treatment of *ŏcŭlu* and *mascŭlu* my serve as an illustration of the importance of such factors. Although the syncope of both *ŏcŭlu* and *mascŭlu* is documented in the *Appendix Probi*: *oculus non oclus; masculus non masclus,* we may assume that *masculu* retained its penult much longer than did *ŏcŭlu* on Rumanian soil, and that it was considered learned as opposed to the popular *ŏcŭlu,* hence the difference in evolution: *ŏcŭlu* > *ochiu* vs. *mascŭlu* > *mascur.*

217. The Nature of Posttonic Non-Final Vowels
The posttonic penult vowels are, of course, short since they would otherwise carry the tonic stress. The following examples may serve as an illustration of the development:

Latin
orphănu, dŭŏdĕcim, VL *dōdĕce, fraxĭnu, arbŏre, lacrĭma, pĕrsĭcu, -a*

Rm.	It.	Sp.	Ptg.	Cat.	Occ.	OFr.	Fr.
orfan	orfano	huér-fano	órfão	orfe,	orfe, orfaniṇ	orfne, orfe	orphelin
	dodici	doce	doze	dotze	dotze	doze	douze
frasin	frassino	fresno	freixo	freixe	fraisse, fraisser	fraisne	frêne
arbore, arbur(e)	albero	árbol	árvore	arbre	arbre, albre	arbre, albre, abre aubre	arbre
lacrămă lacrimă	lacrima, lagrima (dial.)	lágrima	lágrima	llagrima	lagrema, lacrema, larma, lerma	lairme, lerme	larme
piersică	pesca, persico (old)	pérsico, prisco (old)	pêssego	préssec	persega, presega	pesche	pêche

Commentary
Ptg. *órfão*: Portuguese resolves the *-anu* ending as a nasal diphthong (Williams §78.3.c). Retention of the oral *a* may be seen in *stŏmăchu > estômago*.

Cat. *orfe*, Occ. *orfe, orfaniṇ*, OFr. *orfne, orfe*, Fr. *orphelin*: the Old French forms and Cat., Occ. *orfe* are phonological. The French diminutive formation shows dissimilation of the *n – n* sequence in *ŏrphănīnu* to *l – n* (cf. *Bonōnia > Boulogne*), but a non-dissimilated *orfenin* is also documented for the medieval language.

CL *dŭŏdĕcim*, VL *dōdĕce*: the hiatus vowels are resolved as *ō*, which explains the absence of a diphthongization in French. As a rule, tonic *ĕ* and *ŏ* diphthongize in proparoxytones in French, while the corresponding close vowels do not; cf. *tĕpĭdu > tiède* vs. *dēbĭta > dette*. What is clearly implied here is the existence of two chronologically different layers of diphthongization: open vowels diphthongize prior to the fall of the posttonic penult, while the diphthongization of close vowels can be placed at a point in time when this weak vowel had already dropped. A development paralleling that of VL *dōdĕce* may be seen in *trēdĕcim* > *treize* and *sēdĕcim* > *seize,* where *ei* is merely an arbitrary graph for the open *e* obtained in blocked position. The voicing of *c* must have occurred when it was still intervocalic. This late elimination of the penult is linked to the fact that numerals are pronounced with great care in order to avoid any confusion. Voicing is also the norm in Hispanic: OSp. *dodze,* Ptg. *doze.* Sp. *doce* follows from the desonorization feature characteristic of Castilian (§268). The voiceless *tz* of Occ. *dotze* is unusual, while non-voicing is the norm for Italian. For the final *i* of It. *dodici,* see §211. Rumanian forms its numerals above ten by means of the invariable element *-sprezece* lit. 'above ten': *doisprezece* 'twelve', lit. 'two above ten'.

Rm. *frasin,* It. *frassino,* Sp. *fresno*: Rm. *frassin* shows an unexplained reduction of *cs* to *s* (cf. *măseà* < *maxĭlla*), while the Banat dialect has *frapsin,* with *ps* as the regular outcome of the *cs* cluster (§311). In Italian, *cs* is assimilated to *ss,* and the penult shows closure of *e* to *i.* The development of Sp. *fresno* is discussed in §311.

Ptg. *freixo*: the yod from the *cs* group combines with tonic *a* to form an *ei* diphthong which, in Portuguese, is not reduced, and *s* is palatalized to [š], spelled *x* (cf. *saxu* > *seixo*). OPtg. *freixeo* still contains the posttonic penult *e,* which is eventually absorbed by [š]. Several Portuguese words lost their proparoxytone stress through such absorptions: *angĕlu* > *angeo* > *anjo,* or through the coalescence of identical vowels: *pŏpŭlu* > *povoo* > *povo; pĕrīcŭlu* > *perigoo* > *perigo; Bracala* > *Bracaa* > *Braga.* With non-identical hiatus vowels, the posttonic penult usually loses its syllabic value: *macŭla* > *mágoa; nĕbŭla* > *névoa.*

It. *albero*: the consonantal sequence *r–r* is often dissimilated to *l–r* in Italian: *haribergo* > *albergo; peregrīnu* > *pellegrino,* and the Occitan variant *albre* shows a similar development. Non-dissimilated forms *arbore* and *arboro* are documented in Old Italian. The *o* ending represents a morphological adjustment, which may be tied to the change in gender, *arbore* being feminine in Latin, while the alteration of the posttonic penult may have resulted from the influence of the unstressed *-ero* ending, which gains ground in Italian: *cithara* > OIt. *cetera; Casparu* > *Gaspero;* Arabic *sokkar* > *zucchero* (cf. Sp. *azúcar*).

Sp. *árbol*: in Spanish, *r – r* is dissimilated to *r – l,* the opposite sequence of that of Italian: *Mĕrcŭrii (die)* > OSp. *miércores* > *miércoles; carcĕre* > *cárcel; marmŏre* > *mármol.* The retention of the penult vowel *o* is considered learned by Menéndez Pidal (§26.3), irregular by García de Diego (p. 72), while Corominas (I 313–314) appears to accept it as a not infrequent collateral development. Other examples, in addition to *árbol, miércoles* and *mármol,* are *tórtola* < *tŭrtŭre* and *apóstol* > *apŏstŏlu,* and *e* has been replaced by *o* in *víbora* < *vīpĕra.*

Fr. *arbre*: two types of consonantal dissimilation are noted for Old French variants of this word: *abre* with elimination of the first *r* in a sequence (cf. OFr. *herbergier* > *héberger*), and *albre, aubre,* with an early change to *l,* permitting vocalization before a consonant. Similar forms are encountered in Catalan dialects.

Lat. *lacrĭma*: the reflexes of this word are learned in Spanish, Portuguese and Catalan. Rumanian has an earlier form *lacrămă* obtained through vocalic assimilation. Italian has *lacrima* and a Gallo-Italic *lagrima,* and for Occitan Levy (p. 220) lists both *lagrema* and *lacrema.* Retention of the proparoxytone stress is a learned and rare feature in Occitan: *fabrĭca* > *fabrega; pertĭca* > *pertega,* and these forms are found alternating with shortened and more popular variants: *faurga, perga* and the French-type developments *lerma* and *larma.* Old French has *lerme,* while the modern form *larme* owes its existence to the well-known fluctuation between *er* and *ar* (§177).

Lat. *pĕrsĭcu*: *pĕrsĭcu (FEW* VIII 265–268; *REW* 6427, 6429; Corominas IV 654–655) is originally an adjective meaning 'Persian', and *malum persĭcum* thus literally means 'Persian apple'. When the underlying noun (*malum* 'apple' and probably *pōma* 'fruit') is dropped, the adjective becomes a noun of indeterminate gender: *pĕrsĭcu* and *pĕrsĭca.* It is masculine in It. *persico,* Sp. *prisco* and Ptg. *pêssego,* while the feminine *pĕrsĭca* and *pessĭca,* documented in the *Appendix Probi,* is continued in It. *pesca,* Rm. *piersică,* Occ. *persega, presega,* OFr. *pesche,* Fr. *pêche.* The norm is for *rs* to assimilate to *ss,* as confirmed by the *Appendix Probi* entry and by the Portuguese form (cf. *pĕrsōna* > Ptg. *pessoa*), whereupon *ss* simplifies to *s* as in It. *pesca,* OFr. *pesche.* Retention of *rs* is seen elsewhere, occasionally with metathesis of *r*: Sp. *prisco,* Cat. *préssec,* Occ. *presega.* Sp. *prisco* follows from an earlier *priesco* < *pĕrsĭcu.* For the reduction of the *ie* diphthong to *i* before *s* plus consonant, see Menéndez Pidal §10.2; García de Diego, p. 59, and see §173.

218. Proparoxytones and the Chronology of Sound Change

The proparoxytone stress offers ideal conditions for examining the relative chronology of sound changes. We may infer from the development of *tĕpĭdu* to Fr. *tiède* that the tonic vowel diphthongizes at a point in time that antedates the fall of the penult, since a free syllable is required for this change to take place. A comparison between French and Spanish reveals that the penult fell earlier in French than it did in Spanish where the consonant usually remained intervocalic long enough to voice: *sēmĭta* > Fr. *sente* vs. Sp. *senda* (cf. Fr. *sentier* and Sp. *sendero*); *cŏllŏcat* > OFr. *colche* > *couche* vs. Sp. *cuelga*; *dŭbĭtat* > OFr. *dote* > *doute* vs. Sp. *duda*. Voicing of intervocalic occlusives and elimination of the penult took place roughly during the same time period, which accounts for an occasional fluctuating outcome: *cŭbĭtu* > OFr. *cote, code* > *coude*. The treatment of the consonant clusters resulting from the vowel elimination may hold chronological information. Censured in the *Appendix Probi*, the reduction of *vetulus* to *veclus*, with its replacement of the unfamiliar *t'l* cluster by *cl*, dates back to Vulgar Latin, and this secondarily obtained *cl* develops like the primary cluster in the Romance reflexes: It. *vecchio*, Sp. *viejo*, Ptg. *velho*, Occ. *velh*, *vielh*, Fr. *vieil*. The syncope occurred much later in the word *spatula*, so late that *t'l* could no longer merge with *cl*, presumably because the latter had already embarked upon its palatalization course. Each language was thus left to find its own individual solution to the problem of dealing with an unfamiliar cluster. Italian opts for a total assimilation: *spatula* > *spalla*, Spanish for a metathesis of *t* (> *d*) and *l*: *espalda* (cf. *prestalde* for *prestadle* in *Cid*, v. 118), French for the unusual vocalization of *l* before another *l*: *espalle* > *espaule* > *épaule*, Occitan for an assimilation and degemination: *espala*, or for toleration of the *tl* group: *espatla*, whereas Portuguese avoids the problem altogether by retaining the penult and dropping the intervocalic *l*: *espádua*. French shows additional chronological layers in its treatment of the *t'l* cluster, a semi-learned change to *tr*: *tĭtŭlu* > *titre*; *apŏstŏlu* > *apôtre* (cf. E. *title, apostle* borrowed from an earlier stage in the French development), and the elimination of the dental: *rŏtŭlu* > *rôle*, probably obtained via **rodle* and an assimilated *rolle*.

V. INTERTONIC VOWELS

219. Definition and Development

The intertonic vowel is lodged between the pretonic or initial vowel and the tonic stress. It is referred to as *contrefinale* by the French scholar Darmesteter, who had discovered that its treatment in Gallo-Romance parallels that of the final vowel.

Latin
bonĭtāte, memŏrāre, ornamĕntu

Rm.	It.	Sp.	Ptg.	Cat.	Occ.	OFr.	Fr.
bună-tate	*bontà*	*bondad*	*bon-dade*	*bondat*	*bontat*		*bonté*
	(ri)mem-brare	*memo-rar,*	*lembrar, nembrar*	*nembrar*	*mem-brar,*	*(re)mem-brer*	
	rimemo-rare	*mem-brar*	*(old)*		*nembrar*		
	(old)	*(old)*					
ornă-ment	*orna-mento*	*orna-mento*	*orna-mento*		*ornamen*		*orne-ment*

Commentary

Italian keeps intertonic *e* in some words: *Martĭs die > martedì; Venĕris die > venerdì*, but it frequently closes it to *i: montĭcĕllu > monticello; oboe-dīre > ubbidire*. Very often, however, the intertonic *e* is eliminated, specifically when following *r, l* or *n: verecŭndia > vergogna; cerebĕllu > cervello; alĭqu'ūnu > alcuno; bonĭtāte > bontà; sanĭtāte > OIt. santà, (It. sanità* is a Latinism), and *i* and *e* also fall in certain future and conditional formations: **morīre at > morrà; *venīre at > verrà; *venīre habuit > verrebbe; *vīdēre at > vedrà*. As a rule, the velar vowels *o* and *u* are kept: *regŭlāre > regolare; mensūrāre > misurare*, but *matūtīnu* had become *mattīnu* already in Vulgar Latin (> It. *mattino*). The vowel *a* is replaced by *e*, chiefly before *r: margarita > margherita; *widarlōn > guiderdone*, and as a result of this change, *er* becomes a standard ingredient in the future and conditional formations of *-āre* verbs: **parlāre aio > parlerò; *parlāre habuit > parlerebbe*.

Rumanian, like Italian, does not eliminate the intertonic vowels with the same frequency as the West, yet there are several occurrences of this development: *ambulāre* > *umblà; collocare* > *culcà; mandŭcāre* > *mâncà; montĭcĕllu* > *muncel; vĕtĕrānu* > *bătrân; pavĭmĕntu* > *pământ.* The vowel *a* is usually weakened to *ă: lĭgātūra* > *legătură,* and if a palatal precedes, it becomes *e: taliātūra* > *tăietură.* The vowel *e* is retained in *macellāriu* > *măcelar; digĭtāle* > *degetar;* it is closed to *i* before *n: vĕnēnōsu* > *veninos,* and weakened to *ă* following *t, d, n: septĭmāna* > *săptămână; bōnĭtāte* > *bunătate; ĭn dērĕtro* > *ândărăt.* Intertonic *o* and *u* are kept as *u: carbōnāriu* > *cărbunar; medŭllāre* > *mădular.*

Spanish retains *a: paradĭsu* > *paraíso; calamĕllu* > *caramillo,* but drops most other intertonic *vowels: sĕptĭmāna* > *semana; comĭtātu* > *condado; apĕrīre* > *abrir; honŏrāre* > *honrar;* **fabŭlāre* > *hablar;* *consūtūra* > *costura.* Influence of the root word may cause retention of the intertonic vowel in derivations: *matūrāre* > *madurar* from *maduro; mendīcāre* > *mendigar* from *mendigo.* Portuguese drops intertonic *i* and *e* when preceded by *l, m* or *r* or when lodged between *c* and *t: *bĕllĭtāte* > *beldade; delĭcātu* > *delgado; cŏmĭtātu* > *condado; vērĭtāte* > *verdade; rēcĭtāre* > *rezar,* but *e* is kept elsewhere: *capĭtāle* > *cabedal,* and specifically when it stands between *m* and *n: nŏmĭnāre* > *nomear; sēmĭnāre* > *semear.* Retention of *o* and *u* occurs in *sapōrōsu* > *saboroso; Portū Cāle* > *Portugal.* Intertonic *o* usually falls before *r* or *l: mĕmŏrāre* > *lembrar; sĭngŭlāriu* > OPtg. *senlheiro, senheiro,* and in *cŏmpŭtāre* > *contar.* Where the intertonic vowel does not fall through syncope, it may be eliminated later in hiatus position, either through a merger of identical vowels or, in the case of non-identical vowels, the loss of syllabic value: *mĕdĭcīna* > *meezinha* > *mezinha; vŏlŭntāte* > *voontade* > *vontade; salūtāre* > *saudar.* Intertonic *a* survives in *salvatōre* > *salvador; paradĭsu* > *paraíso,* but is merged into the pretonic *a* in *panatariu* > *paadeiro* > *padeiro.*

Occitan and French are less prone to fluctuations since, by and large, they follow the *Lex Darmesteter* very closely, which is to say that all intertonic vowels are dropped, with the exception of *a,* which is kept in the South, but weakened to *e* [ə] in the North, and with the further exception of the use of a supporting vowel with certain consonant clusters. The loss of intertonic vowels occurs more or less simultaneously with the voicing of intervocalic occlusives, which accounts for some hesitation between a voiced and a voiceless outcome for *k.* This makes the syncope of intertonics a fairly late development: *bōnĭtāte* > Occ. *bontat,* Fr. *bonté; dēlĭcātu* > Occ. *delcat, delgat,* OFr. *delgié, deugié;* **carrĭcāre* > Occ. *carcar, cargar,* OFr. *charchier, chargier,* Fr. *charger;* **paraulāre* > Occ. *parlar,* Fr. *parler;* **vŏlēre aio* > Occ. *volrai,* OFr. *voldrai,* Fr. *voudrai.* Intertonic *a* is kept in Occitan and weakened to *e* [ə] in French: *ornamĕntu* > Occ. *orna-men*, Fr. *ornement; paradīsu* > Occ. *paradis*, OFr. *parëis; cantatōre* > Occ. *cantador*, OFr. *chanteor* > Fr. *chanteur* (with absorption of *e* in hiatus). A supporting vowel is present in **quadrĭfŭrcu* > Occ. *caireforc*, OFr. *cadreforc*, Fr. *carrefour; *caprĭfŏliu* > Occ. *cabrefolh*, OFr. *chevrefueil*, Fr. *chèvrefeuille*. Verbs often retain the pretonic vowel through the analogical influence of stem-stressed forms: Occ. *oblidar*, Fr. *oublier* are influenced by Occ. *oblidas*, Fr. *oublies*, and Fr. *occupe* prevents the loss of *u* in *occuper*. Derivations may similarly be influenced by the root word: Occ. *fenimen* has kept its *i* because of *fenir*, Occ. *amoros* < *amōrōsu* is influenced by *amor* < *amōre*, OFr. *onorer* < *hŏnŏrāre* by *onor* < *hŏnōre*, and Fr. *nourriture*, replacing an earlier *norreture*, with a supporting *e*, has undergone an adjustment to the infinitive *nourrir*. The French future *partirai* < **partīre aio* is modeled on the infinitive, while Occitan has both a phonological *partrai* and an analogical *partirai*.

Catalan retains intertonic *a*: *paradīsu* > *paradís*, but drops most other vowels in that position: *molīnāriu* > *molner; bonĭtāte* > *bondat; cĕrĕbĕllu* > *cervell; labōrāre* > *llaurar*. Retention occurs where complex consonant clusters would arise: *hŏrtŭlānu* > *hortolà; pĕtrĭcōsu* > *pedregós;* it is common with *n*: *tĕrmĭnāre* > *termenar*, and in suffixal formations the primitive vowel is generally kept: *sĕntīmĕntu* > *sentiment* retains its *i* through the analogical influence of the infinitive *sentir* < *sĕntīre*.

Lat. *mĕmorāre*, OIt. *membrare*, OIt. *rimemorare*, It. *rimembrare*: unfamiliar consonant clusters, arising when weak vowels fall, are often alleviated through the insertion of transitional consonants or glides: *m'r* > *mbr; m'l* > *mbl; n'r* > *ndr; l'r* > *ldr* (§348). This happens rather infrequently in Italian, where the fall of weak vowels is not very widespread. Old Italian has the compound verb *rimemorare* < *rĕmĕmŏrāre*, while the modern form *rimembrare* is borrowed from OFr. *remembrer*, which is also continued in E. *remember*, but has dropped from French.

OPtg. *nembrar*, Ptg. *lembrar*, Occ. *nembrar*: the *m—m* sequence has been dissimilated in Portuguese, first to *n—m*, then to *l—m*. Old Spanish has the same forms, and Occitan has a variant *nembrar*.

220. Intertonic *u* Becoming Non-Syllabic in Vulgar Latin

It is not uncommon for intertonic *u* to develop into a non-syllabic *u̯ in* Vulgar Latin, and this wau is prone to elimination, specifically when preceded by a double consonant or a consonant cluster. In verbs, intertonic *u* is retained through an analogy with the stem-stressed forms.

Latin
CL *battualia,* VL **battalia,* CL *fĕbruāriu,* VL *febrariu*

Rm.	It.	Sp.	Ptg.	Cat.	Occ.	Fr.
bătaie	*battaglia*	*batalla*	*batalha*	*batalla*	*batalha*	*bataille*
făurar	*febbraio*	*febrero*	*fevereiro*	*febrer*	*feurer,*	*février*
					febrier	

Commentary
In the posttonic penult, *u̯* is similarly eliminated: CL *battuo* > VL **batto;* CL *mortuus* > VL *mortus.*

Sp. *batalla:* since *li̯* normally evolves to [χ] in Spanish: *consĭliu* > *consejo; trapaliu* > *trabajo* (§326), the word *batalla* is easily singled out as a borrowed lexical item, but because palatal *l* enjoys a very wide spread in Romance, it can be difficult to pinpoint the exact source. The word is borrowed either from Gallo-Romance or from Catalan. The native word for 'battle' in Spanish is *lid* < *līte,* continued also in Ptg. *lide,* but not represented elsewhere.

It. *febbraio:* the *b* of the internal *br* cluster is regularly lengthened in Italian: *fĕbre* > *febbre; fabru* > *fabbro; lībra* > *libbra.*

Sp. *febrero:* a popular *hebrero* occurs sporadically in the classical writers (§226).

Ptg. *fevereiro:* the insertion of a parasitic *e* is an infrequent feature occasionally found in clusters containing *r* or *l* (Williams §105.1).

Occ. *feurer, febrier,* Rm. *făurar:* the intervocalic *br* cluster is most often vocalized in Occitan, but is also quite frequently retained: *fĕbre* > *feure, febre; fabru* > *faure, fabre* (Roncaglia, p. 64; Anglade, p. 141; Grandgent §70, and see §292). Rumanian vocalizes *b: fabru* > *faur.*

221. Words Counting Two Intertonic Vowels
The pretonic portion of a word often counts two vowels between the initial and the tonic stress. Whenever this happens, Hispanic and Gallo-Romance concur in eliminating the vowel which immediately precedes the tonic: *recŭpĕrāre* > Sp., Ptg., Cat., Occ. *recobrar,* OFr. *recovrer,* Fr. *recouvrer; commūnĭcāre* > Sp. *comulgar,* Ptg. *commungar,* Occ. *comengar,*

comergar (but also *comenegar,* and cf. Cat. *combregar,* with loss of *u* and retention of *e* for support); *ĭngĕnĕrāre* > Sp., Ptg., Cat. *engendrar,* Occ. *engenrar,* Fr. *engendrer;* *caballĭcāre > Sp. *cabalgar,* Ptg. *cavalgar,* Cat. *cavalcar,* Occ. *cavalgar, cavalcar,* Fr. *chevaucher; lēgalĭtāte* > Sp. *lealtad,* Ptg. *lealdade,* Occ. *lealtat,* OFr. *loialté.* Both vowels are normally retained in Italian: *ricoverare, communicare, ingenerare,legalità,* but there are also occurrences of the elimination of the vowel that stands just before the tonic: *cavalcare.* Rumanian usually retains both vowels: *vīcīnĭtāte* > *vecinătate.*

CONSONANTS

I. INITIAL CONSONANTS

Single Consonants

222. Lat. *p-*

Latin
pīnu, pătre

p: Rm., It., Sp., Ptg., Cat., Occ., Fr.

Rm.	It.	Sp.	Ptg.	Cat.	Occ.	OFr.	Fr.
pin	pino	pino	pinho	pi	pin̦		pin
	padre	padre	pai,	pare	paire,	pedre	père
			pade			pair,	
			(old)			pai	

Commentary

Initial *p* is retained throughout.

Lat. *pătre*: surprisingly, this basic kinship term is not continued in Rumanian, and It. *padre* is non-Tuscan, the voicing of intervocalic *tr* being traceable to the influence of Gallo-Italian dialects. The familiar term in Tuscan is not *padre*, but *babbo*, and Rumanian has *tată*.

Ptg. *pai*: this form appears in the thirteenth century, having arisen from an intermediate *pade*, which is explained by some scholars as analogical from *frade* < *fratre*, where the second *r* has dropped by dissimilation, while others seek its origin in children's language. The corresponding *māi*, Mod. Ptg. *mãe* < *madre* appears a little later; the intermediate form is *made*, formed like *pade* (Williams §86.1.E). Mod. Ptg. *padre* 'priest, father, clergyman' and *madre* 'nun, mother superior' serve solely as religious terms.

Occ. *pair, pai*, Cat. *pare*: the regularly developed form in Occitan is *paire*, but variants without a supporting vowel and without *r* are found in certain dialects (Appel §42b; Anglade, p. 123); *pai* may be Gascon (Anglade, p. 152). Catalan reduces the internal *tr* cluster to *r* in some words: *matre* > *mare; fratre* > *frare*, but a voicing to *dr* is also common: *latro* > *lladre* (§290).

223. Lat. *b-*

b: Rm., It., Ptg., Cat., Occ., Fr.
b and *ƀ:* Sp.

Latin
ba(l)neu, bŏnu

Rm.	It.	Sp.	Ptg.	Cat.	Occ.	OFr.	Fr.
baie	*bagno*	*baño*	*banho*	*bany*	*banh*		*bain*
bun	*buono*	*bueno*	*bom*	*bo*	*boṇ*	*buen*	*bon*

Commentary
Initial *b* is kept unchanged in the languages that have a labiodental *v*: Rumanian, Italian, Portuguese, Catalan, Occitan and French while, in Spanish and Sardinian, initial *b* and *v* are merged. For both *b* and *v*, Spanish has *b* in absolute initial position and a bilabial fricative *ƀ* in intervocalic position. Spanish orthography usually reflects Latin spelling: *vir(i)de* > *verde* vs. *bĕne* > *bien,* but having two letters representing the same sound inevitably led to some confusion, specifically in cases where the Latin origin had become obscured: *vĕrrĕre* > *barrer* (but Ptg. *varrer); vōta* lit. 'vows', plural of the neuter *vōtum* (cf. Fr. *vœu*) > *boda* (Ptg. *boda* may be a Castilianism; *voda* is the written norm in the *Cantigas); versūra* > *basura; vĕrmĭcŭlu* > *bermejo* vs. Ptg. *vermelho* (García de Diego, p. 86; Menéndez Pidal §35.1). In southern Italian dialects, initial *b* evolves to *v* over a wide area (Rohlfs §150). In Medieval Catalan, *b* and *v* are kept apart while, generally speaking, they merge into a bilabial *b* in the modern language, though with a fair amount of dialectal variations (Badía Margarit §67, II).

Lat. *balneu:* the *l* drops everywhere, being absorbed by the palatal *n*. VL *baneum* is documented in an inscription from Pompeii.

OFr. *buen:* for the incipient diphthongization of short *o* before a final nasal in French, see §179.

224. Lat. *m-*

m: Rm., It., Sp., Ptg., Cat., Occ., Fr.

Latin
mānu, mŭltu

Rm.	It.	Sp.	Ptg.	Cat.	Occ.	OFr.	Fr.
mână	mano	mano	mão	mà	maṇ		main
mult	molto	mucho	muito	molt	mọlt,	molt,	
					mout,	mout,	
					mọt,	mot	
					mọn		

Commentary

Initial *m* is kept throughout. In rare instances, it may cause nasalization of the following tonic vowel or diphthong in Portuguese; besides *muito*, this is the case with *madre* > *mãi* > *mãe; mĕa* > *mĩa* > *minha; mĭhĩ* > *mi* or *mĩ* > *mim* (Williams §66.1; Huber §298). This type of nasalization is still encountered in certain dialects. For a similar development of initial *n* in Portuguese, see §229.

Rm. *mână*, Occ. *maṇ*: the feminine gender of Lat. *manu* makes the *-u* ending a morphological anomaly, but Rumanian is alone in formally adjusting this noun to the feminine declension in *-a*. A different development may be seen in Occitan where the form of the noun may occasionally lead to the adoption of the masculine gender: *mas joins* is found alternating with *mans juntas* '(with) folded hands'.

Occ. *mọt*: this reduced form of *molt*, which also occurs in Old French, is encountered sporadically, while *mon* is an extremely rare variant, which has its parallel in OFr. *mont*, OPtg. *muinto*, dial. It. *monto*, dial. Sp. *munto*, *muncho*. These forms have still not been sufficiently elucidated. Von Wartburg (*FEW* VI 210–211) suggests that *l* may have been assimilated to the initial nasal, with *m* subsequently changed to *n* before *t*, while Corominas (IV 178) derives these forms from an extension of the initial nasality.

225. Lat. *v-*

v: Rm., It., Ptg., Cat., Occ., Fr.
b and *ƀ*:   Sp.

Latin
vīnu, vacca, vīce

Rm.	It.	Sp.	Ptg.	Cat.	Occ.	OFr.	Fr.
vin	*vino*	*vino*	*vinho*	*vi*	*viṇ*		*vin*
vacă	*vacca*	*vaca*	*vaca*	*vaca*	*vaca*		*vache*
vęce	*vez*	*vęz*	*vece*	*vętz*	*feiz*	*fois*

Commentary

Latin uses the graph *u*, which originally represents a bilabial fricative. Becoming labiodental over a wide area of Romania, this sound is kept in Rumanian, Italian, Portuguese, Catalan, Occitan and French. A complete merger of *b* and *v* takes place in Spanish, where both consonants evolve to *b* or *ƀ* in a rigid distribution, with the occlusive *b* appearing in absolute initial, the fricative *ƀ* in intervocalic position, as seen in §223. A confusion between *b* and *v* in initial position is widespread in Italian dialects (Rohlfs §167) as well as in Modern Catalan (Badía Margarit §67, II), and there are a few occurrences in Rumanian of the change of *v* to *b*: *větěrānu* > *bătrân;* *vǐtta* > *bată.*

In French, several Latin words with initial *v* were contaminated by related lexical items with an initial Germanic *w*. In their ulterior development these words remain faithful to the Germanic sound, which evolves via [*gʷ*] to *g* (§254): Lat. *věspa* + Frk. **wabsa* > OFr. *guespe* > *guêpe;* Lat. *vădu* + Frk. **wad* > OFr. *guet* > *gué;* Lat. *văstāre* + Frk. **wōsti* > OFr. *guaster* > *gâter;* VL *vŭlpīcŭla* + Frk. **hwelp* > OFr. *goupil.*

Lat. *vǐce*: in Vulgar Latin, the noun *vǐce*, preceded by a cardinal, takes over the function of the classical multiplicativa: *sěmel* 'once', *bis* 'twice', *těr* 'three times', etc., which are not continued. A variant, reconstructed as **vǐcāta*, is continued in OIt. *vicata*, Sp., OPtg., Cat., Occ. *vegada*, OFr. *foiee* (*REW* 9304), and Old Italian has a variant *fiata*, which is borrowed from Old French.

OFr. *feiz,* Fr. *fois*: the problem pertaining to the initial *f* in Fr. *fois* as opposed to the retention of *v* elsewhere has still not been convincingly settled. Rheinfelder (p. 156) and Bourciez (*Phonétique* §163, Rem.) reiterate Holthausen's claim that *v* has become unvoiced in the combinations *cinq fois, six fois, sept fois* (*REW* 9307), but this type of partial assimilation, if it takes place at all, would work in the opposite direction in French, leading to the voicing of the final consonant of the numeral (§373). Other explanations focus on an analogy with corresponding Germanic terms, such as *vart* or *fart* (cf. E. *fold* in *hundredfold*). A likelier source is a contamination with OFr. *fais* 'burden' < *fasce,* the locution *a un fais* 'in one load' having evolved to become the equivalent of 'one time' (*FEW* XIV 410–413). The *f* of *feiz* has been extended to *foiee*.

226. Lat. *f-*

f:	Rm., It., Ptg., Cat., Occ., Fr.
h > ø or *f*:	Sp.

Latin
fŏlia, fīliu, fŏcu

Rm.	It.	Sp.	Ptg.	Cat.	Occ.	OFr.	Fr.
foaie	*foglia*	*hoja*	*fǫlha*	*fulla*	*folha, fuolha, fuelha*	*fueille*	*feuille*
fiu	*figlio*	*hijo*	*filho*	*fill*	*filh*	*fil, fiz*	*fils*
foc	*fuoco*	*fuego*	*fǫgo*	*foc*	*foc, fuoc, fuec*	*fou, fu*	*feu*

Commentary

Initial *f* persists in Rumanian, Italian, Portuguese, Catalan, Occitan and French, and Spanish retains it in spelling until the end of the fifteenth century, at which point it is replaced graphically by *h* which, in the fifteenth and sixteenth century, still marks an aspiration. In Modern Spanish, *h* is still written, although it no longer represents any sound: *fabulare* > *fablar* > *hablar; fŏlia* > *foja* > *hoja; fūmu* > *humo; fātu* > *hado; fīcu* > *higo; ficatu* > *hígado; formīca* > *hormiga*. In northern regions bordering on the Basque domain, the fifteenth-century aspiration persisted, spreading to Burgos, Santander, the upper Pyrenean region, etc., and it was extended to Salamanca and Andalucia. A few of these aspirated forms, mostly from Andalucia, penetrated into the literary language where they were rendered by *j* because of the similarity between the aspiration and the Castilian [χ]: *famelĭcu* > *jamelgo; fŭllīgĭne* > *jollín*. Lat. *f* was not dropped when preceding the diphthong *ue*, the consonant *r* or the semi-consonant *u̯*: *fŏcu* > *fuego; fŏrte* > *fuerte; fŏnte* > *fuente; frēnu* > *freno; frĭcāre* > *fregar; fraxĭnu* > *fresno; fuī* > *fuí*. Some hesitation is noted for the position before the diphthong *ie*: **fĕle* > *hiel; fĕrru* > *hierro* vs. *fĕsta* > *fiesta; fĕbre* > *fiebre,* and *f* may also be retained under a few other, poorly defined circumstances. The loss of *f* is essentially a Castilian feature, extended to neighboring areas as well as to Andalucia in the wake of the *Reconquista,* while the remainder of the Peninsula retains the initial *f* of Latin intact: Portugal, Galicia, Catalonia, Aragón, Navarra, Asturias, etc. In some words, *f* was restored in Castilian either through dialectal or learned influence: *fĕbruāriu* > VL *febrariu* > OSp. *hebrero* > *febrero; falcōne* > OSp. *halcón* > *falcón; foedu* > OSp. *heo* > *feo; fĭde* > OSp. *he* > *fe.*

The traditional explanation for the loss of initial *f* is that of the influence of a Basque-Iberian substratum on Castilian and Gascon, as expounded by Menéndez Pidal in his *Orígenes.* These two languages are geographically contiguous, they have a common Iberian base, and they have evolved in close vicinity of Basque, which lacks *f.* The change to *h* is even more thorough in Gascon, which has *hoec, hüc* vs. Sp. *fuego* and *heret* vs. Sp. *frío.* In support of his substratal theory, Menéndez Pidal adduces examples of the change of initial *f* to *h* dating back to the eleventh century, thereby proving that we have to do with an old development that was widespread in the popular language. Among opponents of the substratal theory are Meyer-Lübke and John Orr, and more recently linguists have turned their attention to internal reasons for this phonological change on the grounds that Spanish does retain *f* under specific circumstances (Menéndez Pidal §38.2; Menéndez Pidal: *Orígenes* §41; García de Diego, pp. 87–89; Bourciez: *Eléments* §336.e; Lausberg §302; Lloyd, pp. 218–223; Tagliavini, pp. 107, 141; Iordan-Manoliu §198). The change of initial *f* to an aspirated *h* is encountered in certain dialects of southern Italy (Rohlfs §154).

OFr. *fiz,* Fr. *fils*: French continues the nominative case *filius* of this noun, most likely because the accusative *fil,* containing a palatal *l,* could easily be confused with the feminine *fille.* OFr. *fiz* is present in such proper nouns as *Fitzgerald,* which were borrowed from the Anglonorman dialect. The *l* of Mod. Fr. *fils* is a learned graph.

Occ. *foc, fuoc, fuec*: the optional diphthongization of *ŏ* is caused by the velar *c.*

OFr. *fou,* Fr. *feu*: the development is not quite clear; *c* drops before a velar vowel, but the lack of a diphthongization is puzzling. *Fu* is a mere spelling variant, while *feu* shows *picard* influence.

227. Lat. *t-*

t: Rm., It., Sp., Ptg., Cat., Occ., Fr.

Latin
tĕmpus, tāle, thesauru

Rm.	It.	Sp.	Ptg.	Cat.	Occ.	OFr.	Fr.
timp	tempo	tiempo, tiempos (old)	tempo, tempos (old)	temps	tems,	tens	temps
tare	tale	tal	tal	tal	tal		tel
	tesoro	tesoro, tresoro (old)	tesouro	tresor	tezaur		trésor

Commentary
Initial *t* is kept everywhere. However, a conditioned change is noted for Rumanian, which assibilates initial *t* to [*ts*] when it stands before *i* < Lat. *ī* or *ie* < Lat.*ĕ: tĕrra > *tiarrǎ > ţarǎ; tĕsta > *tieastǎ > ţeastǎ; sŭbtīle > subţīre; *dĕntī > dinţī.* This palatalization does not occur where *i* is secondarily obtained when followed by a blocked nasal as in *tĕmpus > timp,* since a diphthong *ie* never developed here (§178).

OSp. *tiempos,* OPtg. *tempos*: as early as Berceo, the unusual *tiempos* was changed into a normal singular *tiempo* and similarly for Portuguese. For further details, see OSp., OPtg. *lados* (§152). Other Latin neuters in *-us* are: *ŏpus >* OSp. *huebos; cŏrpus >* OSp. *cuerpos; pĕctus >* OSp. *pechos.*
Lat. *thesaurus*: in this word of Greek origin, Gk. *th-* is treated like Lat. *t-.* For Gk. *thius* (*REW* 8709), however, Italian has *z* [*ts*] as opposed to *t* in Hispanic: It. *zio,* Sp., Ptg. *tio.* The *z* originates from *tį* in **thiane >* S.It. *ziano* 'uncle' and is transferred from there to *tio* and *tía* (Rohlfs §193). A parasitic *r* is present in OSp. *tresoro,* Cat. *tresor* and Fr. *trésor.* Germanic *th* is likewise treated like *t*: Gmc. **thwalja >* It. *tovaglia,* OSp. *tobaja,* Sp. *toalla,* Ptg., Occ. *toalha,* OFr. *touaille* (*REW* 8720).

228. Lat. *d-*

d: Rm., It., Sp., Ptg., Cat., Occ., Fr.

Latin
dūru, dĭgĭtu, dīgĭtu

Rm.	It.	Sp.	Ptg.	Cat.	Occ.	OFr.	Fr.
	duro	*duro*	*duro*	*dur*	*dur*		*dur*
deget	*dito*	*dedo*	*dedo*	*dit*	*det,*	*deit*	*doigt*
					dit		

Commentary

Initial *d* is kept throughout. In Rumanian, however, initial *d* undergoes an assibilation to *dz*, paralleling the conditioned change outlined above for *t* (§227), but with the difference that *dz* is subsequently simplified to *z*. The conditioning factors in this evolution are once again *i* < Lat. *ī* or *ie* < Lat.*ĕ*: *dĕce* > **diece* > *zece; dĕu* > *zeu; dīcĕre* > *zice,* and here, too, the dental remains unaffected by the Rumanian *i* obtained before a blocked nasal: *dĕnte* > *dinte*. For the initial *dḭ-* evolving to *z* before the vowel *a* as in *Diana* > *zănă,* see §256.

Lat. *dĭgĭtu, dīgĭtu*: the quantity of the tonic *i* is fluctuating; It. *dito* and the alternate Occitan form *dit* require an etymon in *ī,* as do also the Sardinian, Catalan, Aragonese, Asturian and Gascon reflexes, while the remaining forms go back to a short *i.* Rohlfs (§49) attributes the long *i* to the influence of the following palatal consonant. The source of the Romance reflexes appears, at least in some instances, to be a shortened **dĭtu* or **dītu* with elimination of *g* at a fairly early stage, but Rm. *deget* continues CL *dĭgĭtu (FEW* III 77). A comparison with **frĭgĭdu* > It. *freddo* would lead one to suspect that a geminate would have evolved in Italian from the *g't* cluster, and *dĭgĭtu* gives *det* in Occitan, not **deit* or **deg.* In Hispanic, *g* regularly drops before a palatal vowel (Menéndez Pidal §43.1; Huber §277; Williams §73.4), but a shortened VL **dĭtu* would, of course, also be acceptable as the etymological source. OFr. *deit* flows easily from VL **dĭtu* with the regular diphthongization of tonic free *ẹ,* but it can also reflect CL *dĭgĭtu.* The elimination of the penult in proparoxytones forms a barrier to the diphthongization of close *e* (cf. *dēbĭta* > Fr. *dette*), but *g,* transformed into yod (cf. **frĭgĭdu* > OFr. *freit*), would combine with *e* to form an *ei* diphthong by coalescence. Fr. *doigt* is Latinizing spelling.

229. Lat. *n-*

n: Rm., It., Sp., Ptg., Cat., Occ., Fr.

Latin
nīdu, nūdu

It.	Sp.	Ptg.	Cat.	Occ.	OFr.	Fr.
nido	*nido*	*ninho*	*niu*	*ni, nit,*	*ni, nit*	*nid*
				nis, niu		
nudo	*nudo*	*nu*	*nu*	*nu, nut*	*nu, nut*	*nu*

Commentary

Initial *n* persists throughout. Rumanian examples are: *nŏcte > noapte; nasu > nas*. Just as with initial *m* (§224), there are rare cases of nasalization in Portuguese caused by initial *n*: *nīdu > nīo > ninho; nec > ne > nem; nūdu > nūu > nu; *nequem > nēguem > nenguem > ninguém* (Williams §66.2B; Huber §298).

Ptg. *ninho*: the resolution of the nasal *ī* as *i* and a palatal *n* is regular; cf. *vīnu > vīo > vinho; farīna > farīa > farinha* (§180).

Occ. *ni, nit, nis, niu*, OFr. *ni, nit*, Fr. *nid*: the norm is for free final *d* to either drop or desonorize in Gallo-Romance: OFr. *ni, nit;* the final dental falls in French, with Mod. Fr. *nid* being nothing more than a case of learned spelling. In Occitan, intervocalic *d* yields a voiced *s*, and the variant *nis* thus seems to imply that this development may at times precede the elimination of the final vowel, perhaps in a regional evolution. In another southern development intervocalic *d* falls early, while final *u* is retained in direct contact with the stressed vowel (Anglade, p. 124; Roncaglia, p. 52; Schultz-Gora §§44, 57; Appel §46c). For other instances of the retention of final *u*, see §210.

Ptg. *nu*: *nu* results from a contraction of *nuu*, which arises with the fall of intervocalic *d* (Huber §156; Williams §§48.5, 99.3). Similar contractions are *crūdu > cruu > cru; mūlu > muu > mu*, the latter coexisting with a learned, regressive *mulo*.

230. Lat. *s-*

s: Rm., It., Sp., Ptg., Cat., Occ., Fr.

Latin
salvāre, sĕx

Rm.	**It.**	**Sp.**	**Ptg.**	**Cat.**	**Occ.**	**Fr.**
	salvare	*salvar*	*salvar*	*salvar*	*salvar*	*sauver*
şase	*sei*	*seis*	*seis*	*sis*	*seis, sieis*	*six*

Commentary

Initial *s* is regularly kept before a vowel (for initial *s* + consonant, see §257). Rumanian examples are: *sōle* > *soare; sĭccu* > *sec*.

A conditioned palatalization of *s* occurs in Rumanian where initial *s* evolves to [š] before the vowel *i*: *sīc* > *şī*, and when followed by the diphthong *ie*, *s* absorbs the yod, likewise becoming [š]: *sĕpte* > **sieapte* > *şapte*. Rm. *şase* owes its palatal *s* to an analogy with *şapte*. The palatalization of initial *s* in **sōrĕce* (CL *sōrĭce*) > *şoarece* is obscure, but could conceivably follow from a partial assimilation with the following [tš]. In Italian, there are a few cases of the palatalization of initial *s* to [š] before the vowels *i* or *e*: *sīmia* > *scimmia; sĭmplus* > *scempio*. The verb *sceverare* may derive its palatal [š] from the prefix *ex-* in **exseperare*. The palatalization of *s* to [š] is widespread in Italian dialects, and there are also occurrences of a change to *z* [ts]: *zufolare* < **sufilare* < *sibilāre* (Rohlfs §165). In Spanish, the occasional change of initial *s* to [š], spelled *x*, may occur before any vowel and is traditionally attributed to Moorish pronunciation. The palatalized [š] evolves to [ǯ] in the modern language: *sapōne* > *xabon* > *jabón; sūcu* > *xugo* > *jugo; sepia* > *jibia*. In regions that had important Moorish populations, this sporadic change is reflected in the toponymy: *Saetabi* > *Játiva; Salōne* > *Jalón; Saramba* > *Jarama* (Menéndez Pidal §37.2.b). There are also sporadic occurrences of [š] in Catalan: *syringa* > *xeringa; simplice* > *ximple*.

Rm. *şase*: the final *e* present in this form is analogical from *şapte* and is introduced early enough to cause the diphthongization of *ĕ*: **siesse* > **sieasse* > *şase* (Nandris, p. 166). For final *e* as an agent in the Rumanian diphthongization process, see §159; for the development of final *x* in Romance, see §358.

231. Lat. *r-*

r: Rm., It., Sp., Ptg., Cat., Occ., Fr.

Latin
rŏta, rāru, rāmu, -a

Rm.	It.	Sp.	Ptg.	Cat.	Occ.	OFr.	Fr.
roată	*ruota*	*rueda*	*rǫda*	*roda*	*rǫda*		*roue*
rar	*raro*	*raro*	*raro*	*rar*	*rar*	*rer*	*rare*
	ramo	*ramo*	*ramo*	*ram*	*ram*	*raim*	
	rama	*rama*	*rama*	*rama*	*rama*	*raime*	

Commentary

Initial *r* is retained throughout, though with varying phonetic properties. The *rr* graph that appears occasionally in Portuguese: *rrainha* = *rainha; rryo* = *rio,* may represent a heavily rolled *r.* An *rr* graph is not uncommon in old Rumanian texts, and in Gascon this quality of *r* may even lead to the addition of a prosthetic *a: rīvu* > *arriu; radīce* > *arraïtz; ramu* > *arram; Rōma* > *Arroume* (Rohlfs: *Le Gascon,* pp. 149–150).

Fr. *roue*: tonic free *ŏ* should have evolved via *ue* to *eu* (§151)*; ou* is unexplained.

OFr. *rer,* Fr. *rare*: the Old French form is phonological, while *rare* is learned with its unchanged *a* and the addition of an unjustified supporting vowel.

Lat. *ramo, rama*: although *ramu* is a masculine noun, it has yielded a collective *rama* analogical from the neuter plural *fŏlia.* French has a diminutive *rameau* and a collective *ramée,* but the standard term for 'branch' in Modern French is *branche,* of uncertain origin.

232. Lat. *l-*

> *l*: Rm., It., Sp., Ptg., Occ., Fr.
> *l'*: Cat.

Latin
lāna, lūna, latrāre

Rm.	It.	Sp.	Ptg.	Cat.	Occ.	Fr.
lână	*lana*	*lana*	*lã, lãa* (old)	*llana*	*lana*	*laine*
lună	*luna*	*luna*	*lua, lũa* (old)	*lluna*	*luna*	*lune*
lătrà	*latrare*	*ladrar*	*ladrar*	*lladrar*	*lairar*	

Commentary

Initial *l* is kept intact everywhere with the exception of Catalan, where it is regularly palatalized: *lacte > llet; lĭngua > llengua; lĕpŏre > llebre* (Badía Margarit §67 III). Initial *l* remains unpalatalized in learned words: *literatura, lògic.*

While retention of initial *l* represents the norm in Rumanian, palatalization occurs before the vowel *i* or before the yod of the *ie* and *ia* diphthongs. The palatal *l* is reduced to *i̯,* which is quickly absorbed into the diphthong while, before the vowel *i,* it is still heard, although it goes unrepresented graphically: *lĕpŏre > iepure; lĩnu > in* [*yin*]. The palatal *l* of Sp. *llevar < lĕvare* is obtained by analogy with the stem-stressed forms, where **lieva < lĕvat* has been misinterpreted as *lleva.*

Lat. *latrāre*: this word is not continued in French, where it is replaced by a verb drawn from a sound-imitating *bai*: OFr. *abaier,* Fr. *aboyer,* and Italian similarly has *abbaiare.*

233. Lat. *c-*

In accordance with Etruscan practice, the *k* sound was rendered graphically in Latin by *c* before *e* and *i,* by *k* before *a* and by *q* before *o* and *u,* but *k* soon fell into disuse and was declared a useless letter by Quintilian and other grammarians. The graphical distinctions borrowed from the Etruscan alphabet do not reflect any major phonetic differences. That *c* was pronounced *k* even before the front vowels *i* and *e* is affirmed by many grammarians, and further proof comes from Greek transcriptions, which consistently use the letter *kappa* to render this sound. Latin lexical items borrowed into Basque, Celtic and Germanic render the *c* before a front vowel by *k* or other graphs reflecting a *k* sound: *pace >* Basque *bake; cēna >* Celtic *cwyn; cellariu >* G. *Keller; cerĕsea >* G. *Kirsche.* Furthermore, the *logudorese* dialect of Sardinian has retained Lat. *k* unchanged before front vowels: *kẹntu* < *cĕntu; kẹrbu* < *cĕrvu; kẹlu* < *caelu*. Elsewhere, *k* later becomes subject to palatalization when followed by *i* and *e*, and in a more recent and less sweeping development, *k* is also palatalized when standing before *a*. It is only before the velar vowels *o* and *u* that the single *c* [*k*] remains unchanged like most other initial consonants. The palatalization before *i* and *e* affects all of Romania with the exception of the *logudorese* dialect of Sardinian, and *k* remains in Dalmatian before the vowel *e* (Rohlfs §152), whereas the palatalization before *a* is restricted to most of the Gallo-Romance and Rhaeto-Romance areas. The stages in this complex evolution have not been conclusively established. While it is generally assumed that a palatalized *k* moves to *ki̯,* perhaps at the end of the third century, which subsequently is fronted to *ti̯,* it is not entirely clear why this stage is superseded by [*tš*] in some regions and by *ts* in others. The chronology of the two waves of palatalization, before *i, e* and before *a,* is uncertain, the conditioning factors are elusive, and the lack of a parallelism between *k* and *g* further complicates the task of theoreticians. Lausberg (§313) seeks the point of departure of the palatalization of *k* before *i, e* in the formation of a *ki̯* cluster, arising when *i* loses its syllabic value in hiatus as in *bracchiu, faceam, facio* (Lausberg §§310–327; Tagliavini, pp. 196–197; Rheinfelder, pp. 159–164; Iordan-Manoliu §§170–180).

234. Lat. *c-* + *i, e*

[*tš*]: Rm., It., *picard* dialect
ts > [*θ*]: Sp.
ts > *s*: Ptg., Cat., Occ., Fr.

Latin
cĕntu, cĕrvu

Rm.	It.	Sp.	Ptg.	Cat.	Occ.	Fr.
	cento	*ciento,*	*cento,*	*cent*	*cẹn*	*cent*
		cien	*cem*			
cerb	*cervo*	*ciervo*	*cervo,*	*cervo*	*cer*	*cerf*

Commentary
 The [*tš*] and *ts* stage may have been reached by the fifth century. The graph mostly remains *c,* however, which makes a precise chronology difficult to ascertain. Occitan may have been the pioneer in the reduction of *ts*

to *s,* judging from the not infrequent occurrences of an *s* graph: *sercar* for *cercar; sert* for *cert; siptat* for *ciutat; sest* for *cest* (Appel §44c). An occasional *s* graph is also found in Portuguese. Spanish has [*θ*], but *s* is common in many dialects and standard in New World Spanish. There are rare occurrences in Spanish of a palatalization to [*tš*] as in Italian: *cīcer* > *chícharo,* while such variants as *chervo* for *ciervo* and *chento* for *ciento* may be attributable to Moorish speech habits (García de Diego, p. 91). There are also sporadic occurrences of [*š*] in Catalan: *cīccu* > *xic; cīmĭce* > *xinxa* (Badía Margarit §67, II; B. Moll §99). The *picard* and *normand* dialects of northern France have [*tš*] as in Italian: *picard chele* = *celle; chent* = *cent.*

Sp. *cien,* Ptg. *cem:* these proclitic forms are normally found when the numeral is used adjectivally before a noun: *cien hombres,* but Sp. *cien* may also appear in pronominal function: *más de cien.* Proclitic forms are very common in Spanish: *un, algún, ningún, mal, buen, primer, tercer, san* < *santo* (Menéndez Pidal §78.1) whereas, in Portuguese, because of the relative strength of unaccented syllables, this feature is only sparsely represented. The few cases that are found mostly reflect Spanish influence: *cem* for *cento; são* for *santo; dom* < *dŏmĭnu.* Some occur only in fixed locutions: *mal tempo, a bel prazer,* or in toponyms: *Monsanto,* with *mon* for *monte; Valverde,* with *val* for *vale* (Williams §107).

Rm. *sută:* of the Latin cardinals only *centum* is abandoned in Rumanian; it is replaced by *sută,* which is very likely of Slavic origin (Nandris, p. 32; Iordan-Manoliu §275). A reflex of *centum* may have been avoided because it could lead to a confusion with *cinci* 'five' < VL *cinque.*

235. Lat. *c- + a*

          k: Rm., It., Sp., Ptg., Cat., *picard* dialect
k or [*tš*]:   Occ.
[*tš*] > [*š*]:   Fr.

Latin
capra, capu

Rm.	It.	Sp.	Ptg.	Cat.	Occ.	OFr.	Fr.
capră	*capra*	*cabra*	*cabra*	*cabra*	*cabra*	*chievre*	*chèvre*
cap	*capo*	*cabo*	*cabo*	*cap*	*cap*	*chief*	*chef*

Commentary

Before *a, k* remains intact in Rumanian, Italian, Spanish, Portuguese and Catalan while, in French, it palatalizes to [*tš*], which is later simplified to [*š*]. The northern regions of the Occitan domain, *limousin, auvergnat, dauphinois,* have [*tš*], whereas *k* is retained intact in Gascon, *languedocien* and other southern areas. The troubadours have both *ca-* and *cha-,* and *cha-* is present already in the earliest texts. The literary terms *chantar* and *chanso* are far more common than *cantar* and *canso,* even in texts which otherwise favor *ca-* (Appel §44c). The *picard* dialect retains *k: cambre* vs. Fr. *chambre* < *camera; cat* vs. Fr. *chat* < *cattu; Cambrai* < *Cameracu.* In some *picard* words the palatal influence is limited to the vowel while *k* itself is kept unchanged: *kief* = *chief* < *capu; keval* = *cheval* < *caballu.* The development of *causa* to *chose* in French throws some light on the chronology of the palatalization, offering proof that it must have taken place prior to the simplification of *au* to *o,* since *k* remains unchanged before a velar vowel. For the occasional voicing of *ca-* to *ga-,* see §236.

236. Lat. *c-* + *o, u*

k: Rm., It., Sp., Ptg., Cat., Occ., Fr.

Latin
cŏllu, cŏxa, cūlu

Rm.	It.	Sp.	Ptg.	Cat.	Occ.	Fr.
	collo	cuello	cǫlo	coll	col	col, cou
coapsă	coscia	coxa (old)	coxa	cuixa	coissa, cueissa, cuoissa	cuisse
cur	culo	culo		cul	cul	cul

Commentary

Overall, *k* is kept unchanged when preceding *o* or *u,* the only exception being a few occurrences of a voicing to *g,* which may also take place before the vowel *a* (§235). This development may have begun with Greek loanwords and seems chiefly to have affected words of non-Latin stock, from where it may then have expanded. Remaining a sporadic feature, voicing occurs mainly in three zones: Italy, the eastern and central Pyrenees with extensions into Occitan and Spanish, and in central and southern Sardinia (Rohlfs: *Estudios*, p. 152, n. 295): *camba* > Sd. *kamba*, Occ., Cat. *camba*, OSp. *cam(b)a* vs. It. *gamba*, Fr. *jambe; cŭbĭtu* > Rm. *cot*, Sp. *codo*, OPtg. *covado*, Cat. *colze*, Occ. *cobde, coide, covedo*, Fr. *coude* vs. OIt. *gombito*, It. *gomito; colaphu* > It. *colpo*, Cat. *cop*, Occ. *colp*, Fr. *coup* vs. Sp., Ptg. *golpe; cattu* > Fr. *chat*, Occ. *cat* vs. It. *gatto*, Sp., Ptg. *gato*, Cat., Occ. *gat*. Voicing of *k* may also occur in the initial *cr* cluster (§244).

Ptg. *cǫlo*: for the open *o*, see §148.

Fr. *col, cou*: French has drawn two separate words from the etymon *collu*: *col* is phonological while *cou* is drawn analogically from the plural *cous* < *cŏllos*.

OIt. *gombito*, It. *gomito*: the etymology being Lat. *cŭbĭtu*, the *m* is unexplained, but once adopted, it enters into an alternation with *mb*, which is characteristic of several southern and central dialects of Italy (Rohlfs §236).

Cat. *colze*: this form does not flow directly from Lat. *cŭbĭtu*, but reveals analogical influence of *polze* 'thumb' < *pŭlĭce* (Badía Margarit §97, I; Fouché: *Phonétique historique*, p. 138).

Sp. *cola*: VL *cōda* evolves regularly to *coa* in Old Spanish, while the modern form *cola* has acquired its *l* from a cross with *cūlu*.

237. Lat. *g- + i, e*

[*dž*]:	Rm., It., OPtg., OCat., Occ., OFr.
i̯ or ⌀:	Sp.
[*ž*]:	Ptg., Cat., Fr.

Latin
gēlu, genŭcŭlu, gĕrmānu

Rm.	It.	Sp.	Ptg.	Cat.	Occ.	OFr.	Fr.
ger	gelo	hielo	gelo	gel	gel		gel
genun-	ginoc-	hinojo	joelho,	genoll	genolh,	genouil	genou
chiu	chio	(old)	jeolho		ginolh		
			(old)				
	ger-	her-	irmão,	germà	german̦		germain
	mano	mano	germão				
			(old)				

Commentary

The velar pronunciation of *g* in Latin may be inferred from the same sources as for velar *k*. Sardinian keeps *g* unchanged: *gĕnĕru* > *gheneru*, and loan-words in Germanic and Basque have *g*: *genĭsta* > G. *Ginster; margĭne* > Basque *márgin*. Outside of Sardinian, *g* is palatalized, although the spelling remains unchanged. The palatalized *g'* merges with initial *i̯* and initial *di̯*, the stages in the palatalization process being *g* > *g'* > *d'* > [*d̆ž*] (Appel §44c). The affricate [*d̆ž*] is retained in Rumanian and Italian, but simplified to [*ž*] *in* Portuguese, Catalan and French. The Occitan pronunciation is difficult to determine, inasmuch as the coexistence of *fogir* and *fozir* and of *borges* and *borzes* (with *g* in initial-of-syllable position) points to a fluctuation between [*d̆ž*] and *dz*, but [*d̆ž*] remains the standard outcome (Anglade, p. 72; Schultz-Gora §83). The most complex development is seen in Spanish, which has *i̯*, though offering many cases of elimination. In *hielo* < *gĕlu*, the yod generated by *g* is absorbed into the first element of the *ie* diphthong while, in *helar* < *gĕlare*, the yod is eliminated, since it would have been interpreted as the first segment of a *ie* diphthong that would be totally unjustified in unstressed position. The letter *h* is a mere graph added to *ielo* because of the reluctance to begin a word with the *ie* diphthong and extended from there to the forms containing a pretonic *e*. Most historical grammars list a dual outcome of initial *g* in Spanish, *i̯* being the norm before a stressed front vowel: *gypsu* > *yeso; gĕnĕru* > *yerno; gĕnte* > OSp. *yente* (Sp. *gente* is learned), while *g* is eliminated before an unstressed front vowel: *genĕsta* > *hiniesta; germanu* > *ermano* > *hermano* (Menéndez Pidal §38.3; Iordan-Manoliu §175). There are indications, however, that *i̯* represents the only phonological outcome of initial *g*, regardless of the stress pattern; the *Glosas de Silos* have *iermano*, and there is documentation for this same form in Burgos and Santander. The loss of yod would thus seem to be analogical rather than phonological in nature: *ielo* and *ielar* are made to conform to the standard pattern of *tierra* and *terreno* (García de Diego, pp. 89–90).

The development of *g- + i, e* does not run parallel to that of *c- + i, e*. French and Portuguese have [*ž*] vs. *s*, and in Spanish where *g- + i, e* is not even assibilated, the opposition is between *i̯* and *∅*. Only Italian and Rumanian show a parallel development, resulting in a rigorous opposition between [*d̆ž*] and [*t̆š*].

Rm. *ger*, It. *gelo*, Fr. *gel*: the initial element of the *ie* diphthong is absorbed into the palatal.

Rm. *genunchiu*: the *n* of *gĕnŭculu* caused the nasalization of the vowel in preliterary times, while a subsequent trend toward denasalization resolved the nasal vowel as *un*. The resulting *n—n* sequence is kept in the word we have here, but it may also undergo a dissimilation to *r—n*: *canūtu* > *cănunt* > *cărunt* (cf. *mărunt* §185).

OSp. *hinojo*: *genŭcŭlu* yields the variant *enojo*, encountered in Berceo, while the change of pretonic *e* to *i* is attributable to the workings of the initial palatal. It soon proved impossible to keep this word separate from the plant name *fenŭcŭlu* (cf. Fr. *fenouil*) > *finojo* > *hinojo*, from which *hinojo* 'knee' took over the aspirated *h*. It is because of this homonymy that *hinojo* was replaced by *rodilla*, drawn from a diminutive of *rŏta* 'wheel': *rŏtula*, and with a suffixal change to **rŏtĕlla* > *rodiella* > *rodilla*. With the meaning of 'knee', *rodiella* is already present in Berceo and Juan Ruiz.

Ptg. *joelho*: in Portuguese, where intervocalic *n* drops, *genŭcŭlu* evolves to *jeolho*, which is subsequently metathesized to *joelho* (Williams §115.1).

Occ. *genolh*, *ginolh*: the initial [*dž*] may or may not close pretonic *e* to *i*.

OFr. *genouil*, Fr. *genou*: the modern form is drawn analogically from the plural *genouz*.

OPtg. *germão*, Ptg. *irmão*: *germão* represents the phonological norm, while *irmão* has been attributed to intervocalic treatment of *g* in the common combinations of *germão* with a preceding possessive adjective: *meu irmão* (Williams §62.4.B; Huber §227.1).

238. Lat. *g-* + *a*

	g:	Rm., It., Sp., Ptg., Cat.
g or [*dž*]:		Occ.
[*dž*]:		OFr.
[*ž*]:		Fr.

Latin
gallīna, gallu

Rm.	It.	Sp.	Ptg.	Cat.	Occ.	OFr.
găínă	*gallina*	*gallina*	*galinha*	*gallina*	*galina*	*geline*
	gallo	*gallo*	*galo*	*gall*	*gal,*	*jal*
					jal	

Commentary
Rumanian, Italian and Hispanic retain *g* before the vowel *a*, French palatalizes *g* to [*dž*], which is later reduced to [*ž*], while Occitan forms a transitional zone, with palatalization occurring in the northern areas, but not in the southern regions, which retain *g* unchanged. This parallels the treatment of *c-* + *a* (§235). In French *g-* + *a* and *g-* + *i, e* evolve in identical fashion, while no such merger occurs with *c-* + *a* (> [*tš*] > [*š*]) and *c-* + *i, e* (> *ts* > *s*). The *normand* and *picard* dialects of French do not palatalize *g* before *a*: *picard gueline* < *gallīna; gal* < *gallu; goie* < *gaudia*. Fr. *joie* < *gaudia* provides proof that the palatalization of *g* before *a* must have occurred prior to the change of *au* to *o*; cf. Fr. *chose* (§235).

OFr. *geline*: this form, which has survived only in north-eastern and eastern dialects, presupposes the existence of a conjectural **galīna*, since the palatal could not change a blocked *a* to *e* [ə] as seen in §196. Fr. *gélinotte* is a derivation of OFr. *geline*.

239. Lat. *g-* + *o, u*

  g: Rm., It., Sp., Ptg., Cat., Occ., Fr.

Latin
gŭstu, gŭtta

Rm.	It.	Sp.	Ptg.	Cat.	Occ.	OFr.	Fr.
gust	gusto	gusto	gosto	gust	gọst	gost	goût
	gotta	gota	gota	gota	gota	gote	goutte

Commentary
Retention of initial *g* before a velar vowel is the norm throughout.

It. *gusto*, Sp. *gusto*, Cat. *gust*: the continuation of *ŭ* as *u* is a learned feature. There is documentation in Old Spanish for *gosto* and *gostar.*

240. Lat. *i̭-*

  [*dž*] > [*ž*]:   Rm., Ptg., Cat., Fr.
        [*dž*]:   It., Occ.

i or ⊘:   Sp. (with front vowels and *a*)
[χ]:   Sp. (with velar vowels)

Latin
januariu, VL *jenuariu, jam, jŏcu, jŭgu, *jūgu*

Rm.	It.	Sp.	Ptg.	Cat.	Occ.	OFr.	Fr.
Ianu-arie	*gen-naio*	*enero*	*janeiro*	*gener*	*genier, ginier, janier*	*jenvier*	*janvier*
	già	*ya*	*já*	*ja*	*ja*	*ja, (des)ja*	*(dé)jà*
joc	*giuǫco*	*juego*	*jǫgo*	*joc*	*jǫc*	*jou*	*jeu*
jug	*giǫgo*	*yugo*	*yugo*	*jou*	*jo, jou*	*jou*	*joug*

Commentary
Generally speaking, initial i evolves like *g-* + *i, e*: Italian, Occitan and the early stages of Portuguese, Catalan and French have [dž], while [ž] is the norm for Rumanian and Modern Portuguese, Catalan and French. The only important difference between the i- and *g-* + *i, e* developments is to be found in Spanish, where i (or ⊘) is the outcome only before front vowels and *a*, while the initial yod of Latin moves via OSp. [ž] to [χ] before *o* and *u: jŏcu > juego; jūniu > junio; Jŏvis > jueves; jūdaeu > judío; jŭnctu > junto* (Menéndez Pidal §38.3). A dialectal explanation is proposed by García de Diego (pp. 90–91), who distinguishes between a *y* (yod) zone and a [ž] (> [χ]) zone: *yuncir* vs. *juncir; yugo* vs. *jugo*, while Lausberg (§333) suggests that only a careful study of each separate word can help us decide whether [χ] is dialectal or learned. The norm with learned words is [χ]: *junio, julio, juicio, general*, but it is not easy to determine whether *gente*, replacing an earlier *yent* or *yente* < *gĕnte*, is learned or is obtained from a dialect. While Spanish retains yod before the stressed vowels *i, e* and *a*, it tends to eliminate it if these vowels are unstressed. Lat. *jacēre* gives OSp. *azer* as opposed to *jacent* > OSp. *yazen*, but an analogical leveling soon generalizes the yod in the conjugation of this verb: *yacer* and *yacen*. This type of fluctuation does not affect the yod that precedes a velar vowel: *jūdĭcāre > juzgar* and *jūdĭcat > juzga*.

In Rumanian, initial *i̯* is continued as [*ž*]: *jūdĭco* > *judec; jūrāre* > *jurà,* but *dz* > *z* is the outcome before the vowel *a*: *jacet* > *zace* (Nandris, p. 159; Rothe §67). Lausberg (§331) draws *zace* from a dissimilation of the [*ž*]—[*tš*] sequence found in this word, but this seems very unlikely.

CL *januariu,* VL *jenuariu*: the change of initial *ja-* to *je-* is treated in §197. For the treatment of the *nu̯* cluster, see §340.

OFr. *desja,* Fr. *déjà*: after the medieval period, *ja* ceases to exist as an independent word in French. It is often encountered in the combination *de-ex-jam* > OFr. *desja* > *déjà,* it coalesces with *magis* to give Fr. *jamais,* and it survives in the adverb *jadis* < *ja a dis* lit. '(il y) a déjà (des) jours'. Sp. *jamás,* with its unusual [*χ*] (cf. *jam* > *ya*), is a borrowing from Occitan (García de Diego, p. 89).

OFr. *jou,* Fr. *jeu*: for this development, see *fou, feu* (§226).

Sp. *yugo*: this word is dialectal on two counts: it has yod instead of [*χ*] before a velar vowel, and it is drawn from an etymon with *ū* instead of *ŭ*.

Occ. *jo, jou*: in the combinations *-gu, -go* and *-cu, -co,* the consonant falls, and final *u* is usually retained in direct contact with the stressed vowel: *fagu* > *fau; lŏcu* > *lou,* but it may occasionally drop: *jou* and *jo;* the variant *joi* is unexplained (Appel §§42.a, 55d).

Fr. *joug*: the final consonant is purely graphical.

241. Lat. *h-*

     ø: Rm., It., Sp., Ptg., Cat., Occ., Fr.

Latin
hōra, habēre

Rm.	It.	Sp.	Ptg.	Cat.	Occ.	OFr.	Fr.
oră	ora	hora	hora	hora	ora	ore	heure
aveà	avere	haber	haver	haver	aver	aveir	avoir

Commentary

H was not pronounced in Latin and therefore was not continued in Romance. Proof of the fact that *h* did not represent any sound in Vulgar Latin may be found in the frequent omission of *h* in inscriptions: *abere* for *habere; onoravit* for *honoravit; omo* for *homo,* as well as in the addition of *h* by hypercorrection, which is to say in cases where it is etymologically unjustified: *hornatus* for *ornatus; habundans* for *abundans.* The influence of Latin spelling has led to the frequent reintroduction of a purely graphical *h* in Romance: Sp. *hombre, honrar, haber*; Ptg. *homen, honrar, haver;* Fr. *homme, honorer.* Italian usually avoids this scribal practice: *uomo, onorare, avere.* Occitan has *honor* and *onor;* *hom* and *om* in random fashion, and it may even extend *h* unetymologically: *hira* for *ira* < *īra; huelh* for *uelh* < *ŏcŭlu.* Whenever Latin *h* is represented graphically in Romance, it is important to bear in mind that it carries no phonetic value. Fr. *l'homme* and *les hommes* are treated like *l'ami* and *les amis,* both nouns beginning phonetically with a vowel. In Fr. *huit* < *ŏcto; huis* < *ūstiu; huître* < *ŏstrea,* the unetymological *h* may serve the purpose of protecting the vocalic initial against any confusion with the consonant *v,* both the vowel and the consonant being represented graphically in Latin by *u. H* is not reintroduced where the etymology had ceased to be clearly perceived: Sp. *invierno* < *hībĕrnu;* Sp. *asta* < **hasta* (but cf. Ptg. *hasta*).

242. Gmc. *h-*

ø:	It., Sp., Ptg., Cat., Occ.
h > *ø*:	Fr.

Latin
VL **hanka,* VL **harpa*

It.	Sp.	Ptg.	Cat.	Occ.	Fr.
anca	*anca*	*anca*	*anca*	*anca*	*hanche*
arpa	*arpa*	*harpa*	*arpa*	*arpa*	*harpe*

Commentary
The aspirated *h* that came into French through Frankish borrowings was dropped from pronunciation in the seventeenth century, but has still kept a trace of its consonantal value as seen from its ability to prevent elision and linking: *le héros* and *les héros* vs. *l'homme* and *les hommes.* Loanwords from French lose the Germanic *h* in the other Romance tongues: It., Sp., Ptg., Cat., Occ. *anca,* although occasionally *h* may persist graphically: Ptg. *harpa.* The only exception here is Spanish, where the aspirated *h* could merge with the *h* obtained from initial *f* (§226); the graph is either *f* or *h* in such cases: Frk. **haunitha* > Fr. *honte* > OSp. *fonta;* Frk. **hapja* > Fr. *hache* > Sp. *hacha.* Generally speaking, Rumanian has no Germanic borrowings.

Consonant Clusters

243. Nature of Consonant Clusters

Initial clusters are formed with *r, l,* yod or wau as the second element, or they consist of *s* and a consonant. It is debatable whether [k^w] and [g^w] represent a single consonant or a cluster; they are treated here as complex sounds consisting of an occlusive and a bilabial fricative. Non-Latin clusters are *h* plus consonant in Frankish words and *ps, pt, pn* in words of Greek origin.

244. Consonant + *r*

no change: Rm., It., Sp., Ptg., Cat., Occ., Fr.

Latin

bracchiu, crēdĕre, frēnu, grŏssu, prātu, trahĕre, VL **tragĕre, trēs*

Rm.	It.	Sp.	Ptg.	Cat.	Occ.	OFr.	Fr.
braţ	*braccio*	*brazo*	*braço*	*braç*	*bratz*		*bras*
crede	*credere*	*creer*	*crer*	*creure*	*creire*	*creire*	*croire*
frâu	*freno*	*freno*	*freio*	*fre*	*fren*		*frein*
gros	*grosso*	*grueso*	*grosso*	*gros*	*gros*		*gros*
	prato	*prado*	*prado*	*prat*			*pré*
trage	*trarre*	*traer*	*trazer,*	*traure*	*traire*	*trere*	*traire*
			trager				
			(old)				
trei	*tre*	*tres*	*três*	*tres*	*tres,*	*treis,*	*trois*
					trei	*trei*	

Commentary

Initial clusters with *r* are retained unchanged. Initial *fr-* is kept in Spanish: *frŏnte > fruente > frente,* as opposed to the loss of single *f* in initial position, and the *b* of *br* is treated like the single *b* in Spanish. The *cr* cluster may occasionally be voiced, chiefly in words of Greek origin, paralleling a similar development of initial *c* before *a* or a velar vowel (§§235, 236): *crypta >* It. *grotta,* Sp., Ptg., Cat. *gruta,* Occ. *crota,* Fr. *grotte; crēta >* Rm. *cretă,* It. *creta,* Sp., Ptg., Cat., Occ. *greda,* Fr. *craie; crassu >* Rm., Occ., Fr. *gras,* It., Ptg. *grasso,* Sp. *graso.* Lat. *crassu* was probably influenced in its evolution by *grŏssu,* with which it was closely associated (cf. Fr. *gros et gras*).

Lat. *crēdĕre*: the unstressed *-ĕre* infinitive is not continued in Spanish and Portuguese; for this area, therefore, the etymon is a hypothetical **crēdĕre.*

Lat. *trahĕre, *tragĕre, *tracĕre*: Sp. *traer* follows regularly from CL *trahĕre,* with the usual shift to a stressed infinitive ending. Since *h* falls early, *traere* loses a syllable, but doubles the *r* through compensatory lengthening to give It. *trarre* (Rohlfs §228). A hypothetical **tragĕre,* built on *agĕre,* is the source of the Rumanian and Gallo-Romance developments. OPtg. *trager* seems likewise drawn from a **tragĕre* base, but may be learned while *trazer* is the popular form. It is drawn from **tracēre,* which is obtained analogically from *placēre* > *prazer* (Williams §200; Huber §378.27), both displaying the stressed infinitive ending characteristic of Hispanic. **Tracēre* is also the etymon required for Cat. *traure* since *ur* reflects a secondary *c'r* cluster and cannot go back to *gr* (§§291, 294): *cŏquĕre* > *cŏcĕre* > *coure; nŏcĕre* > *noure; placĕre* > *plaure* (B. Moll §153; Badía Margarit §95, II).

Lat. *trēs*: this numeral, which is invariable in Latin, develops a nominative in Old French simply through the removal of final *s,* considered an anomaly in the nominative plural. In Occitan, where the removal of *s* would have given **tre,* the *trei—tres* flexion is modeled on *dui (doi)—dos* 'two' (Schultz-Gora §111; Anglade, p. 53; Jensen: *Provençal Philology,* pp. 56–57). This case distinction affects the masculine only.

It. *tre*: in monosyllables, final *s* usually becomes *i̯* in Italian (§357). Given this rule, one would have expected *trēs* to evolve to **trei.* Rohlfs (§308) suggests that the *s* of *tres* may have led to the doubling of a following consonant as in *trēs *cani* > *tre ccani.*

245. Consonant + *l*

These initial clusters are kept unchanged in Gallo-Romance and Catalan, while palatalizations occur in Italian and Hispanic. The palatalization process may have started in the velar clusters *cl* and *gl,* judging from the fact that it does not move beyond that group in Rumanian. Hispanic limits palatalization to the voiceless consonants. These developments are outlined in the following chart:

Lat.	pl-	bl-	fl-	cl-	gl-
Rm.	pl	bl	fl	ki̯	gi̯
It.	pi̯	bi̯	fi̯	ki̯	gi̯
Sp.	l'	bl	l'	l'	l'
Ptg.	[š]	br	[š]	[š]	l
Cat.	pl	bl	fl	cl	gl
Occ.	pl	bl	fl	cl	gl
Fr.	pl	bl	fl	cl	gl

246. Lat. *pl-*

> *pl*: Rm., Cat., Occ., Fr.
> *pi̯*: It.
> *l'*: Sp.
> [š]: Ptg.

Latin
plānu, plĭcāre

Rm.	**It.**	**Sp.**	**Ptg.**	**Cat.**	**Occ.**	**Fr.**
piano	llano	chão, lhano	pla	plan̩	plain	
plecà	piegare	llegar	chegar	plegar	plegar	ployer, plier

Commentary
Initial *pl-* evolves to *pi̯* in Italian, to a palatal *l* in Spanish and to [š] in Portuguese, but suffers no change in Rumanian, Catalan and Gallo-Romance. While the norm for Spanish is a palatal *l*: *plaga* > *llaga*; *plēnu* > *lleno*; *planta* > *llanta*; *plōrāre* > *llorar*, several learned words preserve *pl*: *plangĕre* > *plañir*; *platea* > *plaza*; *plūma* > *pluma*; *plŭmbu* > *plomo*; *placēre* > *placer* (Menéndez Pidal §39.2). Similarly, [š] as the phonological outcome in Portuguese: *plaga* > *chaga*; *plūs* > OPtg. *chus*; *plantāre* > *chantar*; *plŭmbu* > *chumbo*, is flanked by a semi-learned development of *pl-* to *pr-*: *placēre* > *prazer*; *platea* > *praça* (Williams §67.5; Huber §163).

Ptg. *chão, lhano*: *chão* represents the phonological outcome while *lhano*, with its palatal *l* and the retention of intervocalic *n*, is a borrowing from Spanish.

Fr. *ployer, plier*: the phonological outcome of *plĭcāre* and *plĭcat* is *ployer* and *ploie*, while the variant *plier* is an analogical formation modeled on *prier*. **Prĕcāre* evolves to *proyer*, the stem-stressed form **prĕcat* to *prie*. The vocalic alternation or apophony displayed by *prie—proyer* is leveled out through the generalization of *i*: *prie—prier*, and *plier* represents an offshoot of this process (Nyrop I §112).

247. Lat. *bl-*

bl:	Rm., Sp., Cat., Occ., Fr.
bi̯:	It.
br:	Ptg.

Latin
blasphemare, blastimare, *blanku, blandu

Rm.	It.	Sp.	Ptg.	Cat.	Occ.	OFr.	Fr.
bles-temà	biasi-mare	lastimar	lasti-mar, brasfa-mar (old)	blasmar	blasmar	blasmer	blâmer
	bianco	blanco	branco	blanc	blanc		blanc
blând	blando	blando	brando		blan	blant	

Commentary

Initial *bl* gives *bi̯* in Italian, changes to *br* in Portuguese and remains intact elsewhere. Convinced that the two voiced clusters *bl* and *gl* develop in identical fashion, dropping the occlusive, Lausberg (§341) concludes that the phonological norm for Spanish and Portuguese is the reduction of *bl* to *l*, but this rule seems essentially inferred from a single example, the mysterious and obscure Sp., Ptg. *lastimar*. Portuguese offers no further occurrences of the reduction of *bl* to *l*, the regular outcome here being *br* (Williams §67.1), while *blasfemar* is a learned word. For Spanish the rule, as stated by Menéndez Pidal (§39.3), is that *bl* is kept unaltered. Combining these two rules, García de Diego (p. 108) operates with two different outcomes of initial *bl*: retention or simplification to *l,* but the only other instance of *l* that he is able to cite, aside from an unreliable toponym, is *ladilla* 'crab louse' which he relates to *blatta* 'moth', espousing a hypothesis formulated by Meyer-Lübke. This etymology is in error, however, and has been abandoned by Meyer-Lübke himself who, in *REW* 4935, gives the correct source as *latĕlla,* a diminutive of the adjective *latus* 'broad', the latter continued in Medieval Spanish and Portuguese as *lado.* The name refers to the flattened aspect of the insect (Corominas III 553). A major drawback of the simplification rule is that it would make popular Spanish words with initial *bl,* such as *blanco* and *blando,* borrowings or Latinisms.

Lat. *blastimāre*: Meyer-Lübke attributes this variant of *blasphemāre* to a contamination by *aestimāre,* while Corominas (III 552) explains it phonologically as having resulted from a dissimilation of the two labials *f* and *m.*

It. *biaisimare*: this is a borrowing from OFr. *blasmer,* with *i* inserted in order to break up the unfamiliar *sm* cluster; a similar example may be seen in It. *medesimo* < OFr. *medesme* (Rohlfs §338).

Sp. *blanco,* Ptg. *branco*: the etymological source is VL **blancu,* from Gmc. **blank* (cf. G. *blank* 'shining, bright, polished'), which has replaced the Classical Latin color adjective *albus.* It is, however, a generally held belief that the Hispanic forms are borrowed from Gallo-Romance (Meyer-Lübke: *REW* 1152; von Wartburg: *FEW* I 398; Corominas I 598), although Sp. *blanco* makes its appearance as early as in the *Cid.* This assumption has in all likelihood been generated by Cuervo who, in his *Diccionário* (I 881–884), voices the opinion that the retention of *bl* points to a late borrowing. Curiously enough, Corominas does not take issue with Cuervo's statement although elsewhere (cf. *ladilla* above) he dispenses great energy on discrediting the data García de Diego has assembled in support of his claim that *bl* is regularly reduced to *l* in Spanish. Since the reduction of *bl* to *l* is unsupported by evidence, I conclude that Gmc. **blank* was very generally accepted into Vulgar Latin, with direct reflexes occurring in Italian, Hispanic and Gallo-Romance. This early and decisive victory of **blancu* garners further support in the scant traces left in Romance of the Classical Latin adjective *albus,* which has survived only in Rm. *alb,* Sd. *alvu* and Ptg. *alvo.* Though documented as early as 929 and appearing in a few archaic texts, Sp. *albo* is merely a Latinism or a poetic lexical item, and a popularly developed *obo* (cf. *alteru* > Sp. *otro*) seems confined to toponymy: *Torroba.*

Fr. *blanc*: the loss of final *k* from pronunciation follows analogically from the plural **blancos,* where *k* drops between two consonants.

It. *blando*: this word is learned and clearly non-Tuscan (Rohlfs §177). OFr. *blant*: the disappearance of this lexical item from French may be linked to the success of *blanc,* since the two words would merge phonetically with the elimination of the final consonant from pronunciation.

248. Lat. *fl-*

fl:	Rm., Cat., Occ., Fr.
fi̯:	It.
l':	Sp.
[*š*]:	Ptg.

Latin
flamma, flōre

Rm.	It.	Sp.	Ptg.	Cat.	Occ.	OFr.	Fr.
flamă	*fiamma*	*llama*	*chama*	*flama*	*flama*	*flame*	*flamme*
floare	*fiore*	*flor*	*flor*	*flor*	*flǫr*	*flor,*	*fleur*
						flour,	
						flur	

Commentary
Initial *fl-* is continued as *fi̯* in Italian, yields a palatal *l* in Spanish, moves to [*š*] in Portuguese and is left unchanged in Rumanian, Catalan and Gallo-Romance.

It. *fiamma,* Fr. *flamme*: the geminate *m* is retained in Italian whereas in French it is a mere Latinizing graph.

Sp., Ptg. *flor*: the retention of *fl* is a learned feature, traceable to the pronunciation of the educated classes. The word is literary and is widely used in a figurative sense. Old Portuguese has the variant *frol,* which Williams (§115.3.A) believes obtained through metathesis. It may also have evolved through dissimilation: *flōre > fror > frol,* with *fr* as a semi-learned outcome of *fl;* cf. *flŭxu > Ptg. frouxo, froixo.*

249. Lat. *cl-*

ki̯:	Rm., It.

l': Sp.
[*š*]: Ptg.
cl: Cat., Occ., Fr.

Latin
clamāre, clāru, clāve

Rm.	It.	Sp.	Ptg.	Cat.	Occ.	OFr.	Fr.
chemà	*chia-mare*	*llamar*	*chamar*	*clamar*	*clamar*	*clamer*	*(ré)-clamer*
chiar	*chiaro*	*claro*	*claro*	*clar*	*clar*	*cler*	*clair*
cheie	*chiave*	*llave*	*chave*	*clau*	*clau*		*clef, clé*

Commentary

Rumanian and Italian have *ki̯*, Spanish has a palatal *l* and Portuguese [*š*], while the *cl* cluster is kept unaltered in Catalan and Gallo-Romance. Rumanian has *ki̯* here, and for *gl* it has *gi̯*. Since these are the only *l* clusters where a palatalization takes place in Rumanian, it is generally held that the palatalization process of initial *l* clusters began with these groups, from where it then spread to the other *l* combinations. The intervening stages between Latin and the Romance reflexes are largely conjectural, but we may assume that the initial step in the process was that of the palatalization of *l*. This palatalized *l* is kept in Spanish, while Portuguese palatalizes it further via [*tš*] to [*š*], and both languages drop the initial consonant. In Rumanian and Italian, where the initial consonant is kept, the palatal *l* loses its lateral component, leaving only *i̯*.

Rm. *chemà*: a *ia* diphthong arises in *clamat* > *chiamă* through the coalescence of the yod of the *ki̯* cluster with a tonic *a*, but if the *a* is pre-tonic, *i̯a* is weakened to *e*: *clamāre* > *chemà*. These developments thus lead to the creation of a *ia/e* apophony for this verb (Nandris, p. 71).

OFr. *clamer*: in Modern French, this verb has survived only in compounds: *réclamer, proclamer, déclamer.*

Sp., Ptg. *claro*: this word shows learned treatment in Spanish and Portuguese.

Fr. *clair*: the change from OFr. *cler* is merely graphical; cf. *ala* > OFr. *ele* > *aile.*

Rm. *cheie*: the development of Lat. *clāve* to Rm. *cheie* is quite complex. Since *a* is tonic, one would have expected it to remain (cf. *clamat* > *chiamă*), but the weakening to *e* may have come about through the combined workings of the preceding and the following yod, the latter added as a hiatus-separating device when intervocalic *v* falls (cf. *ŏve* > *oaie*).

Fr. *clef, clé*: the norm is for final *v* to desonorize: *clave* > *clef*, while it is eliminated if followed by a consonant: *claves* > *cles*, and hence a new singular *clé*.

250. Lat. *gl-*

gi̯:	Rm., It.
l:	Sp., Ptg.
gl:	Cat., Occ., Fr.

Latin
glīrōne, glīre, glēre, glande, glanda, glandine

Rm.	It.	Sp.	Ptg.	Occ.	OFr.	Fr.
	ghiro	*lirón*	*lirão*	*liron*		*liron, loir*
ghindă, ghindură	*ghianda*	*landre*	*lande*	*glan*	*glandre*	*gland*

Commentary
Rumanian and Italian have *gi̯*, Hispanic simplifies *gl* to *l*, while Catalan and Gallo-Romance retain the cluster unchanged. Examples that can be used for comparative purposes are extremely rare, since many words with initial *gl* are learned or have suffered various interferences. Among words receiving learned treatment are Lat. *gloria* and *globu*: It., Sp. *gloria*, Ptg. *glória* and It., Sp., Ptg. *globo*.

Lat. *glīrōne, glīre, glēre*: Classical Latin has *glīs, glīris*, but the uncertain quality of *i* may be inferred from the French reflex *loir*, which requires a *glēre* base. Lat. *glīrōne*, derived from *glīre*, has adopted the *-o*, *-ōne* noun flexion (cf. *latro—latrōne*).

It. *ghiro*: the *i̯* of *gi̯* has been absorbed into the tonic *i* (*ghii̯ro* > *ghiro*). Rohlfs (§353) explains the *o* ending as a morphological adjustment to the *o* class of nouns (cf. OIt. *fasce* replaced by *fascio*), but in view of the general spread of *glīrōne,* it is tempting to consider the Italian form issued from the nominative of this etymon.

Occ. *liroṇ,* Fr. *liron, loir:* the simplification of *gl* to *l* remains unexplained in these words, which could perhaps be borrowings from Hispanic. Fr. *liron* is extremely rare.

Lat. *glande, glanda, glandine:* The classical form is *glans—glandis,* which may be influenced by the feminine declension in *-a,* as witnessed by the Rumanian and Italian reflexes *ghindă* and *ghianda,* and which may also be replaced by a *glando—glandinis* flexion in Vulgar Latin.

Rm. *ghindă, ghindură:* the change of tonic *a* to *i* occurs when *a* finds itself lodged between a yod and a nasal; cf. *chrĭstiānu > creştin.*

Sp., Ptg. *lande,* Occ. *glan,* Fr. *gland:* these forms follow regularly from the classical *glande,* while *glandĭne* is the source of Sp. *landre* (Corominas III 574–575). Secondarily obtained *d'n* and *g'n* clusters change *n* to *r:* *sanguine > sangne > sangre,* and similarly for French: *ordĭne > ordne > ordre.* OPtg. *lândoa* goes back to a diminutive *glandŭla,* and Rheinfelder (I 191) suggests the same etymon for OFr. *glandre,* but *glandĭne* seems a likelier source.

251. Consonant and Semi-Vowel

A few initial clusters are formed with wau or yod as the second element: [*kʷ*], [*gʷ*] and *di̯.* Many scholars consider [*kʷ*] a single phoneme (Rosetti: *Istoria limbii române,* I, 1960, 61; Iordan-Manoliu §194), while others take it to be a cluster (Lausberg §§344–349). While it seems most logical to assume that [*kʷ*] is, indeed, one sound, I have for purely practical reasons opted to treat it under clusters. What matters in a philological presentation is above all the fact that [*kʷ*] is distinct from *k.* The development of [*kʷ*] depends on the nature of the following vowel. Initial [*kʷ*] does not occur in Latin before the vowel *u,* and in Vulgar Latin the labial element tended to be absorbed by the velar vowel *o.* This development is documented not only through graphs such as VL *cotidianu* for CL *quotidianu* and *como* for VL *quomo* < CL *quomodo,* but also through hypercorrections: *Merqurius* for *Mercurius, quonserva* for *conserva.*

252. Lat. [*kʷ*]- + *i, e*

[*tš*]:	Rm.
k:	It., Sp., Ptg., Cat., Occ., Fr.

Latin
quaerĕre, -ēre, -īre, quiētu, VL *quētu, qui, quĕm*

Rm.	It.	Sp.	Ptg.	Cat.	Occ.	OFr.	Fr.
cere	chiedere	querer	querer		querre, querer, querir	querre	(ac)-quérir
cet	cheto	quedo	quedo	quet	quẹt, quẹt	quei	coi
	chi	quién	quem	qui	qui		qui

Commentary

Before the front vowels *i* and *e*, [k^w] loses its labial component everywhere. This development takes place only after the single *k* had begun its palatalization course before the front vowels, leading it via *k'* and *t'* to [*tš*] and *ts*. A slot was thus left for [k^w] to fill, since the opposition between [k^w] and *k* had ceased to exist, but [k^w] simplified too late for any participation in the patalatalization feature, a notable exception being Rumanian, which has [*tš*] here: *ci* < *quĭd; cer* < *quaero; cet* < VL *quētu,* just as in the case of *k* before *i* and *e: ceară* < *cēra; cer* < *caelu* (Lausberg §346). It. *quindici* < *quindĕcim* is problematic, as one would have expected [k^w] to simplify (Rohlfs §163). To Lausberg (§345), *quindici* offers proof that the norm for Italian is the retention of [k^w]. The simplification process begins in the realm of pronouns, where CL *quod* would phonologically move to **co* in Vulgar Latin. This would pull along other pronouns: *quī* > *chi; quid* > *che,* and spread more generally from there. Based on a single example, this hypothesis is unconvincing. Unrelated to this issue is the fact that Italian possesses a secondarily obtained [k^w]: *eccu—ĭstu* > *questo; eccu—ĭllu* > *quello; eccu—hīc* > *qui.* In northern and northeastern dialects of French: *picard, wallon, lorrain,* a zone referred to by Lausberg (§345) as Belgoromania, [k^w] is retained before *i* and *e: quaerere* > *wallon* [*kwerí*]; *quindĕcim* > *wallon* [*kwēs*].

Lat. *quīnque* had been dissimilated to *cīnque* at an early stage in Vulgar Latin, hence Rm. *cinci,* It. *cinque,* Sp., Ptg. *cinco,* Cat., Occ. *cinc,* Fr. *cinq.* This dissimilation also affects *quīnquaginta,* which becomes VL *cīnquaginta,* continued in It., Cat. *cinquanta,* Sp. *cincuenta,* Ptg. *cinqüenta,* Occ. *cincanta,* Fr. *cinquante,* while Rumanian has an analogical *cincizeci* lit. 'five tens'.

Lat. *quaerēre, -ĕre, -īre*: this verb is encountered in Vulgar Latin as a member of the *-ēre, -ĕre* and *-īre* categories and is continued in all three forms in Occitan.

It. *chiedere*: the *d* may have been obtained through dissimilation, or the verb may have undergone the formal influence of *vendĕre, perdĕre* and *credĕre*.

Fr. *quérir*: this verb has survived in compounds only: *acquérir, conquérir.*

253. Lat. [*k*ʷ]- + *a*

> *k* or *p*:   Rm.
> [*k*ʷ]:   It.
> [*k*ʷ] or *k*:   Sp., Ptg., Cat.
> *k*:   Occ., Fr.

Latin
quando, quattuor, VL *quattor*

Rm.	It.	Sp.	Ptg.	Cat.	Occ.	OFr.	Fr.
când	*quando*	*cuando*	*quando*	*quan*	*can*	*quant*	*quand*
patru	*quattro*	*cuatro*	*quatro*	*quatre*	*catre*		*quatre*

Commentary
Rumanian simplifies [*k*ʷ] to *k* in by far most instances, the change to *p* being a somewhat isolated occurrence. Italian retains [*k*ʷ] unaltered, while Occitan and French simplify it to *k*. The dual outcome in Hispanic depends on the stress. If *a* is stressed, [*k*ʷ] is retained, as seen in the above reflexes of Lat. *quando* and *quattuor* as well as in *quāle* > Sp. *cual,* Ptg., Cat. *qual; quartu* > Sp. *cuarto,* Ptg. *quarto,* Cat. *quart.* When *a* is pretonic, the preceding [*k*ʷ] is simplified to *k*: *qualĭtāte* > Sp. *calidad,* OPtg. *calidade; quantĭtāte* > Sp. *cantidad,* OPtg. *cantidade; quattuordĕcim* > Sp. *catorce,* Ptg., Cat. *catorze. Qualidade* and *quantidade* of Modern Portuguese are regressive forms (Williams §69.2); the spelling *quatorze* is common. Cat. *qualitat* and *quantitat* are *cultismos,* which are often pronounced with *k* as a result of Castilian influence (B. Moll §177). Sp. *cuarenta,* Ptg. *quarenta* and Sp. *cuaresma,* Ptg. *quaresma* have sustained the analogical influence of Sp. *cuatro,* Ptg. *quatro.* The secondary [*k*ʷ], obtained from Lat. *co-* or

cu-, is treated in the same manner as the primitive [*k*ʷ]: Lat. *coagŭlat* > It. *quaglia,* Sp. *cuaja,* Ptg. *coalha,* Occ. *calha,* Fr. *caille.*

The treatment of initial [*k*ʷ] before the vowel *a* varies a great deal from one Romance region to the next. Some languages retain [*k*ʷ] intact, notably Italian and Hispanic. Where a simplification occurs, two avenues are open: the labial component can be sacrificed, leaving *k,* as in Gallo-Romance and under certain circumstances also in Hispanic as seen above, or the labial element can be retained, a rare and somewhat elusive process in Rumanian and Sardinian. By and large, Rumanian joins Gallo-Romance in simplifying [*k*ʷ] to *k: quando* > *când; quale* > *care; quam* > *ca; quantu* > *cât,* while the change to *p* in initial position seems limited to *quattuor* > *patru* and the related derivation *quadragēsima* > *păresimi* (Rothe §83). It hardly seems possible, given this fact, to take the development to *p* to represent the norm. Proponents of this theory (Lausberg §348; Rosetti I 77; Iordan-Manoliu §194; Nandris, p. 164) explain the many cases of *k* as having resulted from an early simplification of [*k*ʷ]. It is clear that the change of [*k*ʷ] to *p* is the rule in intervocalic position, where a syllabic division may have conferred greater independence on the labial component: *ĕqua* > Rm. *iapă; aqua* > Rm. *apă,* and [*k*ʷ] could conceivably be considered internal in such compound numerals as *douăzeci patru* 'two hundred and four'. Conditions in the *logudorese* dialect of Sardinian are similar in nature; in most words [*k*ʷ] evolves to *k: quando* > Sd. *kando; quāle* > Sd. *kale,* while the numerals 'four' and 'fourteen' show a change of [*k*ʷ] to *b: quattuor* > Sd. *battoro; quattuordecim* > Sd. *battórdighi.*

Sp. *cuando,* Fr. *quand*: Spanish represents the [*k*ʷ] sound graphically by *cu,* which is phonologically identical with the *qu* of Italian and Portuguese, while the *qu* of French is learned spelling.

Occ. *can*: Occitan reduces [*k*ʷ] to *k,* but the graphical representation fluctuates between *can* and *quan, catre* and *quatre,* etc. The forms in *qu* merely contain an archaic graph and do probably not reflect a different phonological outcome.

VL *quattor*: u̯ drops in Vulgar Latin when following a geminate or a consonant cluster.

254. Lat. [*g*ʷ]- + *i, e*

        [*g*ʷ]:   It.

        g: Sp., Ptg., Cat., Occ., Fr.

Latin
VL *werra, VL *wīsa, VL *widarlōn

It.	Sp.	Ptg.	Cat.	Occ.	OFr.	Fr.
guerra	*guerra*	*guerra*	*guerra*	*guerra*		*guerre*
guisa	*guisa*	*guisa*	*guisa*	*guiza*		*guise*
guider-	*galardón*	*galardão*		*gazardon,*	*guerredon*	
done				*guerredon,*		
				guizardon,		
				guierdon		

Commentary

Latin does not have an initial [g^w], but this sound, originating from Germanic w-, comes in with Germanic borrowings and thus does not affect Rumanian. Its treatment is roughly parallel to that of its voiceless counterpart [k^w], a notable difference being that Italian keeps [g^w], while [k^w] is reduced to k. Initial Germanic w-, unfamiliar to Latin speakers, came to be pronounced with an auxiliary g. The resulting sound [g^w] is retained in Italian before i and e, but simplified to g in Hispanic and Gallo-Romance.

Frk. *widarlōn: this Germanic term meaning 'reward' consists of widar, which marks reciprocity or exchange (cf. wieder, which may mean 'in return'), and lon 'payment, reward, recompense' (cf. G. Lohn). Romance speakers mistook lōn for Lat. dōnu 'gift', as evidenced in all the Romance continuations of this term.

It. *guiderdone*, Occ. *guierdon, gazardon*: these forms exemplify the common er—ar fluctuation. Occitan may have dropped the first d by dissimilation, while the standard development of intervocalic d to a voiced s may be observed in the other Occitan reflexes. The pretonic a present in some forms is obtained by vocalic assimilation.

Sp. *galardón*, Ptg. *galardão*: Hispanic has metathesized d and l. Corominas (III 29–30) derives the Hispanic forms from Goth. *wĭthralaun, but adds that widarlon would also be acceptable as etymon.

255. Lat. [g^w]- + a

[g^w]: It., Sp., Ptg., Cat.
g: Occ., Fr.

Latin
Gmc. and VL *wardôn, *wantu

It.	Sp.	Ptg.	Cat.	Occ.	OFr.	Fr.
guardare	guardar	guardar	guardar	gardar	guarder	garder
guanto	guante	guante	guant	gan	guant	gant

Commentary

Italian and Hispanic retain [g^w] unaltered. For both Occitan and Old French, it is not easy to determine whether the *gu* spelling is a mere archaic graph, or whether it indicates the retention of the *u̯* element in pronunciation. Considering the spellings *guarda* (v. 132) and *guarnit* (v. 56) in the earliest Occitan text, the *Boeci,* merely traditional, Appel (§44g) believes that *u̯* had fallen from pronunciation already in preliterary times. This is difficult to prove, and Rheinfelder (I 173) concludes, quite to the contrary, for Old French that the *gu-* spelling must have represented [g^w], at least until the middle of the eleventh century. Before *i* and *e,* the *u* spelling is not normally abandoned, although there certainly are cases in Old French of such spellings as *gerre* and *gise,* but even before *a, u* persisted in spelling for quite some time, as evidenced in the English borrowing *guard* from OFr. *guarder.* Germanic lexical items were not borrowed into Rumanian.

Gmc. *wardôn*: verbs of foreign origin were adapted to the Latin conjugation system. Most Germanic verbs ending in *-ôn* and *-an* joined the *-āre* conjugation: *wardôn* > It. *guardare*; *wîtan* > It. *guidare,* Sp. *guiar,* Fr. *guider,* while those ending in *-jan* were by and large absorbed into the *-īre* category: *warnjan* > It. *guarnire,* Cat. *guarnir,* Fr. *garnir.*

VL *wantu*: Gothic probably had the form *wantu,* which cannot be the direct source of Hispanic *guante* with its final *e.* Both *guante* and It. *guanto* are very likely Gallicisms (*DEI* III 1883), the Hispanic forms probably with Catalan as the intermediary in the transfer process. The word does not come into Spanish until the fourteenth century.

256. Lat. *di̯-*

[*dž*] > [*ž*]:	Rm., Ptg., Cat., Fr.	
[*dž*]:	It., Occ.	
i̯:	Sp.	

Latin
deōrsu, diŭrnu

Rm.	It.	Sp.	OPtg.	Cat.	Occ.	OFr.	Fr.
jos	*giuso*	*yuso*	*juso*	*jus* (old)	*jos*	*jus*	
	giorno			*jorn*	*jorn*	*jorn*	*jour*

Commentary

The initial *dị* evolves like initial *ị-* or *g-* before *i* and *e*. Italian, Old Portuguese and Old French have [*dž*], and it is generally assumed that the early stages of Rumanian and Catalan also had the affricate. A simplification to [*ž*] occurs in Rumanian, Portuguese and French as well as in Catalan, although here certain dialects still favor a [*dž*] pronunciation. In Rumanian, initial *dị-* is continued as *z* before the vowel *a*; this rule, however, seems based on a single example: *Diana* > *zână* (§228). Spanish has *ị*. Examples of this cluster are far from plentiful and are mostly restricted to learned words, in which *dị-* undergoes no palatalization or assibilation: *diabolu* > Rm. *diavol*, It. *diávolo*, Sp. *diablo*, Ptg. *diabo*, Occ., Fr. *diable*; *diacŏnu* > It. *diacono*, Sp., Ptg. *diácono*, OPtg. *diagoo*, Occ. *diague*, Fr. *diacre*. In the early Greek borrowing *zelōsu*, initial *z* merges with Lat. *dị-* in a popular evolution: Lat. *dielōsu* or *jelōsu* > Rm., Occ. *gelos, gilos*, It. *geloso*, Cat. *gelós*, Fr. *jaloux*. In later borrowings, *z* receives learned treatment, evolving to a voiced *s*: *zelu* > Rm., Occ. *zel*, It. *zelo*, Fr. *zèle*. Castilian unvoices *dz*, which then evolves from *ts* to [*θ*]: *celo* and *celoso*, and Portuguese has *zelo*, replacing an older *zeo*, while the adjective is *zeloso*.

dĕōrsu: the *e* in hiatus loses its syllabic value, becoming *ị*. Some reflexes show involvement with the popular *sūsum* for CL *sūrsum*, which accounts for the change of tonic *o* to *u* in Italian, Hispanic and Old Catalan, to [*y*] in Old French. The assimilation and subsequent reduction of *rs* to *ss* and *s* represents the phonological norm; cf. *dŏrsu* > It. *dosso*, Rm., Occ., Fr. *dos*. Sp., Ptg. *dorso* is learned.

257. Lat. *s-* + Consonant

      s or [*š*]:   Rm.
      s: It.

es: Sp., Ptg., Cat., Occ., OFr.
e: Fr.

Latin
schŏla, spatha, stēlla

Rm.	It.	Sp.	Ptg.	Cat.	Occ.	OFr.	Fr.
şcoală	*scuola*	*escuela*	*escola*	*escola*	*escola*	*escole*	*école*
spată	*spada*	*espada*	*espada*	*espasa*	*espada,*	*espee*	*épée*
(dial.)					*espaza*		
stea	*stella*	*estrella*	*estrela*	*estela*	*estela*	*esteile*	*étoile*

Commentary

Initial *s* before a consonant, the so-called impure *s*, remains intact in Rumanian and also, generally speaking, in Italian, but develops a prosthetic vowel *e* in Hispanic and Gallo-Romance, with the resulting *es-* combination retained in Spanish, Portuguese, Catalan and Occitan. In French, *s* having become internal, drops before a consonant, leaving only the prosthetic vowel. In Vulgar Latin, the *s* followed by a consonant began to acquire syllabic force, and this quality was given formal expression in writing through the addition before *s* of a vowel which, in Vulgar Latin, was usually *i*, but which becomes *e* in the western Romance languages, while Italian and Sardinian have *i*. In Italian, however, the occurrence of vowel prosthesis is limited to a few cases of syntactic phonetics, common prepositional phrases such as *per iscritto, in iscuola, in Isvizzera* vs. *lo scritto, la scuola, la Svizzera,* and Rumanian has no vestige of this feature at all. The consonants that form a group with initial *s* in Latin are *p, t* and *k*, and the earliest examples of vowel prosthesis occur, characteristically enough, in Greek borrowings with an unfamiliar *sm* cluster: *Ismurna* for *Smyrna,* found at Pompeii, and *Ismara(g)dus,* documented in Rome in A.D. 105. An examination of the eleventh-century Old French text, *la Vie de Saint Alexis,* reveals that the prosthetic vowel was used following a word ending in a consonant: *ad espous* (v. 66), *out esposede* (v. 237), but not after a vowel: *la spouse* (v. 102), *ta spouse* (v. 53). With the loss of certain final consonants, specifically *d* and *t*, the conditions for the use of prosthetic vowels become unclear, and as a result this phonological feature is generalized in the West. In Italian, the feminine article *la,* coupled with the creation of the article *lo,* used before the impure *s*, renders a prosthetic vowel needless in most instances. The prosthetic *i* of Italian is not an archaic feature continued from Vulgar Latin, but represents the normal development of pretonic *e* (§185). An isolated occurrence of *i* may be seen in Occ., OFr. *isnel,* a Germanic borrowing (< Gmc. **snel;* cf. G. *schnell*) with an *sn* cluster that was unfamiliar to Latin speakers.

Italian may drop the original *i* or *e* before *s* plus consonant: *aestimāre* > *stimare; *excadēre* > *scadere; Hispania* > *Spagna; historia* > *storia.* This follows analogically from the treatment of impure *s* in the language. In French, learned words carry no prosthetic vowel: Fr. *statue, spatial, scribe.* In Italian, initial *s* becomes voiced if it stands before a voiced consonant, but this change remains unexpressed graphically: *sventura, sbarcare, sdentato,* with *s-* stemming from the prefix *ex-* (Meyer-Lübke, p. 96; Rohlfs §189). Rumanian similarly voices the *s* of the prefix *ex-* if followed by a voiced consonant: **exvŏlāre* > *zburà; *exmŭlgēre* > *smulge.* Although voicing is the norm here, the spelling shows some hesitation between *z* and *s* (Nandris, p. 132). Before a voiceless stop, a strong trend is noted in Rumanian toward the palatalization of *s* to *ş: şcoală, şpital, şstafetă, şstatut* (Nandris, pp. 131–132).

Ptg. *escola,* Fr. *école:* the learned nature of this word may account for the retention of intervocalic *l* in Portuguese as well as for the non-diphthongization of tonic free *ŏ* in French.

It. *spada:* northern influence is evident in the voicing of intervocalic *t* (§267).

Occ. *espada, espaza:* in its normal evolution, intervocalic *t* voices to *d* in Occitan: *vīta* > *vida; catēna* > *cadena,* but it is not uncommon for it to move one step further, merging with the primitive *d* into a voiced *s: pŏtestāte* > *podestat, pozestat;* Frk. **wītan* > *guidar, guizar; mĕt-ĭpsu* > *meteis, medeis, mezeus* (§267).

Cat. *espasa:* this word is probably a borrowing from Occitan (Badía Margarit §10, II).

258. Gmc. *h* + Consonant

In Frankish borrowings into French, *h* (or the Germanic *ach*-Laut) may be preconsonantal. Such groups are simplified in various ways; the change of *hl* to *cl* occurs in a few proper nouns, while a later change of *hl* to *fl* and of *hr* to *fr* has left traces in the French lexicon: **hlank* > *flanc; *hrōk* > *froc.* In more recent borrowings, the unfamiliar grouping of *h* with *l, n* or *r* was alleviated through the insertion of an epenthetic vowel: **hring* > *harangue,* or through the elimination of *h: *hring* > OFr. *renc* > *rang* (Rheinfelder I 176–178; Lausberg §357).

259. Greek *pn-, ps-, pt-*
These initial clusters came into Latin with Greek borrowings. With only very few exceptions, these loan-words never developed popular reflexes in Romance. A reduction of *ps-* to *s-* and of *pt-* to *t-* may be seen in *psalmu* > Sp. *salmo,* Cat., Occ. *salm,* OFr. *saume; psaltēriu* > Sp. *salterio,* Cat. *saltiri,* Occ. *sauteri,* OFr. *sautier; ptisana* > Sp., Ptg., Cat. *tisana,* Occ. *tizana,* Fr. *tisane.* The original graph is often reintroduced, which usually brings back the pronunciation of the primitive Greek clusters in French: Occ. *psalm, psalteri,* Fr. *psaume, psautier.* Spanish has both *seudo* and *pseudo,* French only *pseudo,* and to Sp. *neumonía* corresponds Fr. *pneumonie.* The Greek clusters are retained in learned words: Sp. *psicología,* Fr. *psychologie.*

260. Special Developments
A few sporadic and unpredictable occurrences may interfere with the development of initial consonants or consonant clusters or lead to the addition or elimination of initial consonantal elements. Dissimilation has taken place in Persian *nāranğ(a)* > Ptg. *laranja* vs. Sp. *naranja;* CL *lībĕlla* > VL **lībĕllu* > OFr. *livel* (cf. E. *level*) > OFr. *nivel* > *niveau; memŏrāre* > OSp. *lembrar, nembrar,* Ptg. *lembrar; clavīcŭla* > **cavīcŭla* > Occ. *cavilha,* Fr. *cheville; flēbĭle* > Occ. *frevol, freble,* OFr. *feible, foible,* Fr. *faible.* The opposite trend is assimilation which, in the realm of initial consonants, is a rather infrequent feature: *cĭrcāre* > OFr. *cerchier* > *chercher; gloria* > OPtg. *groria.* The development of *jejūnu* to Cat. *dejú* may be explained as a case of consonantal dissimilation, or the word may have suffered the influence of the prefix *de-.* Metathesis occurs most often with the consonant *r: formaticu* > Fr. *fromage* vs. It. *formaggio; capra* > Occ. *cabra* and *craba.* Initial *l* may be mistaken for the definite article and consequently removed in a process known as deglutination: *lauribacca* > It. *orbacca; lusciniŏlus* > It. *usignuolo.* The reduction of OIt. *narancia* to *arancia* is usually explained as a case of deglutination of *n,* erroneously taken to be part of the indefinite article, but it seems likelier that the modern form may have arisen through haplology in the combination *una narancia.* The same change has also affected the outcome of *nāranğ(a)* in French: *orange.* Agglutination, or the addition of the article *l* to the beginning of a word, results from a false interpretation: *hĕdĕra* > OFr. *l'ierre* > *lierre; in de mane* > OFr. *l'endemain* > *lendemain; Insula (Căstrum)* > OFr. *Lisle* > *Lille.* Other cases of consonant addition may follow from a variety of sources, such as from a merger with the preposition *de: (poule)*

d'Inde > Fr. *dinde,* or from children's language: *amita* > OFr. *ante, anglo-normand aunte* (cf. E. *aunt*) > *tante.*

II. *INTERVOCALIC CONSONANTS*

261. The Lenition Feature

Traditionally, the Romance languages are divided up into an eastern group which keeps the intervocalic voiceless stops intact (Rumanian, Italian), and a western group which sonorizes them (Spanish, Portuguese, Catalan, Occitan and French). The dividing line between East and West based on this phonological feature runs approximately from La Spezia to Rimini. This cuts Italy into a southern-central section belonging to the eastern group, and a northern region whose dialects are aligned with the West. The term lenition refers to the weakening which the intervocalic voiceless occlusives *p, t, k* undergo in the western group of languages. Latin grammarians applied the term *fortis* 'strong' to the voiceless occlusives and the term *lenis* 'weak, soft' to the voiced, since they were cognizant of the fact that *b,* which is here taken to represent the voiced series, was pronounced with less muscular tension and with less energy than *p.* It was, in other words, perceived as being weaker than its voiceless counterpart. In some languages, the weakening may lead beyond voicing to fricativization or to complete elimination: *sapēre* > It. *sapere,* Ptg. *saber,* Fr. *savoir; vīta* > It. *vita,* Occ. *vida,* Sp. *vida,* Fr. *vie.* The diphthong *au* may in some areas close the syllable, thereby preventing lenition: *paucu* > Sp. *poco* (§155), and similarly with secondary *au* and *ai* diphthongs in Spanish: *sapui* > **saupi* > *supe; sapiam* > **saipa* > *sepa,* but intervocalic development is seen in *audīre* > Sp. *oír; causa* > OSp. *cosa,* with a voiced *s* in the old language. Aspiration is a lenition feature encountered in Pop. Tuscan: *sapēre* > *saphere; matūru* > *mathuro; sēcūru* > *sikhuro,* with *h* representing an aspirated pronunciation. Syntactic phonetics accounts for the weakening in Tuscan of consonants across word boundaries: *illa carne* > *la xarne* (with *x* pronounced much like Sp. [*χ*] or the German *ach*-Laut). Some areas of Gascony and Aragon form "archaic islands" (Lausberg §363), in which no lenition of intervocalic *p, t* and *k* occurs: *apértu* > Gasc. *aperto,* Arag. *apierto; spatha* > Gasc. *espato,* Arag. *espata; formīca* > Gasc. *rumiko,* Arag. *fornika* (Rohlfs: *Le Gascon,* pp. 130–137).

Sardinian presents a varied picture in its treatment of the voiceless occlusives. No lenition takes place in the *nuorese* and *gallurese* dialects, while sonorization and fricativization occur in *logudorese, campidanese* and *sassarese.* The *logudorese* and *campidanese* dialects have an unstable initial, which means that lenition occurs across word boundaries: *ĭpsa pĭra* > *logudorese sa ƀĭra* vs. *sa pira* in the central dialects (§373).

Single Consonants

262. Lat. -*p*-

p:	Rm., It.
b̵:	Sp.
b:	Ptg., Cat., Occ.
v:	Fr.

Latin
capĭllu, rīpa, apĭcŭla

Rm.	It.	Sp.	Ptg.	Cat.	Occ.	OFr.	Fr.
	capello	*cabello*	*cabelo*	*cabell*	*cabel*	*chevel*	*cheveu*
râpă	*ripa,*	*riba*	*riba*	*riba*	*riba*		*rive*
	riva						
	pecchia	*abeja*	*abelha*	*abella*	*abelha*		*abeille*

Commentary

Intervocalic *p* is retained in Rumanian and Italian, while it voices to *b* in Portuguese, Catalan and Occitan and moves to the labiodental fricative *v* in French. Spanish at first has the voiced occlusive *b*, but the pronunciation later changes to the bilabial fricative *b̵* (Menéndez Pidal §40). Lausberg (§367) dates this development to the sixteenth century, but since the graphical representation remains the same, it is quite difficult to establish a chronology for this change. There are a few words in Portuguese, in which Latin intervocalic *p* has moved beyond *b* to *v*: *pŏpŭlu > poboo > povo; scōpa > escova* (Williams §72.4.A). The loss of *p* in *sapūtu >* OFr. *sëu > su* does not follow from regular phonological development, as stated by Lausberg (§369), but is analogical from the past participles *dēbūtu > dëu > dû* and **habūtu > ëu > eu* [y], for while *b* drops intervocalically before a velar vowel, this rule does not apply to *p*: *tabōne >* Fr. *taon* vs. *sapōne >* Fr. *savon* (§263; Rohlfs: *Vom Vulgärlatein*, p. 149; Rheinfelder I 262). Though intervocalic in VL *capu, p* becomes final in its Gallo-Romance and Catalan development: *capu > *cabu >* Cat. *cap.* Such cases are treated under final consonants, even though the initial stages of the evolution are those of the intervocalic position.

It. *riva*: northern, Gallo-Romance influence is responsible for the change of intervocalic *p* to *v* in some Italian words: *recĭpĕre* > *ricevere; pauper* > *povero; epĭscŏpu* > *vescovo; *ex-seperare* > *sceverare* (Rohlfs §205).

It. *pecchia*: in this word, which appears sporadically in Tuscan and Neapolitan, the initial *a* of *apĭcŭla* has suffered deglutination, *l'a* having been erroneously perceived as the feminine article. This development changes *p* from intervocalic to initial, which makes no difference for Italian anyway, since *p* is retained in either position. The more common term is *ape*, which is present in all dialects.

Fr. *abeille*: the *b* instead of the expected *v* is an indication that the word is not native, but borrowed from Occitan.

It. *sceverare*: the initial [š] has evolved from the prefix *ex-*. While the widespread fluctuation between *ar* and *er* may conveniently account for the change of CL *separāre* to VL *seperāre*, it seems likelier that we have to do with yet another instance of the weakening or ablaut that affects Latin stem vowels when a prefix is added: *parāre* vs. **compĕrāre; aptus* vs. *ineptus; damno* vs. *condemno*. For the change of intervocalic *p* to *v*, see *riva* above. Occitan has *sebrar,* French *sevrer* (hence E. *sever*), while Fr. *séparer* is learned.

263. Lat. -*b*-

∅:	Rm.
v:	It., Ptg., Occ.
ƀ:	Sp.
v or ∅:	Cat., Fr.

Latin
faba, caballu

Rm.	It.	Sp.	Ptg.	Cat.	Occ.	Fr.
	fava	*haba*	*fava*	*fava*	*fava*	*fève*
cal	*cavallo*	*caballo*	*cavalo*	*cavall*	*caval*	*cheval*

Commentary
Intervocalic *b* and *v* merged throughout Romania, acquiring fricative pronunciation as early as the first century of our era, whereupon a labio-dental *v* evolved in Italian, Rumanian, Portuguese, Catalan and Gallo-

Romance, while Spanish developed a bilabial fricative ƀ (Lausberg §§366, 373; Iordan-Manoliu §§188–189). A fricative pronunciation ƀ is common in Catalan dialects. Intervocalic *b* and *v* drop in Rumanian: *caballu > cal;* **ŏvu > ou*, and in the *logudorese* and *campidanese* dialects of Sardinian: *caballu >* Sd. *kaḍḍu; nĭve >* Sd. *nie.* In French, *-b-* and *-v-* are continued as *v*, but they drop before a velar vowel: *dēbūtu > dëu > dû; tabōne > taon*, rarely when the velar vowel precedes and perhaps only as a dialectal feature: VL **nūba > nue* (Rheinfelder I 264). Catalan eliminates intervocalic *b* and *v* before a tonic *o* or *u*: *pavōre > paor > por; sabūcu > saüc.* In Occitan, intervocalic *b* often falls both before and after the vowels *o* and *u*, but this development is optional only: *abŭndāre > aondar, abondar; prŏbāre > proar, provar; sŭbĭnde > soen, soven.* Retention of *b* in *abondar* is learned or dialectal.

Rm. *aveà, avem, aveţĭ, avut*, etc.: in the reflexes of Lat. *habēre, habēmus, habētis, *habūtu*, etc., intervocalic *b* has not dropped, but shows a partial weakening to *v*. While the reasons for this deviation from the norm are unclear, it seems likely that the labial was not allowed to fall as this would have seriously reduced the phonetic substance of this very important verb. Rosetti theorizes that the change of *b* to *v* is phonological before *u*, and that *v* would then have spread analogically from *avut* to *aveà, avem*, etc. This is unconvincing since it is precisely before a velar vowel that *b* and *v* are most prone to elimination in Romance.

264. Lat. *-v-*

⊘:	Rm.
v:	It., Ptg., Occ.
ƀ:	Sp.
v or ⊘:	Cat., Fr.

Latin
lĕvāre, nŏva

Rm.	It.	Sp.	Ptg.	Cat.	Occ.	OFr.	Fr.
luà	levare	llevar	levar	llevar	levar		lever
nouă	nuova	nueva	nǫva	nova	nǫva	nueve	neuve

Commentary

The development is the same as for intervocalic *b:* elimination in Rumanian, *v* in Italian, Portuguese, Catalan and Gallo-Romance, *ƀ* in Spanish. French drops *v* before a velar vowel: *pavōne* > *paon; pavōre* > *paour* > *poour* > *peeur* > *peur,* while *v* is rarely eliminated when the velar vowel precedes (§263): *ŏvĭcŭla* > *oeille* > *ouaille,* with *-aille* representing a suffixal change. In Occitan, intervocalic *v* drops when standing before a velar vowel: *pavōre* > *paor; pavōne* > *paon,* and it may be eliminated optionally when the velar vowel precedes: *Provĭncia* > *Proensa, Provensa; nŏvĕllu* > *noel, novel.* Catalan follows Gallo-Romance in eliminating intervocalic *v* before a velar vowel (§263). Intervocalic *v* tended to drop in Vulgar Latin when part of the *-īvu* ending: *rivus non rius* (*Appendix Probi*), and the corresponding Castilian suffix goes back to this reduced form: *aestīvu* > *estío; vacīvu* > *vacío* (García de Diego, p. 95; Menéndez Pidal §43.2). The same development takes place in Portuguese: *aestīvu* > *estio; rīvu* > *rio.* Also in Portuguese, *v* has fallen between two *i*'s in *cīvĭtāte* > *cidade* (Williams §72.2.A). Elimination of *v* through dissimilation has occurred in *vīvĕnda* > *vīvanda* > Occ. *vianda,* Fr. *viande* and in *vīvaciu* > Occ. *viatz,* OFr. *viaz.* Occ. *vivatz* and Fr. *vivace* are learned. Graphical confusion between *b* and *v* is commonplace, specifically where the two consonants are pronounced alike. Latin inscriptions have *brebis* for *brevis,* and *nuve* is a frequent Old Spanish graph for *nube.* A fricative pronunciation of *v* is common in Catalan dialects.

Rm. *luà*: Lat. *lĕvare* yields a form **leuà.* The insertion of *u̯* serves to separate the hiatus which arises when intervocalic *v* drops (cf. *nŏva* > Rm. *nouă*), whereupon the resulting triphthong *eua* is resolved as *ua.*

265. Lat. *-f-*

Rules are difficult to write since Latin did not have an intervocalic *f,* except in compounds where it mostly evolves as in initial position, while intervocalic treatment is limited to cases where the notion of a composition is lost. In such instances, *f* is kept in Rumanian and Italian, it voices to *v* in Portuguese, Catalan and Gallo-Romance and becomes a fricative in Spanish. Like intervocalic *b, f* drops in Gallo-Romance before a velar vowel.

Latin
*defēnsa, -u, profĕctu, malifātiu, *refūsāre*

It.	Sp.	Ptg.	Cat.	Occ.	OFr.	Fr.
difesa	*dehesa,* *defensa*	*defesa,* *devesa*	*defensa,* *devesa*	*defesa,* *defensa,* *defes,* *deves*	*defois*	*défense*
profitto	*pro-* *vecho*	*proveito*	*profit*	*prof(i)ech*		*profit*
				malvatz	*malvais*	*mauvais*
	refusar, *rehusar*	*refusar*	*refusar*	*refuzar,* *reüzar,* *raüzar*	*rëfuser*	*ruser,* *refuser*

Commentary

Examples of the retention of intervocalic *f* in Rumanian and Italian are: *scrōfa* > Rm. *scroafă,* It. *scrofa; tūfa* > Rm. *tufă; trĭfŏliu* > Rm. *trifoiu,* It. *trifoglio.* Italian retains *f* in a few well-known Osco-Umbrianisms: *būbalu* > **bufalu* > *bufalo; būbŭlcu* > **būfŭlcu* > *bifolco; tabānu* > **tafanu* > *tafano; scarabaeu* > **scarafaiu* > *scarafaggio.* In Hispanic, the intervocalic *ph* of Greek loan-words usually undergoes a voicing which may be traceable to the Latin pronunciation *p* of Greek *ph*; the spelling fluctuates between *b* and *v*, specifically in Spanish where a fricative pronunciation *ƀ* prevails: *raphanu* > OSp. *rávano,* Sp. *rábano,* Ptg. *rábão; Stephanu* > OSp. *Estevan,* Sp. *Esteban; Christophoru* > OSp. *Cristóval,* Sp. *Cristóbal.* Catalan has *rave* and *Esteve.* Loss of *f* before a velar vowel has occurred in *profŭndu* which, with a prefixal change, is continued as OCat., Occ. *preon.* In Mod. Cat. *pregon,* a *g* has been inserted to separate the hiatus.

Lat. *defēnsa, -u*: the listed examples show initial treatment of *f*, while the voicing that has occurred in the variants Ptg., Cat. *devesa* and Occ. *deves* reveals a loss of the notion of compounding. The *ns* cluster was reduced to *s* in early Vulgar Latin, but Sp., Cat., Occ. *defensa,* Fr. *défense* owe their *n* to the influence of the verb *defĕndĕre.*

Sp. *provecho,* Ptg. *proveito*: the sonorization reveals early loss of the notion of composition.

Lat. **refūsāre*: Thurneysen draws this hypothetical form from a cross between *recūsāre* and *refūtāre,* while other scholars consider it drawn from *refūsum,* past participle of the verb *refŭndĕre* (*FEW* X 198–200; Corominas II 977).

266. Lat. *-d-*

d:	Rm., It.
đ or *ø*:	Sp.
ø:	Ptg., Fr.
ǿ or *z*:	Cat., Occ.

Latin
vĭdēre, audīre

Rm.	It.	Sp.	Ptg.	Cat.	Occ.	OFr.	Fr.
vedeà	*vedere*	*ver*	*ver*	*veer*	*vezer*	*veeir*	*voir*
auzì	*udire*	*oír*	*ouvir*	*oir*	*auzir*	*oïr*	

Commentary
Intervocalic *d* is retained in Rumanian and Italian, becomes a fricative *đ* or drops in Spanish, drops or becomes *z* in Catalan, evolves to a voiced *s* or is eliminated in a few cases in Occitan, while it falls very generally in Portuguese and French. Spanish shows a great deal of hesitation between a weakening arrested at the fricative stage and total loss of the dental. Many scholars have accepted the rule established by Meyer-Lübke (*Grammatik* I 382), in terms of which *đ* is the norm when *d* stands immediately after the stress: *nĭdu > nido; nūdo > (des)nudo; crūdu > crudo; vadu > vado; sūdat > suda,* except when it is placed between two *e*'s: *fĭde > fee > fe; vĭidet > vee > ve; pĕde > pie,* whereas it drops before the stress: *radīce > raíz; laudāre > loar; paradīsu > paraíso; cadēre > caer.* Exceptions are quite numerous, however. Some find their explanation in stress alternations: *cae < cadit* is analogical from *caer < cadēre, loas < laudas* from *loar < laudāre, sudor < sūdōre* and *sudar < sūdāre* from *suda < sūdat.* It is not clear why OSp. *hedo < foedu* is replaced by *feo,* and there is a strong possibility that *crudo, nudo, vado, nido* could be *cultismos,* since the old language has *crúo, núo, vao, nío* (García de Diego, pp. 96–98). The importance of stress in the development of consonants has thus not been convincingly proven with Meyer-Lübke's rule, since it suffers far too many exceptions. Menéndez Pidal (§41.2) states simply that "la D (i.e., intervocalic *d*) . . . vacila mucho." We have to do with a weak sound-law that was not carried

through, a development which seems to have somehow been curbed by learned reaction.

Fluctuations in the treatment of intervocalic *d* are not limited to Spanish, but they also extend into the Occitan-Catalan domain. In Occitan, the weakening of *d* via a fricative stage *đ* to *z* takes place during the literary period. The archaic *Sainte Foi* still has *d*: *audir* (v. 228) < *audīre; vedon* (v. 381) < *vĭdunt* while, in the *Boeci*, *d* is found alternating with *z* and with complete elimination, the latter basically a northern dialectal feature: *tradatiōne* > *tradazo, traazo* (Appel: *Chrest.* 105.57); *fīdāre* > *fidar, fiar* (ibid., 105.82). The change to *z* may be dated approximately to the twelfth century: *laudāre* > *lauzar; adōrāre* > *azorar; alauda* + *-ĭtta* > *lauzeta*. This late date accounts for the relative frequency of alternate solutions in the literary language: *vĭdēre* > *vezer, veder, ver; crūdēle* > *cruzel, crudel, cruel; *tradīre* > *trazir, tradir, trair; audīre* > *auzir, audir, auir*. Catalan scholars (B. Moll §111; Badía Margarit §70, II) relate the alternations in that language to the stress pattern: *d* drops early before unstressed vowels: *tĕpĭda* > *tèbea; nĭtĭda* > *nèdea;* it falls before the stress: *jūdaeu* > *jueu; sūdore* > *suor; crūdēle* > *cruel; redĭmĕre* > *reembre; laudāre* > *lloar,* but is more resistant when following the stress, where it is modified to *z*: *alauda* > *alosa; lampreda* > *llampresa*. Just as for Spanish, the importance of the stress pattern in this evolution is to be viewed with some reservation, however. It is clear that the Catalan lenition of intervocalic *d* parallels that of Occitan, moving via *đ* and *z* to elimination, and this makes it quite difficult to determine whether forms with *z* represent native developments or are borrowings from Occitan. Archaisms with *s* are common in thirteenth-fourteenth-century documents: *juseu, crusel, veser.*

Rm. *auzì*: a conditioned change in Rumanian, paralleling the development in initial position (§228), leads to the assibilation of intervocalic *d* via *dz* to *z* before the vowel *i*: *audīre* > *auzì; vĭdes* > *vedi* > *vezi*. This change has important morphological implications in that it creates stem alternations in the declensions of nouns and adjectives whose plural ends in *-ī*: *crūde* > *crud* vs. *crūdī* > *cruzi*. The primitive opposition *d/z* is changed later to *d/[ž]: cruji* (Nandris, p. 136).

Sp., Ptg. *ver*: this form has resulted from the contraction of an earlier *veer;* cf. OFr. *veoir* > *voir.*

Occ. *vezer* and *veire*, OCat. *veer* and Cat. *veure*: the alternate infinitives Occ. *veire* and Cat. *veure* come from *vĭdĕre*, which does not have intervocalic *d*, but a secondary *d'r* cluster which, in Occitan, evolves to *ir*, while the Catalan outcome is *ur* in this particular instance. The Catalan

200 A Comparative Study of Romance

treatment of the *d'r* cluster is lacking in uniformity as seen in §293. The final *e* is kept for support.

267. Lat. -*t*-

t:	Rm., It.
đ:	Sp.
d:	Ptg., Cat., Occ.
ø:	Fr.

Latin
vīta, prātu

Rm.	It.	Sp.	Ptg.	Cat.	Occ.	OFr.	Fr.
vită	*vita*	*vida*	*vida*	*vida*	*vida*	*vidhe*	*vie*
	prato	*prado*	*prado*	*prat*	*prada*		*pré*

Commentary
    Intervocalic *t* is retained in Rumanian and Italian, it sonorizes to *d* in Portuguese, Catalan and Occitan, becomes a dental fricative *đ* in Spanish and drops in French. The voicing of intervocalic *t* to *d* is not uncommon in Italian under the influence of northern dialects: *lītu > lido; spatha > spada; strāta > strada; scūtu > scudo*. In very popular pronunciation, Spanish may eliminate *đ*: *cantao* for *cantado; soldao* for *soldado*. Portuguese tends toward a fricative pronunciation of *d* in intervocalic position (Williams §74.1; Iordan-Manoliu §183); in a recent description of Portuguese pronunciation, Teyssier concludes that intervocalic *d* remains an occlusive in Brazil, but has become a fricative in Portugal (P. Teyssier: *Manuel de langue portugaise*. Paris: Klincksieck, 1984, 33). The intervocalic *t* of second-person plural verb forms in -*tis* drops in Spanish: *amātis > amades > amaes > amáis; partītis > partides > partís; amabātis > amábades > amábais*. In the thirteenth century, *d* is still present graphically; it drops in the fifteenth and, for the forms with proparoxytone stress, in the seventeenth century (Menéndez Pidal §107.1). Portuguese treats intervocalic *t* of these verbal endings in a similar manner, dropping *d* at the latest during the first half of the fifteenth century (Huber §190.1.Anm. 2; Williams §74.2.A). Early Old French still had the fricative *đ*: *vīta > vidhe* (*Vie de Saint Alexis*, v. 63).

It is not uncommon in Occitan for intervocalic *t* to voice early enough for this secondarily obtained *d* to participate in the change of Lat. *d* to *z*: *spatha* > *espada* and *espaza;* **wītan* > *guidar, guizar* and even *guiar; pŏtĕstāte* > *podestat* and *pozestat; metĭpsu* > *medeis* and *mezeis* (the variant *meteis* could flow from a **mĕttĭpsu* base) (Jensen: *Provençal Philology,* pp. 272–273). An early sonorization may also affect *t* in its Catalan evolution; merging with *d*, it drops: *patĕlla* > **padĕlla* > *paella; spatha* > OCat. *espaa* (B. Moll §110; Badía Margarit §69, III). Corominas bases his explanation on a different chronology; the *d* was already present in Vulgar Latin, which means that what we are dealing with here is the loss of intervocalic *d* and not that of intervocalic *t: graella* < *gradīcŭla* and not *craticula; quaern* < *quadernu* and not *quaternu;* OCat. *espaa* < **spada* and not *spat(h)a,* and he considers *paella* a borrowing from French.

If intervocalic *t* is followed by the vowel *i* from Lat. *ī* or by *ie* from Lat. *ĕ* in Rumanian, it assibilates to [*ts*]: *vītĕllu* > **vitiel* > *viţel.* The assibilation of *t* before *-ī* is a prominent feature of the plural formation in *-ī,* where it generates a stem alternation between *t* and *ţ: barbātu* > *bărbat* vs. *barbātī* > *bărbaţi; cognātu* > *cumnat* vs. *cognātī* > *cumnaţi; fratre* > *frate* vs. **fratrī* > *fraţi* (with loss of *r* through dissimilation).

Occ. *prada:* Occitan continues the plural form *prāta* of the neuter *prātum.*

Cat. *prat,* Fr. *pré:* in these developments, the dental has become final.

268. Lat. *-s-*

s: Rm., It., Sp.
z: OSp., Ptg., Occ., Fr.
z or ø: Cat.

Latin
causa, spōnsa, VL *isposa*

Rm.	It.	Sp.	Ptg.	Cat.	Occ.	Fr.
cauză	*cosa*	*cosa*	*coisa, cousa* (old)	*cosa*	*cauza*	*chose*
	sposa	*esposa*	*esposa*	*esposa*	*espoza*	*épouse*

Commentary

Rumanian keeps voiceless *s* unchanged: *casa* > *casă; mēnsa* > *masă; -ōsa* > *-oasă. Cauză,* with its voiced *s,* is learned, and similar cases of the sonorization of *s* in learned words are: *curiozitate, epizod.* In a conditioned development, Rumanian palatalizes *s* to [š] before *-i: -ōsī* > *-oşĭ; formōsī* > *frumoşĭ; rēsīna* > *răşĭnă.*

The norm for Italian is similarly to retain the voiceless *s,* while the languages of the western group sonorize it. Latin did not have a voiced *s* since, in intervocalic position, *s* had become *r* in a development known as rhotacism: *flos—*flozem* > *flos—flōrem; honos* (archaic)—*honozem* > *honor—honōrem.* Italian quite often voices intervocalic *s* under the influence of northern dialects; this parallels a similar development for the voiceless occlusives *p, t* and *k,* but the fact that voiced *s* receives no separate graphical representation may lead to a fluctuating pronunciation in some instances. Words that are part of the core vocabulary have a voiceless *s: asino, cosa, casa, mese, peso, naso,* and the same is true of such basic morphological features as verbal endings: *presi, offesi, misi, chiusi, chiuso, sceso,* and the suffixes *-oso: pietroso,* and *-ese: pistoiese, genovese* although, for this last suffixal group, some words carry a voiced *s: francese, cortese, paese.* A few past participles in *-so* are pronounced with a voiced *s: ucciso, fuso.* Verb forms, which are not easily subject to borrowing or to dialectal influence, represent the normal evolution, as do also basic vocabulary items. Where the voiced *s* gains the upper hand is in learned or borrowed words: *chiesa, battesimo, bisogno, lasagna, musica, paradiso, deserto* (Rohlfs §210).

Old Spanish distinguishes between a voiceless and a voiced *s,* the former spelled *ss* intervocalically and *s* following a consonant: *passar, mensage,* the latter spelled with a single *s: casa* (Menéndez Pidal §35 bis 1), but the voiced *s* becomes voiceless in the sixteenth-seventeenth century as a result of the Castilian desonorization (Lausberg §381). Spanish thus no longer has a voiced *s.* In Catalan, intervocalic *s* basically follows the same evolution as intervocalic *d* (§266): it is retained as a voiced *s* following the stress: *asinu* > *ase; *lausa* > *llosa; pausāre* > *posar,* while it tends to fall when it precedes the stress (B. Moll §112): *accūsāre* > *acuar; resīna* > *reina; rasōre* > *raor.* To Badía Margarit (§71, II), however, the loss of *s* is essentially a dialectal feature.

OPtg. *cousa,* Ptg. *coisa:* the modern form *coisa* is obtained through a dissimilation of the two velar elements.

Fr. *épouse*: tonic *o* gives *eu,* not *ou* in French (§150), and Fr. *époux, épouse* remains unexplained. Some scholars suggest that the influence of the language of the troubadours may have affected such words as *amōre* > *amour; spōnsu* > VL *isposo* > *époux; zelōsu* > *jaloux* (Rheinfelder I 25). That derivations such as *amoureux, épouser, jalousie* could have exerted an influence on the vocalism of the basic terms seems highly unlikely, as one would have expected the analogy to work in the opposite direction; cf. *calōrōsu* > OFr. *chaloureux,* which is replaced by *chaleureux* under the influence of *chaleur* < *calōre.*

269. Lat. *-r-*

r: Rm., It., Sp., Ptg., Cat., Occ., Fr.

Latin
pĭra, cara

Rm.	It.	Sp.	Ptg.	Cat.	Occ.	OFr.	Fr.
parǎ	*pera*	*pera*	*pera*	*pera*	*pera*	*peire*	*poire*
	cara	*cara*	*cara*	*cara*	*cara*	*chiere*	*chère*

Commentary
Intervocalic *r* remains throughout, although the pronunciation may vary. Modern French has a uvular *r,* but that the French *r* was pronounced much farther front in the medieval language may be inferred from the insertion of dentals as glides in clusters containing *r*: **essĕre* > OFr. *estre; cinĕre* > Fr. *cendre.* In a few instances, intervocalic *r* is assimilated to *n* in Rumanian: *cŏrōna* > *cununǎ; sērēnu* > *senin.* The loss of *r* in *farīna* > *fǎīnǎ* can possibly be accounted for through an assimilation to **fǎnī-nǎ* followed by a dissimilation.

270. Lat. *-l-*

r: Rm.
l: It., Sp., Cat., Occ., Fr.
ø: Ptg.

Latin
mŏla, vŏlāre, sōle, sōlĭcŭlu

Rm.	It.	Sp.	Ptg.	Cat.	Occ.	OFr.	Fr.
moară	*mola*	*muela*	*mó*	*mola*	*mola*	*muele*	*meule*
	volare	*volar*	*voar*	*volar*	*volar*		*voler*
soare	*sole*	*sol*	*sol*	*sol*	*sol,*		
					solelh	*souleil*	*soleil*

Commentary

Intervocalic *l* is generally kept, but it drops in Portuguese: *colŏbra* > *coovra* > *cobra; caelu* > *céu; palātiu* > *paaço* > *paço; dŏlōre* > *door* > *dor; salīre* > *sair.* Portuguese keeps *l* in learned words: *calōre* > *calor; schŏla* > *escola,* and in many instances regressive forms with *l* have re- placed popular words: *sĭlĕntiu* > *seenço* and *silêncio; zēlu* > *zeo* and *zelo; dŏlōrōsu* > *doroso* and *doloroso.* Other occurrences of the preservation of *l* have to be considered separately: *pêlo* < *pĭlu* may have been influenced by *cabelo* < *capĭllu,* where *l* represents the normal outcome of double *l, palavra* < *parabŏla* may be a borrowing from Spanish, etc. (Williams §75.1, Huber §251). Resulting from an instance of syntactic phonetics, the Portuguese definite articles *o, a* and *os, as* are derived from *lo, la, los, las* which, when preceded by *de* or *a,* contain an *l* in intervocalic position, since articles are not independently stressed. In another noteworthy Ro- mance development, Rumanian changes intervocalic *l* to *r: fīlu* > *fir; pūlĭce* > *purece; caelu* > *cer; scala* > *scară; salīre* > *sărì.* This devel- opment occurs prior to final-vowel loss as seen in *fir* and *cer,* while Portu- guese retains the *l* of *sol* < *sōle* and *mal* < *male,* because it had become final.

It. *mola*: this word reveals learned treatment in its stressed vowel, which should have diphthongized (§151).

Ptg. *mó*: when tonic *ŏ* comes into hiatus with final *a* through the loss of intervocalic *l,* the final vowel is assimilated and then absorbed into the tonic open *o: mŏla* > *moo* > *mó.* This development does not take place if it is an intervocalic *n* that drops, since nasalization closes *ǫ* to *o̧: bŏna* > *bõa* > *bǫa* (Williams §45.2).

Occ. *sol, solelh*: the diminutive form may have been chosen in order to add more phonetic substance to the monosyllable *sol.* There is further the possibility that the speakers may have felt a need to keep *sol* 'sun' < *sōle* differentiated from *sǫl* 'alone' < *sōlu,* or the diminutive form may have been chosen simply for its affective value.

271. Lat. *-m-*

> *m*: Rm., It., Sp., Ptg., Cat., Occ., Fr.

Latin
amōre, clamāre

Rm.	It.	Sp.	Ptg.	Cat.	Occ.	OFr.	Fr.
amore	*amor*	*amor*	*amor*	*amor*			*amour*
chemà	*chia-*	*llamar*	*chamar*	*clamar*	*clamar*	*clamer*	*(ré)-*
	mare						*clamer*

Commentary

Intervocalic *m* is kept throughout. Nasalization of the preceding vowel may occur infrequently in French, but is abandoned later, as in *pōma* > *pomme;* for details, see §179. If *m* becomes final in French, nasalization is the norm: *hŏmo* > *on.*

Fr. *amour*: for the irregular development of the tonic vowel, see §§150, 268.

272. Lat. *-n-*

> *n*: Rm., It., Sp., Cat., Occ., Fr.
> ∅: Portuguese

Latin
bŏna, lāna

Rm.	It.	Sp.	Ptg.	Cat.	Occ.	OFr.	Fr.
bună	*buona*	*buena*	*boa*	*bona*	*bona*	*bone*	*bonne*
lână	*lana*	*lana*	*lã,*	*llana*	*lana*		*laine*
			lāa				
			(old)				

Commentary

Intervocalic *n* is kept everywhere, with the exception of Portuguese where it nasalizes the preceding vowel. The nasalization is either abandoned later: *lūna > lūa > lua; cŏrōna > corōa > coroa; persōna > pessoa,* or it is retained, notably where the two vowels that come into contact are identical: *lana > lāa > lā; bŏnu > bōo > bom,* or where a nasal diphthong arises: *mānu > mão.* For details, see §180, and see Williams §78 and Huber §244. Nasalization in French follows the same pattern as for *-m-* above: it is inceptive and soon abandoned where *n* is intervocalic, but remains if *n* becomes final: *dōnu > don; ūnu > un.* The loss of intervocalic *n* in *grānu* > Rm. *grâu* and *frēnu* > Rm. *frâu* remains unexplained.

273. Lat. *-k-* + *i, e*

[*tš*]:	Rm.
[*š*] or [*tš*]:	It.
[*θ*]:	Sp.
z:	Ptg., Occ.
ø:	Cat.
i̯ + *z*:	Fr.

Latin
vīcīnu, VL **vēcīnu, placēre*

Rm.	It.	Sp.	Ptg.	Cat.	Occ.	OFr.	Fr.
vecin	vicino	vecino	vizinho	veí	vezin	veisin	voisin
plăceà	piacere	placer	prazer	plaer	plazer		plaisir

Commentary
    The intervocalic *k* before front vowels evolves to [*tš*] in Rumanian, to [*š*] or [*tš*] in Italian, to the voiceless dental fricative [*θ*] in Spanish, to a voiced *s* in Portuguese and Occitan and to a voiced *s* accompanied by a yod release in French. It drops in Catalan, while it is kept unchanged in central Sardinian dialects. The prevailing pronunciation is [*š*] in Tuscan, while the affricate [*tš*] is characteristic of the dialects of the South. This [*š*] is kept distinct from the lengthened [*šš*] that arises from *-sc-: pesce < pĭsce* (Rohlfs §213; Lausberg §389, n. 2). Old Spanish has the voiced affricate *dz: dīcit > dize; facis > hazes; placēre > plazer.* This sound evolves in the direction of the interdental pronunciation [*θ*] approximately in the sixteenth century. With the Castilian desonorization, which sets in about a century later, Spanish acquires its voiceless interdental [*θ*]. If [*θ*] becomes final, it is spelled *z* in Spanish: *vōce > voz; pace > paz; lūce > luz.* For the details of

this complex evolution, see Menéndez Pidal §§35bis 2; 42.3; Lausberg §391. The intermediate stage in the Portuguese, Catalan and Gallo-Romance developments is the affricate *dz* just as in Spanish; this *dz* is subsequently simplified to a voiced *s*. In Catalan, the voiced *s* regularly drops: *jacĕnte > jaent; *racīmu > raïm; *facenda > faena > feina; recĭpĕre > reebre > rebre*, but the *s* stage is fairly well documented in old manuscripts: *jasent, fasena, resebre*. In French, the palatal element is released as yod before the consonant and thus left free to form a diphthong with the preceding vowel (Rheinfelder I 277–278).

Lat. *placēre, placĕre*: both infinitives are continued in French, the first yielding the noun *plaisir*, while the second is the source of the infinitive *plaire*. Ptg. *prazer* comes from Occitan, and OSp. *plazer* and Sp. *placer* are learned or borrowed forms, as seen from the treatment of the initial *pl*-cluster (§246).

274. Lat. *-k-* + *a*

k:	Rm., It.
g̶:	Sp.
g:	Ptg., Cat.
g, [*dž̬*] or *i̯*:	Occ.
i̯ or *ø*:	Fr.

Latin
pacāre, formīca

Rm.	It.	Sp.	Ptg.	Cat.	Occ.	OFr.	Fr.
pagare	pagar	pagar	pagar	pagar, paiar	paiier	payer
furnică	formica	hormiga	formiga	formiga	formiga	formi	fourmi

Commentary
Intervocalic *k* remains unchanged before the vowel *a* in Rumanian and Italian, voices to *g* in Portuguese and Catalan and moves on to a fricative *g̶* in Spanish. Occitan has *g*, [*dž̬*] or *i̯*, and French mostly has *i̯*.

While retention of *k* represents the norm for Italian: *caeca > cieca; amīca > amica*, there are not infrequent occurrences of a voicing to *g* under northern influence: *spīca > spiga; lactūca > lattuga; *prĕcāre > pregare*

(Rohlfs §194). The Occitan developments are complex; the spellings *g, j, y, i* indicate that the evolution may take three directions, perhaps in geographical distribution: a voicing to *g*, a palatalization to [*dž*] or a change to the semi-vowel *i̯*: *pacāre* > *pagar, pajar, paiar, payar; bracas* > *bragas, brajas, braias, brayas; *prĕcāre* > *pregar, prejar, preiar, preyar.* Nonvoicing after *au* is the norm in Hispanic and Occitan: *pauca* > Sp., Cat. *poca,* Ptg. *pouca,* Occ. *pauca; av(i)ca* > *auca* > Sp., Cat. *oca,* Occ. *auca.* French mostly has *i̯*: *baca* > *baie; nĕcāre* > *neiier* > *noyer,* but where the preceding vowel is *ī*, the yod is absorbed: *amīca* > *amie* (via a hypothetical *amiie); pīca* > *pie.* If the vowel that precedes is velar, which is to say in the combinations *-oca, -uca, k* moves via *g* and *ǧ* to complete elimination: *lactūca* > *laitue; lŏcāre* > *louer; carrūca* > *charrue* (Rheinfelder I 272).

Occ. *formiga,* Fr. *fourmi,* Rm. *furnică*: Occitan continues Lat. *formīca* regularly as *formiga,* while Fr. *fourmi* goes back to a hypothetical masculine form **formīcu.* In fact, OFr. *formi* was originally masculine, and it was only in the seventeenth century that the feminine gender of the Latin etymon was restored. The *picard, wallon* and *dauphinois* dialects continue a Late Latin **formīce;* reflexes of this form are Occ. *formitz* and a metathesized OFr. *fromiz.* The change of *m* to *n* that has occurred in Rm. *furnică* shows influence of the labiodental *f.*

Ptg. *charrua*: cannot be drawn directly from Lat. *carrūca;* it is a borrowing from Fr. *charrue* as clearly shown by the treatment of both initial and intervocalic *k.* The word *carrūca* is of Gaulish extraction, the Classical Latin term for 'plough' being *aratru* (> It. *aratro,* Sp., Ptg. *arado,* Occ. *araire*).

275. Lat. *-k-* + *o, u*

k: Rm., It.
g̸:   Sp.
g: Ptg., Cat., Occ.
ø: Fr.

Latin
fŏcu, acūtu

Rm.	It.	Sp.	Ptg.	Cat.	Occ.	OFr.	Fr.
foc	*fuoco*	*fuego*	*fǫgo*	*foc*	*foc, fuoc, fuec*	*fou*	*feu*
	acuto	*agudo*	*agudo*	*agut*	*agut*	*agut, agu*	*aigu*

Commentary

Lat. *k* followed by a velar vowel is retained in Rumanian and Italian, voices to *g* in Portuguese, Catalan and Occitan, becomes a fricative *g* in Spanish and drops in French. In Cat. *foc* and Occ. *foc, fuoc, fuec, g* has regularly desonorized to *k* upon becoming final.

Lat. *fŏcu*: for the Romance reflexes of this word, see §226.

Cat., Occ. *agut*: the intervocalic *t* of Latin voices to *d* in Catalan and Occitan, then unvoices in final position (cf. *foc* above). The feminine form of the adjective is Cat., Occ. *aguda*.

Fr. *aigu*: this development remains largely unexplained; the *g* points to southern influence, but the presence of an *i* is puzzling. It is a late addition, the norm being *agu* until the thirteenth century. Other instances in French of the change of *-k-* to *g* before a velar vowel are of a learned nature: *cĭcūta* > OFr. *cëue*, but Fr. *cigüe; cĭcōnia* > OFr. *ceogne*, but Fr. *cigogne; sĕcūndu* > OFr. *segond*, Fr. *second*, with *c* as a mere graph for *g*.

276. Lat. *-g-* + *i, e*

[*dž*]:	Rm.
[*dž*] (lengthened)	
or ø:	It.
ø:	Sp.
ø or [*ž*]:	Ptg.
i̯, [*dž*] or ø:	Occ.
ø, i̯ or [*ž*]:	Fr.

Latin
sagĭtta, magĭstru, magister, lēge

Rm.	It.	Sp.	Ptg.	Cat.	Occ.	OFr.	Fr.
săgeată	*saetta*	*saeta*	*sẹta*	*sageta*	*saeta, saieta, sageta*	*saete*	
maestru	*maestro*	*maestro*	*maestre, mestre*	*maestre, mestre*	*maestre, maiestre, magestre, mestre*	*maistre*	*maître*
lege	*legge*	*ley*	*lei*	*llei*	*lei, leg*	*lei*	*loi*

Commentary

The development of intervocalic *g* before a palatal vowel is extremely complex. It is generally assumed that the intervocalic palatal *g* had evolved to *i̯* in Vulgar Latin, thus following the same evolution as the primary *i̯*. The elimination of the palatal *g* mostly occurs before a stressed *i* or *e* (*sagĭtta, magĭstru*), but *g* also drops elsewhere (*sartāgĭne, lēge*).

Rumanian has [*dž*], the only exceptions being *magis* > *mai*, and *magĭstru* > *maiestru* > *maestru*, where *g* evolves to *i̯* and is absorbed. *Mai* is proclitic, and *maestru* is similarly weak through its frequent use as a title. Italian has [*dž*] which, because of the intervocalic position, is lengthened: *lĕgit* > *legge; grĕge* > *gregge*. Before a stressed *i* or *e* the norm is for *g* to drop: *saetta, maestro; pagēnse* > *paese*. Forms with *i̯* may represent an earlier stage in this evolution: OIt. *maiestro, paiese*. Intervocalic *g* drops in Spanish before a stressed front vowel: *saeta, maestro; sigĭllu* > *seello* > *sello; rūgĭtu* > *ruido; rēgĭna* > *reina; sexagĭnta* > *sesaenta* > *sesenta*, and in the *-āgĭne* suffix: *sartāgĭne* > *sartén*. For the final position, Lausberg (§395) proposes a separate rule, in terms of which the Vulgar Latin *i̯* that comes from *g* before a palatal vowel is retained: *lēge* > *ley; rēge* > *rey; grĕge* > *grey*. However, the existence in Old Leonese of the forms *lee* and *ree* proves that *g* has dropped here, too, and that the yod stems from the final *e* in hiatus with the stressed vowel (Menéndez Pidal §28.2; García de Diego, p. 80). Portuguese follows Spanish very closely, with the loss of *g* representing the norm: *magĭster* > *maestre* > *mestre; sigĭllu* > *seello* > *selo; rēgĭna* > *rainha*. Cases with a final yod: *lei, rei, grei*, are obtained in the same manner as the corresponding Spanish forms. Portuguese differs from Spanish, however, in that it offers a few occurrences of a learned change to [*ž*] from an earlier [*dž*]: *fūgĭre* > *fugir* (vs. Sp. *huir*); *vĭgĭlāre* > *vigiar*. Catalan shows loss of *g* in *magistru* > *maestre, mestre*, but elsewhere it mostly has [ž] from an earlier [dž] in what appears to be a learned evolution: *pagēnse* > *pagès; sigĭllu* > *segell; fūgīre* > *fugir* (B. Moll §§117–118; Badía Margarit §72, II). Occitan has *i̯,* [dž] or ∅: *saieta, sageta, saeta; maiestre, magestre, maestre.* Loss of *g* may occur before a stressed *ī: rēgīna* > *reina* and *regina* (Appel §46a; Roncaglia, p. 63). French drops *g* before a tonic *i* or *e: sagĭtta* > OFr. *saete; fūgīre* > *fuir; rēgīna* > *reïne* > *reine,* while [ž] appears in learned words: *fūgĭtīvu* > *fugitif; lĕgĕnda* > *légende.* A change to *i̯* may be seen in **negĕnte* > OFr. *neient.* Occ. *lei, leg* and Fr. *loi* are treated in the section on final consonants.

Sp. *maestro, maestre,* Ptg. *maestro:* Williams (§73.4) draws Ptg. *mestre* from *magĭstru,* while Menéndez Pidal (§74.6), more convincingly, lists Sp. *maestre* as a continuation of the Latin nominative *magister,* a form which was in common use in the Latin chancellery. The variant Sp., Ptg. *maestro* represents the accusative *magistru.*

277. Lat. -*g*- + *a*

g:	Rm., It., Ptg.
g:	Sp.
g or ∅ (or *i̯* ?):	Cat.
g, i̯ or [dž]:	Occ.
i̯ or ∅:	Fr.

Latin
plāga, nĕgāre, rūga

Rm.	It.	Sp.	Ptg.	Cat.	Occ.	OFr.	Fr.
plagă	*piaga*	*llaga*	*chaga*	*plaga*	*plaga, plaia, plaja, playa*		*plaie*
negà	*negare*	*negar*	*negar*	*negar*	*negar, neiar*	*neiier, noiier*	*nier*
	ruga	*arruga*	*rua*	*rua*	*rua, ruga*		*rue*

Commentary

Intervocalic *g* remains unchanged before *a* in Rumanian, Italian and Portuguese, but acquires fricative pronunciation in Spanish. Catalan may keep *g* or drop it: *plāga > plaga* vs. *rūga > rua*. Occitan largely keeps *g*, but the fairly common *i* graph is an indication that *g* may also evolve to *i̯* or undergo a palatalization to [*dž*] (Appel §46a; Roncaglia, p. 63). French mostly has *i̯*: *plaga > plaie; rēgāle > reial > royal*, but elimination of *g* is the norm when a velar vowel precedes: *rūga > rue*, and *i̯* is absorbed into a preceding long *i*: *castīgat > *chastiie > châtie*. There are sporadic occurrences of the loss of intervocalic *g* before *a* in Romance, mostly in Hispanic, but also in Occitan: *līgāre >* Sp., Ptg., Occ. *liar; lītīgāre >* Sp. *lidiar,* Ptg. *lidar; navīgāre >* OSp. *navear; fūmīgāre >* Sp. *humear,* Ptg. *fumear; lēgāle >* Sp., Ptg. *leal* and *legal,* Occ. *lial, leal, leial;* Sp., Ptg. *real,* Occ. *real, reial.*

The dual outcome in Catalan, retention or elimination, is explained by scholars as related to the stress pattern (Fouché: *Phonétique historique,* p. 113). Before the stress *g* disappears: *rūmīgāre > rumiar; lēgāle > lleial; rēgāle > reial* (with *i* in a hiatus-separating function or analogical from *llei, rei*), following the stress it is kept: *castīgat > castiga; rĕnĕgat > renega.* Analogical levelings, specifically within verb paradigms, account very handily for exceptions to this rule: *rumia < rūmīgat* is analogical from *rumiar,* and *lligar < līgāre* is drawn from *lliga < līgat.* Applied to verb paradigms, the rule as formulated by Badía Margarit (§70, III) is thus infallible, but it offers no justification for the elimination of *g* in an isolated word such as *rūga > rua.* It further seems quite plausible that the *i̯* of *lleial* and *reial* could represent a third development of *g* before *a,* since such a change has parallels in Occitan and French: *rēgāle >* Occ. *reial,* Fr. *royal.* Direct contact with a velar vowel offers an explanation for the loss of *g* in *rūga > rua.*

Lat. *līgāre,* It. *legare,* Sp. *ligar:* the Italian resolution of Lat. *i̯* as *e* is analogical from the tonic position, while Spanish obtains its *i* through analogical pressure from *castīgāre.*

278. Lat. -*g*- + *o, u*

g:	Rm., It., Ptg.
g̶:	Sp.
g or ∅:	Cat., Occ.
∅:	Fr.

Latin
lĕgūmen, jŭgu, *jūgu

Rm.	It.	Sp.	Ptg.	Cat.	Occ.	OFr.	Fr.
legumă	*legume*	*legum-bre*	*legume*	*llegum*	*leum, legum*	*leun*	*légume*
jug	*giogo*	*yugo*	*jugo*	*jou*	*jou, jo*	*jou*	*joug*

Commentary
When preceding a velar vowel, *g* is retained in Rumanian, Italian and Portuguese, becomes a fricative *g̶* in Spanish. In Occitan, it is either kept or dropped: VL *agosto > agost, aost; lĕgūmen > legum, leum;* VL **agūru > agur, aür,* while French eliminates it consistently: *lĕgūmen >* OFr. *leun.* Catalan shows the same dual outcome as Occitan: VL *agosto > agost* vs. *jŭgu > jou.*

Rm. *legumă*: neuter in Latin, this noun has become feminine in Rumanian, formally joining the first declension.
Fr. *légume*: on the verge of being reduced to a monosyllable, OFr. *leun* was replaced by *légume,* which may be a borrowing from Italian.
Lat. *jŭgu*: see §240.
Lat. *augŭstu*: see §192.

279. Lat. *-i̯-*

i̯:	Rm.
[*dž*] (lengthened):	It.
i̯ or *ø*:	Sp.
[*ž*] or *ø*:	Ptg.
[*ž*]:	Cat.
i̯ or [*dž*]:	Occ.
i̯ or [*ž*]:	Fr.

Latin
majōre, pējōre, maju

Rm.	It.	Sp.	Ptg.	Cat.	Occ.	OFr.	Fr.
mag-giore	*mayor*	*maor, mór*	*major*	*maior, major, mayor*	*maiour*	*majeur*	
peg-giore	*peor*	*pior, peor* (old)	*pitjor*	*peior, pejor*	*peiour*		
maiu	*maggio*	*mayo*	*maio*	*maig*	*mai*		*mai*

Commentary

By and large, intervocalic i̯ evolves like *g* before a front vowel. It is not always easy, however, to distinguish between popular and learned treatment, and the interpretation of the *i* graph is fraught with its share of uncertainty. Rumanian has i̯. Italian has a lengthened [*dž*]: *maju* > *maggio; pĕjus* > *peggio; scarafaju* > *scarafaggio,* the only exceptions being *trŏja* > *troia* and *majāle* > *maiale,* which both show retention of yod. Since both of these lexical items are of a rustic nature, they can easily be dispensed with as dialectalisms, which may have found their way into the language from Umbria or Latium (Rohlfs §220). Spanish mostly keeps i̯: *maju* > *mayo;* VL *(j)ajūnāre* > *ayunar,* but there are also cases of elimination: *pĕjōre* > *peor;* Late Lat. *mĕjāre* > *mear* (Menéndez Pidal §43.1). Portuguese has [*ž*], spelled *j: cuju* > *cujo; jejūnāre* > *jejuar;* CL *habeat* > VL **aiat* > *aja.* Loss of i̯ has occurred in *pĕjōre* > *peor* > *pior* and, analogically from there, in *majōre* > *maor* > *moor* > *mór* (cf. *Montemor*). The standard form of this comparative adjective in Portuguese is not *mór,* however, but *maior,* which does not appear to flow from a popular development (Williams §73.5). A different explanation is proposed by Huber (§229), who considers retention of i̯ or its elimination to represent the norm when Lat. i̯ stands before the stressed vowel: *mayor* and *mor, peyor* and *peor,* while [*ž*] represents the regular outcome following the stress. Catalan has [*ž*]: *majōre* > *major; die Jŏvis* > *dijous; *plŏia* > *pluja.* An earlier affricate pronunciation [*dž*] seems proven by the graphical representation in *pitjor* < *pĕjōre* as well as by the desonorization to [*tš*] that has occurred in *maju* > *maig.* Occitan has i̯ or [*dž*]: *pĕjōre* > *peior, pejor, peyor,* French mostly i̯: *pĕjōre* > OFr. *peiour; majōre* > OFr. *maiour.* The interpretation of the *i* graph is uncertain, however, and a [*dž*] pronunciation may have come about as a learned feature (cf. Fr. *majeur*). In *jejūnu* > *jëun* > *jeun,* the intervocalic i̯ has dropped by dissimilation.

Sp. *ayunar,* Fr. *déjeuner: jajūnare* is a documented Vulgar Latin variant of CL *jejūnāre.* In the Spanish development, as well as in Rm. *ajuna,* the initial *j* has been removed by dissimilation, while Portuguese *jejuar* has evolved regularly from the Classical Latin form. Fr. *déjeuner* goes back to Pop. Lat *disjūnāre* for *disjejūnāre.*

Internal Consonant Clusters

280. Primary and Secondary Clusters

Primary clusters are those which exist already in Latin, while secondary clusters arise in the Vulgar Latin period or during the formation of the individual Romance languages as the result of the fall of weak vowels. It is customary to mark the secondary clusters by introducing an apostrophe between the two elements: *tr* vs. *t'r.* A primary *tr* is found in *patre, latrōne,* a secondary *t'r* in *arātor, quattŭor.* Quite often, the syllabic division separates the elements of a cluster in such a way that the first consonant finds itself at the end of a syllable, while the second assumes initial position in the following syllable. This initial-of-syllable position after a consonant is very strong, paralleling that of the absolute initial position. This means that the *d* of *ardĕnte* receives the same treatment as the *d* of *dĕnte,* and that the second *b* of *barba* develops like the first.

281. Lat. *r* + Consonant

Latin

pŏrta, hĕrba, cŏrvu, *cŏrbu, dŏrsu,* VL *dŏssu, deōrsu,* VL *deōsu, vĕrsus, ŭrsu, spargĕre*

Rm.	It.	Sp.	Ptg.	Cat.	Occ.	OFr.	Fr.
poartă	porta	puerta	porta	porta	porta		porte
iarbă	erba	hierba	erva	herba	erba	erbe	herbe
corb	corvo	cuervo	corvo	corb	corp	corp, corbel	corbeau
dos	dosso	dorso	dorso	dòs, dors	dos		dos
jos	giuso, gioso (old)			jus (old)	jos	jus, jos	

Rm.	It.	Sp.	Ptg.	Cat.	Occ.	OFr.	Fr.
	verso	*verso,* *vies(s)o* (old)	*vesso* (old)	*vers*	*ves,* *vas*		*vers*
urs	*orso*	*oso,* *osso* (old)	*urso,* *usso* (old)	*os*	*ors*	*ors*	*ours*
sparge	*spar-* *gere*	*espar-* *cir,* *esparzer* (old)	*espar-* *gir*	*espar-* *gir*	*espar-* *zer*	*espardre*	

Commentary

Overall, the *r* + consonant clusters are left intact in Romance, with *r* closing the first syllable, and with the consonant following *r* receiving initial-of-syllable treatment in the next. In Hispanic, however, *b* is subject to the fricativization one normally associates with the intervocalic or consonant plus *r* position, and *v* moves to ƀ in Spanish. The assimilation of *rs* to *ss* dates back to Vulgar Latin. The *rg* + *i, e* cluster shows some breaks in the parallelism that is usually observed between initial and initial-of-syllable development.

Sp. *hierba,* Ptg. *erva*: a fricative pronunciation ƀ is the norm in Spanish, while Portuguese changes the occlusive *b* to the labiodental fricative *v*. This parallels the treatment of intervocalic *b*: *faba* > Sp. *haba,* Ptg. *fava.* Neither Menéndez Pidal nor García de Diego seems to emphasize the fricative pronunciation of *b* and *v* in Spanish in the particular position discussed here. Characteristically, the spelling fluctuates in Spanish: *yerba* in the *Cid* vs. *yerva* in Berceo. Another example containing the Latin *rb* sequence is *arbŏre* > Sp. *árbol,* Ptg. *árvore* (§217).

Sp. *cuervo*: *v* is pronounced just like *b* in *hierba;* the spelling is etymologically determined.

Occ., OFr. *corp,* Fr. *corbeau*: since final *v* evolves to *f* in Gallo-Romance: *sĕrvu* > Occ., Fr. *serf; salvu* > Occ. *salf,* Fr. *sauf,* the development to *corb* presupposes the existence in Vulgar Latin of a hypothetical **cŏrbu,* as further demonstrated by the diminutive formation **cŏrbĕllu,* continued as OFr. *corbel,* Fr. *corbeau.* Another example of final *b* may be seen in *ŏrbu* > Occ., OFr. *orp* (Appel §53; Rheinfelder I 189).

CL *dŏrsu, deōrsu*: a total assimilation of *rs* to *ss* takes place early, and the resulting geminate is kept if the preceding vowel is short (*dŏssu*), simplified to *s* if it is long (*deōsu* > **diūsu*). The initial *de-* in hiatus position merges with *di͡-;* for this development and for the replacement of *ō* by *ū*, see §256. Hispanic *dorso* is learned.

Lat. *versus*: the retention of *rs* in Italian, Spanish and French is learned. The vocalic fluctuation evident in Occ. *ves, vas* may be attributed to the fact that the preposition is not independently stressed. This preposition is not continued in Portuguese, *para* having taken over most of its functions, nor in Rumanian where *spre* < *sŭper* is used.

Lat. *ŭrsu*: with the exception of Sp. *oso,* OPtg. *usso* and Cat. *os,* the Romance reflexes of this word show learned retention of the *rs* cluster. In Portuguese, the tonic vowel *u* points to learned treatment.

Lat. *spargĕre*: although in some languages *g* + *i, e* is treated as initial when following *r*: Rm. *sparge,* It. *spargere,* Ptg., Cat. *espargir,* deviations from this principle are noted elsewhere. Old Spanish does not have *i͡* (cf. §237), but *dz*: *esparzer,* and since *dz* is not normally encountered in absolute initial position, it is later replaced by *ts* > [*θ*]: *esparcir.* Portuguese has an old and popular variant *esparzir.* Occitan has *z*: *esparzer,* although the norm for the initial position is [*dž*]: **sŭrgīre* > *sorgir.* Appel (§45) views the difference as determined by the position in relation to the tonic stress: *z* after the stress, [*dž*] before. Be that as it may, a general confusion inevitably set in, and this at a fairly early stage: *sorzer* and *sorger* < *sŭrgĕre; borzes* and *borges* < *bŭrgēnse* (Appel §44c). In the Old French development, *g* soon became interconsonantal due to the loss of the weak *e,* and the resulting *rgr* cluster was regularly resolved as *rdr;* cf. *fŭlgŭre* > **folgre* > *foldre* > *foudre.* A similar development may occur in Occitan, where the treatment of the weak vowel is not uniform: *fŭlgĕre* > Occ. *folgre, foldre* vs. *folzer.* The Old French verb *espardre* disappears in the sixteenth century, but the past participle *espars* has survived in the adjective *épars.*

282. Lat. *l* + Consonant

Latin
talpa, talpu, alteru, alba, altu, mŭltu

Rm.	It.	Sp.	Ptg.	Cat.	Occ.	OFr.	Fr.
topo	*topo*	*toupo*	*talp,* *top* (old)	*talpa*			*taupe*
alt	*altro*	*otro*	*outro*	*altre*	*autre,* *altre*		*autre*
albă	*alba*	*alba*	*alva*	*alba*	*alba*		*aube*
înalt	*alto*	*alto*	*alto*	*alt*	*aut,* *naut* *alt,* *nalt*		*haut*
mult	*molto*	*mucho*	*muito*	*molt*	*molt,* *mout*	*molt,* *mout*	

Commentary

Latin *l* was velar when standing before a consonant, and this pronunciation is continued in Catalan and Portuguese. For the move toward vocalization of velar *l* in Brazilian Portuguese, see P. Teyssier: *Manuel,* p. 38. The preconsonantal *l* vocalizes very generally to u in French while, in Occitan, vocalization occurs only if the following consonant is dental or palatal, and it remains an optional feature. Occurrences of this development in Spanish and Portuguese are limited to cases where *l* is preceded by the vowel *a*. Vocalization of *l* does not occur in Rumanian and Italian, and *l* is mostly retained in Catalan.

It. *topo,* which is a totally isolated example of the vocalization of *l* in Italian, must have come in from a Gallo-Romance dialect. The *au* that results from the vocalization of *l* evolves like the primary *au* to *o* in Spanish and French and to *ou* in Portuguese, while it is retained in Occitan (§155). Other examples in Spanish of the vocalization of *l* are *saltu* > *sauto* (tenth century) > *soto; calce* > *coz; falce* > *hoz.* Exceptions to this development are too numerous to be termed semi-learned (Menéndez Pidal §9.3): *altu* > *alto; saltāre* > *saltar; calvu* > *calvo; salvu* > *salvo,* and a dialectal explanation runs counter to the existence in the same geographical regions of the toponyms *Villalta* and *Villota,* with *ota* as a popularly developed variant of *alta* (García de Diego, p. 119; Menéndez Pidal: *Orígenes,* pp. 103–122). The intermediate forms *auto, sauto, autro,* common in the tenth and eleventh centuries, have vanished, but *cauce* < *calĭce* and *sauce* < *salĭce* came into existence at a later date and thus were able to survive. Portuguese vocalizes preconsonantal *l* in environments that are by and large identical with those of Spanish; the preceding vowel has to be *a*, and the following consonants are chiefly *t*, *c*[*s*] or *p*: *alteru* > *outro; saltu* > *souto; calce* > *couce; falce* > *fouce; palpāre* > *poupar.* The existence of *poupar* and *palpar* points to the instability of *l* in this position. Huber (§245.2.a) attempts unconvincingly to prove that *l* is kept only in the pretonic syllable: *alĭquem* > *alguém;* *alĭcūnu > *algum; saltāre* > *saltar.* Vocalization of *l* does not seem to affect Romance clusters (cf. *cal(i)du* > Sp., Ptg. *caldo*).

In Catalan, the preconsonantal *l* is basically retained: *auscŭltāre* > VL *ascoltāre* > *escoltar; saltare* > *saltar,* but a strong tendency toward the vocalization of *l* to *u̯* is noted for the old language, specifically before a dental consonant and mostly following a velar vowel, but also elsewhere (Badía Margarit §78, II; Fouché: *Phonétique historique,* pp. 155–156; Griera: *Gram. hist.,* pp. 70–71; B. Moll §164): *alteru* > OCat. *autre;* *mŭltones > OCat. *moutós; falda* > OCat. *fauda;* *dŭlca > *Dousa.* A learned reaction, which had its inception in the fourteenth century, led to the restoration of *l*: Cat. *altre, moltons, falda, dolça.* And *l* was even "restored" by hypercorrection in *male habĭtu* > OCat. *malaute* > Cat. *malalt; dĕcĭmu* > OCat. *deume* > Cat. *delme.* In some instances, *l* was not restored where *u̯* had been absorbed by a preceding velar vowel: *cŏlaphu* > *colpu > *cop; pūlĭce* > *puça; ŭlmu* > *om.* Monophthongization of the *au* diphthong obtained secondarily through the vocalization of *l* has occurred in *talpu* > *taupu > OCat. *top,* but the standard form is *talp.*

In Occitan, vocalization of *l* occurs most frequently after the vowel *a* and before the dentals *t, d, s* and *n,* and it remains optional only. The process is difficult to circumscribe chronologically and dialectally, since *l* continues to be written long after the vocalization had taken place. None of these restrictions applies to French, where vocalization is an ongoing process from the beginnings of the language down through the twelfth century. Only learned words or late borrowings retain *l* unchanged. *L* drops when the preceding vowel is *ī* or *ū*: *gentīles* > OFr. *gentis,* spelled *gentils* in the modern language; *pūlĭce* > *pulce* > *puce; nūllos* > OFr. *nus.* The vocalization feature, coupled with syntactic phonetics, leads to the creation of such double forms as *bel—beau; fol—fou; à l'—au.*

Ptg. *alva,* Sp. *alba*: the change of *lb* to *lv* parallels that of *rb* to *rv* (§281); Spanish *alba* is pronounced with a fricative *ƀ.*

Rm. *alt* < *alteru*: in most instances where the loss of *r* in the consonant + *tr* combination occurs, it does not seem to rise above the level of a careless pronunciation. *Fereastă,* for example, is found alternating with the standard form *fereastră* < *fĕnĕstra*. The permanent loss of *r* in this environment seems limited to the word we have here.

Lat. *altu*: in the languages that drop final *u*, the reflexes of this adjective had insufficient phonetic substance, which may account for the various reinforcements that occurred. In Rumanian, homonymy with *alt* 'other' < *alteru* led to the creation of a prepositional construction *in altu* > *înalt* (cf. *în altu* + *-iāre* > Rm. *înălţà*). Catalan practices a similar agglutination with the preposition *de* (or perhaps *ad*): *de altu* > *d'alt* > *dalt*. The aspirated *h* of Fr. *haut* comes from a contamination with Frk. **hôh* (cf. G. *hoch*).

Sp. *mucho*, Ptg. *muito*: for the palatalization of *l* in the *-ŭlt-* cluster in Spanish and Portuguese, see §165.

283. Lat. *n, m* + Consonant

Latin
cantāre, campu

Rm.	**It.**	**Sp.**	**Ptg.**	**Cat.**	**Occ.**	**Fr.**
cântà	cantare	cantar	cantar	cantar	c(h)antar,	chanter
câmp	campo	campo	campo	camp	c(h)amp	champ

Commentary
    With the exception of a few specific clusters, the nasal + consonant combinations remain unchanged in Rumanian, Italian, Spanish, Catalan and Occitan, but are subject to nasalization in French and Portuguese in accordance with the rules outlined in §§179, 180. In French, *n* and *m* nasalize the preceding vowel, losing their consonantal value in the process. In certain environments, specifically before *t, d, p, b, k, g*, the nasals have not been completely stripped of their consonantal characteristics in the Portuguese nasalization process, but are present as a vague consonantal nasal offglide (Williams §95.1). The nasal vowels which they give rise to are, however, "nasalisées dans la totalité de leur émission" (Teyssier: *Manual*, p. 31).

284. Lat. *-mb-, -nd-*
    In Spanish and Catalan the *mb* cluster is assimilated to **mm* and then reduced to *m*: *lŭmbu* > Sp. *lomo*, Cat. *llom* vs. Ptg. *lombo; lŭmba* > Sp. *loma* vs. Ptg. *lomba; palŭmbu* > Sp. *palomo* vs. Ptg. *pombo; plŭmbu* > Sp.

plomo, Cat. *plom* vs. Ptg. *chumbo*. In Spanish, *tamién* is a fairly common popular pronunciation for *también*. Sp. *ambos* < *ambos* is learned or dialectal (cf. OSp. *amos*), and Sp. *tumba* < *tŭmba* is learned. The reduction of *mb* to *m* is characteristic of Castilian, Catalan and Aragonese, while the Leonese dialect retains the cluster. The conjectural intermediate stage *mm* is encountered in southern Italian dialects (Menéndez Pidal §47.2.a; García de Diego, p. 121; Lausberg §416; Väänänen §119). In his *Orígenes* (pp. 295–305), Menéndez Pidal explains the reduction of *mb* to *m* and of *nd* to *n* as linked to an Oscan substratum, which existed in the area around Huesca. Another assimilation, which is characteristic of the south-central dialects of Italy, is that of *-nd-* to *-nn-*, which is documented in Oscan: *úpsannam* for CL *operandam*, in Pompeii: *Verecunnus* for *Verecundus*, and in the *Appendix Probi*: *grundio non grunnio* (Väänänen §119).

285. Lat. *-ns-*, *-nf-*, *-nv-*

Latin

mēnse, VL *mese*, *pēnsāre*, VL *pēsāre*, *pēnsu*, VL *pēsu*, *spōnsu*, VL *isposo*

Rm.	**It.**	**Sp.**	**Ptg.**	**Cat.**	**Occ.**	**OFr.**	**Fr.**
mese	*mes*	*mês*	*mes*	*mes*	*meis*		*mois*
pesare	*pesar*	*pesar*	*pesar*	*pezar*			*peser*
peso	*peso*	*peso*	*pes*	*pes*	*peis,*	*pois*	*poids*
sposo	*esposo*	*esposo*	*espos*	*espos*	*espous*		*époux*

Commentary

The loss of *n* before *s* in Vulgar Latin is a very early change that is documented as far back as the third century B.C.: *cosol* (=*consul*) and *cesor* (= *censor*) on the Scipio epitaph. Numerous examples from Pompeii and several entries in the *Appendix Probi*: *ansa non asa; mensa non mesa,* including a few hypercorrections: *occasio non occansio; formosus non formunsus,* confirm the importance of this change. This development is completed in the Vulgar Latin period as evidenced throughout in Romance, where only learned words preserve *ns* intact.

Rumanian examples of the reduction of *ns* to *s* are: *dēnsu > des; mēnsa > masă; mēnsūra > măsură*. The retention of *ns* is learned or caused by analogical influences. *Pēnsāre* is continued as a learned variant of *pēsāre*, yielding It. *pensare*, Sp., Ptg., Cat., Occ. *pensar,* Fr. *penser.* Fr. *poids* has

222 A Comparative Study of Romance

acquired an unetymological and purely graphical *d* through a false association with Lat. *pondus* 'weight'. Fr. *défense* is influenced by *défendre* < *defĕndĕre*. In Rumanian *n* is kept before *s* in many strong past participles by analogy with the infinitive and other verb forms where *n* is not subject to elimination: *prehensu* > *prensu* > *prins* (cf. inf. *prinde*); *respŏnsu* > *răspuns* (cf. inf. *răspunde*); *absconsu* > *ascuns* (cf. inf. *ascunde*). The elimination of *n* before *f* and *v* is much less common than before *s*, occurring only in compounds formed with the prefixes *in-* and *con-*, and the original clusters have usually been restored: *înfante* > OSp. *ifante*, found in the *Cid* and later replaced by *infante;* *confŭndĕre* > OSp. *cofonder,* replaced by *confundir;* *infĕrnu* > OSp. *ifierno*, now *infierno*. Old Portuguese similarly has *ifante, iferno* and *cofortar* < *confortāre*, and in Occitan *efan, ifern, cofondre, covenir* are found alternating with *enfan, infern, confondre, convenir*. French examples are *convĕntu* > OFr. *covent* > *couvent;* VL *convĕnit* > OFr. *covient*, now *convient*, and Rumanian has *cuveni* < *convĕnīre* and *cuvânt* < *convĕntu*. Specifically for Rumanian, the internal *nt* cluster is reduced to *t* in a few unstressed words: *quantu* > *cât; contra* > *câtră* (Nandris, p. 121; Rothe §94). The fall of *n* is accompanied by a change in the preceding vowel. The large-scale restoration of *n* in the *ns*, *nf* and *nv* clusters may be attributed to the strong pressure exerted by the prefixes *in-* and *con-*, which were resistant to change in all combinations other than the three clusters treated here. Occ. *cosselh* < *consīliu* and Occ. *essenhar* < **insĭgnare* revert to *conselh* and *ensenhar* under the influence of *condemnar, concluire, conoisser, enamorar, encantar, entendedor,* etc. (Väänänen §121; Menéndez Pidal §47.2.a; Appel §56a; Williams §85.7; Rheinfelder I 143, 226).

286. Lat. *-mn-, -m'n-*

mn:	Rm.
nn:	It.
ñ (< *mn*) or *mbr*	
(< *m'n*):	Sp., Cat.
n:	Ptg.
nn, mn:	Occ.
m:	Fr.

Latin
damnu, sŏmnu, dŏmĭna, fēmĭna, homĭnes, VL **homĭnī*

Rm.	It.	Sp.	Ptg.	Cat.	Occ.	OFr.	Fr.
daună	*danno*	*daño*	*dano*	*dany*	*dan*	*dam, dan*	*dam*
somn	*sonno*	*sueño*	*sono*	*son*	*son, som*		*somme*
doamnă	*donna*	*doña, dueña*	*dona*	*dona*	*domna, dona*		*dame*
	fem- mina	*hembra*	*fêmea*	*fembra*	*fenna, femena, femna*		*femme*
		hombres	*homens*	*homes*	*omes, homens*		*hommes*
oameni	*uomini*						

Commentary

The evolution of the *mn* and *m'n* clusters presents a varied picture, often with two or more outcomes in the individual languages. Rumanian keeps *mn* unchanged, but a significant conditioned change occurs if the cluster is preceded by the vowel *a*, in which case *mn* evolves to *u̯n*: *damna* (neuter plur. of *damnu*) > *daună; scamnu* > *scaun; damnāre* > *dăună*. An intermediate stage in this evolution may be the bilabial fricative *ƀ* (Rothe §91; Lausberg §418). There are also instances of this rare and unusual development in Occitan, specifically in Gascon: *damnu* > Old Gascon *daun; domĭna* > *dauno; *scamnĕllu* > Old Gascon *escaunèt. Daun* < *damnu* is also documented for the Hérault, Toulouse and Rouergue regions (Rohlfs: *Le Gascon*, pp. 117, 233; Pfister, *Vox Rom. 17*, 130). The most homogeneous development is found in French, which has *m* throughout, obtained via an assimilation of *mn* to *mm* whereas, in the other areas where assimilation takes place, it works in favor of *n*. The assimilated *nn* is retained in Italian, but simplified in Portuguese. Weak-vowel retention works against the formation of a secondary *m'n* cluster in Italian, Portuguese and Rumanian, and there are also occurrences of this feature in Occitan as seen in the chart of the reflexes of *fēmĭna* and *hŏmĭnes*, **hŏmĭnī*. A major exception is the word *domĭna* which, because of its proclitic status as a title, suffered an early loss of its posttonic penult, thus aligning itself with the primary cluster.

In Spanish, the primary and the secondary clusters follow different paths in their evolution. The primary *mn*, but including the *m'n* of *dŏmĭna*, is assimilated to *nn*, whereupon a palatalization to *ñ* takes place: *daño*, *sueño, doña, dueña.* In the Romance cluster, quite to the contrary, *m'n* dissimilates to *mr* with the subsequent insertion of *b* as a glide: *hembra, hombre; sēmĭnāre > sembrar; nōmĭne > nombre.* There is documentation for earlier stages in this evolution: *nomne* and *nomre* (Menéndez Pidal §69.1). Catalan basically follows the pattern outlined for Spanish; the Latin cluster yields a palatal *n*: *damnāre > danyar; damnōsu > danyós,* while the Romance group evolves via *mr* to *mbr*: *sēmĭnāre > sembrar; commūnĭcāre > combregar.* Suffering an early syncope, *dŏmĭna* becomes *dona* in Catalan. The only major difference between the Catalan and the Spanish developments resides not in the treatment of the consonants themselves, but in the greater tendency in Catalan to retain weak vowels, whereby an *m'n* cluster fails to materialize: *lūmĭnāria >* Cat. *llumenera* vs. Sp. *lumbrera.* Some fluctuation is noted for Catalan: Old Catalan has both *femna* and *fembra < fēmĭna,* and in final position both *ñ* and *n* are found: *damnu > dany* vs. *sŏmnu > son.* An even greater fluctuation is noted for Occitan where *mn, nn, n* and *mpn* are found alternating: *domna, fenna, dona, dompna,* and in the case of *femena, m* and *n* may also be kept separate. It is not clear whether *p* in *dompna* is a mere graphical device utilized to keep *m* and *n* separate, or whether it marks a dissimilation between the two nasals. In final position, Occitan has *n* or *m*: *son, som < sŏmnu.*

Fr. *dam, dan*: French has either *m* or *n* graphs in final position. In most instances, final *m* requires a supporting vowel: *sŏmnu > somme* (Rheinfelder I 190, 304).

Sp. *doña, dueña*: the use of *dŏmĭna* as a title explains the existence of a non-diphthongized variant; it usually precedes a proper noun: *Doña Sol.*

It. *femmina*: gemination is a common feature in Italian in proparoxytones: *macchina, legittimo, sabbato,* but it is not consistently observed: *rapido, camera, pecora.* A Vulgar Latin example may be seen in the *Appendix Probi: cammera non camara* (Rohlfs §§227–228).

Ptg. *fêmea, homens*: an *m'n* cluster is not formed in Portuguese, and as a result *n* drops in intervocalic position: *nomĭnāre > nomear; semĭnāre > semear.* The loss of *n* may also lead to the creation of a nasal diphthong; this happens where final *e* comes into contact with a preceding *e*: *hŏmĭnes > homēes > homens* (Williams §46.5).

287. Lat. -*ng*- + *i, e*

The *ng* cluster may be treated like other *n* + consonant groups, with *g* evolving as initial of syllable, but quite frequently *ng* merges, just like *ni,* into a palatal *n*: *ŭngit >* Rm., It., Ptg. *unge* vs. It. *ugne* (dialectal and poetic), Occ. *onh*. The reasons for this dual development are unclear, but the problem shows an obvious similarity with the treatment of the *n̦* cluster in French, which mostly evolves to a palatal *n* as in *vīnea* > *vigne;* *līnea* > *ligne*, but which may also treat *g* as initial of syllable as in *extrāneu* > *étrange;* *līneu* > *linge* (§324). Rumanian which reduces *n̦* to *i̦* (§324) has only [*n ž*] here: *gingīva* > *gingie; frangĕre* > *frânge*. There is ample documentation in Medieval Italian for both developments: *plangĕre* > *piangere* and *piagnere; fingĕre* > *fingere* and *fignere*, but the modern written language has only [*nd ž*], while a palatal *n* is commonly found in the dialects (Rohlfs §256).

In Spanish, *ng* + *i*, *e* may evolve via *ndz* to [*n θ*] with a syllable-initial treatment of *g* that parallels that of the *rg* cluster (§281): **sĭngĕllu* > OSp. *senziello* > *sencillo; gingīva* > OSp. *enzía* > *encía*. In an alternate evolution, however, *n* and *g* are not kept separate, but merge into a palatal *n*. This dual outcome is illustrated in the following examples: *jŭngĕre* > *uncir* and *uñir; frangis* > *franzes* and *frañes; frangĭmus* > *franzemos* and *frañemos; frangĕre* > *franzer* and *frañer*. The *ñ* variant is very quickly successful in ousting its competitor in these verb paradigms, but the opposite outcome of the struggle may be seen in certain relics: *rĭngĕre* is continued as *reñir*, while the noun **rĭngĕlla* survives as *rencilla* (< OSp. *renziella*) alongside an antiquated *reñilla*. Learned words have *n* + [*χ*]: Sp. *ángel, longitud*. Portuguese has *n* + [*ž*]: *angĕlu* > *angeo* > *anjo; lŏnge* > *longe*, while cases of a palatal *n* seem restricted to Castilian borrowings: **rĭngīre* > Sp. *reñir* > Ptg. *renhir* (Williams §92.3). Catalan mostly has a palatal *n*: *plangĕre* > *plànyer; fingĕre* > *fènyer*, but no merger of *n* and *g* took place in *ĭngĕniu* > *enginy*, where *ĭn-* had maintained its independence as a prefix. As a result, *g* is assibilated to [*ž*], and the same treatment obtains for learned words: *àngel, evangeli*. The Occitan norm calls for a palatal *n*: *plangĕre* > *planher; fingĕre* > *fenher; fingit* > *fenh*. French has a palatal *n* in intervocalic position: *ŭngĭtis* > *oignez*, but examples are rare since the palatal *n'* is resolved as *in* whenever it comes into direct contact with a consonant through weak-vowel loss: *plangĕre* > *plaindre; plangit* > *plaint*.

288. Consonant + *r*

Overall, the consonant which stands before *r* is treated as if it were intervocalic. This is specifically true of the groups containing voiceless occlusives, *pr, tr, cr*, while certain disagreements between the two positions are noted for the voiced occlusive series *br, dr, gr*. The voiceless occlusives become voiced, as if *r* were endowed with a certain vocalic quality (Meyer-Lübke: *Gramm.* I 313). García de Diego (p. 113) seeks proof of the separation of the two elements in inscriptions such as *pateres* for *patres* and *retoro* for *retro*, which would assure the occlusive of true intervocalic treatment.

289. Lat. *-pr-*

> *pr*:　Rm., It.
> *b̆r*:　Sp., Cat.
> *br*:　Ptg., Occ.
> *vr*:　Fr.

Latin
*capra, apĕrīre, *ŏpĕrīre, lĕpŏre*

Rm.	It.	Sp.	Ptg.	Cat.	Occ.	OFr.	Fr.
capră	*capra*	*cabra*	*cabra*	*cabra*	*cabra*	*chievre*	*chèvre*
	aprire	*abrir*	*abrir*	*obrir*	*obrir,*	*ovrir*	*ouvrir*
					ubrir		
iepure	*lepre*	*liebre*	*lebre*	*llebre*	*lebre*		*lièvre*

Commentary

In the *pr* cluster, the treatment of the occlusive parallels that of the intervocalic position (§262): *p* is retained in Rumanian and Italian and voiced to *b* in Portuguese and Occitan, while Spanish and Catalan have a bilabial fricative *b̆* and French a labiodental fricative *v*. A secondary cluster did not form in *lĕpŏre* > Rm. *iepure*, dial. Tuscan *lepora* (Rohlfs §§87, 381).

Lat. *capra*: see §235.

Cat. *obrir,* Occ. *obrir, ubrir,* Fr. *ouvrir*: the Catalan and Gallo-Romance forms go back to a Pop. Lat. *ŏpĕrīre*, obtained analogically from *coopĕrīre* > Fr. *couvrir,* with which *apĕrīre* forms a semantic contrast. The alternation between *o* and *u* in Occitan is common in the pretonic position: *morir* and *murir* (§187).

It. *lepre*: noteworthy is the lack of diphthongization in an open syllable.

Cat. *coure*: an early sonorization of Lat. *cŭpru* to *cŭbru* accounts for the change to *ur* in this word (B. Moll §139), since this represents the normal outcome for the *br* cluster in Catalan (§292).

290. Lat. *-tr-*

tr:	Rm., It.
[*đr*]:	Sp., Cat.
dr:	Ptg.
i̯r:	Occ.
r:	Fr.

Latin
pĕtra, pătre

Rm.	**It.**	**Sp.**	**Ptg.**	**Cat.**	**Occ.**	**Fr.**
piatră	*pietra*	*piedra*	*pedra*	*pedra*	*peira*	*pierre*
	padre	*padre*	*padre*	*padre,*	*paire*	*père*
				pai,		
				pare		

Commentary

The *tr* cluster is kept in Rumanian and Italian, but voices to *dr* in Portuguese. In Spanish and Catalan the occlusive becomes a fricative *đ*, while French drops the *t* altogether. The only language that does not show parallelism with the treatment of intervocalic *t* is Occitan, which voices *t* to *d*, but changes it to *i̯* in the *tr* grouping. The occasional loss of the dental in Spanish may be seen in certain toponyms: *Peralta < pĕtra alta; Perona < pĕtrōna* (Américo Castro, *RFE, 7* (1920), 57–60). There are several instances of the loss of the dental in Catalan: *patre > pare; matre > mare; de rĕtro > darrera,* and *Pera* for *Pedra* is encountered in toponyms: *La Pera, Peralada, Perafita* (cf. Sp. *Piedrahita.)* Another outcome of the *tr* cluster is *i̯r*, a change which Catalan shares with Occitan. Medieval texts have *layre* for *lladre < lātro* and *noyrir* for *nodrir < *nūtrīre* (cf. Occ. *laire* and *noirir).* Examples from the dialects are *rosellonés araire < arātru* and *veire < vĭtru.*

Lat. *patre*: see §222.

Fr. *pierre, père*: the graphical variation in French between a single and a double *r* appears to be of no phonological importance.

291. Lat. *-cr-*

cr:	Rm., It.	
g̱r:	Sp.	
gr:	Ptg., Occ.	
g̱r or *u̯r*:	Cat.	
i̯r:	Fr.	

Latin
lacrĭma, acru

Rm.	It.	Sp.	Ptg.	Cat.	Occ.	OFr.	Fr.
lacrimă,	*lacrima,*	*lágrima*	*lágrima*	*llàg-*	*lagrema*	*lairme,*	*larme*
lacrămă	*lagrima*			*rima*		*lerme*	
acru	*agro*	*agrio,*	*agro*	*agre*	*agre*	*aire*	*aigre*
		agro					
		(old)					

Commentary

While the expected norm in Italian is the retention of *cr,* most occurrences of the *cr* cluster show the voicing to *gr* that is characteristic of northern dialects. Spanish and Catalan have *gr,* with fricative pronunciation of the velar, while voicing is characteristic of Portuguese and Occitan, and French has *i̯r.* The change of *cr* to *gr* in Occitan parallels the voicing of intervocalic *k* to *g* before a velar vowel, but no such symmetry obtains for French. In Catalan, the secondary *c'r* cluster evolves to *u̯r*: *nocĕre > noure; placĕre > plaure; cŏquĕre > cŏcĕre > coure* (B. Moll §153). Cases of *i̯r* in Catalan are characteristic of *rossillonés* and neighboring dialects, which have *playre* for *plaure.*

Lat. *lacrĭma*: see §217.

VL *acru*: the Romance forms go back to VL *acru,* which had completely replaced CL *acer,* as seen from the final *o* of Italian and Hispanic and the final *u* of Rumanian. Admittedly, the Gallo-Romance reflexes could fit either etymon, but the *Appendix Probi* entry *acre non acrum* lends strong support to the very general nature of this substitution. The final *u* of Rumanian and the final *e* of Catalan, Occitan and French are retained for support following the *muta cum liquida* cluster.

OSp. *agro,* Sp. *agrio:* the regularly developed *agro* dominates until the seventeenth century, at which time it is replaced by *agrio,* which is modeled on the verb *agriar* < **acriāre.*

Fr. *aigre: acru* should have given *aire* in French, but this is a very rare form, which soon yields to the obscure *aigre.* While *gr* is indicative of Occitan influence or of learned treatment, the *i̯* remains unexplained.

292. Lat. *-br-*

u̯r:	Rm.
bbr:	It.
b̶r:	Sp.
vr:	Ptg., Fr.
b̶r or *u̯r:*	Cat.
u̯r or *br* or *i̯r:*	Occ.

Latin
labru, labra, fabru

Rm.	It.	Sp.	Ptg.	Cat.	Occ.	OFr.	Fr.
	labbro	labro	labro		laura,		lèvre
		(old)			labra		
faur	fabbro				faure,		(or)fèvre
					fabre		

Commentary

Italian has a lengthened *bbr,* Spanish *b̶r,* and Portuguese and French have *vr,* while the Rumanian, Catalan and Occitan development shows vocalization of the occlusive to *u̯.* Only Hispanic and French show parallelism with the intervocalic treatment. Lengthening of *br* to *bbr* is the norm in Italian: *lībra* > *libbra;* VL *febrariu* > *febbraio; fĕbre* > *febbre,* which makes *libro* < *lībru* a learned, Latinizing form. In Catalan, *br* is either retained or vocalized to *u̯r,* but the distribution of these two developments is difficult to determine. B. Moll (§140) considers vocalization the norm and retention a learned feature, while Badía Margarit (§82, III), taking retention to represent the popular development, simply adds that vocalization occurs in a few instances. The primary cluster is kept in: *fĕbre* > *febre; fabrĭca* > *fàbrega; febr(u)ariu* > *febrer; lībru* > *llibre* while, generally speaking, the secondary *b'r* is vocalized: *bibĕre* > *beure; rōbŏre* > *roure;*

dēbĕre > *deure*, but this division still leaves exceptions: *lībra* > *lliura*. A few occurrences of *i̯r* are noted for Occitan: *ŏctōber* > *ochoure* and *ochoire*; *rōbŏre* > *roure* and *roire*. The vocalization of *b* to *u̯* in Occitan seems to be carried through quite consistently in the secondary *b'r* cluster: *bĭbĕre* > *beure*; *scrībĕre* > *escriure*; *lībĕrāre* > *liurar*, while the primary group is open to a fair amount of hesitation: *fabru* > *faure* and *fabre*; *fabrica* > *fabrega* and *faurga*; VL *febrariu* > *feurer* and *febrier*. Lat. *fĕbre* is continued only as *febre*, perhaps because *feure* is documented as a member of the *febrariu* family.

293. Lat. *-dr-*

dr:	Rm., It., Ptg.
đr:	Sp.
i̯r or *u̯r*:	Cat.
i̯r:	Occ.
r:	Fr.

Latin
quādru, quadrātu

Rm.	**It.**	**Sp.**	**Ptg.**	**Cat.**	**Occ.**	**Fr.**
codru	quadro	cuadro	quadro	caire	caire	cadre
	quadrato	cuadrado	quadrado	cairat	cairat	carré

Commentary
Rumanian, Italian and Portuguese retain *dr*, while Spanish changes the occlusive to a fricative *đ*; Catalan has *i̯r* or *u̯r*, Occitan has *i̯r*, French *r*. Examples of this cluster are few in number, and some of the words in which it occurs have suffered an early loss of *d*: *quadragĭnta* > It., Cat. *quaranta*, Sp. *cuarenta*, Ptg. *quarenta*, Occ. *caranta*, Fr. *quarante*; *quadragēsĭma* > It. *quaresima*, Sp. *cuaresma*, Ptg., Cat. *quaresma*, Occ. *caresma*, Fr. *carême*. A popular form *quarranta* is documented in an inscription (Väänänen §267; Appel §47). The reflexes of Lat. *quadragĭnta* and *quadragēsĭma* thus cannot serve as bona fide examples of the treatment of the *dr* cluster in the individual Romance languages, the reduction to *r* being a Vulgar Latin and hence pan-Romance feature.

Rm. *codru*: the change of *a* to *o* is obscure.

Fr. *cadre*: this word is borrowed from Italian.

Sp. *cairel*: García de Diego (p. 114) draws this word from **quadrĕllu*, explaining that the vocalization of *d* is caused by a syllabic division which has separated *d* from *r*, but he makes no attempt to justify the irregular treatment of the *-ĕllu* suffix. This explanation is unacceptable, and everything points to a borrowing from Occ. *cairel*. The regular Castilian reflex of Lat. **quadrĕllu* is *cuadrillo* (*REW* 6921).

Lat. *cathĕdra*: the non-diphthongization of *ĕ in* Sp. *cadera* is explained through an obscure vocalization of *d* to *i̯*, since the presence of a palatal element would prevent a diphthongization from taking place (Menéndez Pidal §48). In terms of this explanation, the yod represents an intermediate non-documented stage prior to the complete elimination of the dental: *cathĕdra* > **cadedra* > **cadeira* > Sp. *cadera*. Menéndez Pidal looks to Ptg. *cadeira* for an example of the yod stage. However, an analogical explanation seems preferable to the theory of a purely conjectural vocalization. The early removal of the second *d* of **cadedra* through dissimilation would very quickly draw the word into the orbit of the *-aria* suffix, which would account for both Sp. *cadera* and Ptg. *cadeira*.

The tonic vowel of Cat. *cadira* can only be accounted for if we assume that *dr* has evolved to *i̯r*, in which case the yod would cause the diphthongization of *ĕ* to *ie* with subsequent reduction of **iei* to *i* (B. Moll §36). Elsewhere (§145), B. Moll considers the phonological norm to be the simplification of *dr* to *r*, but the examples he quotes in support of this hypothesis can all be dismissed. We can immediately eliminate *quarenta* and *quaresma* from consideration, and the *r* of *consirar* < *consīdĕrāre* could easily follow from *i̯r*, with the yod absorbed into the preceding *ī* (cf. Occ. *dezirar* < *desīdĕrāre* and Occ. *cossir(e)* < *consīdĕro*). The obscure *cadira* cannot serve as a reliable instance of the reduction of *dr* to *r* either, since *d* could have evolved to *i̯* and been absorbed into the tonic vowel, or else the yod may have come from the *-aria* suffix. *R* can thus be dismissed as a reflex of *dr*, but there is documentation for another development emanating from the secondary *d'r* cluster which may move to *u̯r*: *cadĕre* > *caure*; *crēdĕre* > *creure*; *hĕdĕra* > *eura*. Occ. *cadiera* can only be explained on the basis of a *cathĕdra* plus *-aria* source, since *ĕ* does not diphthongize in the South. It is the only form listed by Levy, while Appel (§33a) further offers *cadieira*, which he draws from *cathĕdra* + *-ariam*. Roncaglia (p. 45) proposes a regular development of *cathĕdra* to *cadeira*, with *dr* evolving to *i̯r* and with subsequent formation of an *ei* diphthong through coalescence, but no such variant is listed by Levy. Anglade (p. 40) gives both *cadiera* and *cadeira* as regular outcomes of *cathĕdra*, but offers no explanation, while Schultz-Gora (§15) only has *cadieira*. In French, a similar analogical pressure did not materialize, and the *ĕ* was regularly diphthongized: *cathĕdra* > OFr. *chaiere* > *chaire*. This form is the source of E. *chair*, while French itself adopted the form *chaise* from a central dialect in the fifteenth century, keeping *chaire* only as an ecclesiastical or academic term.

294. Lat. *-gr-*

gr:	Rm.
r:	It.
[ǥr]:	Sp.
i̯r:	Ptg., Fr.
i̯r, r or *gr*:	Cat.
i̯r or *gr*:	Occ.

Latin
nĭgru, ĭntĕgru, pĭgrĭtia, pĕrĕgrīnu, pēlĕgrīnu

Rm.	It.	Sp.	Ptg.	Cat.	Occ.	OFr.	Fr.
negru	*nero*	*negro*	*negro*	*negre*	*neir, negre*	*neir*	*noir*
întreg	*intero, intiero*	*entero*	*inteiro*	*enter, entir*	*entier*	*entir*	*entier*
	pigrizia	*pereza*	*pre-guiça*	*peresa*	*pereza, pigreza*	*perece*	*paresse*
	pelle-grino	*pere-grino*	*pere-grino*	*pelegrí*	*pelerin, pelegrin, peregrin*		*pèlerin*

Commentary

Examples of the intervocalic *gr* cluster are few in number, and since some of the words in which it appears have received learned treatment in their evolution or are obscure, it becomes quite difficult to establish precise rules. The chart disregards the reflexes of *pĭgrĭtia* and *pĕrĕgrīnu/pēlĕgrīnu*, since these are essentially of a learned nature, and *ĭntĕgru* is somewhat unreliable because of its ties to the *-ariu* suffix.

Rumanian keeps *gr* intact. Italian simplifies the cluster to *r*: *nero, intero, peritare* < *pĭgrĭtāre* (Rohlfs §261), in an evolution which Wiese (§92) curiously qualifies as suggestive of Gallo-Romance influence, but *gr* is kept unaltered in *pellegrino* and *pigrizia,* most likely as a learned feature. The rules for Spanish, as outlined by Menéndez Pidal (§48), are that *g* is either kept or lost before *r,* the only important case of elimination being *pereza* > *pĭgrĭtia,* which also loses its occlusive in Cat. *peresa,* Occ. *pereza,* OFr. *perece* and Fr. *paresse.* Sp., Ptg. *peregrino* is learned, the popular term in Hispanic being Sp. *romero,* Ptg. *romeiro.* Portuguese has *ir̯: fragrāre >* *flagrāre > cheirar,* while *gr* survives unchanged in learned words: *negro, peregrino.* Catalan retains *gr* in *nĭgru > negre* and in learned words, while the loss of *g* in *pĭgrĭtia > peresa* is an early change shared by several Romance languages. The *gr* cluster is reduced to *r* in **agraniōne > aranyó,* while a change to *ir̯* occurs in *fragrat > flagrat > flaira* (B. Moll §153). Occitan has either *ir̯* or retention of *gr,* the latter an evolution which Appel (§47) hesitates to term learned: *nĭgra > neira* and *negra; acru > aire* and *agre.* The popular *pereza* and *pelerin̯,* showing elimination of the velar, are flanked by the learned *pigreza* and *pelegrin̯.* French has *ir̯: nĭgru > neir >* *noir; fragrāre > flagrāre > flairier > flairer; lĕgĕre >* **lieire > lire;* VL *ĭntĕgru > *entieir >* OFr. *entir,* with the modern form *entier* obtained through the influence of the *-ariu* suffix. Besides in *paresse,* loss of the velar has occurred in *pĕlĕgrīni > pèlerin.*

Lat. *ĭntĕger, ĭntĕgru:* in some continuations of this word, *r* has suffered metathesis: Rm. *întreg,* OSp. *intrego.* In Hispanic and Gallo-Romance, the word is influenced in its development by the *-ariu* suffix.

It. *intẹro:* a close *e* is characteristic of Tuscan pronunciation, while the Roman dialect has *intẹro,* and there is also documentation in the dialects for a regularly diphthongized *intiero,* comparable to OFr. *entir < *entieir* (Iordan-Manoliu §146).

Sp. *entero:* Corominas (II 642–643) does not have recourse to any suffixal analogies in order to account for Sp. *entero* as the reflex of *ĭntĕgru,* explaining instead that the norm for *gr* is to evolve to *ir̯.* The yod traditionally forms an obstacle to the diphthongization of *ĕ,* and the *ei* diphthong that arises through coalescence is reduced to *e.* A purely phonological explanation of the development is, however, unconvincing, and scholars do not seem to share Corominas' view that *ir̯* represents the regular outcome of *gr* in Spanish. Sp., Ptg. *íntegro* is an entirely learned form.

Ptg. *preguiça:* the Portuguese reflex of *pĭgrĭtia* shows metathesis of *r* and learned treatment of the tonic vowel.

295. Consonant + *l*

The internal consonant plus *l* clusters participate in the palatalizations outlined in §245 for the initial position, but a major difference is that, for *cl* and *gl,* the palatalization feature also extends to Gallo-Romance and Catalan, which keep the corresponding initial clusters intact. The *cl* and *gl* combinations yield a palatal *l* in the West, which then evolves in different directions in the individual languages. Italian changes *l* to *i̯,* just as in the initial cluster, but the consonant that precedes *i̯* in the internal position is doubled or rather lengthened. Examples of these clusters are often scarce, which makes it difficult in some instances to infer precise rules for their development. The following chart presents the developments in outline form:

Lat.	*pl*	*bl*	*fl*	*cl*	*gl*	*scl*	*ngl*
Rm.	*pl*	*u̯l*	*fl*	*ki̯*	*gi̯*	*ški̯*	*ngi̯*
It.	*ppi̯*	*bbi̯*	*ffi̯*	*kki̯*	*l'l'* or *ggi̯*	*ski̯*	*ngi̯*
Sp.	*ƀl*	*ƀl* (or *l'?*)	*l'*	*l'* > [ž] > [χ]	*l'* > [ž] > [χ]	[tš]	*n'*
Ptg.	*br*	*br* or *l*	[š]	*l'*	*l'*	[š]	*n'*
Cat.	*bl*	*u̯l* or *bl*	*fl*	*l'*	*l'*	*skl*	*ngl*
Occ.	*bl*	*u̯l* or *bl*	*fl*	*l'*	*l'*	*skl*	*ngl*
Fr.	*bl*	*bl*	*fl*	*l'* > *i̯*	*l'* > *i̯*	*sl* > *l*	*ngl* > nasalization + *gl*

296. Lat. -*pl*-

pl:	Rm.
ppi̯:	It.
ƀl:	Sp.
br:	Ptg.
bl:	Cat., Occ., Fr.

Latin
dŭplu, cōpŭla

It.	Sp.	Ptg.	Cat.	Occ.	Fr.
doppio	*doble*	*dobro*	*doble*	*dǫble*	*double*
coppia			*cobla*	*cǫbla*	*couple*

Commentary

Lausberg (§422) gives the Rumanian reflex as *pl,* but offers no examples. Lat. *dŭplu* and *cōpŭla* have left no popular continuations in Rumanian, and a *p'l* cluster never developed in *pŏpŭlu,* which is continued as *popor* in an evolution showing intervocalic treatment of *l.* The *REW* (2801) offers Rm. *înduplecà,* traced to Lat. *dŭplĭcāre.* Internal *pl* evolves to *ppi̯* in Italian with gemination of *p,* the intermediate stage in this evolution being *p* and a palatal *l.* Lengthening of *p* does not take place if the cluster is postconsonantal: *tĕmplu* > *tempio; amplu* > *ampio* (Rohlfs §252; Meyer-Lübke, p. 107). Spanish has *bl,* Portuguese *br,* and Catalan, Occitan and French have *bl.* Lausberg (§422) gives *bl* and *pl* as alternate popular outcomes in French while Rheinfelder (I 222–223), more convincingly, considers the retention of *pl* to be a learned feature: *cōpŭla* > *couple; pŏpŭlu* > OFr. *pueble* vs. Mod. Fr. *peuple; trĭplu* > OFr. *treble* vs. Mod. Fr. *triple.* Spanish similarly has a few learned words in *pl: duplo* vs. *doble; triple* vs. OSp. *treble.* B. Moll (§167) and Badía Margarit (§94 I) give a palatal *l* as the outcome of the secondary *p'l* cluster in Catalan, but there is no reason to consider *bl* learned, and examples such as **manupulu* (B. Moll has *manŭplu*) > *manoll* and *scōpŭlu* > *escull* are easily accounted for through a suffixal change to *-ŭcŭlu.*

Sp. *doble: dŭplu* > *doble* is a rare example in Spanish of a gender-distinguishing adjective which has joined the uniform category (Menéndez Pidal §78.1). The etymon could conceivably be *dŭplex* > **dŭples* > **dŭple,* but all other Romance forms are derived from *dŭplu.* Another solution would be to consider *doble* derived from *doblo* through dissimilation. *Golpe* for OSp. *golpo* < *colaphu* may have been similarly obtained, or else it is a Provençalism or a deverbal from *golpar.* For other examples of the hesitation between final *o* and final *e,* see Menéndez Pidal §29.2.d.

Fr. *double:* the presence of a labial consonant has prevented the change of *ou* to *eu;* cf. *lŭpa* > Fr. *louve* (§181).

297. Lat. *-bl-*

$\underset{\frown}{u}l$:   Rm.
$\underset{\frown}{bb}i$:   It.
[*ƀl*] (or *l'?*):   Sp.
br or *l*:   Ptg.
$\underset{\frown}{u}l$ or *bl*:   Cat., Occ.
bl: Fr.

Latin
stabulu, -a, trībŭlāre, *trēbŭlāre, *fabŭlāre, ŏblītāre

Rm.	**It.**	**Sp.**	**Ptg.**	**Cat.**	**Occ.**	**Fr.**
staul	*stabbio*	*establo*	*estabulo*	*estable*	*establa*	*étable*
	trebbiare	*trillar*	*trilhar*			
	favolare	*hablar*	*falar*			
	(old)					
uità		*olvidar,*	*olvidar,*	*oblidar*	*oblidar,*	*oublier*
		oblidar	*obridar*		*emblidar*	
		(old),	(old)			
		olbidar (old)				

Commentary

Rumanian vocalizes *bl* to $\underset{\frown}{u}l$. Italian has $\underset{\frown}{bb}i$: *nĕbŭla* > *nebbia; fībŭla* > *fibbia*. Spanish has either *ƀl* or *l'*, but opinions are divided as to which is the popular outcome. Menéndez Pidal (§48) cites only *ƀl*: *oblāta* > *oblada*, along with the occasional fall of the occlusive in dialects, while García de Diego (p. 113), taking *oblada* to be learned, considers *l'* the sole outcome: *trībŭlu* > *trillo; sībīlāre* > *chillar*. He makes no mention of **fabŭlāre* > *hablar*, although this word can hardly be considered learned. The change of *b'l* to a palatal *l* in Spanish is inferred from a couple of words that present severe phonological problems. Lat. *trībŭlu* evolves to Sp. *trillo* 'harrow for thrashing', documented in 1222 for the Valladolid region, but Meyer-Lübke, convinced that *b'l* does not give a palatal *l* in Spanish, circumvents this difficulty by proposing a hypothetical **trīflom* and **trī-flāre* as etymon; he does not, however, repeat this explanation in the *REW* (8885–8886). Corominas (V 633) defends the evolution to *l'*, which he justifies on the basis of the stress, an argument which seems immaterial. He is better inspired when he emphasizes the social character of the word, since this may be taken to mean that this rustic lexical item could very easily have come in from a dialect. The verb *sībǐlāre* has undergone a series of changes that are either onomatopoeic in nature, or which stem from analogies with semantically related words. The variant *sīfǐlāre*, documented in the fourth-fifth century, could be Oscan or onomatopoeic; the *Appendix Probi* makes mention of this popular pronunciation: *sibilus non sifilus*. For Sp. *chillar,* Corominas dismisses *sībǐlāre* as the source outright. The details of the argumentation are complex and cannot be reviewed here; see *FEW* XI 564–572 and Corominas I 359–360. Suffice it to say that it is only with the greatest reluctance that I would list *l'* as a regular outcome of *b'l* in Spanish. A metathesis accounts for *olvidar* as the reflex of **ŏblītāre;* a non-metathesized *oblidar* is encountered in Berceo, and the most common graph in the medieval period is *olbidar.*

In Portuguese, *bl* mostly changes to *br* in accordance with the treatment of the initial *bl* cluster (§247): *nōbǐle* > *nobre; ŏblītāre* > OPtg. *obridar; ŏblǐgāre* > *obrigar.* Lausberg (§422) makes no mention of *br,* and Williams (§86.2.A) labels this development semi-learned, considering instead the reduction of *bl* via *ll* to *l* to represent the norm. If, however, **fabǔlāre* > *fablar* > *falar* offers the only reliable evidence of the simplification of *bl* to *l,* it would seem more logical to base *falar* on an analogy with its antonym *calar* 'to remain silent' < *callāre* (Huber §167). The other examples listed by Williams all have a conjectural dimension that tends to make them unsuitable as evidence. *Trilha* is borrowed from Spanish, which removes *l'* as a phonological outcome. Quite frequently, a secondary *b'l* cluster never arose in Portuguese because of the lack of syncope: *nēbǔla* > *névoa; stabǔlu* > *estabulo; diabŏlu* > *diaboo* > *diabo.*

Catalan has *u̯l: fabula* > *faula; nebula* > *neula; parabŏla* > *paraula; sībǐlat* > *siula,* or *bl: stabǔlu* > *estable; nōbǐle* > *noble,* with no predictable pattern being discernible between the two developments. For Occitan, *u̯l* is the norm while, by and large, *bl* represents a learned or semi-learned development: *fabǔla* > *faula* and *fabla; nēbǔla* > *neula* and *nebla; sībǐlāre* > *siular* and *siblar; parabŏla* > *paraula* and *parabla; flēbǐle* > *freule* and *feble* and also *frevol.* Appel (§48), however, expresses some hesitation about terming *feble* learned. Lausberg (§422) gives *bl* as the sole outcome for Occitan, while Roncaglia (p. 66) considers *bl* the norm for the primary cluster, limiting the fluctuation between *bl* and *u̯l* to the secondary group. The obscure *trilhar* surfaces here, too, but Appel questions the etymology, rejecting the idea that *b'l* could evolve to *l'.* In French, *bl* is retained: *ŏblītāre* > *oublier; ēbǔlu* > *hièble; tābǔla* > *table; diabŏlu* > *diable.* Vocalization of *b* to *u̯* is a characteristic feature of the *picard* dialect (cf. *diaule*

< *diabolu* in the *Sainte Eulalie*), but some words displaying this develop-
ment have found their way into the standard language: *parabŏla* >
*paraula > *parole; tăbŭla* > **taula* > *tôle.*

Rm. *staul*, Ptg. *estabulo*: the syncope of *stabulu* to *stablu* is attested in
the *Appendix Probi*: *stabulum non stablum;* it is an early development
antedating the change of intervocalic *l* to *r* in Rumanian. Yet in spite of this
early dating, Ptg. *estabulo* reflects the non-syncopated form.

Lat. **ŏblītāre*: this infinitive, replacing CL *oblivisci*, is drawn from the
past participle *oblītu*. It is continued in most areas, with Italian forming the
major exception. OIt. *ubbliare* is a borrowing from French, and Ptg. *olvidar*
has come in from Spanish. The basic term for 'to forget' is *dimenticare* in
Italian, built on *mĕnte* 'mind', in Portuguese *esquecer* < **ex-cadescĕre*,
derived from *cadēre* 'to fall'. The existence of the Occitan variant *emblidar*
lends support to Appel's suggestion (§48) that the *o* of *oblītāre* may have
been taken to be a prefix, rendering *bl* initial rather than internal and thus
preventing the change to *u̯l*. The Rumanian reflex *uită*, however, which also
seems to imply the removal of initial *o* in its evolution, does not show
initial treatment of *bl; b* is continued as *u̯*, while *l* is absorbed into the
vowel *i* in the same manner as *līnu* evolves to *in* pronounced [*yin*].

298. Lat. *-fl-*

fl:	Rm., Cat., Occ., Fr.
ffl̯:	It.
l̯':	Sp.
[*š*]:	Ptg.

Latin
sŭfflāre, afflāre

Rm.	It.	Sp.	Ptg.	Occ.	Fr.
suflà	*soffiare*	*soplar,*	*soprar*	*soflar*	*souffler*
		sollar			
		(old)			
aflà		*hallar*	*achar*		

Commentary

Internal *fl* does not appear between vowels, but is preceded by *f* in the above examples. Italian has *ffi̯*, Spanish a palatal *l* and Portuguese [*š*], while retention is the norm in Rumanian, Catalan, Occitan and French. Sp. *soplar* and Ptg. *soprar* show an unexplained development of *fl* to *pl* and to *pr* respectively, and a change of *fl* to *pl* and *pi̯* is noted for certain Italian dialects (*FEW* XII 407–413; Rohlfs §249). If the *fl* cluster is preceded by *n*, Italian has *fi̯*, with a single *f*, Spanish has [*tš*] and Portuguese [*š*]: *īnflāre* > It. *enfiare*, Sp. *hinchar*, Ptg. *inchar*, while the Gallo-Romance treatment of the group remains the same: Occ. *enflar*, Fr. *enfler* (*REW* 4406). Catalan has *inflar*, Rumanian *umflà*.

Lat. *sŭfflāre*: derived from *sŭb-flāre*, *sŭfflāre* had replaced *flāre* in Late Latin as evidenced in the *Glossary of Reichenau* entry: *flare: sufflare*. The change of *fl* to *pl* in Sp. *soplar* is not as common an alternation as Corominas (V 305–308) seems to believe, and Ptg. *soprar* is a late form, dating from the end of the fifteenth century.

299. Lat. *-cl-*

$$
\begin{array}{ll}
ki̯: & \text{Rm.} \\
kki̯: & \text{It.} \\
l' > [\check{z}] > [\chi]: & \text{Sp.} \\
l': & \text{Ptg., Cat., Occ.} \\
l' > i̯: & \text{Fr.}
\end{array}
$$

Latin
ŏcŭlu, genŭcŭlu, aurĭcŭla, VL *orĭcla*

Rm.	It.	Sp.	Ptg.	Cat.	Occ.	OFr.	Fr.
ochiu	occhio	ojo	olho	ull	olh, uolh uelh	ueil	œil
genun- chiu	ginoc- chio	hinojo (old)	joelho, jeolho (old)	genoll	genolh, ginolh	genouil	genou
ureche	orec- chio	oreja	orelha	orella	aurelha		oreille

Commentary
Rumanian has *ki̯*, Italian a lengthened *kki̯*, and Spanish has [χ], while a palatal *l* is characteristic of Portuguese, Catalan, Occitan and Old French. This palatal *l* is reduced to *i̯* in French in the seventeenth century. The Spanish development is quite complex. With the loss of the weak vowel, *k* became a yod which palatalized the *l*, whereupon *l'* evolved via [ž] and [š] to [χ], spelled *j*. The *c'l* cluster reached the *l'* stage at approximately the same time as the *l* + yod cluster did, which explains why the two groups merged in an evolution that ultimately took them to [χ]. The change to [χ] is usually dated to the late sixteenth century. The Aragonese dialect has a palatal *l*, while Leonese has yod: *ŏcŭlu* > Arag. *uello*, Leon. *ueyo*. For these and other dialectal developments, see Menéndez Pidal §57.2 and García de Diego, pp. 111–113. Contrasting with the above-mentioned merger of *cl* and *li̯*, the geminate *ll* achieved its palatal quality too late for any participation in further development and thus remained at the *l'* stage; cf. *ŏcŭlu* > *ojo* and *alliu* > *ajo* vs. *sĕlla* > *silla*.
Italian has a series of words, in which *c'l* has evolved to *l'* instead of *kki̯*: *conĭcŭlu* > *coniglio; vermĭcŭlu* > *vermiglio; bŭttĭcŭla* > *bottiglia; vĕntacŭlu* > *ventaglio; quacŏla* > *quaglia*. They are undoubtedly borrowings from French (Rohlfs §248). The ecclesiastical vocabulary items *mīracŭlu* and *saecŭlu* have received learned treatment throughout; *mīracŭlu* > Rm. *miracol*, It. *miracolo*, Sp. *milagro*, Ptg. *milagre*, Cat., Occ., Fr. *miracle; saecŭlu* > Rm. *secol*, It. *secolo*, Sp. *siglo*, OPtg. *segre*, Ptg. *século*, Cat., Occ. *segle*, Fr. *siècle*.
The creation of the *c'l* combination through vowel syncope took place so early that the cluster rates as a primary Latin group (Menéndez Pidal §57.2; García de Diego, p. 110; Väänänen §§63–72). Numerous entries in the *Appendix Probi* deal with the syncope feature affecting the *-cŭl-* segment; *speculum non speclum; oculus non oclus; articulus non articlus; masculus non masclus*, and it is well documented in Pompeii (Väänänen §67).

Lat. *genŭcŭlu*: see §237.
Lat. *aurĭcŭla*: see §189.

300. Lat. *-t'l-*
This cluster, which arose through vowel syncope, was unfamiliar to speakers of Latin. Already in Vulgar Latin, *t'l* had been replaced by the familiar *cl* group in some words, as we learn from a couple of *Appendix Probi* entries: *vetulus non veclus; vitulus non viclus*. The development of

cl in *vĕclu* is identical with that of the original *cl* cluster: Rm. *vechiu,* It. *vecchio,* Sp. *viejo,* Ptg. *velho,* Cat. *vell,* Occ. *velh, vielh,* Fr. *vieil.* Other examples are **ad-rŏtŭlāre* > Sp. *arrojar; sĭtŭla* > It. *secchia,* Occ. *selha.* In a later development, *tl* is kept at first, then assimilated to *ll* and simplified to *l: rŏtŭlu* > Occ. *rotle,* OFr. *rolle,* Occ. *role,* Fr. *rôle.* Some learned words in French at first retained *tl,* then substituted the more familiar *tr* for it: *tĭtŭlu* > OFr. *title* > *titre; apŏstŏlu* > OFr. *apostle* > *apôtre.* E. *title* and *apostle* were borrowed at the earlier stage in the French development. In a few learned words, a late syncope allows for the voicing of *t'l* to *d'l* in Spanish, whereupon the cluster is metathesized to *ld: capĭtŭlu* > *cabildo; tĭtŭlu* > *tilde.* Because of its *-e* ending, Sp. *tilde* cannot go directly back to Latin, but may have been obtained via Catalan or Occitan; Sp. *título* is learned.

301. Lat. *-gl-*

gi̯:	Rm.
l'l' or *ggi̯*:	It.
l' > [*ž*] > [*χ*]:	Sp.
l':	Ptg., Occ.
l' or *gl*:	Cat.
l' > *i̯*:	Fr.

Latin
coagŭlāre, tēgŭla, vĭgĭlāre

Rm.	It.	Sp.	Ptg.	Cat.	Occ.	OFr.	Fr.
	cagliare	*cuajar*	*coalhar*		*calhar*		*cailler*
	teglia,	*teja*	*telha*	*teula*	*teula*	*teule,*	*tuile*
	tegghia			*tella*		*tiule*	
veghià	*vegliare,*	*velar*	*velar,*	*vetllar*	*velhar*	*veillier*	*veiller*
	vegghi-		*vigiar*				
	are						
	(old)						

Commentary
Rumanian has *gi̯,* which forms a perfect parallel with the development of *cl* to *ki̯* (§299), and it is the only language that shows identical outcomes of these two clusters in the initial and internal positions (§§249–250).

Italian does not show uniform treatment of the *gl* cluster. The norm is for *gl* to merge with *l̦i̦* (§326) in an evolution whose outcome is a lengthened palatal *l*: *cagliare, vegliare, teglia,* but the change to *ggi̦,* spelled *gghi,* is quite common in Tuscany. Some of these forms are old or dialectal: *vegghiare, tegghia,* but one exception is *mugghiare* < **mūgŭlāre,* which has ousted *mugliare* as the predominant form in the modern language (Rohlfs §250). In Spanish, *gl* evolves like *cl* and *l* plus yod via [ž] and [š] to [χ]: *cuajar, teja; rĕgŭla* > *reja.* Retention of *gl* in *regla* is learned, while the elimination of *g* before *i* in *vĭgĭlāre* > *velar* indicates that no *g'l* cluster ever formed here. Portuguese has a palatal *l*: *coalhar, telha. Rĕgŭla* > *regra* is semi-learned and may have evolved from Sp. *regla,* and Ptg. *vigiar* lends strong support to the fact that *g* and *l* never formed a cluster in *vĭgĭlāre* in Hispanic, but were treated separately, with *g* palatalizing to [ž] (§276) and with elimination of intervocalic *l* in Portuguese (§270). Ptg. *velar* is a borrowing from Spanish. The scarcity of data coupled with a diversity of outcomes makes it particularly difficult to establish any rules for the development of the internal *gl* cluster in Catalan. In fact, Badía Margarit (§82, II) refrains from proposing any rules, citing only the learned retention of *gl* in words such as *negligentia* > *negligència.* B. Moll (§171) gives *tll* as the graphical outcome, for which he suggests a lengthened palatal *l* as the pronunciation, but the problem with this finding is that the rule is inferred from a single example: *vĭgĭlat* > *vetlla,* and furthermore this is a verb whose evolution in Hispanic is far from transparent. Nor is it clear why *tēgŭla* is continued both as *tella* (< **teg'la*) and *teula,* with early loss of *g* before a velar vowel (B. Moll §169). Occitan and French generally have a palatal *l,* but some of the words containing the *g'l* cluster have not received popular treatment. This is the case with Occ. *teula* (Appel §48) and with OFr. *teule, tiule,* Fr. *tuile; rĕgŭla* > OFr. *reule, riule* (cf. E. *rule*). Rheinfelder (I 125) proposes that, in *tēgŭla* and *rĕgŭla, g* dropped early before a velar vowel and thus did not form a cluster with *l,* but the question as to whether this represents popular or learned treatment is left open. Both *reule* and *règle* are documented in the twelfth century. In another development, *rĕgŭla* did allow for the formation of a *g'l* cluster, evolving via OFr. *reille* to Fr. *rail.* E. *rail* is borrowed from the Old French form. For another example of the change of [ej] to [aj] in French, see *ovĭcŭlas* > *oeilles* > *ouailles* (§264).

　　While *c'l* formed a cluster so early that there is general consensus among scholars that it must be considered a primary group (§299), it will be seen from the treatment of *vĭgĭlāre, tēgŭla* and *rĕgŭla* that the same thing cannot be said about the *g'l* combination. It would seem somehow that *g'l* evolved into a cohesive group at a slower pace, so slow in fact that in some words no cluster ever came into existence, and these reflexes cannot all be dismissed as learned.

302. Lat. *-scl-*

ʂki̯:	Rm.
ski̯:	It.
[tš]:	Sp.
[š]:	Ptg.
skl:	Cat., Occ.
sl > *l*:	Fr.

Latin
mascŭlu, mĭscŭlāre

Rm.	It.	Sp.	Ptg.	Cat.	Occ.	OFr.	Fr.
mascur	maschio	macho	macho	mascle	mascle	masle	mâle
mis-chiare	mezclar	mesclar	mesclar	mesclar	mesler	mêler

Commentary
The internal *scl* cluster evolves to *ski̯* in Italian, to *ʂki̯* with a palatalized *s* in Rumanian, to [tš] in Spanish and to [š] in Portuguese; it is retained in Catalan and Occitan, simplified to *sl* in Old French and to *l* in Modern French. For the clusters *rlc* and *ncl*, see below *sarcŭlu* and *conchŭla*.

Rm. *mascur, muʂchiu*: quite often an *scl* cluster does not arise in Rumanian because of weak-vowel retention. This is the case with *mascŭlu* > *mascur*, where *u* is kept, and *l* is treated as intervocalic. If a cluster does form as in *muscŭlu* > *muʂchiu*, the *s* is usually palatalized in the *sk* combination.

Sp. *mezclar*, Ptg. *mesclar*: these forms are semi-learned rather than borrowings from Catalan as maintained by Meyer-Lübke (*REW* 5606). The reduction of *scl* to *sl* in *mūscŭlu* > Sp. *muslo* and the metathesis of *sl* to *ls* in *mascŭlu* > OSp. *malso* constitute aberrant developments in the Spanish domain (Menéndez Pidal §3.3). The norm is represented by *macho*, which is regularly obtained and not a *portuguesismo*, as Meyer-Lübke claims (*REW* 5392).

Lat. *sarcŭlu*: just as *s* drops before the [*tš*] and [*š*] originating from *cl* in Hispanic, so *r* may be eliminated in the same surroundings: *sarcŭlu* > Sp., Ptg. *sacho* vs. It. *sarchio* (*REW* 7602). Occitan has *sarcle* and an assimilated *salcle*.

Lat. *conchŭla*: if *n* precedes the *cl* cluster, it is retained in Hispanic before [*tš*] and [*š*]: *conchŭla* > Sp., Ptg. *concha; *trŭncŭlu* > Sp. *troncho*.

303. Lat. *-ngl-*

> ngi̯: Rm., It.
> n̉': Sp., Ptg.
> ngl: Cat., Occ.
> ngl > nasalization
> + gl: Fr.

Latin
ŭngŭla

Rm.	It.	Sp.	Ptg.	Cat.	Occ.	Fr.
unghie	unghia	uña	unha	ungla	ongla	ongle

Commentary

Rumanian has *ngi̯*. This is also the norm for Italian: *sĭngulāre* > *cinghiale; *sĭnglŭttiāre* > *singhiozzare*, but many dialects have a palatal *n*: *uña, ciñale* (Rohlfs §250). Spanish mostly has *n'*: *sĭngŭlos* > OSp. *seños; Rivi Angŭlu* > *Riaño*, but a change of *ngl* to *nd* is seen in *sĭngŭlos* > *sendos*, which has replaced OSp. *seños*. Portuguese has *n'*, while Catalan and Occitan keep *ngl* intact. In the French cluster, *n* ceases to be a consonant, serving instead to mark nasalization of the preceding vowel, and *gl* is retained. Where *n* is kept before *g*, it usually has a velar pronunciation.

304. Lat. *-s* + Consonant

> *s* or [*š*]: Rm.
> *s*: It., Sp., Cat., Occ.
> [*š*] or [*ž*]: Ptg.
> ø: Fr.

Latin
věspa, fěsta, pǐscāre

Rm.	It.	Sp.	Ptg.	Cat.	Occ.	OFr.	Fr.
viespe	*vespa*	*avispa*	*vespa*	*vespa*	*vespa*	*guespe*	*guêpe*
	festa	*fiesta*	*festa*	*festa*	*festa*	*feste*	*fête*
	pescare	*pescar*	*pescar*	*pescar*	*pescar*	*peschier*	*pêcher*

Commentary

When standing before a consonant in internal position, *s* is mostly kept in Rumanian, Italian, Spanish, Catalan and Occitan. A palatal pronunciation [*š*] prevails in Portuguese, with voicing to [*ž*] occurring before a voiced consonant. The Spanish anteconsonantal *s* also tends to have a certain palatal quality to it (Menéndez Pidal §10.2), but the graphical representation remains *s* in Hispanic whereas, in Rumanian, palatalization is a conditioned feature marked graphically by *ş*. In French, *s* gradually drops during the medieval period. Before voiced consonants this happens as early as the middle of the eleventh century, perhaps via a voiced stage which remains unmarked graphically, but it takes two more centuries for *s* to drop before voiceless consonants. This chronological difference may be inferred from French words borrowed into English. By the time these borrowings were introduced, following the conquest of England by William the Conqueror in 1066, *s* had ceased to be pronounced before voiced consonants, thus leaving no trace in English, but contrasting with this, English has kept *s* before voiceless consonants in loanwords from French: *blasphemāre* > OFr. *blasmer* > Fr. *blâmer* and E. *blame;* CL *īnsula* > VL *isola* > OFr. *isle* > Fr. *île* and E. *isle* (with a purely graphical *s*); *mascŭlu* > OFr. *masle* > Fr. *mâle* and E. *male* vs. *fěsta* > OFr. *feste* > Fr. *fête* and E. *feast; castēllu* > OFr. *chastel* > Fr. *château* and E. *castle* (from *normand castel*) (Rheinfelder I 219). Outside of French where *s* drops in anteconsonantal position, *sp* and *st* are usually kept intact as illustrated above, and the same is true of *sk,* except when followed by a front vowel. A Rumanian example is *pǐscāriu* > *pescar.* A conditioned change occurs in Rumanian where *st* becomes *şt* before a front vowel: *castīgāre* > *câştigà; *accu-istī* > *aceşti.* For the change of *sk* to *şt* before a front vowel, see §305.

Rm. *viespe*: this form cannot go back to *věspa,* but reflects an undocumented variant **věspe.*

Sp. *avispa*: the initial *a* is analogical from *abeja;* the palatal quality of *s* before a consonant has caused the reduction of the diphthong *ie* to *i* (cf. OSp. *aviespa*). A similar development occurs when tonic *ĕ* is followed by *ll: sĕlla* > OSp. *siella* > *silla*.

Fr. *guêpe*: for the influence of Gmc. *w-* on the initial *v* of Latin, see §§225, 254.

305. Lat. *-sc-* + *i, e*

ʂt:	Rm.
[šš]:	It.
[θ]:	Sp.
[i̯š]:	Ptg.
[š]:	Cat.
i̯s:	Occ., Fr.

Latin
pĭsce, *nascĕre, *-ēre

Rm.	**It.**	**Sp.**	**Ptg.**	**Cat.**	**Occ.**	**OFr.**	**Fr.**
peşte	*pesce*	*pez*	*peixe*	*peix*	*peis*	*peis*	
naşte	*nascere*	*nacer*	*nascer*	*néixer*	*naisser*	*naistre*	*naître*

Commentary

The internal *sc* + *i, e* combination evolves to *şt* in Rumanian and to a lengthened [šš] in Italian. Old Spanish has a voiced *z* which unvoices later, but the *z* graph is kept if the consonant becomes final: *pez, haz*. Portuguese has a palatal [š], which releases a yod in front: *pĭsce* > *peixe*, and this yod influences the vowel *a*, altering it to *e: fasce* > *feixe*. The change to *s* as in **nascēre* > *nascer* is semi-learned and characteristic of the inchoative ending **-escēre* > *-ecer* or *-escer* (an *-*ēre* ending is required for Hispanic): **florescēre* > *florescer; *cognōscēre* > *conhecer; *warnjan* + **-escēre* > *guarnecer; *patescēre* (from *patīre*) > *padecer* (Williams §92.2; Huber §359). Catalan has [š], which is spelled *x* or *ix: crēscĕre* > *créixer; vascĕllu* > *vaixell; dĭscĭpŭlu* > *deixeble*. In Occitan, *k* palatalizes the *s* to [š], which is mostly resolved as *i̯s*, spelled *iss* or *is* internally, *is* in final position: *pĭsciōne* > *peissoṇ; crēscĕre* > *creisser; dēscĕndĕre* > *deissendre; pĭsce* > *peis; crēscit* > *creis*. Forms with [š] or [i̯š] are dialectal: *creyssher, deshendre* (Appel §§53, 56a). In French, the development follows the same path as in Occitan via a palatalized [š] to i̯s: *pĭsciōne* > *peisson* > *poisson*. Where an *s'r* cluster arises through vowel syncope, a *t* is inserted as a glide: *crēscĕre* > *creistre* > *croître; *nascĕre* > *naistre* > *naître*.

OFr. *peis, pois*: the Old French form was replaced by a suffixated *poisson* < *pĭsciōne* because of the homonymy with *pois* 'pea' < *pĭsu* and *poids*, OFr. *pois* 'weight' < *pēnsu*. OFr. *peis, pois* forms part of the compounds *craspois* 'whale' < *crassu pĭsce* lit. 'fat fish' and *porpois*, continued in E. *porpoise*, < *pŏrcu pĭsce* lit. 'pig-fish'.

It. *fascio*: the *o* ending represents a morphological adjustment.

306. Lat. *-pt-*

> *pt*: Rm.
> *tt*: It.
> *t*: Sp., Ptg., Cat., Occ., Fr.

Latin
sĕpte, scrīptu

Rm.	It.	Sp.	Ptg.	Cat.	Occ.	OFr.	Fr.
şapte	sette	siete	sete	set	set	set	sept
	scritto	escrito	escrito	escrit	escrit	escrit	écrit

Commentary
The *pt* cluster is kept in Rumanian, assimilated to *tt* in Italian and simplified to *t* elsewhere. Fr. *sept* is merely a case of learned spelling, but *p* has been reintroduced in pronunciation in *sĕptĕmber* > OFr. *setembre* > *septembre*. Vocalization of *pt* to u̯ occurs sporadically in Portuguese (Williams §92.7.3) and in Occitan (Appel §56b), mostly as a semi-learned feature.

It is fairly common in Spanish for the secondary *p't* cluster to voice to *bd* with subsequent vocalization of *b* to u̯: *capĭtĕllu* (diminutive of *caput*) > *cabdiello* > *caudillo; capĭtāle* > *cabdal* > *caudal*. Ptg. *caudal* is a borrowing from Spanish. Following the vowel *e*, *pt* seems to have been interchanged with *ct* in Portuguese (Williams §92.7.c): *concĕptu* > *conceito; praecĕptu* > *preceito*. In Catalan, the secondary *p't* cluster is retained with early weak-vowel loss: *repŭtāre* > *reptar*, while voicing occurs if the vowel falls later: *capĭtāle* > *cabdal; capĭtĕllu* > *cabdell.* A secondary *p'd* cluster has great difficulty establishing itself in Romance. French reduces *p'd* to *d,* probably via a voicing of *p* to *b*: *tĕpĭdu* > *tiède; sapĭdu* > OFr. *sade* (kept in *maussade* < *mal* + *sade*). There is no syncope in Italian: *tiepido, sapido,* while Spanish usually drops *d* from the *-ĭdu* suffix: *tibio.* Sp. *raudo* may reflect *rapĭtu* (Corominas IV 781) rather than *rapĭdu* (Menéndez Pidal §60.1 and *Orígenes,* p. 270).

Lat. *sĕpte*: see §148.

Occ. *escrit*: this is the most common form of the participle, while *escrich* or *escrig* is analogical from *dich, dig* < **dīctu.* The variant *escriut* may have been built on the infinitive *escriure* < *scrībĕre;* there are, however, genuine occurrences of the vocalization of *p* to *u̯* in the *pt* cluster; *adaptu* > *azaut; captīvu* > *cautiu.* It is difficult to determine whether the form *escript* is merely learned spelling, or whether *p* was actually pronounced (Appel §56b; Anglade, p. 138).

Lat. *captīvu*: It. *cattivo* shows the normal assimilation of *pt* to *tt* while, in Hispanic and Occitan, *p* has vocalized before *t*: Sp., OPtg. *cautivo* (but Mod. Ptg. *cativo*), Occ. *cautiu.* This may represent a semi-learned development, while the retention of *pt* is entirely learned: It. *captivo,* Fr. *captif;* Sp., Ptg. *raptar* < *raptāre* (Huber §165). In a more popular Gallo-Romance development, *captīvu* is reshaped to **cactīvu* under the influence of a Gaulish root (cf. OIrish *cacht* and E. *caught*), hence Occ. *caitiu* and Fr. *chétif* (Appel §56b; Rheinfelder I 107).

307. Lat. *-ps-*

> *s*:   Rm., Sp., Ptg., Occ., Fr.
> *ss*: It.
> *ps*: Cat.

Latin
ĭpse, ĭpsu, gypsu

Rm.	It.	Sp.	Ptg.	Cat.	Occ.	OFr.	Fr.
îns	*esso*	*ese, esse* (old)	*esse*	*es, eix*	*es, eps, eis*	*es*	
	gesso	*yeso*	*gesso*	*guix*	*geis*		

Commentary

The *ps* cluster is retained in Catalan, assimilates to *ss* in Italian and simplifies to *s* elsewhere, with *ss* in Hispanic being a mere graph. Occ. *eps* is an archaic form or a case of learned spelling.

There are not infrequent occurrences in Occitan and Hispanic of a palatal development, which is traditionally attributed to a confusion between *ps* and *cs* (Lausberg §429; Appel §56b; Williams §85.3.A; García de Diego, pp. 116–117): *capsa* > Sp. *caja*, Ptg., Cat. *caixa*, Occ. *caissa*, as opposed to the regular development represented by It. *cassa* and Fr. *châsse*. Other instances of this palatalization are: *ĭpsu* > Cat. *eix*, Occ. *eis; gypsu* > Cat. *guix*, Occ. *geis.* Convinced that *-iss, -ix* represents the regular phonological development in Occitan and Catalan, Corominas (I 740–741) considers the Spanish and Portuguese palatalized forms to be borrowings from there, an explanation already proposed by Meyer-Lübke (*REW* 1658), but this is mere conjecture. Von Wartburg (*FEW* II 314) upholds the theory of an adjectival **capsea* as the direct source of all Romance forms, but an adjectival formation is hard to defend for the basic word for 'box' and even less so for Ptg. *queixo* 'chin, jaw', which has differentiated itself semantically from the base. Since French is immune to this palatal infiltration, Fr. *caisse* must be considered a borrowing from Occ. *caissa*.

Rm. *îns*, Cat. *es*: the Rumanian form is drawn from the combination *ĭn-ĭpsu*, while proclitic use may account for the loss of *p* in Cat. *es*.

Lat. *gypsum*: in this word of Greek origin, *y* is represented by *ę* in Italian, Spanish, Portuguese and Occitan, while Catalan has *i*. OFr. *gip* shows learned treatment of the vowel and loss of *s*, mistaken for a flexional ending.

308. Lat. *-b't-, - v't-*

t:	Rm., Fr.
tt:	It.
ud or *bd* > *d* > *đ*:	Sp.
no cluster formed	Ptg.
ut:	Cat.
ut, ud or *pt, bd*:	Occ.

Latin

dŭbĭtāre, cīvĭtāte

Rm.	It.	Sp.	Ptg.	Cat.	Occ.	OFr.	Fr.
dubitare,	*dudar*	*duvidar*	*dubtar*	*doptar*	*doter*	*douter*	
dottare (old)							
cetate	*città*	*ciudad*	*cidade*	*ciutat*	*ciutat, ciptat*		*cité*

Commentary

The rare occurrences of these secondary clusters in Rumanian show a reduction to *t*: *cŭbĭtu* > *cot; cīvĭtāte* > *cetate*. Rules are difficult to formulate for Italian and Portuguese due to the frequent lack of a syncope, but where a cluster does come about, Italian assimilates to *tt*. Portuguese does not normally eliminate the vowel; this lack of syncope allows for the voicing of the dental, and the labial receives intervocalic treatment as well: *cŭbĭtu* > OPtg. *covedo,* except that it drops between two *i*'s in *cīvĭtāte* > *cidade*. Ptg. *dívida* < *dēbĭta* and *dúvida* < **dŭbĭta* are learned. In Spanish, the labial may vocalize, but only after intervocalic voicing of the dental has taken place: *dēbĭta* > *debda* > *deuda; cīvĭtāte* > *ciudad,* or it may drop before the dental, again only after voicing has occurred: *cŭbĭtu* > *cobdo* > *codo*. Catalan shows vocalization to *u̯t*: *dēbĭtu* > *deute; male habĭtu* > OCat. *malaute; bt* is retained in learned words, though with a *pt* pronunciation: *dubte, dubtar, dissabte*. Occitan has a variety of outcomes, showing vocalization or retention of the labial and voicing or non-voicing of the dental: *sabbatu (die)* > *sabde, sapte; male habĭtu* > *malaute, malaude, malapte; dēbĭtu* > *deute, deude, depte*. French drops the labial following syncope, but shows some hesitation between voiced and voiceless outcomes: *cŭbĭtu* > OFr. *code, cote* > *coude; dēbĭta* > OFr. *dete* > Fr. *dette*.

Rm. *cetate,* Ptg. *cidade*: the combination of *ī* and *ĭ* that arises through the loss of *v* in *cīvĭtāte* is resolved in favor of *e* in Rumanian and of *i* in Portuguese.

Ptg. *dúvida,* Sp. *duda*: *u* results from learned treatment in Portuguese while, in Spanish, the vowel closure may be attributed to the following labial plus dental cluster (Menéndez Pidal §20.2), unless it is simply learned here, too.

Lat. *male habĭtu*: the phonological development of *male habĭtu* in Gallo-Romance poses severe problems; Thomas suggests as etymon a form **malabĭdu,* showing analogical influence of the *-ĭdu* suffix, while Richter believes we have to do with a learned medical term syncoped at the **mala-*

vidu stage (*FEW* VI 93*)*. It., OSp., OPtg. *malato* are borrowed from French or Occitan.

309. Lat. *-ct-*

pt:	Rm.
tt:	It.
[*tš*]:	Sp.
i̯t:	Ptg., Cat., Fr.
i̯t or [*tš*]:	Occ.

Latin
tēctu, nŏcte, lacte, frūctu

Rm.	It.	Sp.	Ptg.	Cat.	Occ.	OFr.	Fr.
	tetto	*techo*	*teito*		*tech*	*teit*	*toit*
noapte	*notte*	*noche*	*noite*	*nit,*	*noch,*		*nuit*
				nuit	*noit,*		
				(old)	*nuoch,*		
					nuech,		
					nuoit, nueit		
lapte	*latte*	*leche*	*leite*	*lleit*	*lach*		*lait*
frupt,	*frutto*	*fruto,*	*fruto,*	*fruit*	*fruch,*		*fruit*
fruct		*fruito*	*fruito*		*frut*		
		(old),	(old)				
		frucho					
		(old)					

Commentary

The *ct* cluster gives *pt* in Rumanian, assimilates to *tt* in Italian and evolves to [*tš*] in Spanish. The area in which *ct* becomes *i̯t* comprises Portuguese, Catalan and French, while Occitan forms a transitional zone between the Spanish and French developments, having both [*tš*] and *i̯t*. Generally speaking, [*tš*] is characteristic of the southern zones of the Occitan domain, *i̯t* of the northern (Roncaglia, p. 68; Anglade, p. 166). It is generally assumed that *k* was pronounced as a fricative before a consonant, presumably the equivalent of the German velar *ach-Laut*. This velar sound is continued in Rumanian and Italian, while a palatal pronunciation prevailed elsewhere. The nature of the preceding vowel may have determined the original pronunciation, with a velar fricative being the norm following back vowels, while a palatal fricative appeared after front vowels. The individual Romance languages then opted for one or the other of these sounds (Lausberg §§430–435; Iordan-Manoliu §168; Rohlfs §258).

The stages in the development that leads from *ct* to [*tš*] in Spanish are the transformation of *c* to *i̯*, the palatalization of *t* to [*tš*] caused by *i̯* and, finally, the absorption of *i̯* into [*tš*]: *pĕctus > pecho; profĕctu > provecho*. When preceded by *i*, the *i̯* coming from *c* is absorbed: *frīctu > frito*. If the preceding vowel is *a*, it will contract with *i̯* into **ai* and hence *e*: *lacte > *laiche > leche; factu > hecho; lactūca > lechuga*. In Portuguese, the loss of *i̯* when preceded by *u* is general: *frūctu > fruito > fruto; trŭcta > truita > truta*. The reduction of *ct* to *t* may also be a learned feature: *vīctĭma > vítima*. The *-oct-* combination evolves to *-oit-* in some regions, to *-out-* in others: *nŏcte > noite* and *noute*. The secondary *c't* cluster yields a voiced *s* in Portuguese, while Castilian desonorizes to [*θ*]: *recĭtāre >* Ptg., Sp. *rezar*. In Catalan, the yod is active in reducing a preceding *a* to *e* via *ei*: *factu >* OCat. *feyt > fet*, and the reduction of *ei* to *e* seems to have gained further momentum through an analogy with this particular development: *strĭctu >* OCat. *estreyt > estret; dīrēctu > dret*. In French, the secondary *c't* in final position moves to *i̯st*: *placet > plaist > plaît; lūcet > luist > luit*, while *facit > fait* and *dīcit > dit* are obscure.

Cat. *nit*: for the reduction of OCat. *nuit* to *nit*, see §163.

Lat. *lac, lacte*: neuter in Latin, this noun becomes feminine in Spanish, Catalan, Gascon and in a few dialects of Languedoc, masculine in Italian, Portuguese, Occitan, French, Rumanian and the Leonese dialect. The source of the Romance forms is the popular *lacte*, not CL *lac*.

Lat. *frūctus*: in Old Spanish, the popular form is *frucho*, encountered in Berceo, and there is also documentation for *fruito*, but both of these forms soon yield to a semi-learned *fruto*. For Portuguese, the reduction of the earlier *fruito* to *fruto* is regular, and other popular developments are It. *frutto*, Occ. *fruch* and Fr. *fruit*. The Occitan variant *frut* may have lost its *i* to an analogy with *fruch*.

310. Lat. *-nct-*

nt:	Rm., It., Sp., Ptg., Cat.
[*ntš*], *n'* or *n' + t*:	Occ.
n' + t > i̯nt:	Fr.

Latin
sanctu

It.	Sp.	Ptg.	Cat.	Occ.	Fr.
santo	santo	santo	sant	sanch, sanh, saint	saint

Commentary

Rumanian, Italian, Spanish, Portuguese and Catalan reduce *nct* to *nt* whereas, in Gallo-Romance, the *k* palatalizes the *n*. In French, the palatal element is released in front as *i*, which combines with the preceding vowel, and *n* causes nasalization to occur. Occitan has a variety of outcomes: [*ntš*], a palatal *n* or *int*: *sanch, sanh, saint* and *sant* (Appel §58). The simplification of *nct* to *nt* follows a trend that is already noted for Latin: *quintus* for *quinctus* 'fifth' (cf. *quinque* 'five'). For Italian, Rohlfs (§272) postulates an intermediate palatalized stage *n' + t;* however, documentation for such a development is limited to the northern dialects. A Rumanian dialectal form is *sânt*.

311. Lat. -*cs*-

ps:	Rm.
ss or [*šš*]:	It.
i̯ + [*š*] > [*š*] > [*χ*]:	Sp.
[*š*]:	Ptg., Cat.
i̯ + *s*:	Occ., Fr.

Latin
maxĭlla, cŏxa

Rm.	It.	Sp.	Ptg.	Cat.	Occ.	OFr.	Fr.
măseà	mas- cella	mejilla	maxila		mais- sela	mais- sele	
coapsă	coscia		coxa	cuixa	coissa, cueissa, cuoissa		cuisse

Commentary

The fricative pronunciation of *k* before *s* follows the same pattern as for *ct*. Rumanian has *ps: cŏxa > coapsă; frīxit > fripse.* A reduction of *cs* to *s* has occurred in *frasin < fraxĭnu* and in *măseà* (§217). Of the dual outcome in Italian, *ss* and a lengthened [š], it is the former that represents the norm (Rohlfs §225). Not only does it parallel the development of *ct* to *tt* and the general trend in Italian toward total assimilation of a variety of contiguous consonants, but it is also the only form encountered in verb paradigms. This is important since these tend to be genuinely Tuscan and are very seldom borrowed from dialects: *cŏxī > cossi; vīxī > vissi; dūxi > dussi.* Other examples are *axe > asse; prŏxĭmu > prossimo; saxu > sasso; sĕxagĭnta > sessanta.* Examples of the development to [šš] are: *cŏxa > coscia; laxāre > lasciare; exīre + ūstiu > uscire; axĭlla > ascella.* Lausberg (§441) holds the opposite view from that of Rohlfs: [šš] represents the popular development, and perfects in *ss* are analogically obtained: *cossi* is modeled on *scrissi < scrīpsī,* etc. In an attempt to account for the heterogeneous development in Italian, Meyer-Lübke (*Ital. Gramm.* §225) establishes the rule that *cs* evolves to [š] before the stress before or after front vowels, and he offers explanations for some of the exceptions to this principle: *lasciare* is derived from **laxiare, coscia* from **coxea.* These explanations, however, are not repeated in the *REW.* The dialectal distribution of *ss* and [šš] is quite complex and does not provide any solution to the problem. In the final analysis, no clear distinction between the two developments can be established; we have to do with two tendencies that are strongly intertwined.

In Spanish, *k* palatalizes, being ultimately transformed into a yod, and this yod then palatalizes the *s* to [š] and is absorbed into it. This stage is represented graphically by *x* while the change to [χ], spelled *j*, comes about with the Castilian velarization in the seventeenth century: *ks > k's > i̯s > [i̯š] > [š] > [χ]* (Menéndez Pidal §50.2; García de Diego, p. 117). If the preceding vowel is *a*, the yod combines with it, forming the diphthong **ai* which soon evolves to *e: *maxĕlla* (for CL *maxĭlla*) *> mexiella > mejilla; taxu > texo > tejo.* At the end of a syllable, the chain of developments as outlined above comes to a halt at the *i̯s* stage with no subsequent palatalization of *s: fraxĭnu > *fraisno > freisno > fresno.* The same is true of the word-final position: *sĕx > seis.* Portuguese has [š], spelled *x*, and a release of yod toward the vowel *a* is the norm, just as in Spanish: *cŏxa > coxa; saxu > seixo.* There are rare occurrences of *ss* in Portuguese: *dīxit > disse* vs. *dixe < dīxī,* but this seems to be limited to third-person singular perfects. In Catalan, *cs* moves via *i̯s* and [i̯š] to [š], spelled *ix: cŏxa > cuixa; axĭlla > aixella; ĕxīre > eixir; exāmen > eixam.* Occitan and French both have *i̯ss*: *cŏxa* > Occ. *coissa,* Fr. *cuisse; exīre* > Occ., OFr. *eissir; laxāre* > Occ. *laissar,* OFr. *laissier,* Fr. *laisser.* Occ. *laishar* and *laichar* are dialectal. OFr. *laissier* shows the regular release of a yod toward the free tonic *a* (§171).

Lat. *exīre*: OFr. *eissir* is flanked by a variant *issir,* obtained by analogy with the stem-stressed forms where *ĕ* + palatal regularly evolves to *i*: *ĕxit* > OFr. *ist* (§162). Occitan shows the same fluctuation between *eiss-* and *iss-* (Anglade, p. 290). It. *uscire* owes its initial vowel to the influence of the noun *uscio.*

Lat. *maxīlla*: the Spanish and Occitan developments require the replacement of *-īlla* by the *-ĕlla* suffix.

312. Lat. *-g'd-*

?:	Rm.
dd:	It.
no cluster formed:	Sp., Ptg.
d:	Cat.
i̯d or [*dž*]:	Occ.
i̯d:	Fr.

Latin
*frīgĭdu, *frĭgĭdu*

It.	Sp.	Ptg.	Cat.	Occ.	OFr.	Fr.
freddo	*frío*	*frio*	*fred*	*freg, freit*	*freit*	*froid*

Commentary
The *g'd* cluster is encountered in **frĭgĭdu* and derivations from there. It forms the voiced counterpart to *ct* and evolves accordingly, giving *dd* in Italian, *i̯d* or [*dž*] in Occitan and *i̯d* in French. In Spanish and Portuguese, *d* drops early in the *-ĭdu* suffix (§146), while Catalan has *d,* perhaps from an earlier *i̯d.* The voiceless outcomes in Occitan and French are brought about by the final position; the corresponding feminine forms are Occ. *freja, freida* and Fr. *froide.* There do not appear to be any Rumanian examples of this rare cluster.

Lat. *frīgĭdu,* see §146.

313. Lat. -gn-

> mn:　Rm.
> n'n':　It.
> n':　Sp., Ptg., Cat., Occ., Fr.

Latin
pŭgnu, lĭgnu, -a

Rm.	It.	Sp.	Ptg.	Cat.	Occ.	OFr.	Fr.
pumn	*pugno*	*puño*	*punho*	*puny*	*ponh*	*poin*	*poing*
lemn	*legno,*	*leño,*	*lenho,*	*lleny,*	*lenh,*	*lein,*	
	legna	*leña*	*lenha*	*llenya*	*lenha*	*leigne*	

Commentary

　　Lat. *gn* evolves to a lengthened palatal *n* in Italian and a single palatal *n* in the western languages, while Rumanian has *mn*.

　　Just as for *ct* and *cs*, Lausberg distinguishes between a velar pronunciation continued in Rumanian and in southern Italian dialects, and a palatal pronunciation elsewhere (Lausberg §444; Rohlfs §259). Rumanian has *mn*: *sĭgnu > semn; cognātu > cumnat; agnĕllu > mniel > miel* (with aphaeresis of *a*). This peculiar case of mutation is a late development characteristic of Rumanian alone. Intermediate stages in the evolution leading from *gn* to *mn* are difficult to establish. Lausberg (§445) proposes *gn > *g̯n > *ᵬn > mn*, but it is perhaps safer to assume that we have to do with a sudden change rather than with a progressive evolution (Nandris, pp. 154–155, 261–263). Italian has a lengthened palatal *n*, obtained via *i̯n*, and Spanish and Portuguese obtain their palatal *n* in a similar manner. In Spanish, this *ñ*, differing from the palatal emerging from *ct* and *cs*, does not inflect a preceding *a*: *tam magnu > tamaño; stagnu > estaño* vs. *lacte > leche; taxu > tejo*. The *gn* cluster is retained in learned words: Sp. *pugnar* vs. OSp. *puñar < pŭgnare;* Sp. *signar < sĭgnāre* vs. *enseñar < *in-sĭgnāre. G* fell in semi-learned words: *dĭgnu >* OSp., OPtg. *dino; malĭgnu >* OSp., OPtg. *malino,* but it was later restored in both spelling and pronunciation: Sp., Ptg. *digno, maligno.* The same feature may also be observed in fifteenth-sixteenth century French, which has *dine* and *sine* for *digne* and *signe* (Nyrop I §335). Sp., Ptg. *reino < rēgnu* was arrested at the *in* stage due to the analogical influence of Sp. *rey,* Ptg. *rei < rēge* (Williams §92.5). Catalan has a palatal *n* spelled *ny: jŭngit > juny.* Occitan retains *n'* very generally while, in French, this palatal *n* is kept intervocalically only but resolved as *i̯n* and with nasalization in final position: *dĭgnat* > *daigne* vs. *sĭgnu* > OFr. *sein* > *seing; pŭgnu* > OFr. *poin* > *poing.*

The vowel *ǫ* preceding the palatal *n* that comes from *gn* is inflected to *u* in Italian, Spanish, Portuguese and Catalan, but remains intact in Occitan and French, while the Rumanian *u* follows regularly from Lat. *ŭ.* The close *e* suffers no inflection anywhere in this position.

OFr. *lein, leigne*: these representatives of the *lĭgnu* family have not survived in Modern French; they were replaced by *bois,* drawn from Gmc. **bosc* (cf. E. *bush*).

CL *cognōscĕre*: this Classical form had been reduced to *conōscĕre* in Vulgar Latin through the influence of the simple verb *noscĕre.* The Romance reflexes thus follow from an etymon with intervocalic *n*: Rm. *cunoaşte,* It. *conoscere,* Sp. *conocer,* Cat. *conéixer,* Occ. *conoisser,* OFr. *conoistre,* Fr. *connaître,* the sole exception being Ptg. *conhecer,* which goes back to a literary *cognōscĕre.*

314. The -*gm*- Cluster

The *gm* cluster is unfamiliar to Latin speakers, appearing only in borrowings from Greek. It is resolved as *u̯m* in *sagma* > VL *sauma* > It. *soma,* Occ. *sauma,* Fr. *somme; phlegma* > OSp., Ptg. *fleuma,* Occ. *fleuma,* OFr. *fleume.* This points to a velar quality of *gm* in Latin. Learned forms retain *gm* intact, while a reduction to *m* signals a more popular development: Sp. *flema,* Fr. *flegme.*

315. Consonant + Yod

A Vulgar Latin yod arises when a syllabic *i* or *e,* following a consonant, is in hiatus position: CL *filia* > VL *fīli̯a;* CL *area* > VL *ari̯a.* The yod frequently merges with the preceding consonant into a palatalized or assibilated sound, and some consonants are lengthened in the process, specifically in Italian and Sardinian. The outcome of the yod cluster may be voiced or voiceless depending on whether the group is intervocalic or postconsonantal, or it may relate to the nature of the cluster or to other factors.

316. Lat. -*ti̯*-

ts:	Rm.
tts or [*dž*]:	It.
dz:	OSp.

[θ]:   Sp.
z or s: Ptg.
∅:   Cat.
z: Occ.
i̯ + z: Fr.

Latin
prĕtiu, ratiōne

Rm.	It.	Sp.	Ptg.	Cat.	Occ.	OFr.	Fr.
preţ	*prezzo*	*precio*	*preço*	*preu*	*pretz*	*pris*	*prix*
	ragione	*razón*	*razão*	*raó*	*razoṇ*		*raison*

Commentary

   The *ti̯* cluster is palatalized and assibilated very early, with a *tz* graph documented in second and third century inscriptions: *Vincentzo, ampitzatru* < *amphiteatrum* (Väänänen §99). Rumanian has [*ts*]. The norm for Italian is *tts*, but an alternate evolution, leading to a voiced [*dž*] is also well represented in the language. Spanish goes through a voiced stage *dz*, which unvoices to [θ] with the Castilian desonorization in the seventeenth century. Portuguese has *z*, but occurrences of a voiceless *s* are quite numerous. The cluster usually drops in Catalan. Occitan has a voiced *s*, French a voiced *s* accompanied by a yod release, while cases of a voiceless *s* are only very sporadically found in Gallo-Romance.

   Rumanian has [*ts*]: *nĭgrĭtia > negreaţa; pŭteu > puţ*, but with isolated occurrences of [*tš*]: **fētiŏlu > fecior; tītiōne > tâciune*. Italian has a voiceless *tts*, spelled *zz*: *palatiu > palazzo; Aretiu > Arezzo; pŭteu > pozzo*. The alternate development to a voiced [*dž*] is encountered in borrowings from French: *prĕtiāre > pregiare; statiōne > stagione; mĭnūtia > minugia*. Overall, It. [*dž*] corresponds to a voiced *s* in the French source: OFr. *preisier,* Fr. *priser,* Fr. *saison* (< *satiōne*), Fr. *menuise* (Rohlfs §289). Spanish moves via *dz* to [θ], spelled *z*: *pŭteu > pozo; tītiōne > tizón; trīstĭtia > tristeza; satiōne > sazón*. There is no yod-caused inflection of the vowel. *Palatiu > palacio* is learned. Intervocalic *ti̯* is subject to voicing in Portuguese, the regular outcome being a voiced *s,* for which the traditional spelling is *z*: *prĕtiāre > prezar; ratiōne < razão; satiōne > sazão,* yet a voiceless *s* spelled *ç* is even more common (Lausberg §454); *palatiu > paço; pŭteu > poço; *mētio > meço; oratiōne > oração*. This difference in treatment is hardly attributable to the place *ti̯* assumes in relation to the stress, as suggested by Huber (§§191.1, 192), who considers *ç* the norm following the stress, *z* the regular outcome if *ti̯* precedes the stress. This is contradicted by *oração* vs. *razão* and by the common *-eza* suffix, and as far as verb forms are concerned, the stress hypothesis tends to engender an unreasonable amount of analogical explanations. A widespread confusion between *ki̯* and *ti̯* offers a far more acceptable solution to the problem (Williams §89.5.A), and there is further the possibility that, at least in some instances, a double *t* may be involved. A case in point is *praça*, from a hypothetical **plattea* influenced by the adjective *plattu*, where Occitan and French, too, have voiceless outcomes: Occ. *plassa*, Fr. *place*.

In Catalan, *ti̯* mostly falls, in the view of some scholars specifically when it stands before the stress: *satiōne > saó; prĕtiāre > prear*. The intermediate stage in this evolution is a voiced *s*, which is well documented in Old Catalan: *acūtiāre > agusar, aguar; attitiāre > atisar, atiar*. Phonologically, it thus merges with the outcome of intervocalic *d* (§266) and *s* (§268), and as a rule the voiced *s* resulting from any of these sources tends to drop. It seems somewhat doubtful, however, that position in relation to stress is of any importance here, for the two examples Badía Margarit (§87, II) cites as proof of the alternate change to a voiceless *s*, spelled *ç* or *ss*: *platea > plaça* and **pĕtia > peça*, flow not from an intervocalic *ti̯*, but from a *tti̯* cluster: **plattea* and **pĕttia*, and these same forms with a geminated *t* are required for other Romance evolutions as well. In final position, the cluster evolves to *u̯*: *pŭteu > pou; palātiu > palau; Dalmatiu > Dalmau*. While this is the explanation that is traditionally proposed (B. Moll §183, Badía Margarit §87, II), it is certainly tempting to view *u* as a continuation of the final vowel, retained as *u̯* in direct contact with the stressed vowel after the elimination of *ti̯*, and this would appear to be the interpretation implicit in the example Lausberg (§453) cites of the loss of *ti̯*: *prĕtiu > preu*. Fouché (*Phonétique historique*, p. 190), on the other hand, considers *s*, spelled *ç*, the sole reflex of intervocalic posttonic *ti̯*, but this forces him into playing a cumbersome analogical game: *preu* is drawn analogically from *prĕtiāre > prear*, and *pou* is based on a hypothetical **pŭteāre* which does not even appear to be continued anywhere. The isolated *arbŭteu > arboç* on which Fouché's argumentation is based could be analogical from the feminine form *arbŭtea*, where *ti̯* is not final (B. Moll §183). The voiceless *s* of Cat. *arboça* points to postconsonantal treatment of *ti̯*, however, which makes Antoine Thomas' suggested etymon **arbŭttiu* the likeliest source (*Romania*, 25 (1896), 382). For the Romance continuations of Lat. *arbuteus*, see Jensen: "*Arbuteus* and the ty Cluster in Romance", *RPh*, 48 (1994), n°2, 136–144. Corominas (I 253) suggests that the intermediate stage prior to elimination was not *s*, but the voiced interdental *đ* from -*d*-, -*ti̯*- and -*c* + *i, e*.

Occitan has *z*: *satiōne* > *sazoṇ; bĕllatiōre* > *belazor; prĕtiāre* > *prezar;* **acūtiāre* > *aguzar;* -*ĭtia* > -*eza*. Desonorization takes place in word-final position: *palatiu* > *palatz*. The fact that it is not *s* that appears here, but *tz,* is a sure sign that the primitive intervocalic stage is not represented by *z,* that *z* must have been secondarily obtained from the simplification of an earlier *dz* (Appel §59b). It follows that, in Occitan, affricates were reduced earlier internally than in final position. French regularly has a voiced *s* accompanied by a yod release: *satiōne* > *saison; prĕtiāre* > OFr. *preisier, proisier* (Fr. *priser* is obtained analogically from the stem-stressed forms of the paradigm: *prĕtiat* > *prise,* etc.); *Vĕnĕtia* > *Venise.* The -*i̯tia* suffix is regularly continued as -*eise,* -*oise:* **prōdĭtia* > OFr. *proeise,* but it mostly receives learned treatment: *justice, prouesse.* As in Occitan, a voiceless *s* is the norm in final position: *palatiu* > *palais; prĕtiu* > OFr. *pris* > *prix.* Internally, a voiceless outcome appears limited to learned words and to *place,* for which the etymon is **plattea* rather than *platea*.

Lat. *prĕtiu*: this word receives popular treatment in most areas of Romania, but Sp. *precio* is learned, and so is perhaps Ptg. *preço* (*FEW* IX 370–375), although this is debatable in view of the frequency of the voiceless outcome of the *ti̯* cluster. The *x* of Fr. *prix* is arbitrary spelling.

317. Consonant + *ti̯*

    ts or [*tš*]:   Rm., It.
    [*θ*]:   Sp.
    s: Ptg., Cat., Occ., Fr.

Latin
fŏrtia

It.	Sp.	Ptg.	Cat.	Occ.	Fr.
forza	*fuerza,* *fuerça* (old)	*força*	*força*	*forsa*	*force*

Commentary

If the *ti̯* cluster is preceded by a consonant, the outcome is voiceless throughout; there is no lengthening in Italian, and *ts* may be posited as the intermediate stage in the Hispanic and Gallo-Romance developments. The *sti̯* cluster is treated separately.

Rumanian has [*ts*]: *pŏtĕntia* > *putinţa*; **in-altiāre* > *înălţà; scŏrtea* > *scoarţa*, but a variant development to [*tš*] is also found: **matteŭca* > *măciucă*, which Nandris (pp. 124–125) links to the position before the stress. See below for Italian, where the opposite distribution has been proposed. Italian likewise vacillates between *ts* and [*tš*]: **altiāre* > *alzare* (but also OIt. *alciare*); *sperantia* > *speranza; Florentiae* > *Fiorenze* > *Firenze; cantiōne* > *canzone; Martiu* > *marzo; tĕrtiu* > *terzo* vs. **tractiāre* > *tracciare; *cum-initiāre* > *cominciare; *captiāre* > *cacciare; corrŭptiāre* > *corrucciare*. It is quite difficult to account for this dual outcome; it cannot be tied to the stress, as suggested by Meyer-Lübke, who holds that *ts* is the norm before the stress, [*tš*] after the stress. This theory is easily contradicted by the example material. It seems that *cti̯* may have flowed together with *ci̯*, which accounts for the very general evolution to a lengthened [*tš*] here, an exception being **dīrectiāre* > *drizzare*. Elsewhere, *ts* seems to represent the norm, while [*tš*] may stem from dialectal or foreign influences (Rohlfs §291). Where the posited cluster is *tti̯*, Italian lengthens the *ts*: **mattea* > *mazza; *pĕttiu* > *pezzo*.

In Spanish, *ti̯* evolves to a voiceless *ç* [*ts*]; this sound later changes to [*θ*], and the old *ç* spelling gives way to *z*: *Martiu* > *março* > *marzo; *pĕttia* > *pieça* > *pieza; -antia* > *ança* > *-anza; *captiāre* > *caçar* > *cazar*. Portuguese has *s*, obtained via the affricate *ts*: *tertiāriu* > *terceiro; lĕnteu* > *lenço; silĕntiu* > OPtg. *seenço*, and the same development is characteristic of Catalan, which represents its voiceless *s* graphically by *ç*: *lĕctiōne* > *lliçó; lĭnteōlu* > *llençol; mattiāna* > *maçana; *altiāre* > *alçar*. In the primary *pti̯* cluster, *p* is assimilated to *t*, whereupon the resulting *tti̯* combination evolves to *s*, mostly spelled *ç*: **captiāre* > *caçar; *nŏptias* > *noces*, while the secondary *p'ti̯* cluster retains *p* before *ç*: *capĭtiāle* > *capçal; *excapĭtiāre* > *escapçar*. In Occitan, the post-consonantal *ti̯* moves via *ts* to *s*: *cantiōne* > *cansoṇ; -antia* > *-ansa; *captiāre* > *cassar; nĕptia* > *nessa*, and French shows the same evolution: **captiāre* > *chacier* > *chasser; Martiu* > *marz* > *mars; cantiōne* > *chanson; *matteŭca* > *massue; nĕptia* > *nièce*.

Lat. **pĕttia* or **pĕttiu*: this word, though considered of Gaulish extraction, is pan-Romance and not limited to areas of Gaulish settlement. In

French, *pĕttia* regularly evolves to *pièce*, with the diphthongization caused by the palatal, and Italian has *pezza* and *pezzo*. For Sp. *pieza,* Corominas declares that the etymology *pĕttia* presents no difficulty whatsoever (IV 539). One would, however, have expected the palatal to prevent any diphthongization from occurring (§164).

318. Lat. *-sti̯-*

[š]:	Rm., Cat.
[šš]:	It.
[θ]:	Sp.
s? or [tš]*?* or [š]*?*:	Ptg.
i̯ + *s*:	Occ., Fr.

Latin
VL *ūstiu, angŭstia*

Rm.	It.	Sp.	Cat.	Occ.	OFr.	Fr.
uşa	*uscio*	*uço* (old)		*uis*	*uis*	*huis*
	angoscia	*angoxa* (old)	*angoixa*	*angoissa*		*angoisse*

Commentary

Rumanian has [š]: *pastiōne > păşune; ōstiŏlu > uşor,* and it shares this evolution with Catalan, which uses an *ix* spelling: *angoixa; *pŏstius > puix.* Words that retain *sti̯* are learned: *bēstia > bèstia; christiānu > cristiá.* The *sti̯* group gives a lengthened [šš] in Italian: *bīstia > biscia.* Spanish has [θ]: *ūstiu >* OSp. *uço, uzo* (§169); Sp. *angustia* is learned, and OSp. *angoxa,* with *x* and not *ç,* is probably borrowed from Catalan (Corominas I 270). Reliable Portuguese examples are hard to come by; one would expect *s,* but unfortunately *ūstiu* is not continued in Portuguese, and *bīstia > bicha* may have been borrowed from the Galician dialect (Huber §193.1). Gallo-Romance has *s* plus a yod release.

319. Lat. *-di̯-*

z or [ž]:   Rm.

[*dž*] (lengthened) or
    zz (voiced):   It.
        i̯:   Sp., Fr.
       [*ž*]:   Ptg.
   [*dž*] > [*ž*]:   Cat.
i̯ or [*dž*] (or [*dz*]?):   Occ.

Latin
hŏdie, radiu, mŏdiu

It.	Sp.	Ptg.	Cat.	Occ.	OFr.	Fr.
oggi,	*hoy*	*hoje*	*avui,*	*oi,*	*hui*	*(aujourd')hui*
ogge			*huy*	*uoi,*		
(old)			(old)	*uei*		
raggio,	*rayo*	*raio*	*raig*	*rai,*	*rai*	*rai*
razzo				*rag*		
moggio,	*moyo*	*moio*		*moi,*	*mui*	*muid*
mozzo				*mog*		

Commentary

Intervocalic *di̯* and *i̯* merge in Vulgar Latin. Rumanian has *z* or [*ž*]. Italian has a lengthened [*dž*], but also rare cases of a lengthened *dz* (§320). Spanish, Occitan and French all have *i̯*, while Portuguese and Catalan have [*ž*] obtained from an earlier [*dž*] (§320).

Rumanian has *z*: *mĕdiu > miez; sĕdeo >* ORm. *șez; audio >* ORm. *auz* (replaced in the literary language by the analogically obtained *sed, aud*), but there are also instances of [*ž*]: *adjutāre > ajutà*, specifically before a tonic velar vowel: **rotŭndiōre > rotunjor; *rapĭdiōre > răpejor.* The norm for Italian is a lengthened [*dž*]: *vĭdeo >* OIt. *veggio; Claudia > Chioggia; pŏdiu > poggio,* but certain words show a development to a lengthened *dz*: *radiu > razzo; mŏdiu > mozzo; mĕdiu > mezzo.* The *-ĭdiāre* suffix evolves regularly to *-eggiare,* corresponding to Fr. *-oyer:* It. *verdeggiare,* Fr. *verdoyer;* It. *guerreggiare,* Fr. *guerroyer,* but it is also the source of a learned *-izzare* or *-ezzare,* paralleling Fr. *-iser:* It. *moralizzare,* Fr. *moraliser;* It. *battezzare,* Fr. *baptiser;* It. *fraternizzare,* Fr. *fraterniser.* *Mezzo < mĕdiu* may not be popular; there is no documentation for **meggio,* and Spanish similarly has a learned *medio,* and no trace of a popular **meyo.* No acceptable phonological explanation has as yet been found for the alternate evolution to *zz.* Rohlfs (§276) suggests that the *zz* forms may have come in from northern dialects, since *razzo* and *mozzo* are technical terms from the cartwright and wheelwright industry in Lombardy, but it remains a mystery why also *mezzo* and *rozzo* < *rŭdiu* have adopted this dialectal shape. *Annoiare* is borrowed from Occ. *enoiar* < *in-ŏdiāre*, and the noun *noia* is derived from the same source.

Spanish resolves *dị* as *ị*: *radiāre* > *rayar; pŏdiu* > *poyo; mŏdiu* > *moyo,* but this *ị* disappears if it is placed after the vowels *e* and *i: vĭdeo* > *veo; fastīdiu* > *hastío; perfĭdia* > *porfía; -ĭdiāre* > *-ear,* as in *guerrear, verdear* (Menéndez Pidal §§53.3, 125.2.C). Sp. *enojar* and It. *annoiare* pay tribute to the power of expansion of Occ. *enojar* which, along with the noun *enueg* or *enoi,* serves to express a concept of great prominence in troubadour lyrics. There can be no doubt that Sp. *enojar* is a borrowing (Corominas II 635–636), yet based on this sole evidence, García de Diego (pp. 131–132) makes the unfounded claim that [χ] represents an alternate development of intervocalic *dị* or *ị* in Spanish. A native evolution of Lat. *ĭnŏdiāre* would give Sp. *enoyar,* a form which is actually documented in Berceo. For the dual outcome in Old Spanish of *dị* in *badiu* > *bayo* and *baço* and *radia* > *raya* and *raça,* see §320. Portuguese has [ž]: *adjutāre* > *ajudar; vĭdeo* > *vejo; hŏdie* > *hoje,* but *dị* is resolved as *ị* in the same words for which Italian shows the deviant evolution to a lengthened *dz: moio, raio; mĕdiu* > *meio.* These words are usually considered to be either semi-learned or borrowings from Spanish (William §89.5.A). Catalan has [ž] spelled *j* from an earlier [*dž*]: *adjūtat* > *ajuda; videāmus* > *vejam; radiāre* > *rajar.* Desonorization to [*tš*] spelled *ig* is the norm in final position: *radiu* > *raig; gaudiu* > *goig; mĕdiu* > *mig; pŏdiu* > *puig.* A notable exception is *hŏdie* > OCat. *huy,* Mod. Cat. *avui,* which may have obtained its *i* by analogy with *hĕrī* > *i, ir,* Mod. Cat. *ahir.*

The Occitan spelling for the sound issuing from Lat. *dị* is consistently *i,* but this graph covers at least two pronunciations, yod and an assibilated [*dž*]: *ĭnvĭdia* > *enveia* and *enveja; *in-ŏdiāre* > *enoiar* and *enojar; pŏdiare* > *poiar* and *pojar* (Roncaglia, pp. 66–67; Anglade, p. 179). To this, Appel (§59b) adds *dz,* no doubt a rare form which he probably extrapolates from the existence of word-final *tz* in *in-ŏdiu* > *enueitz,* an infrequent variant of *enoi, enueg.* It is *enueg* (with *g* = [*tš*]) which represents the normal desonorization of [*dž*] in final position. In French, *dị* is reduced to *ị*: *radiu* > OFr. *rai; gaudia* > *joie; pŏdiu* > *pui* (cf. *Puy-de-Dôme*); *hŏdie* > OFr. *hui; audio* > OFr. *oi* (Nyrop §475.4).

It. *oggi*: the final *i* is obtained analogically from *ieri* < *hĕrī.*

OCat. *huy,* Cat. *avui*: while the final *i* can very handily be drawn from an analogy with *hěrī,* and while the inflection of *o* to *u* is the norm when a yod follows, there are certain details in the evolution that have still not been fully elucidated. The initial *a* may follow from *anit < ad nŏcte* (B. Moll §219), but unexplained is the epenthesis of *v* before a velar vowel which, besides in *avui,* also occurs in *ŏcto > vuit* and *hōra > vora.* This feature is also documented for Occitan, where *von, vostar, vuelh* are encountered as variants of *on, ostar, uelh.*

Lat. *pŏdiu: pui,* as the reflex of *pŏdiu,* has been abandoned in the North of France where it could not be kept separate from *puits < pŭteu,* whose *u* vocalism is irregular and unexplained. In the South, where *pŭteu > potz* runs no risk of being confused with the reflexes of *pŏdiu,* Occ. *poi, pog, puech,* these forms have not fallen into disfavor.

320. Lat. *-rdi̯-*

rdz:	Rm., It.
rts:	OSp., OPtg.
[*rθ*]:	Sp.
rs:	Ptg.
[*rž*]:	Cat.
rdz or [*rdž*]:	Occ.
[*rdž*] > [*rž*]:	Fr.

Latin
hŏrdeu, hŏrdeŏlu

Rm.	It.	Sp.	Ptg.	Cat.	Occ.	OFr.	Fr.
orz	*orzo*		*orjo* (old), *orge* (old)	*ordi*	*orge, ordi*		*orge*
		orzuelo			*orjol, orzol*	*orjuel*	

Commentary

When *di̯* follows the consonant *r,* it evolves to a voiced *dz* in Rumanian and Italian, while Old Spanish and Old Portuguese have *ts,* which is simplified to [*θ*] in Spanish, *s* in Portuguese. Catalan has [*ž*], Occitan *dz* or [dž] or retention of a vocalic *i* with no cluster formed. Old French [dž] is simplified to [ž] in the modern language.

Following the consonant *r,* the *di̯* cluster evolves to a voiced *s* in Rumanian: *ardeo* > *arz.* The Italian outcome of the postconsonantal *di̯* is a voiced *dz,* spelled *z*: *hŏrdeu* > *orzo; vir(i)dia* > *verza.* This development leads Rohlfs (§276) to suggest that It. *mezzo* and *razzo* may go back to a reinforced **meddiu* and **raddiu.* The rule showing a dual outcome of intervocalic *di̯* in Italian (§319) could thus be reformulated to read that [dž] is the norm in intervocalic position, *zz* if *di̯* is postconsonantal.

For Old Spanish and Old Portuguese, a primitive voiced stage *dz* was replaced by *ts* early on, a change which may have been hastened by the lack of a correlation between the absolute initial and the syllable-initial position, with *ts* alone capable of assuming either position (Lausberg §§407, 457). Old Spanish has *ts,* spelled *ç*: *orçuelo; vir(i)dia* > *berça,* while the modern pronunciation [θ] is rendered graphically by *z*: *orzuelo, berza; *admŏrdiu* > *almuerzo.* Since the intervocalic *di̯* is resolved as *i̯* in Spanish (§319), while the postconsonantal *di̯* moves to *ts* and [θ], Menéndez Pidal (§53.3) explains the few cases in which the intervocalic *di̯* becomes OSp. *ç* as having resulted from the gemination of *d* before yod: *badiu* > *bayo* vs. **baddiu* > *baço; radia* > *raya* vs. **raddia* > *raça.* This parallels the interpretation suggested by Rohlfs for Italian. Old Portuguese has *ts,* which is simplified to *s* in the modern language; the spelling is *ç*: *ardeo* > OPtg. *arço; *pĕrdeo* > OPtg. *perço; vĭr(i)dia* > OPtg. *verça.* Ptg. *orje* or *orge* or *orjo* is a borrowing from French. We may also note postconsonantal treatment of *di̯* following *au*: *audio* > *ouço.*

Catalan has [ž]: *vĭr(i)diāriu* > *verger,* while retention of *d* and a vocalic *i* is a learned feature: *hŏrdeu* > *ordi; studiu* > *estudi; ŏdiu* > *odi.* A variety of outcomes is noted for Occitan. Lat. *hŏrdeu* is mostly continued as *ordi* with a vocalic *i* signaling that no *di̯* cluster ever arose here. Since this form is quite common, it cannot be dispensed with as the result of an entirely learned process. Lat. *hŏrdeŏlu* evolves to *orjol* and *orzol,* with *di̯* continued either as [dž] or *dz* (Appel §59b). French has [ž]: *vĭrĭdiariu* > OFr. *vergier* > *verger; hŏrdeu* > *orge.*

321. Lat. -*ndi̯*-

n ž(?):	Rm.
n'n':	It.
nts or *n'*:	OSp.
[nθ]:	Sp.

nts > *ns*: OPtg.
n': Ptg., Cat., Occ., Fr.

Latin
verecŭndia

It.	Sp.	Ptg.	Cat.	Occ.	Fr.
vergogna	*vergüenza,* *vergüença* (old), *vergoiña* (old), *vergüeña* (old)	*vergonha,* *vergonça* (old)	*vergonya*	*vergonha*	*vergogne*

Commentary

The lack of homogeneity in the evolution of this cluster is caused by two contrasting trends: on one hand, a desire to maintain separate treatment for each of its two constituent elements *n* and *di̯*, and on the other a powerful attraction to the *ni̯* cluster with which *ndi̯* could very easily merge through the elimination of *d*. Italian has *ndz* or a lengthened palatal *n*. A palatal *n* is the norm for Portuguese, Catalan, Occitan and French, while Spanish has [*nθ*]. Alternate developments are noted, however, both for the Hispanic domain and for Occitan, while the French evolution to a palatal *n* appears to have no competitors. A lack of examples makes it impossible to establish rules for the development of the *ndi̯* cluster in Rumanian. The suggested outcome [*nž*] is inferred from *rotunjor,* which may reflect **rŏtŭndiōre.*

For Italian, Lausberg (§458) takes a lengthened palatal *n* to represent the popular development, while Rohlfs (§276) lists *ndz* encountered in *mandiu* > *manzo* as the norm. The voiceless *nts* of *pranzo* < *prandiu* remains unaccounted for. In a rare attempt to explain diversity on the basis of the stress pattern, Rohlfs claims that the occasional change to a palatal *n* is restricted to the position before the stress: **grandiŏla* > *gragnuola; Mindiōne* > *Mignone*. This rule is, however, contradicted by one of the three examples he gives: *verecŭndia* > *vergogna,* but this word could be a borrowing from Occitan, as seen from the lenition of intervocalic *k* to *g*.

In Old Spanish and Old Portuguese, *ndi̯* evolved to *nç* [*nts*]: *verecŭndia* > OSp. *vergüença,* OPtg. *vergonça.* Modern Spanish has [*nθ*], spelled *nz*:

vergüenza, but forms with a palatal *n* are not uncommon in the old language: *vergoiña* is encountered in the *Glosas Silenses*, and there is also documentation for a form *vergüeña* in the medieval period. Portuguese has *vergonha*, but the implied loss of *d* that underlies this form is rated a regional phenomenon by Williams (§89.6.A). A palatal *n* appears to be the sole outcome in Catalan, but examples of the cluster are rare. Occitan mostly has a palatal *n*: *vergonha*, but it also offers cases of a development to [*ndž*]: *vergonja; *rŏtŭndiāre* > *redonhar* and *redoniar* (Appel §59b). French has a palatal *n* throughout: *verecŭndia* > *vergogne; Bŭrgŭndia* > *Bourgogne; *rŏtŭndĭāre* > OFr. *rooignier, reoignier* > *rogner.*

Sp. *vergüenza*, OSp. *vergüeña, vergoiña*: the hesitation demonstrated here between [*nθ*] and *n'* has a parallel in the development of *-ng-* + *i, e* (§287). Malkiel (*Studies in Philology, 41* (1944), 501–502) considers *vergüenza* semi-learned, characteristic of the conservative pronunciation encountered in an ecclesiastical milieu. The yod release yields an *oi* diphthong (*vergoiña*), raised to *ui* because of the yod and ultimately drawn into the orbit of the *ue* diphthong (Corominas V 788–789).

322. Lat. *-sį̆-*

$[š]$:   Rm., It.

į̆ + *z*:   OSp., Cat., Occ., Fr.

į̆ + *s*:   Sp.

į̆ + [*ž*]: Ptg.

Latin
basiāre, basiu, camīsia, caseu

Rm.	It.	Sp.	Ptg.	Cat.	Occ.	OFr.	Fr.
băşà (dial.)	*baciare*	*besar, bezar* (old)	*beijar*	*besar*	*baizar*	*baisier*	*baiser*
	bacio	*beso*	*beijo*	*bes*	*bais*		
cămaşă	*camicia*	*camisa*	*camisa*	*camisa*	*camiza*		*chemise*
caş	*cacio*	*queso*	*queijo*				

Commentary

The *si̯* cluster, being intervocalic, undergoes voicing in the western languages, and it is not subject to gemination anywhere. The yod palatalizes the *s*, and the [š] that results from this process remains in Rumanian and Italian. Elsewhere, the palatal element is released in front in the form of a yod. In Spanish, the *s* is unvoiced in accordance with the principle of Castilian desonorization. Portuguese releases a yod, yet at the same time it preserves a palatal [ž]. Catalan, Occitan and French have *i̯* plus a voiced *s*.

In Rumanian, where consonantal length is not a distinguishing feature, intervocalic *si̯* and *ssi̯* both evolve to [š]. Examples of *si̯* > [š] are: *ceresea* > *cireaşă; basiāre* > dial. *băşà; roseu* > *roş.* Italian has [š]: *bacio, cacio, camicia.* In the old language this sound is often rendered graphically by *sci: bascio, camiscia* (Rohlfs §286), while the *ci* graph may be analogical from words such as *vicino,* where *ci* reflects the same sound, the Tuscan pronunciation in both instances being [š] and not [tš] (Lausberg §461). Several Italian words show a development to [ž], the voiced counterpart of [š] and usually spelled *sgi* in the medieval period, paralleling the *sci* graph: *prĕhĕnsiōne* > *prigione; occasiōne* > *(ac)cagione; pēnsiōne* > *pigione; *pertūsiāre* > *pertugiare; Parisii* > *Parigi; phasiānu* > *fagiano.* These are most likely borrowings from French, or they have come in from Gallo-Italian dialects. In most instances, each of these lexical items corresponds to a French word with voiced *s: prison, occasion, faisan.* An explanation based on stress: [š] after the stress, [ž] before it, is attempted by Meyer-Lübke, but examples contradicting this rule are quite easy to find (Rohlfs §286).

Spanish shows voicing and subsequent desonorization of *s;* the palatal element is released, causing inflection of the preceding vowel if it is an *a: beso, queso; mansiōne* > *maisón* > *mesón.* If the preceding vowel is an *i,* the yod is absorbed: *camisa.* Portuguese has [ž] and the same yod release and inflection feature as Spanish with the difference, however, that the yod survives its palatalizing and inflecting roles: *beijo, queijo.* The yod is absorbed by *i* in *camisa,* as it is also in Catalan and Gallo-Romance.

Catalan has a voiced *s,* while the palatal element is released in front, where it inflects *a: basiat* > **baisa* > *besa.* Badía Margarit (§87, II) draws *nosa* from a reduced Vulgar Latin form *nausa* instead of CL *nausea,* while both *nauza* and *noiza* are documented for Occitan. The palatal element has perhaps dropped here because of the difficulty of combining a yod with the *au* diphthong.

Occitan regularly has yod plus a voiced *s: baizar; fūsiōne* > *foizon,* but a dialectal development to *i̯* or [ž] or [i̯ž] is not uncommon: *basiāre* >

baiar; phasiānu > faian; mansiōne > maio, maijo (Appel §59a). French has yod and a voiced *s*: *baiser; mansiōne > maison.* Unvoicing occurs in final position in both Occitan and French: *basiu >* Occ. *bais; *pĕrtūsiu >* Fr. *pertuis.*

Fr. *baiser*: French does not continue *basiu,* using instead the infinitive *baiser* as a noun.

Lat. *camīsia*: the quality of the tonic *i* is uncertain; the primitive form may have been *ĭ,* while the long *i,* required for the developments in western Romance, may have come in through ecclesiastical use (*REW* 1550). *Camĭsia* is reflected in Rm. *cămaşă* and Old *padovano camesa.* The word is a relative late-comer in the Latin vocabulary, being first documented in the fourth century.

323. Lat. *-ssi̯-*

[š]:	Rm.
[šš]:	It.
[š] > [χ]:	Sp.
i̯ + [š]:	Ptg., Cat.
i̯ + s:	Occ., Fr.

Latin
bassiāre

Sp.	Ptg.	Cat.	Occ.	OFr.	Fr.
bajar, baxar (old)	baixar	baixar	baissar	baissier	baisser

Commentary

Examples of a popularly developed *ssi̯* cluster are very few in number since most words containing the group are of a learned nature. Rumanian has [š]: *ingrŏssiāre > îngroşà,* while a lengthened [šš] is the norm for Italian: *prĕssia > prescia; Cassia > Cascia; *revĕrsiāre > *revĕssiāre > rovesciare.* Spanish transforms *ssi̯* via [š], spelled *x,* to [χ]: *rŭsseu > roxo > rojo; *bassiāre > baxar > bajar.* In Portuguese, the palatalization of *s* to [š] is accompanied by a yod release: *baixar; passiōne > OPtg. paixom > paixão.* Ptg. *baixo* does not come from *bassu,* but is derived from the verb *baixar* (Huber §205). Absorption of the yod has occurred in *rŭsseu > roixo*

> *roxo*. Catalan has [š] spelled *ix*, and a yod is released from the cluster: *baixar;* *crasseu > *greix*. It seems quite possible that [i̯š] may represent an earlier stage in the pronunciation. The *ssi̯* cluster evolves to yod and a voiceless *s* in Occitan: *baissar;* *pressia > *preissa, prieissa,* while *baichar* and *preicha* are dialectal (Appel §59a). French likewise has yod and a voiceless *s: baissier* > *baisser; mēssiōne* > *meisson* > *moisson*.

324. Lat. -*ni̯*-

i̯:	Rm.
n'n':	It.
n':	Sp., Ptg., Cat., Occ.
n' or nasalization +	
[ž]:	Fr.

Latin
vīnea, montanea, extrāneu

Rm.	It.	Sp.	Ptg.	Cat.	Occ.	Fr.
vie	*vigna*	*viña*	*vinha*	*vinya*	*vinha*	*vigne*
	mon-	*mon-*	*mon-*	*mun-*	*mon-*	*mon-*
	tagna	*taña*	*tanha*	*tanya*	*tanha*	*tagne*
strano	*extraño*	*estra-nho*	*estrany*	*estranh*	*étrange*

Commentary

Rumanian reduces *ni̯* to *i̯*, Italian has a lengthened palatal *n*, while simplification to *n'* occurs in the western languages. In Italian and in the western Romance group, intervocalic *ni̯* and intervocalic *gn* evolve in identical fashion (§313), but this identity does not extend to Rumanian, where *gn* gives *mn*, while the palatal *n* obtained from *ni̯* is reduced to *i̯*: *cŭneu* > *cuiu; aranea* > *râie; līnea* > *ie*. A palatal *n* does not come about in the *logudorese* dialect of Sardinian, which has *ndz: vīnea* > *bindza* (Lausberg §463).

In Italian, the yod doubles the preceding consonant: *vīnea* > *vinnia, and the resulting lengthened *ni̯* is spelled *gn: vīnea* > *vigna; jūniu* > *giugno; campānia* > *campagna; sĕniōre* > *signore*. Non-palatalization of the *ni̯* cluster is a rare feature, which may be seen in *extraneu* > *straino* > *strano*, but Old Italian also knows the form *stragno*. Retention of *ni̯* is learned: *Germania* as opposed to *Spagna* < *Hispania* (Rohlfs §282). The Hispanic development is straightforward: *aranea* > Sp. *araña*, Ptg. *aranha*, Cat. *aranya*. Catalan and Occitan have *n'*, not only intervocalically: *sĕniōre* > Cat. *senyor,* Occ. *senhor; ba(l)neāre* > Cat. *banyar,* Occ. *banhar,* but also in final position: *ba(l)neu* > Cat. *bany,* Occ. *banh,* whereas French retains the palatal *n* in intervocalic position only: *montanea* > *montagne, ba(l)neare* > *baigner,* but resolves it as *in* when it becomes final, with *n* causing nasalization: *ba(l)neu* > *bain; tĕstĭmōniu* > *témoin.* In an alternate development in French, *n* and *i̯* do not merge; instead, *n* nasalizes the preceding vowel, while *i̯* receives initial-of-syllable treatment, evolving to [ž] with *e* added for support: *extraneu* > *étrange; līneu* > *linge.* A syllabic division appears to have prevented the fusion of *n* and *i̯* into *n'* (Rheinfelder I 202). The Romance *ni̯* cluster, which arises in Catalan in the *-nĭcu* ending following the loss of the velar consonant, evolves to [*nž*]: *canonĭcu* > *canonge; die domĭnĭcu* > *diumenge.*

325. Lat. *-mni̯-*

?:	Rm.
n'n':	It.
n':	Sp., Ptg.
mn' or [*mdž*] or	
mni or *n':*	Cat., Occ.
nasalization + [*dž*]:	OFr.
nasalization + [*ž*]:	Fr.

Latin
sŏmniu, sŏmniāre

It.	Sp.	Ptg.	Cat.	Occ.	Fr.
sogno	*sueño*	*sonho*	*suny,*	*somnhe,*	*songe*
			somni	*somni*	
sognare	*soñar*	*sonhar*	*somniar,*	*somnhar,*	*songer*
			somiar	*somiar,*	
				somjar	

Commentary
   No Rumanian examples are available. Italian has a lengthened palatal *n* and Hispanic a simplification to *n'*. The Occitan evolution is complex,

comprising a variety of outcomes: *m* followed by a palatal *n*, retention of *m* accompanied by the change of the palatal element to either [*dž*]: *somjar,* or *i̯: somiar,* or *mni,* a combination in which *mn* and *i* have not merged, *i* having maintained syllabic value, and finally the cluster may be resolved as a palatal *n*: *calŭmniare* > *calomniar, calonjar, calonhar* (Appel §59a; Anglade, pp. 181–182). Catalan shares most of the Occitan developments (Badía Margarit §87, III). In French, the preceding vowel is nasalized, while the palatal component moves via [*dž*] to [*ž*].

326. Lat. *-li̯-*

i̯:	Rm.
l' (lengthened)	It.
l' > [*ž*] > [*χ*]:	Sp.
l':	Ptg., Cat., Occ.
l' > *i̯:*	Fr.

Latin
fŏlia, palea, alliu

Rm.	It.	Sp.	Ptg.	Cat.	Occ.	OFr.	Fr.
foaie	*foglia*	*hoja*	*folha*	*fulla*	*folha*	*fueille*	*feuille*
paie	*paglia*	*paja*	*palha*	*palla*	*palha*		*paille*
aiu	*aglio*	*ajo*	*alho*	*all*	*alh*		*ail*

Commentary
Italian has a lengthened *l'*, while a single palatal *l* is characteristic of Portuguese, Catalan and Occitan. Rumanian reduces the palatal *l* to *i̯,* and in a very late development dating no further back than to the seventeenth or eighteenth century, French similarly eliminates the lateral component, altering *l'* to *i̯.* In Spanish, *l'* assibilates to [*ž*], which becomes [*χ*] in the sixteenth century. In a development that is characteristic of Catalan and Occitan, learned words do not form a palatal cluster; instead, *l* is kept unchanged, and it is followed by a syllabic final *i*: *ŏleu* > Cat., Occ. *oli; līliu* > Occ. *lili; concīliu* > Cat. *concili* (Appel §59d; Badía Margarit §87, IV).

The reflexes of *alliu* show that the combination *lli̯* is not treated any differently from the simple *li̯.* The rare *kli̯* cluster, which exists in the word *cŏchleāre* or *cochleāriu,* is treated like *li̯* in most areas, evolving to a palatal *l* in Ptg. *colher,* Cat. *cullera,* Occ. *culhier(a),* Fr. *cuiller* (with the usual reduction to *i̯*). In Italian, however, it merges with the *cl* cluster (§299): *cŏchleāriu* > *cucchiaio.* In Spanish, the *kli̯* cluster does not voice, but evolves to [*tš*]: *cŏchleāre* > *cuchara,* with the *a* ending representing a morphological adjustment. The word is not continued in Rumanian, which has *lingură* as a reflex of CL *lĭngŭla* (§87).

327. Lat. *-ri̯-*

r: Rm.
i̯: It.
i̯r: Sp., Ptg., Cat., Occ., Fr.

Latin
area, cŏriu

Rm.	It.	Sp.	Ptg.	Cat.	Occ.	Fr.
arie	*aia*	*era*	*eira*	*era*	*aira*	*aire*
	cuoio	*cuero*	*coiro,*	*cuir*	*cuer,*	*cuir*
			couro		*cuor,*	
					cor	

Commentary
In the *ri̯* sequence, *r* did not double anywhere when palatalized by the yod. A complex evolution is seen in Rumanian, one of the outcomes being retention of the palatal *r,* a feature which also occurs in certain dialects of southern Italy and central Sardinia. An unusual development is found in Italian, where the *r* is completely absorbed into the yod, which alone survives. In the western zone, the palatal component of *ri̯* is released in front as *i̯,* a development which, in Hispanic, is accompanied by the inflection of the vowel *a.*

It is difficult to find one's way in the maze of Rumanian developments. The loss of the palatal element is common if the final vowel is *a.* Before disappearing, the yod changes *-a* to *e*: *caldaria* > *căldare; venatōria* > *vânătoare.* This rule, as formulated by Nandris (p. 234), does not, however, account for the masculine form of the suffixes, where the yod also drops: *-ariu* > *-ar* and *-ōriu* > *-or* as in *pĭscāriu* > *pescar; adjutōriu* > *ajutor.* A reduction to *i̯* takes place in certain verb forms: *pareo* > *paiu,* while retention of *ri̯* is seen in *area* > *arie* (ORm. *are*). Lausberg (§466), who lists only the example *arie*, takes retention of *ri̯* to be the norm. The most satisfactory interpretation is proposed by Rothe (§100): the rule is for *ri̯* to be reduced to *r*, the change to *i̯* in certain verb forms is not a phonological feature, and the presence of an *ri̯* cluster in *arie* finds an analogical explanation in such variations as *fune—funie* and *unghe—unghie* (Rothe §60, n. 1).

In Italian, the *ri̯* cluster is reduced to *i̯*: *-ariu > -aio; pareo > paio; variu > vaio; fŭrnariu > fornaio; notariu > notaio*. Forms in *-aro* are, however, quite common: *notaro, scolaro, danaro*. Some of these words are new singular formations drawn from the plural where Lat. *-arii* is at first continued as *-ari*, whereupon *calzolaio—calzolari* is regularized to *calzolaro—calzolari*. This morphological adjustment finds additional support in the existence of *-aro* in the neighboring dialects of Umbria and Latium as the popular outcome of *-ariu*. Tuscan eventually favors the opposite leveling, drawing a plural *fornai* from the singular *fornaio* (Rohlfs §284; Wiese §98). Learned words retain *ri̯* unchanged: *memoria, purgatorio, gloria*, while OIt. *memora, purgatoro, ghiora* are semi-learned.

In the Spanish evolution, the yod is attracted to the preceding syllable where its presence causes certain changes in the vocalism. It combines with *a*, inflecting it to *e*: *-ariu > -airo > -ero*, as in *fŭrnariu > hornero and fĕrrariu > herrero; area > era*, and if the tonic vowel which it is attracted to is a close *o*, the resulting unfamiliar *oi* diphthong is replaced by *ue*, obtained via *ui*: CL *augŭriu > VL agŭriu > agoiro > agüiro > agüero*. Both *agoiro* and *agüiro* are documented in the *Fuero Juzgo*. Another instance of the change of *oi* to *ue* is: *Dōriu > Duero* (the Leonese form is *Doiro*). With an open *o* the result is the same: *cŏriu > cuero;* cf. Ptg. *coiro* (Menéndez Pidal §§13.3d, 14.2). *Coiro* seems preferable to the stage *coero* proposed by Menéndez Pidal. Yod may have fallen already in Latin in *coriācea > coraza; ŏstrea > Sp., Ptg. ostra* (cf. CL *pariĕte > VL parēte*), but Catalan and Galician have *ostria*. In Portuguese, the yod of the *ri̯* cluster exerts the same inflecting role in regard to the vowel *a* as in Spanish, with the difference, however, that the yod does not drop in the process: *-ariu > -airo > eiro*, as in *primāriu > primeiro; fĕrrariu > ferreiro*. The *-oriu* combination evolves to *-oiro*, with *-ouro* as a dialectal variant: *cŏriu > coiro* and *couro; aratōria > aradoira* and *aradoura* (Williams §37.2).

Catalan releases the palatal element, which generally inflects the preceding tonic vowel: *caldaria > caldera; fĕria > fira; *monĭstĕriu > monestir*. Occitan resolves the palatal *r* from *ri̯* as *ir*: *fĕriat > feira; *exclariāre > esclairar*. Examples of the *i̯* from *ri̯* as a diphthongization-causing agent are: *fĕrio > fier; *mŏrio > muer; cŏriu > cuer, cuor*, but also a non-diphthongized *cor* (Appel §59a). *Lavatōriu* > *lavador* shows the characteristic loss of *i̭* in the development of the *-ōriu* suffix in Occitan (Appel §59a; Anglade, p. 182). Occ. *memoria* and *gloria* are learned. Release of the yod is also the norm in French: *fēria* > *feire* > *foire; variu* > *vair; ŏstrea* > **ueistre* > *huître*. The change of the *-ariu* suffix to *-ier* is obscure (§174). Non-formation of an *r'* cluster and the resulting independent assibilation of *i̭* to [*dž*] and [*ž*] may be seen in *cēreu* > *cerge, cirge* > *cierge; sŏrōriu* > OFr. *sororge, serorge* (cf. *extraneu* > *estrange* for a similar development of the *ni̭* cluster (§324)). The assibilation of *ri̭* to *rdz* is the norm in the *logudorese* and *campidanese* dialects of Sardinian.

Sp. *ostra*: the etymology suggested for Sp. *ostra* by Menéndez Pidal (§30.2) is a reduced *ostra* for CL *ŏstrea*. The pivotal role of the palatal in preventing any diphthongization of *ŏ* from taking place does put some time constraints on the elimination of yod, however. Prior to dropping, the yod may have caused the closure of the open vowel.

328. Lat. -*ki̭*-

[*tš*]:	Rm.
[*tš*] (lengthened):	It.
dz or *ts* > [*θ*]:	Sp.
ts > *s*:	Ptg., Cat., Fr.
ts or *s*:	Occ.

Latin
bracchiu, bracchia, laqueu, VL **laceu*

Rm.	It.	Sp.	Ptg.	Cat.	Occ.	OFr.	Fr.
braţ	*braccio*	*brazo,* *braço* (old)	*braço*	*braç*	*bratz*	*braz*	*bras*
	braccia	*braza,* *braça* (old)	*braça*	*braça*	*brassa*	*brace*	*brasse*
laţ	*laccio*	*lazo*	*laço*	*llaç*	*latz*	*laz*	*lacs*

Commentary

Rumanian has [tš], Italian a lengthened [tš] while, in the West, *ts* represents the medieval pronunciation from which Spanish [θ] and Portuguese, Catalan, Occitan and French *s* evolved. Occitan usually maintains the original affricate stage in final position while [*ts*] is reduced to *s* when intervocalic. The *ki̯* cluster is palatalized and assibilated everywhere, even in Sardinian where initial *k* is kept before the vowels *i* and *e*. This palatalization is consequently very old, preceding that of *k* before a front vowel. While most areas testify to a confusion between *ki̯* and *ti̯*, Italian has been able to keep the two clusters separate (§316).

In Rumanian, *ki̯* is treated like *ti̯* (§316), assibilating to [*ts*]: *laţ; acia* > *aţa; sŏciu* > *soţ,* and just as in the case of *ti̯,* there are sporadic occurrences of [*tš*]: *ŭrceŏlu* > *urcior, ulcior.* The *ki̯* cluster and *k* before *i, e* follow different paths in their evolution, with *ki̯* > *ts* ranking as an earlier process than that of *k + i, e* > [*tš*] (cf. *cēra* > *ceară*). In Italian, assibilation to [*tš*] represents the norm: *mĭnācia* > *minaccia; *facia* (for CL *facies*) > *faccia,* and similarly in cases where the cluster is preceded by a consonant: *ŭrceu* > *orcio; *Frankia* > *Francia.* A few exceptions showing a postconsonantal *ts*: *lŭncea* (from Gk. *lynx*) > *lonza; calcea* > *calza,* may have come in from northern dialects (Rohlfs §275).

A very complicated question posed by the Spanish development is whether the assibilated outcome of the *ki̯* cluster is voiced or voiceless. Modern Spanish can be of no help in settling this issue because of the Castilian desonorization. There seems to be general consensus that voicing represents the normal outcome: *erīciu* > *erizo; aciāriu* > *azero; mĭnācia* > *amenaza.* Cases such as OSp. *braço* and *braça* can very conveniently be accounted for because of the geminate present in the etymon (Menéndez Pidal §53.c; Lloyd, p. 260), but *arzón* < **arciōne* with its voiced *s* in spite of the postconsonantal position of the *ki̯* cluster cannot be considered obtained through normal evolution, the more so as a voiceless outcome is found elsewhere: It. *arcione,* Ptg. *arção,* Cat. *arçó,* Occ. *arson,* Fr. *arçon* (Corominas I 369). Additional cases of a voiceless development of intervocalic *ki̯* in Spanish are: *saetaceu* > *sedaço; pellīcea* > *pelliça.* Here, however, a confusion of suffixes may offer an explanation. Corominas rates *pelliça* as dialectal, and *cedazo* is a common old graph for *sedaço.* Voicing thus definitely rates as the norm for the intervocalic *ki̯* cluster, and Lausberg (§470) speculates that we have to do with a very early sonorization on Spanish soil, antedating the gemination of *ts* to *tts.* For further details on this thorny issue, see Lloyd, pp. 259–263 and Malkiel: "Derivational

Transparency as an Occasional Co-Determinant of Sound Change: A New Causal Ingredient in the Distribution of -*ç*- and -*z*- in Ancient Hispano-Romance" (*RPh*, 25 (1971), 1–52). Portuguese, quite consistently, has a voiceless *ts* which, in the course of the sixteenth century, evolves to *s*: *braço, laço; facio > faço; pĕllīcea > peliça; aciāriu > aceiro. Juizo < jūdĭciu* may be learned; for this word and a couple of additional exceptions, Williams (§89.2.B) suggests that a confusion with *tį* may have occurred. *Facie > faz* is regular; what is involved here is merely the graphical tradition of not using *ç* in word-final position. The verb *praza < placeat* is built analogically on the infinitive *prazer < placēre* (Huber §225).

In Catalan, the intervocalic *kį* cluster evolves via the affricate *ts* to a voiceless *s*: *aciariu > acer; ericiōne > eriçó; facio > faç*, and following most consonants, *s* likewise represents the normal outcome: *bĭlancia > balança; calceāre > calçar*, the only exception being the *scį* combination, which evolves to [*š*], spelled *ix*: *ascia > aixa; fascia > faixa*. Learned words in both Catalan and Occitan form no cluster, retaining *i* as vocalic: *jūdĭciu >* Cat. *judici*, Occ. *juzizi; officiu >* Cat. *ofici; beneficiu >* Occ. *benefici*.

In Occitan, *kį* moves via *ts* to a voiceless *s* in preliterary times: *faciat > fassa; placeat > plassa; erīciōne > erissoṇ*, but if the cluster becomes final, the affricate is retained: *bratz, latz; facio > fatz; facie > fatz*. This provides proof that *brassa* was obtained from an earlier, but undocumented **bratza*. A postconsonantal *kį* evolves to a voiceless *s*: **arciōne > arsoṇ; *balancia > balansa*. In French, *kį* becomes *ts*, which later evolves to *s*: *facia > face; faciat > face > fasse; bracchiu > braz > bras; bracchia > brace > brasse*, and the postconsonantal *kį* behaves similarly: **arciōne > arçon*. OFr. *laz* evolves regularly from **lăceu*, and the modern form *lacs* is merely a case of capricious spelling influenced by *lacer, lacet* (Nyrop I §§98, 476.2). Cases presenting a yod-release and a voicing of *s* are all susceptible to an analogical explanation: OFr. *croisier*, Fr. *croiser* does not go back to **crŭciāre*, but is based on *croix*, and in its normal evolution *placeat* evolves to OFr. *place*, which is later replaced by *plaise*, drawn from the indicative *plais* on the model of *vent—vende, pert—perde*.

329. Lat. -*gį*-

∅ or *į*:	Rm.
[*d ž*] (lengthened):	It.
į or ∅:	Sp.
[*ž*] or *į*:	Ptg.

[ž]:　Cat.
i̯ or [dž]:　Occ.
　i̯:　Fr.

Latin
fageu, -a, corrĭgia

Rm.	It.	Sp.	Ptg.	Cat.	Occ.	OFr.	Fr.
	faggio	*haya*	*faia* *faia*	*faig,*	*faia*		
curea	*correggia*	*correa*	*correia*	*corretja* *correya*	*correja,*	*correie*	*courroie*

Commentary

Since intervocalic *gi̯* tended to merge with *i̯* in Vulgar Latin (Rohlfs §279), the developments are essentially the same as those outlined for intervocalic *i̯* (§279). Rumanian has ø: *corrĭgia > curea,* or *i̯: plagiu > plaiu,* but examples are very scarce, rules consequently difficult to formulate. Italian has a lengthened [dž]: *exagiu > saggio; (casa) regia > reggia.* Spanish has *i̯: exagiu > ensayo,* but this yod drops when following a front vowel: *corrĭgia > correa.* Portuguese has [ž]: *fūgio > fujo; pŭlēgiu > poejo.* An alternate development to *i̯* may be seen in *faia, correia, ensaio;* Williams (§89.7), however, considers *correia* and *ensaio* to be borrowings from Spanish. In Catalan, the intervocalic *gi̯* is continued as [ž]: **exagiāre > assajar; fageŏlu > fajol,* while [tš] is the norm in final position: *fageu > faig; exagiu > assaig.* Occitan has *i̯* or [dž] intervocalically: **exagiāre > assayar, assajar; corrĭgia > correya, correja,* or [tš] or *ts* in final position: *corrĭgiu > correi, correg, corretz* (Appel §59b). In French, *gi̯* is reduced to *i̯: corrĭgia > courroie; exagiu > essai.*

The *ngi̯* cluster, which appears limited to the word *spongia,* is treated like *ni̯* (§324) in It. *spugna,* OFr. *espongne.* A reduced **sponga (REW* 8173) is probably the source of Occ. *esponga,* Fr. *éponge,* while Sp., Ptg., Cat. *esponja* may be borrowed from French.

330. Lat. *-pi̯-*

i̯p(?):　Rm.
ppi̯:　It.
i̯p or ƀi̯:　Sp.

$$i\underset{\frown}{b}: \quad \text{Ptg.}$$
$$p\underset{\frown}{i}: \quad \text{Cat.}$$
$$[pt\check{s}], \ p\underset{\frown}{i} \ \text{or} \ [t\check{s}]: \quad \text{Occ.}$$
$$[t\check{s}] > [\check{s}]: \quad \text{Fr.}$$

Latin
sapiam, sēpia

It.	Sp.	Ptg.	Cat.	Occ.	Fr.
sappia	*sepa*	*saiba*	*sàpia* (old)	*sapcha, sapia, sacha*	*sache*
seppia	*jibia*	*siba*	*sípia*	*sepcha, sepia, sipia*	*seiche*

Commentary

The Rumanian development is uncertain. In Italian, the yod causes doubling of the *p*. Spanish lets the palatal element slip through: *sapiam > sepa*, but it may also remain: *sēpia > jibia*. In the first instance, *p* remains intact while, in the second, it voices to *b* and then moves to a fricative pronunciation. Portuguese shows a similar fluctuation in its treatment of the yod, which either combines with the preceding vowel: *sapiam > saiba*, or inflects it: *sēpia > siba*. Catalan keeps *p*i. Occitan has a variety of developments: [*ptš*], *p*i, or [*tš*]; Old French has [*tš*], which is simplified to [*š*] in the modern language.

Since there are no reliable examples of this cluster in Rumanian, Lausberg (§§472–473) and Rothe (§100) refrain from offering any discussion. Nandris (p. 222) cites one conjectural occurrence of the group: **succupiu > scuip*. Based on this fragile evidence, but with further support from the general trend in the language toward a yod release in labial + yod clusters, I tentatively suggest *ip* as the outcome. The Italian development of *p*i involves merely a doubling of *p* to *ppi*, but the palatalization feature is encountered in southern dialects. It. *saccente < sapiente* and *piccione < pīpiōne* are thus likely borrowings from the South.

The heterogeneous development that is characteristic of Spanish is quite difficult to account for. The yod may be attracted to the preceding vowel while *p* itself remains unchanged; this metathesis of *p*i to *ip* occurs in *săpiam > sepa* and *căpiam > quepa*. In both instances the attracted yod combines with the vowel *a*, altering it to *e*. Elsewhere, the *p* undergoes its traditional lenition process via *b* to *ƀ*, and the yod remains in spite of the inflection role it has performed: *sēpia* > *jibia*. The paucity of examples makes it almost impossible to provide an explanation for this divergence. Lausberg (§472, n. 1), espousing a theory formulated by Meyer-Lübke (*Gramm.* I §506), suggests that it may be linked to the quantity of the tonic vowel: if this vowel is short, the *pi̯* cluster is doubled to *ppi̯*, which prevents any lenition of *p* from taking place; if the tonic vowel is long, *p* receives intervocalic treatment. This, however, does not explain why *ăpiu* becomes *apio*, but this word may perhaps, like Ptg. *aipo*, be semi-learned. In Portuguese, *pi̯* evolves to *i̯b*: *capiam* > *caiba*. The consonant is treated as intervocalic, but this should not have happened if there is doubling of *p* following a short vowel, as seen for Spanish above. The *b* could then have spread analogically from forms that do not contain a yod, such as *saber*, *caber*. *Aipo* is semi-learned rather than based on a hypothetical **appiu* (Williams §88.A). Catalan has *i̯p*, but the documentation for this development is very limited: *sapiat* > OCat. *sàpia; capiat* > OCat. *càpia*.

In Occitan, the *pi̯* cluster suffers a variety of changes, the most common being an assibilation to [*ptš*] or the retention of *pi̯*, but there are also instances of the reduction of [*ptš*] to [*tš*]: *sapiātis* > *sapchatz, sapiatz, sachatz; apprŏpiāre* > *apropchar, apropiar* (Appel §59b; Anglade, p. 177). *Sai* does not reflect *sapio*, but is analogically obtained as seen below, and *pīpiōne* suffers lenition to **pībiōne* or **pīviōne* prior to the formation of a yod cluster, hence the voiced outcome *pijon̦*. In French, *p* is eliminated before the yod, but it determines the voiceless outcome [*tš*], reduced to [*š*] in the modern language: *sēpia* > *seiche* (with a purely graphical *i*); *appropiāre* > *aprochier* > *approcher*. Fr. *pigeon* is obtained in the same manner as Occ. *pijon̦*, and lenition also affects **săpiu* > **sabio* > *sage*. OFr. *sai*, Fr. *sais* does not go back to *sapio*, but to the reduced form **saio* in Vulgar Latin, which derives from an analogy with VL **aio* for CL *habeo*. Characteristic of Occitan is the ability of the postconsonantal *i* to retain its syllabic value in final position. What this amounts to is in essence the non-formation of a yod cluster (Appel §59d). This occurs with semi-learned words, an example from the *pi̯* group being *api* < *apiu* (*REW* 526; Lausberg §473); this form, however, is not listed by Levy. Catalan has *àpit*, with a *t* that may be epenthetic or of analogical origin (B. Moll §223; Badía Margarit §207, III).

282 *A Comparative Study of Romance*

331. Lat. -bi̯-, -vi̯-

i̯b:	Rm.
bbi̯:	It.
bi̯ or i̯:	Sp.
i̯v:	Ptg.
[u̯ž] or bi̯:	Cat.
[u̯dž] or [dž]; [tš] or i̯ when final:	Occ.
[dž] > [ž]:	Fr.

Latin
rabia, rŭbeu, cavea

Rm.	It.	Sp.	Ptg.	Cat.	Occ.	OFr.	Fr.
	rabbia	rabia	raiva	ràbia	rauja, rabia		rage
roib	robbio (old)	rubio	ruivo	roig	rog, roi		rouge
	gabbia	gabia		gàbia	gabia	chage	cage

Commentary

The *bi̯* and *vi̯* clusters fell together in *vi̯* or perhaps *ƀi̯* throughout Romania, with labiodental pronunciation prevailing in Rumanian, Italian, Portuguese and Gallo-Romance, while Spanish has a bilabial fricative. See §§263–264 for a similar merger of intervocalic *b* and *v*. Rumanian has *i̯b*, Italian a lengthened *bbi̯*, while Spanish has *ƀi̯* and Portuguese *i̯v*. Catalan has either [u̯ž] or retention of *bi̯*. In Occitan the cluster assibilates to [dž], and the same is true of Old French, while the modern language simplifies the affricate to [ž]. There are occurrences in Occitan of the consonant vocalizing to *u̯* instead of being simply absorbed by the following [dž].

Rumanian releases the yod of the *bi̯* group: *rŭbeu > roib; scabia > zgaibă*. Rm. *aibă* reflects CL *habeat*, while elsewhere only the reduced Vulgar Latin form **aiat* is continued. I have found no examples of the *vi̯* cluster. The norm in Italian is for *bi̯* and *vi̯* to evolve to *bbi̯*: *dēbeat > debbia; trĭviu > trebbio*. An early reduction of *bi̯* to *i̯* has occurred in CL *habeo > VL *aio > OIt. aggio; CL habeat > VL *aiat > OIt. aggia; CL dēbeo > VL *deio > OIt. deggio*, and CL *plŭvia* was replaced in Vulgar

Latin by *plŏia* > It. *pioggia* (§279). Southern Italian dialects have a lengthened [*dž*]: *rabia* > Calabrese *raggia; cavea* > Sicil. *caggia.* The Spanish norm is *ƀi̯*: *rabia, gabia, rubio; labiu* > *labio; plŭvia* > *lluvia.* An alternate evolution, the reduction of *ƀi̯* to *i̯*, is considered more popular both by Menéndez Pidal (§53.1) and by García de Diego (p. 129), but it occurs only in a very limited number of words: *rŭbeu* > *royo* (cf. *Peñarroya*); *fŏvea* > OSp. *fovia* > *hoya.* The subjunctive *haya*, quoted by García de Diego, does not offer a valid example of the *bi̯* cluster, since it does not reflect CL *habeam*, but flows from the abridged VL **aia* (cf. OIt. *aggia*). Portuguese has *i̯v*: *raiva, ruivo.* The dual outcome in Catalan is in the opinion of some scholars linked to stress conditions: [*u̯ž*] is the norm before the stress: *abbreviāre* > *abreujar; *lěviāriu* > *lleuger; allěviāre* > *alleujar,* while retention occurs if the cluster follows the stress: *cavea* > *gàbia* (Badía Margarit §87, I; B. Moll §180). In final position, a voiceless [*tš*] occurs in *roig*, but retention of a vocalic *i*, characteristic of learned words, is more frequently found: *labiu* > *llavi; *glaviu* (for CL *gladiu*) > *glavi.*

Occitan mostly has [*dž*]: *rŭbea* > *roja*, often accompanied by the vocalization of *b* or *v*: **lěviāriu* > *leugier; *brěviāre* > *breujar; *grěviāre* > *greujar.* It seems quite plausible, however, as suggested by Schultz-Gora (§86), that these latter forms may have undergone the formal influence of *leu* < *lěve; breu* < *brěve; greu* < **grěve* (§363). Some of Anglade's examples of [*dž*] are poorly chosen: CL *habeat, debeat* and Lat. **plŏvia,* since these forms were reduced to **aiat, *deiat* and **plŏia* in Vulgar Latin. An alternate development is the retention of *bi̯*: *rabia, gabia.* In final position, [*tš*] is found competing with *i̯*: *rog, roi.* In the *mbi̯* combination, *bi̯* is either retained or changed to [*dž*]: *cambiāre* > *cambiar, camjar;* an occasional variant in palatal *n* is also found, stemming from the alternation of [*ndž*] and *n'* that is noted for the *ng* cluster (§287): *plŭmbiāre* > *plombiar, plonjar, plonhar.* French has [*ž*] from an earlier [*dž*]: *tībia* > *tige; Dīviŏne* > *Dijon; sěrviente* > *sergent.* CL *habeo, dēbeo* and *plŭvia* are reduced in Vulgar Latin to **aio, *deio* and **plŏia* and are thus instances of *i̯* and not of *bi̯* or *vi̯.* In French, the [*dž*] cluster requires a supporting vowel: *rŭbeu* > *rouge* and thus does not become final.

Fr. *cage*: the retention of *k* before *a* shows this to be a dialectal form from the northern regions of the French domain.

CL *plŭvia*, VL **plŏia*: Lat. *plŭvia*, the feminine form of the adjective *plŭviu*, based on the verb *plŭĕre*, is the source of Sp. *lluvia*, Ptg. *chuva.* The alternate infinitive form *plŏvĕre* leads to the creation of the noun **plŏvia* which, reduced to *plŏia*, is continued in Rm. *ploaie*, It. *pioggia*, Cat. *pluja*, Occ. *plǫja*, Fr. *pluie*.

332. Lat. -*mi̯*-

i̯m:	Rm.
mmi̯:	It.
mi̯:	Sp., Cat.
mi̯ or *i̯m*:	Ptg.
mi̯, *mn'*, *n'* or [*md ž*]:	Occ.
nasalization + [*d ž*]:	OFr.
nasalization + [*ž*]:	Fr.

Latin
vĭndēmia, sīmiu, -a

It.	Sp.	Ptg.	Cat.	Occ.	Fr.
vendemmia	*vendimia*	*vindima*	*venímia* (old)	*vendemia*	*vendange*
	simio,				
scimmia	*ximio, -a* (old), *jimia* (old)	*simio, -a*	*simi*	*simi, simia*	*singe*

Commentary

Rumanian has *i̯m*: **famia* > *faimă; *diffamio* > *defaim*. Italian lengthens the *m* before *i̯*: **blastemia* > *bestemmia; commeātu* > *commiato*. Spanish retains *mi̯*: *vendimia*. Portuguese *vindima* may serve as an example of the *i̯m* development, since the yod here has been released in front where it disappears after causing inflection. Retention of *mi̯*, which may simply be learned or semi-learned, occurs in *sīmiu* > *simio*. Catalan retains *mi̯*: *commeātu* > *comiat; vĭndēmia* > OCat. *venímia*. The normal form in Catalan is *verema*, and the verb is *veremar*, reflecting an early loss of the yod. Retention of a syllabic *i* is the traditional outcome in learned words when the cluster becomes final: *sīmiu* > *simi; praemiu* > *premi*. Occitan is the only language where *m* and *i̯* may coalesce into a palatal *n*, but there are complex outcomes as well: *mi̯*, *mn'* and [*md ž*]: *vĭndēmia* > *vendenha, vendemia, vendemnha; commeātu* > *comnhat, comjat*. The yod has kept its syllabic value in *sīmiu* > *simi*, which is semi-learned, while *simia* is an entirely learned form (Appel §59a; Schultz-Gora §89). In French, the nasal receives end-of-syllable treatment, nasalizing the preceding vowel, but losing its consonantal value. The yod engenders a syllable-initial [*dž*], which is subsequently reduced to [*ž*]: *sīmiu* > *singe* (with a supporting vowel); *commeātu* > OFr. *congié* > *congé*. The yod thus does not merge with the nasal here, as opposed to the *nĭ* cluster which, in by far most instances, coalesces into a palatal *n*, while independent treatment of the two elements represents a fairly infrequent alternate development (§324).

Lat. *sīmiu, sīmia*: the more frequent form is *sīmia*, continued in It. *scimmia*, OSp. *ximia, jimia*, Ptg., Occ. *simia*, but other reflexes go back to *sīmiu*: OSp. *ximio*, Occ., Cat. *simi*, Fr. *singe*. The influence of the following palatal vowel is responsible for the change of initial *s* to [*š*] in Italian (cf. *sĭmplu* > *scempio*), while Mozarabic speech habits may offer an explanation for the Old Spanish forms. *Simio* is retained only as a learned word in Spanish, the popular term for 'monkey' being *mono*, which is of Persian extraction (*REW* 5242).

Lat. *commeātu*: the phonological development in Italian is represented by *commiato*, while OIt. *congiato* and It. *congedo* are borrowed from French.

333. Consonant + *u̯*: [*kʷ*] and [*gʷ*] and Other *u̯* Clusters

Lat. [*kʷ*] had been reduced to *k* before the vowel *u* in preliterary times: **quum* > *cum*, and in Vulgar Latin a similar reduction took place before the vowel *o*: CL *quotidiānu* > VL *cotidiānu*. To this may be added further simplifications of analogical origin. Thus, when *cŏquo* is reduced to **cŏco*, it causes the change of *cŏquĕre* to **cŏcĕre*, hence It. *cuocere*. The *Appendix Probi* warns against this reduction: *coquens non cocens; equs non ecus*. In the case of CL *laqueu*, an unfamiliar and cumbersome *ku̯* cluster was reduced to *kĭ* in Vulgar Latin, yielding the form *laceu*, which is the source of the Romance forms (§328). Lat. *quīnque* is reduced to *cinque* in the popular language through dissimilation. Aside from these and similar specific changes, [*kʷ*] keeps its velar element in Vulgar Latin before the vowels *i, e* and *a*, and it may appear either in postconsonantal or intervocalic position. Lat. [*gʷ*] is postconsonantal only, the initial [*gʷ*] being of Germanic origin. Examples of the [*kʷ*] cluster in internal position are scarce, and in many instances the phonological development is poorly elucidated. It becomes quite difficult therefore to establish broad rules; in the following, a brief examination of a few words will have to suffice.

334. Intervocalic [k^w] + *i, e*

[*tš*]:   Rm.
[g^w]:   It.
[$g̑$]:   Sp.
g: Ptg., Cat., Occ.
u̯:   Fr.

Latin
**séquĕre, *-īre*

It.	Sp.	Ptg.	Cat.	Occ.	OFr.	Fr.
seguire	*seguir*	*seguir*	*seguir*	*segre,*	*siure,*	*suivre*
				seguir	*sivre,*	
					sieure	

Commentary

An intervocalic [k^w] before a front vowel is encountered in the Vulgar Latin infinitives *séquĕre* and *séquīre,* which have replaced CL *séquī.* Italian voices the occlusive and retains the labial component. In Hispanic and Occitan, the occlusive voices and *u̯* drops, and Spanish as usual moves to a fricative pronunciation. The French developments are extremely complex and often obscure, but essentially the occlusive has dropped here, while the labial element is retained as *u̯* or changed to *v* (Rheinfelder II 299–300; Ineichen, pp. 61, 94). The retention of *u̯* is archaic or dialectal, while the modern language has *v.* Rumanian is the only language that drops the labial element early enough to allow for participation of the secondarily obtained *k* in the palatalization process; [k^w] + *i, e,* in other words, evolves to [*tš*] just like initial *k* + *i, e* (§234). The word we have here is not continued in Rumanian, but *aquĭla > aceră* may serve as an example. §252 may be consulted for the same development in initial position.

335. Consonant + [k^w] + *i, e*

[*tš*]:   Rm.
[k^w]:   It.
k: Sp., Ptg., Cat., Occ., Fr.

Latin
quīnque, VL *cīnque*

Rm.	It.	Sp.	Ptg.	Cat.	Occ.	Fr.
cinci	*cinque*	*cinco*	*cinco*	*cinc*	*cinc*	*cinq*

Commentary
Following a consonant, there can be no voicing. Rumanian has [*tš*], Italian retains [*kʷ*] intact, while a reduction to *k* occurs elsewhere. Sardinian *(logudorese)* changes [*kʷ*] to *b* and assimilates the nasal to *m: kimbe.* In Hispanic, *cinco* is modeled on Sp. *cuatro,* Ptg. *quatro* and does not represent an extraordinary mutation of *u̯* to a syllabic *o,* as maintained by Lausberg (§482).

336. Intervocalic [*kʷ*] + *a*

$$
\begin{aligned}
p\text{:} & \quad \text{Rm.} \\
[kk^w]\text{:} & \quad \text{It.} \\
[g^w]\text{:} & \quad \text{Sp., Ptg., Cat.} \\
g \text{ or } i̯g\text{:} & \quad \text{Occ.} \\
i̯w \text{ or } i̯v\text{:} & \quad \text{Fr.}
\end{aligned}
$$

Latin
aqua, ĕqua

Rm.	It.	Sp.	Ptg.	Cat.	Occ.	OFr.	Fr.
apă	*acqua*	*agua*	*água*	*aigua*	*aiga, agua*	*eaue, aive, eve*	*eau*
iapă		*yegua*	*égua*	*egua*	*ega*		*ive*

Commentary
In Rumanian, [*kʷ*] evolves to *p.* A lengthened *acqua,* documented for Vulgar Latin in the *Appendix Probi,* is the source of It. *acqua* with its internal [*kkʷ*], and it further seems required for Cat. *aigua* and Occ. *aiga,* with the yod stemming from the first *k,* while [*kʷ*] itself is voiced to [*gʷ*] in Catalan, simplified to *k* and then voiced in Occitan. A voicing of [*kʷ*] to [*gʷ*] takes place in Hispanic, including Catalan, as well as in the rare Occitan

variant *agua*. The normal development in Occitan calls for the voicing of *k* to *g* and the elimination of *u̯*: *ĕqua* > *ega; aequāle* > *egal; *sĕquat* > *sega*. The French reflexes of *aqua* are mostly unexplained, and dialectal interferences are much in evidence. In the West and later in *francien*, [*kʷ*] evolves to *i̯v*: *aqua* > *aive* > OFr. *eve* (cf. Fr. *évier*), while eastern and northern dialects have *eaue* > Fr. *eau*. The loss of the final vowel is obscure, and *w* here seems to have played the same role as the velar *l* in *bĕllos* > *beals* (§175), breaking the tonic *ę* of **ęwe* into *ea* (Rheinfelder I 214). The change of [*kʷ*] to *i̯v* seems to be characteristic of *francien*: *ĕqua* > **ieive* > OFr. *ive; aequāle* > OFr. *ivel* (Fr. *égal* is learned). In *antīqua* > OFr. *antive*, the yod has been absorbed into the tonic *ī*. A masculine *antif* is drawn analogically from *antive*, but these forms are replaced in the fourteenth century by the Latinism *antique*. In Sardinian, intervocalic [*kʷ*] evolves to *bb*: *aqua* > *abba; ĕqua* > *ebba*.

337. Consonant + [*kʷ*] + *a*
This combination is very rare; the simplification of [*kʷ*] to *k* appears to be the norm, and there is no voicing: *nŭmquam* > Sp., Ptg. *nunca*, Occ. *nonca*, OFr. *nonque*. The form that predominates in Medieval Spanish is *nunqua*, but this is probably a learned graph which does not reflect a [*kwa*] pronunciation. Learned also is the *u* of Sp., Ptg. *nunca*.

338. Consonant + [*gʷ*] + *i, e*

[*dž*]:	Rm.
[*gʷ*]:	It.
g:	Sp., Ptg., Cat.
g > k:	Occ., Fr.

Latin
sangue, sanguĭne

Rm.	**It.**	**Sp.**	**Ptg.**	**Cat.**	**Occ.**	**Fr.**
sânge	*sangue*	*sangre*	*sangue*	*sang*	*sanc*	*sang*

Commentary
In Rumanian, [*gʷ*] yields to a palatal [*dž*] in an evolution which parallels that of [*kʷ*] (§335). Italian retains [*gʷ*], while the labial element drops elsewhere. Desonorization occurs in Gallo-Romance due to the final

position; the *g* of French and Catalan is merely learned spelling for an occlusive that is left unpronounced. It is *k* that appears in French in linking.

Lat. *sanguĭs—sanguĭne*: the Rumanian, Italian, Catalan and Gallo-Romance forms are drawn from a Vulgar Latin declension *sanguis—sangue*, based on the short nominative form, while Sp. *sangre* and Ptg. *sangue* are reflexes of the longer oblique form *sanguĭne*. Spanish resolves the *g'n* cluster as *gr*, with *sangre* being the standard form as early as the *Cid*. There is, however, documentation in Berceo and in the *Fuero de Avilés* of an earlier stage in this evolution: *sanguĭne > sangne*. Portuguese drops the final *n*, presumably via a nasalized stage **sanguē* (Williams §124.6). Sardinian has *sambene*.

339. Consonant + [*gʷ*] + *a*

> *b*: Rm.
> [*gʷ*]: It., Sp., Ptg., Cat.
> *g*: Occ., Fr.

Latin
lĭngua

Rm.	It.	Sp.	Ptg.	Cat.	Occ.	OFr.	Fr.
limbă	*lingua*	*lengua*	*língua*	*llengua*	*lenga*	*lengue*	*langue*

Commentary

In Rumanian and Sardinian, [*gʷ*] evolves to *b*, paralleling the development of the voiceless [*kʷ*] to *p* (cf. *ĕqua >* Rm. *iapă*). This change causes the partial assimilation of the preceding *n* to *m*: *lĭngua >* Rm. *limbă*, Sd. *limba*. Italian and Hispanic keep the [*gʷ*] cluster intact, while Gallo-Romance simplifies it to *g*.

It. *lingua*, Ptg. *língua*: before the clusters *ng* and *nc*, tonic *e* closes to *i* in Italian, regardless of the nature of the following vowel: *lĭngua > lingua; fĭngĕre > fingere; vĭncĕre > vincere; vĭnctu > vinto* (Rohlfs §49), and the same rule applies to Portuguese: *lĭngua > língua; (die) domĭnĭcu > domingo* (Williams §35.10), whereas Lat. *lĭngua* suffers no inflection in Castilian or Catalan. In Fr. *langue*, *an* is merely a variant spelling for the etymological *en*.

340. Other u̯ Clusters

In Italian, the u̯ in hiatus doubles the preceding consonant. If this consonant is *k*, u̯ is retained: *tacuī* > *tacqui; placuī* > *piacqui; *nacuī* > *nacqui*. With consonants other than *k*, a doubling takes place, but u̯ itself drops: **stĕtuī* > *stetti; *caduī* > *caddi; vŏluī* > *volli;* VL *jenuāriu* > *gennaio*. In some verb forms, u̯ becomes *v*, and the preceding liquid consonant is not doubled: *paruī* > *parvi; dŏluit* > OIt. *dolve. Genŭa* > *Genova; Mantŭa* > *Mantova; Padŭa* > *Padova; vĭdŭa* > *vedova* are Latinizing forms.

The change of *u* to *v* also occurs in French: VL *jenuāriu* > OFr. *jenvier* > *janvier; vĭdŭa* > OFr. *veve* > *veuve*. Occ. *genoier* and *genier* < *ienuāriu* show that u̯ may either assume vocalic quality or drop. In Sp. *enero* and Ptg. *janeiro*, the Latin u̯ has dropped, perhaps by analogy with VL *febrariu* for CL *februāriu*.

The French *-ui* perfect formation poses severe phonological problems (Nyrop II §193; Lausberg §487). *Placuī* moves to a hypothetical **plawi*, whereupon this secondarily obtained *au* monophthongizes to *o*, giving OFr. *ploi*. This development implies the elimination of *k* before u̯, but the second person singular *placuistī* > OFr. *ploüs* > *plëus* > Fr. *plus* can hardly be explained in the same manner, since the stress has shifted in Vulgar Latin to **placústī*, which thus presents the vowel *u* and no longer the semi-vowel u̯. In this position, *k* drops and *a* is weakened and absorbed in hiatus position; the *o* of *ploüs* may be analogical from *ploi*. The perfect *habuī* undergoes an assimilation of *bu̯* with subsequent simplification and change of *au* to *o*: **awwi* > **awi* > OFr. *oi*, while the third person may retain the gemination: *habuit* > **awwit* > OFr. *out* vs. *habuit* > **awwit* > **awit* > OFr. *ot*, and *habuerunt* > **awwerent* > OFr. *ourent* vs. *habuerunt* > **awwerent* > **awerent* > OFr. *orent*.

Sp. *viuda*, Ptg. *viúva*: documented in the *Cid* as *bibda*, a form which still keeps the original accentuation on *i*, the word soon undergoes a metathesis, whereby the stress shifts to *u*, while *i* loses its syllabic value. The same process takes place in Portuguese, where an assimilation accounts for the replacement of *d* by *v*, while the Galician dialect keeps the form *viuda*.

OFr. *veve*, Fr. *veuve*, Occ. *veva, veuza, veuva, vepda, bepda, vezoa*: in Old French, the *du̯* cluster evolves to *dv* and is subsequently reduced to *v*. The ulterior change to *veuve* is usually attributed to the rounding influence of labials, but a comparison with the Occitan and Hispanic evidence suggests that the French reflex, too, must have undergone a metathesis. Whereas in Hispanic the transposed u̯ becomes a full-fledged vowel, it merges with ẹ in French to form the diphthong *eu*, which is later resolved as [œ].

The numerous Occitan forms have their counterparts elsewhere in Romance: *veva* corresponds to OFr. *veve, vepda* and *bepda* to OSp. *bibda, veuza* to Sp. *viuda, veuva* to Ptg. *viúva,* and *vezoa* recalls It. *vedova.* The stress pattern is difficult to sort out, but we may take note of the intervocalic treatment of *d* in *veuza.*

341. Geminates

Double consonants occur only in internal position, where they are characterized by a prolonged rather than by a double articulation or, in the case of occlusives, by a delayed explosion. This pronunciation is retained in Italian and Sardinian, while a simplification takes place in the rest of Romania. In addition to the geminates inherited directly from Latin, Italian creates several others through a process of total assimilation: *factu > fatto; *frīgĭdu > freddo; sŭbtu > sotto; rŭptu > rotto; saxu > sasso,* or through the influence of the postconsonantal ų: *jenuāriu > gennaio.*

In Latin, consonantal quantity is a phonemic feature: *ănnus* 'year' vs. *ănus* 'old woman'; *stēlla* 'star' vs. *stēla* 'stone column', but in Late Latin the geminates tend to simplify: *garrulus non garulus (Appendix Probi).* Typical of Latin is a sequence of long vowel and short consonant or of short vowel and long consonant, and some words are actually found to hesitate between these two sequences: *glūtus* vs. *glŭttus; cūpa* vs. *cŭppa.* Length is rarely found together in both the vocalic and the consonantal segments: *stēlla,* VL *tōttī.* Geminates form a blocked syllable, and chronologically they simplify too late in the Western languages for any participation in the lenition of the corresponding single consonants. The lengthened pronunciation becomes superfluous, as the former geminates fill the slots vacated by the single consonants whose pronunciation had been altered through the lenition process.

342. Lat. *-ll-*

l or ∅:	Rm.
ll:	It.
l':	Sp.
l:	Ptg., Occ., Fr.
l' or *l*:	Cat.

Latin
caballu, gallīna

Rm.	It.	Sp.	Ptg.	Cat.	Occ.	OFr.	Fr.
cal	*cavallo*	*caballo*	*cavalo*	*cavall*	*caval*		*cheval*
găină	*gallina*	*gallina*	*galinha*	*gallina*	*galina*	*geline*	

Commentary

Double *l* is retained in Italian, palatalized to *l'* in Spanish and Catalan and simplified to *l* in Rumanian, Portuguese and Gallo-Romance. A cacuminal pronunciation of *l* is characteristic of Sardinian and certain southern Italian dialects: *caballu* > Sd. *kaḍḍu* (Lausberg §§496–498).

The norm for standard Italian is the retention of *ll;* the dialects, however, show a variety of developments, which are described in great detail by Rohlfs (§§233–235). In Spanish, *ll* is palatalized: *cŏllu* > *cuello; pŭllu* > *pollo; valle* > *valle.* Learned words show a simplification of *ll* to *l*: *collēgiu* > *colegio; vacillāre* > *vacilar,* and there are occurrences of the transformation of *ll* to *ld*: *cĕlla* > *celda; rebĕlle* > *rebelde; *pillŭla* > *píldora.* Portuguese simplifies the double *l*, but the resulting single *l* is kept separate from the intervocalic *l* of Latin (§270). Chronologically, the intervocalic *l* drops prior to the simplification of the geminate, which allows for the secondarily obtained *l* to be retained: *caballu* > *cavalo* vs. *fīlu* > *fio.* Words in which *ll* is palatalized are borrowings from Spanish: *castĕllānu* > OPtg. *castelão* and Ptg. *castelhano: caballariu* > *cavalheiro* and *cavaleiro.* Ptg. *rebelde* may be a borrowing from Spanish. Rumanian, which changes the intervocalic *l* to *r,* observes the same chronological distinction between -*ll*- and -*l*-, as does Portuguese: *caballu* > *cal* vs. *fīlu* > *fir.*

A palatal pronunciation of the reflex of *ll* is noted for Gascony and the Ariège and Aude regions of the Occitan domain and is documented in some manuscripts through the use of an *lh* graph: *bĕlla* > *belha; ĕlla* > *elha.* Gascon may also change the internal *ll* to *r*: *bĕlla* > *bera; appĕllāre* > *aperar,* as opposed to *t* in final position: *gallu* > *gat* (Appel §49). There are a couple of words in French that point to a very early reduction of *ll* to *l,* allowing for open-syllable treatment of the preceding tonic vowel: *stēlla* > **stēla* > OFr. *esteile* > *étoile; ōlla* > **ōla* > OFr. *eule.* Both *l* and *ll* are resolved as *l* in French, but the modern language favors a Latinizing graph, which does not imply length: OFr. *bele* vs. Fr. *belle.*

In Rumanian and Catalan, a set of conditioned changes interferes with the phonological development of the geminate *l*. The situation in Rumanian is particularly complex. Before the vowel *i, ll* becomes *i̯* and falls: *gallīna* > *găină; caballī* > *cai,* as opposed to the regular development to *l* before *u* and *e*: *caballu* > *cal; valle* > *val.* Stress becomes a conditioning factor when *ll* stands before the vowel *a*. If *a* is tonic, *ll* is absorbed and disappears: *stēlla* > *stea; catēlla* > *cǎţea.* There is no proof that a vocalization to *u̯* forms an intermediate stage in this evolution (Lausberg §498). Conditions in Catalan are relatively simple compared to the intricacies of Rumanian. The norm is for *ll* to palatalize: *sĕlla* > *sella; ampŭlla* > *ampolla,* but if the preceding vowel is a tonic *i, ll* undergoes a simplification to *l*: *anguīlla* > *anguila; argīlla* > *argila; vīlla* > *vila.* Fouché (*Phonétique historique,* p. 164) adds the vowel *ẹ* as a conditioning factor, but this rule is inferred solely from *stēlla* > *estela,* an archaic form that could reflect a hypothetical **stēla,* which is also required for the French development. Mod. Cat. *estrella* is a Castilianism.

Sp. *rebelde, celda*: the controversy surrounding the change of *ll* to *ld* in a few Spanish words dates back to Leite de Vasconcelos and Gonçalves Viana, who explain Sp., Ptg. *rebelde* as a derivation from the hypothetical verb **rebĕllītāre* > **rebeldar.* The trouble with this interpretation is that no such verb has ever been documented. García de Diego turns to a cross with *umilde* for an explanation, while Malkiel draws *rebelde* from the noun *rebeldía,* formed analogically from *osadía* and other cases of the *-adía* suffix, all very rare. OSp. *rebele* or *rebelle* is a learned reflex of Lat. *rebĕlle,* based on *bĕllum* 'war', and forms such as *rebelarse* and *rebelión* are pure Latinisms. The learned character is evident in the lack of a diphthongization (cf. *cĕlla* > *cella,* for which Berceo offers a popular variant *ciella*), and Corominas (II 19) concludes that the change to *ld* may simply have resulted from an unsuccessful attempt to pronounce the double *l* of Latin. Corominas' explanation may be expanded upon, for there existed another cluster that caused pronunciation problems in late Medieval Spanish, the unfamiliar *t'l* group (§300) which, following the voicing of *t* to *d,* suffered a metathesis of *dl* to *ld* in a few learned words: *tĭtŭlu* > Sp. *tilde; capĭtŭlu* > Sp. *cabildo.*

Lat. *ōlla*: this form, used already by Cicero, replaces an earlier *aula* and is the source of Rm. *oalǎ,* Sp. *olla,* Ptg. *ola,* while OFr. *eule* reflects a reduced *ōla,* which is documented in inscriptions.

343. Lat. *-rr-*

r: Rm., Fr.

rr: It., Sp., Ptg., Cat., Occ., OFr.

Latin
tĕrra, carru

Rm.	It.	Sp.	Ptg.	Cat.	Occ.	Fr.
ţară	terra	tierra	terra	terra	terra	terre
car	carro	carro	carro	carro	car,	char
					carre	

Commentary

Double *r* is kept distinct from the single *r* in Italian, Hispanic, Occitan and Old French, while the two merge in Rumanian. In French, the simplification of *rr* to *r* occurs as late as the seventeenth century in internal position but it is an early change where *rr* becomes final: *carru* > *char,* while Occitan hesitates between a simplification to *r* in final position and retention of the geminate accompanied by a supporting *e*: *car* and *carre*. In many areas of Romance, the difference between *rr* and *r* tends to be of a qualitative rather than a quantitative nature.

344. Lat. *-nn-*

$$
\begin{aligned}
&n\text{:} && \text{Rm., Ptg., Occ.}\\
&nn\text{:} && \text{It.}\\
&n'\text{:} && \text{Sp., Cat.}\\
n \text{ or nasalization:} && &\text{Fr.}
\end{aligned}
$$

Latin
annu

Rm.	It.	Sp.	Ptg.	Cat.	Occ.	Fr.
an	anno	año	ano	any	an	an

Commentary

The geminate is retained in Italian, palatalized in Spanish and Catalan and simplified elsewhere. In Portuguese, this secondarily obtained *n* is prevented chronologically from participating in the elimination process that affects the single *n*. Words in which Latin *nn* shows palatalization in Portuguese are borrowings from Spanish: *pĭnna* > Sp. *peña* > Ptg. *penha;* **ante-annu* > Sp. *antaño* > Ptg. *antanho*. French has *n* internally: **an-*

nāta > *année* (*nn* is learned spelling), and nasalization in final position: *annu* > *an.*

345. Secondary Consonant Clusters

Secondary consonant clusters arise through vowel syncope and are particularly common in French, where the elimination of weak vowels occurs with greater frequency than elsewhere. Vowel syncope often leads to the formation of consonant clusters that are unfamiliar to Latin speakers. Such clusters may either be transformed into familiar groups, or they may be tolerated. The change to well-known combinations is usually done in unpredictable fashion, involving such sporadic features as assimilation and metaphony, etc., or sudden leaps in quality.

346. Changes in Quality

When *vĕtŭlu* is reduced to **vetlu,* the unfamiliar *t'l* cluster is replaced by *cl* already in Vulgar Latin: *vĕtulus non veclus* (*Appendix Probi*), and *veclu* is the source of the Romance forms. A postconsonantal *g'n* is replaced by *gr* in *sanguĭne* > Sp. *sangre* and in the French toponym *Langres* < *Langŏnes,* and *pr* is substituted for *p'n* in *pampĭnu* > Fr. *pampre.* A change from a palatal to a dental consonant occurs in French in the clusters *nc'r, ng'r, rc'r* and *rg'r*: *vĭncĕre* > OFr. *veintre; plangĕre* > *plaindre; carcĕre* > OFr. *chartre; sŭrgĕre* > *sourdre,* and *sc'r* becomes *i̯* + *str*: **nascĕre*> OFr. *naistre.*

347. Consonant Loss

If a cluster of three consonants exists in Latin or arises through vowel syncope, the middle element usually falls, unless the last consonant is a liquid. This process is known as *la loi des trois consonnes*: **aestĭmāre* > Cat., Occ. *esmar,* OFr. *esmer; campsāre* > Sp., Ptg., Cat. *cansar; hōspĭte* > Cat. *hoste; fŏrte mĕnte* > OFr. *forment.* No reduction occurs if the last element is a liquid: *amplu* > Cat., Fr. *ample; ŭmbra* > Rm. *umbră,* It., Cat., Occ. *ombra,* Fr. *ombre.* In *pŏrcos* > OFr. *pors* > *porcs, c* is reintroduced in spelling only. Consonant loss is also a common occurrence outside of the three-consonant rule: *dēbet* > Fr. *doit; naves* > OFr. *nes; colaphu* > **colpu* > Cat. *cop.*

348. Consonant Addition

The addition of a transitional consonant, referred to as a glide, occurs with the regularity of a sound-law in French between *m, n, l, s* or *z* as the first element and *r* as the second as well as in the *m'l* group. These clusters evolve as follows: *m'r* > *mbr; m'l* > *mbl; n'r* > *ndr; l'r* > *ldr; s'r* > *str; z'r* > *zdr.* Examples of these developments are: *camĕra* > *chambre; cŭmŭlu* > *comble; cĭnĕre* > *cendre; mŏlĕre* > OFr. *moldre* > *moudre; pascĕre* > OFr. *paistre* > *paître; mīsĕrunt* > OFr. *misdrent; Lazaru* > OFr. *lasdre* > *ladre.* Occitan inserts a *b* in the *m'r* and *m'l* groups: *camĕra* > *cambra; sĭmŭlāre* > *semblar; cŭmŭlāre* > *comblar,* but shows a decided preference for leaving the *n'r* and *l'r* clusters unchanged: *die Vĕnĕris* > *divenres; mĭnor* > *menre; honorāre* > *onrar; tollĕre* > *tolre; *vŏlēre aio* > *volrai.* These forms are found alternating with the French-type development: *mendre, ondrar, toldre,* etc. *S'r* gives *str* in **essĕre* > Occ. *estre,* but examples of this change are infrequent due to the specific rules governing weak-vowel syncope and retention in Occitan (§215): **essĕre* > *esser; *nascĕre* > *naisser; pascĕre* > *paisser.* *Prezeron* < *prehenserunt* is more common than *presdrent.* The secondary *m'n* cluster is dissimilated to *m'r,* whereupon a *b* is inserted as a glide in *hŏmĭne* > Sp. *hombre; fēmĭna* > Sp. *hembra,* Cat. *fembra; sēmĭnāre* > Sp., Cat. *sembrar,* and *n'r* evolves to *ndr* in *tĕnĕru* > Cat., Fr. *tendre; ĭngenerāre* > Sp. *engendrar,* Fr. *engendrer.* An example of the change of the unfamiliar *s'l* cluster to *scl* may be seen in: *īnsŭla* > Occ. *iscla,* It. *Ischia.*

349. Metathesis

This device is rarely used as a means to eliminate unfamiliar clusters. The example most often quoted of this feature is *gĕnĕru* > Sp. *yerno.* French overcomes the difficulty by inserting a glide: *gendre,* while Portuguese tolerates the cluster: *genro.*

350. Retention of Unfamiliar Clusters

New clusters arising through vowel syncope may be retained. This occurs most readily where liquids are present: *mŏrdĕre* > Fr. *mordre; Monte Martyrum* > Fr. *Montmartre.* Occitan and Catalan keep unfamiliar clusters with greater ease than French: *septĭmana* > Cat., Occ. *setmana* vs. Fr. *semaine; repŭtāre* > Cat., Occ. *reptar* vs. OFr. *reter.* Many such clusters are often reintroduced in learned words: Fr. *captif, précepte, sceptre, Egypte;* here, however, Italian seems less prone to retention: *cattivo, precetto, scettro, Egitto.* Secondary geminates exist in such compounds as Sp. *innatural, ennegrecer.*

351. Relative Chronology of Sound Changes

In French, the secondary *m'n* of *hŏmĭne* is treated in exactly the same manner as the primary *mn* of *sŏmnu,* the two words being continued as *homme* and *somme*. This proves that the syncope had arisen when *mn* was still pronounced *mn*, allowing for a complete merger of the two outcomes. A different chronology surfaces in Spanish, where the primary *mn* palatalizes to *n'*: *sŏmnu* > *sueño*, while the secondary *m'n*, obtained too late for any participation in the palatalization process, evolves to *mbr*: *hŏmĭne* > *hombre*. In Occitan, the primary *pt* cluster is simplified to *t*: *sĕpte* > *set;* *scrīptu* > *escrit*, while the secondary *p't* group survives: *reputāre* > *reptar;* *capĭtāle* > *captal.*

A close link exists between vowel syncope and the feature of lenition. An early syncope rules out lenition, while a late vowel loss allows for intervocalic treatment of the following consonant. French usually shows an early syncope, as opposed to Spanish where lenition has time to take hold: *cīvĭtāte* > Fr. *cité*, vs. Sp. *ciudad; dŭbĭtāre* > Fr. *douter* vs. Sp. *dudar; dēbĭta* > Fr. *dette* vs. Sp. *deuda; sēmĭta* > Fr. *sente* (cf. Fr. *sentier*) vs. Sp. *senda* (cf. Sp. *sendero*); *pūlĭce* > Fr. *puce* vs. *pūlĭca* > Sp. *pulga: collō-cāre* > OFr. *colchier* > *coucher* vs. Sp. *colgar.* Occitan shows a fair amount of hesitation between voiced and voiceless outcomes: *sabbatu* > *sabde* and *sapte; dēbĭtōre* > *deudor* and *deptor,* and a similar fluctuation may at times be observed in Old French: *cŭbĭtu* > *coude* and *coute; carrĭcātus* > *chargiez* and *charchiez.*

352. Retention of Transitional Stages

Closely linked to the chronology feature is the retention of transitional stages in the phonological evolution. This happens when a sound change suddenly finds itself obstructed by the workings of another phonological rule. Lat. *sŭbĭtānu* counts an intervocalic *t*, which in its normal evolution in French will voice to *d*, whereupon fricativization to *đ* will take place prior to complete elimination as in *vīta* > OFr. *vidhe* > Fr. *vie*. In the case of *sŭbĭtānu*, however, the evolution is arrested at the *d* stage by the elimination of the weak intertonic vowel, which deprives the consonant of the intervocalic position necessary for any further change. The end result is thus Fr. *soudain*, in which a transitional stage in the evolution of *t* is retained.

It may also happen that a consonant cluster is generated too late for any merger to take place with the same cluster created earlier from other sources. The treatment of the *-atĭcu* suffix in French is a case in point. The intervocalic position of the consonants leads to their voicing, yielding a form **-adegu*, whereupon the occlusive drops before the velar vowel. As a result of this loss, a hiatus position is created, in which *e* loses its syllabic value, becoming yod. The *dį* cluster generated in this manner appears too late, however, for any participation in the normal reduction of $d\underset{\cap}{i}$ to $\underset{\cap}{i}$ (§319). Instead, it joins the $b\underset{\cap}{i}$ cluster at some point in its trajectory toward [$d\check{z}$] as in *rabia > rage* (§331): *-atĭcu > *-adego > *-ad\underset{\cap}{i}o > -age.*

III. *FINAL CONSONANTS*

353. Vocalic Word Endings; Primary and Secondary Final Consonants

Vulgar Latin is characterized by a decisive preference for vocalic word endings, and this trend remains very strong in Italian, is less pronounced in Spanish and Portuguese, even less so in Catalan, Occitan and Rumanian, and it is weakest in French. A vocalic ending can be obtained through the loss of the final consonant: *pĭper* > It. *pepe,* through metathesis: *quattuor* > Sp. *cuatro,* or through the addition of a paragogical vowel: *crēdunt* > It. *credono.* The shape of this added vowel may be determined by the preceding vowel as in It. *credono,* but *-o* soon achieves a greater spread: *cantant,* for example, does not give **cantana,* but *cantano* in Italian.

The final consonant may be present in Latin, in which case it is termed primary, or a consonant may become final secondarily through final-vowel loss. Secondary final consonants are above all common in Gallo-Romance, where final vowels other than *a* regularly fall.

354. Lat. *-m*

The loss of final *m* in words of more than one syllable ranks as one of the earliest consonantal changes in Vulgar Latin. CL *mūrum* becomes *muro* in early Vulgar Latin, and in Latin versification the presence of a final *m* forms no barrier to synalepha, the reduction of two adjacent syllables into one. Final *m* thus leaves no trace in Romance: CL *mūrum* > VL *muro* > It., Sp., Ptg. *muro,* Occ., Fr. *mur,* with the exception, however, that in monosyllables the final nasal is retained, usually in the form of *n.* Italian has *n,* but cases are limited to a couple of words: *cŭm* > *con* and *sŭm,* which yields a rare *son* that soon evolves to *sono* by adopting the standard *-o* ending of first-person singular verbs. Spanish similarly has *n: cŭm* > *con; quĕm* > *quién,* while nasalization is the norm in Portuguese: *cŭm* > *com; quĕm* > *quem,* as well as in French: *rĕm* > *rien; mĕum* > *mon* and *mien.* The outcome in Occitan is an unstable *n: mĕum* > *mom > *moṇ; rĕm* > *reṇ; sŭm* > *soṇ. Cŭm* evolves to *cun* in Old Rumanian, but is reduced to *cu* in the modern language. It is unclear how Rm. *cine* relates to Lat. *quĕm;* it may have been modeled on *mine, tine.* The adverb *jam* has lost its final nasal throughout: It. *già,* Sp. *ya,* Ptg. *já,* Cat., Occ., OFr. *ja,* Fr. *déjà* < **de-ex-jam.*

355. Lat. *-n*

Outside of monosyllables final *n* drops: *nōmen* > It., Ptg. *nome,* Cat., Occ., Fr. *nom* (Sp. *nombre* comes from *nōmĭne* with an internal *m'n* group);

lūmen > Rm., It., Ptg. *lume*, Cat. *llum*, Occ. *lum*. In monosyllables *n* occurs in *ĭn* and *nōn*. The preposition *ĭn* retains the nasal in Rm. *în*, It. *in*, Sp. *en*, while nasalization occurs in Ptg. *em* and Fr. *en*. Occitan has *en* which, in anteconsonantal position, may be reduced to *e* (Appel §52). *Nōn* evolves to *nu* in Rumanian, to a weak *non* or a tonic *no* in Italian; Old Spanish has *non*, which is reduced to *no* in the modern language, while Ptg. *não* shows transition to a nasal diphthong. Occitan has *non̦* with an unstable *n*, while French shows a dual outcome based on stress: a tonic *non* and a proclitic *ne*, the latter obtained via a weakening to *nen*, with the removal of *n* beginning in anteconsonantal position and then generalized.

356. Lat. -*s* in the West

Final *s* is retained in the West and in Sardinian, but drops in Italian and Rumanian. The pronunciation of final *s* in Latin was linked to morphological factors and to problems of syntactic phonetics. Generally speaking, however, final *s* was restituted in Classical Latin, no doubt as a result of its important morphological functions. The Romance languages that innovate are thus those that drop *s*, not those that have a final *s*. Final *s*, in other words, is not restored in western Romania through the influence of the schools and of the literary language; its presence follows from a direct continuation of the stability achieved within Classical Latin itself (Väänänen §§128–129; Lausberg §§534–535; Rohlfs §308; von Wartburg: *Ausgliederung*, p. 21, and *Evolution et structure*, p. 51).

Latin final *s* is kept in Sardinian and in the western Romance group (Hispanic, Gallo-Romance, Rhaeto-Romance): *fēmĭnas* > Sd. *feminas*, Sp. *hembras*, Ptg. *fêmeas*, Cat. *fembras*, Occ. *femnas*, Fr. *femmes; nōs* > Sd., Sp., Ptg., Cat., Occ. *nos*, Fr. *nous; cantas* > Sd., Sp., Ptg., Occ. *cantas*, Cat. *cantes*, Fr. *chantes*. The Portuguese pronunciation is [*š*]; this palatalization has its inception in the thirteenth century, and [*š*] is voiced to [*ž*] in proclitics if a voiced consonant follows: *os* [*uš*] *pêlos* vs. *as* [*až*] *mãos*. Occitan retains final *s*, but drops it for morphological reasons in the first-person plural ending -*mus*: *amāmus* > *amam; vendĭmus* > *vendem*, as does also Catalan: *amam, venem*. A somewhat similar reduction of -*mus* to -*mo* occurs in Spanish and Portuguese when enclitic pronouns are added: Sp., Ptg. *levantémonos*, Sp. *vámonos*, but in this case it may be explained as a dissimilation feature (García de Diego, p. 155). Lat. *magis* evolves to *mais* or *mai* in Occitan, the latter a feature of syntactic phonetics, and final *s* drops in enclitic constructions: *no·n* < *nos ne; vo·n* < *vos ne*. The secondary *t's* and *d's* combinations are retained as *ts;* the spelling is *tz*: *lātus* > *latz; nūdos* > *nutz*, and Old French similarly has *ts*, spelled *z*: *lez, nuz*. In French, final *s* ceases to be pronounced in the thirteenth century, but it is still kept as a voiced *s* in linking: *nous avons; les amis.*

357. Lat. *-s* in the East

In Italian final *s* drops: *mĕlius* > *meglio; tĕmpus* > *tempo; lātus* > *lato; sentīs* > *senti,* but it normally leaves a yod in monosyllables: *nōs* > *noi; vōs* > *voi; stas* > *stai; das* > *dai; cras* > OIt. *crai; pŏs(t)* > *poi.* Monosyllables showing no trace of *s* are very few in number: *plūs* > *più* is a reduced form of OIt. *piui.* Italian usually eliminates falling diphthongs (Meyer-Lübke, p. 54), and furthermore, the loss of *i̯* here can easily be accounted for through syntactic phonetics: *piui bello* > *più bello* (ibid., p. 116). Lat. *trēs* is continued as *tre,* while southern Italian dialects have *trei;* the verb *è* < *ĕst* is pan-Italian. Final *s* probably became *i̯,* and this yod was kept in monosyllables where retention of phonetic substance was critical, but it was eliminated elsewhere. This development is not entirely clear, however, and opinions are divided concerning the provenance of the final *i̯* present in Italian and Rumanian monosyllables that had *s* in Latin. Among the proponents of a purely phonological explanation is Lausberg (§§539–545) who, linking the fate of final *s* overall to considerations of syntactic phonetics, theorizes that *s* would voice before a word beginning with a voiced consonant. The next stage would then be the transformation of the voiced *s* to *i̯,* and he seeks proof of these developments in certain dialectal areas of Occitan and Gascon, where *las rodas* (with the *s* of *las* voicing before *r*) becomes *lai rodas* (cf. *asne* > Gascon *aine*). The final stage is a general elimination of final *s,* with yod remaining only in monosyllables. Terming the phonological evolution unclear, Rohlfs (§308) suggests in a note that *-i* could reflect the *i* of *nobis, vobis,* but this does not account for *cras* > *crai,* which Rohlfs draws from a paragogical **crae,* nor for *pŏs(t)* > *poi.* In this last word, *t* drops early when followed by a word beginning with a consonant.

The origin of the Italian second-person singular *-i* ending: *cantas* > *canti; vĭdes* > *vedi; dormīs* > *dormi,* has been the subject of a great deal of controversy. Meyer-Lübke (p. 56) is convinced that the process leading from *-as* and *-es* to *-i* is phonological: *cantas* > **cantēs* > *canti; vĭdēs* > *vedi.* In his explanation of this development, Lausberg (§542) suggests that *-as* first evolves to **-ai,* which subsequently becomes *-e* as in OIt. *cante,* whereby the ending merges formally with that of the *-ēre* group: *vĭdēs* > OIt. *vede.* The change to *-i: canti, vedi,* is very old as confirmed by Rm. *vezi,* since Rumanian assibilates *d* to *z* before *i,* but not before *e* (§266). The manner in which *-es* moves to *-i* is not explicitly stated, however. The change of -*as* to -*es* as well as that of -*e* to -*i* cannot be justified on purely phonological grounds, and it is Rohlfs' analogical interpretation of the shift, as it applies to both verb and noun morphology, that offers the most coherent analysis of the problem (§§142, 365, 528). There are dialectal occurrences of -*a* in the -*āre* conjugation: *pēnsas* > *(tu) pensa; lāvas* > *(tu) lava*, but in Old Tuscan texts, this -*a* is replaced by -*e* by analogy with the -*ēre* verbs: *vĭdes* > *(tu) vede*. The -*e* ending of *vede* and *cante* yields to -*i* in an ultimate analogy with the victorious -*īre* group, where *dŏrmīs* phonologically evolves to *dormi*. Forms in -*i* are present already in the oldest Tuscan texts. In the realm of declensions, analogical influences coupled with determined efforts to establish a differentiation between the singular and the plural have led to the elimination of the regular phonological outcome of nouns such as *canes* and *dentes* which, with the loss of final *s*, would yield *cane* and *dente*. An analogy with the masculine declension in -*o*, -*i*: *il gallo—i galli; il lupo—i lupi*, leads to the creation of an *il cane—i cani* formation, perhaps with added pressure exerted by the masculine plural article *i*. The feminine declension in -*a* forms its plural from the nominative: *portae* > *porte; caprae* > *capre; aquae* > *acque*, and not from the accusative in -*as* (Rohlfs §362).

Rumanian similarly drops final *s*: *tĕmpus* > *timp; cŏrpus* > *corp; dormīs* > *dormi*, but continues it as *į* in monosyllables: *nōs* > *noi, vōs* > *voi; trēs* > *trei; das* > *dai; stas* > *stai; ad pŏst* > *apoi*, an evolution which Tiktin (§156) terms unclear, and for which Rothe (§80) rules out a phonological explanation. Instead, he suggests linking *i* to the plural -*i* of nouns and drawing *trei* analogically from *doi*. The treatment of the verbal endings in *cantas* > *cânţi; vĭdes* > *vezi; dormīs* > *dormi* parallels that of Italian.

358. Lat. -*x*

s:	Rm.	
įs > *į:*	It.	
įs:	Sp., Ptg., Cat., Occ., Fr.	

Latin
sĕx

Rm.	**It.**	**Sp.**	**Ptg.**	**Cat.**	**Occ.**	**Fr.**
şase	*sei*	*seis*	*seis*	*sis*	*seis, sieis*	*six*

Commentary

The Latin numeral *sĕx* offers an isolated occurrence of final *x (cs)* in a word that belongs to the core vocabulary. Rm. *şase* is entirely dependent in its evolution on an analogy with the neighboring numeral *şapte* (§230). While *cs* normally evolves to *ps*: *cŏxa* > *coapsă* (§311), there are rare instances of a simplification to *s* as in *frasin* < *fraxĭnu* and *măseà* < *maxĭlla* (§217). In the other languages, final *x* is resolved as *i̯s* with ulterior elimination of *i̯* in Catalan and French and with loss of final *s* in Italian. Lausberg (§546) explains the final yod of Italian as derived from a palatal [*š*], but the details of the phonological process remain somewhat unclear (Rohlfs §308). Spanish treats final *x* like the syllable-final *x*, which is resolved as *i̯s*: *fraxĭnu* > **fraisno* > *fresno*, as opposed to the treatment of intervocalic *x*, which moves via [*š*] to [*χ*]: *taxu* > *texo* > *tejo* (§311). The presence of a palatal prevents a diphthongization from taking place, while in Italian the blocked position has the same effect. Overall, Spanish tends to avoid having palatal consonants in word-final position; cf. *pĕlle* > *piel;* *domĭnu* > *don* vs. *dueño*. The Catalan and French forms follow from a reduction of **sieis*.

359. Lat. Vowel + -*t*

Following a vowel, the final *t* of Latin survives in Old French until the beginning of the twelfth century; it was probably pronounced like the voiceless interdental fricative [*θ*]. It is encountered in the *Vie de Saint Alexis: aimet* (v. 250) < *āmat; donet* (v. 28) < *dōnat; achatet* (v. 40) < **adcaptat,* and in the *Chanson de Roland: aimet* (v. 7) < *āmat; reclaimet* (v. 8) < *reclāmat.* It disappears in the twelfth century. Elsewhere, the postvocalic final *t* of Latin is not continued: *cantat* > Rm. *cântă,* It., Sp., Ptg., Cat., Occ. *canta,* Fr. *chante* vs. OFr. *chantet; dat* > Rm. *dă,* It., Sp., Ptg., Occ. *da.* Totally isolated structurally, the noun *caput* drops its final *t* at a very early stage, which means that the Romance forms are reflexes of VL *capu*: Rm., Cat., Occ. *cap,* It. *capo,* Sp., Ptg. *cabo,* OFr. *chief,* Fr. *chef.* Only Sd. *cápute* continues the Classical Latin form.

The *t* of the conjunction *et* was subject to assimilation when standing before a consonant, whereby a geminate was created Maintained in Italian: *e Pietro* [*eppi̯etro*], it is simplified elsewhere, yielding a preconsonantal *e*. Before a vowel, *et* was replaced by *ed,* obtained analogically from *a—ad* (Lausberg §§551, 559), and as a result the treatment becomes that of intervocalic *d*. Italian has *ed,* Occitan *ez* and the earliest stages of Old French have [*eθ*]: *et amōre* > It. *ed amore,* Occ. *ez amor,* OFr. [*eθ*] *amor.* Italian has *e,* while *ed* is limited in use to the position before the vowels *e* and *i*:

ed ecco lui, lei ed io, and it has disappeared from the spoken language (Rohlfs §759). Old Spanish and Portuguese have *e* before consonants as well as before vowels, but Spanish later closes *e* to *i* before vowels other than *i,* and this form, spelled *y,* is then generalized, with the exception that *e* is retained before *i* or *hi: aguja e hilo.* Catalan has *i* from an earlier *e,* and Old Rumanian has *e,* which is now replaced by *şi.* Occitan shows a variety of forms: *e, ed, ez, et.* Of these, *e* is anteconsonantal, *ed* antevocalic, *ez* antevocalic and analogical from *az* (§361) and *et* is learned. From the twelfth century on, French has only the form *e,* but the spelling remains a Latinizing *et.* The treatment of *aut* parallels that of *et,* with the Romance reflexes based on an antevocalic *aud*: Rm. *au,* It. *o, od,* Sp. *o, u,* Ptg. *ou,* Cat. *o,* Occ. *o, oz,* Fr. *ou.* It. *od* is a little used antevocalic form, and Occitan similarly has *o* before a consonant and *oz* before a vowel. Spanish uses the variant *u* before *o* or *ho: siete u ocho; española u holandesa.* In French, *o* is closed to *u* before a vowel, and this sound is then generalized. Ptg. *ou* [*ọ*] represents the regular outcome of the *au* diphthong.

360. Lat. Consonant + *-t*

French is the only language which retains the final *t* of the Latin third-person plural ending; it is pronounced in the thirteenth century: *cantant > chantent,* and it still surfaces in linking: *chantent-ils.* Vulgar Latin hesitated for reasons of syntactical phonetics between *-nt* and *-n,* a fluctuation which found its way into Sardinian. Elsewhere in Romania *-n* prevails, except in Rumanian, which reduces *-ant* to *-ă,* and Portuguese, which shows nasalization: *cantant >* Rm. *cântă,* It. *cantano,* Sp., Occ. *cantan,* Ptg. *cantam,* Cat. *canten* vs. Fr. *chantent.* Lat. *sŭnt* is continued as Rm. *sunt,* OIt. *son,* It. *sono,* Sp., Occ. *son,* Ptg. *são,* Cat. *són* vs. Fr. *sont.* The reflexes of Lat. *ĕst* are Rm. *este,* It. *è,* Sp., Occ. *es,* Ptg. *é,* Cat. *és,* Fr. *est,* with the final *t* of French appearing in linking: *est-il.*

361. Lat. *-b, -d, -r, -l, -c*

A final *b* exists in the Latin preposition *sŭb,* continued in Spanish as *so* with a variant *son,* which draws its *n* from the common prepositions *en, con, sin.* Old Portuguese has *so,* while the modern form *sob* is learned. Rm. *sub* may also be a learned form.

A final *d* is encountered in *ad, apud, quĭd* and *quod. Ad* causes gemination before a consonant just like *et* (§359). Before a consonant, *ad* is reduced to *a,* whereas *d* receives intervocalic treatment when a vowel follows: It. *a* and *ad,* Occ. *a* and *az* and also *ad,* which may follow from an analogy with *ed* and *od* where an intervocalic *t* is involved (Appel §52).

French has generalized *a,* but *ad* was used before a vowel until the beginning of the twelfth century. From *quĭd* Italian draws *ched* before a vowel and *che* before a consonant, whereupon *que* is generalized, Old French has *qued* and *que* in a similar distribution, and Occitan has *quez* and *que.* The same pattern may be observed for *od* and *o* as Old French reflexes of the preposition *apud.*

R is often removed from the final position. In monosyllables this can be achieved by adding a paragogical or morphologically determined *e*: CL *cŏr > *cŏre >* It. *cuore.* In words of more than one syllable, final *r* may drop in Italian: *pĭper > pepe; cĭcer > cece; marmor > marmo,* but it is difficult to determine whether this is a purely phonological process, or whether certain morphological adjustments are involved: a popular **cĭcis— **cĭce* flexion, a change of *marmor* to **marmus,* analogical from *tempus,* etc. (Rohlfs §307). OIt. *suoro* does not go back to CL *sŏror,* but to a morphologically reshaped **sŏru,* later replaced by **sŏra >* It. *suora.* Old French, on the other hand, with its *suer—serour* flexion does offer a bona fide example of the elimination of final *r*: *sŏror > suer > soeur.* Occitan has *sor* or *sorre.* In a more common development final *r* may become internal through metathesis: *sĕmper >* It., Ptg., Cat., Occ., OFr. *sempre,* Sp. *siempre; quattuor >* Rm. *patru,* It. *quattro,* Sp. *cuatro,* Ptg. *quatro,* Occ. *catre,* Cat., Fr. *quatre.*

Final *l* of Latin is often followed by a paragogical *e* (§157), which probably has its origin in a morphological adjustment: CL *mĕl > *mĕle >* Rm. *miere,* It. *miele;* CL *sal > sale >* Rm. *sare,* It. *sale.* This has led to intervocalic treatment of *l* in Rumanian (§270), but not in Portuguese where the original final position has prevented *l* from falling in *mel* (§367).

A final *c* is encountered in a few adverbs and pronouns; it is subject to a mixed evolution involving mostly loss, but also retention or paragogical extension: **eccu-hīc >* It. *qui; *eccu-hac >* It. *qua; ĭllac >* It. *là; *accu-hīc >* Sp. *aquí; *ecce-hīc >* Fr. *ici; *ecce-hŏc >* It. *ciò,* OFr. *iço, ceo > ce; ab hŏc >* OFr. *avuec > avec; *eccu-hīnc >* It. *quinci; ĭntŭnc >* OSp. *entón* and *ĭntuncce >* OSp. *entonce > entonces. Hŏc* is continued as Occ. *o,* but also as *oc,* which may reflect a reinforced **hŏcc,* and some scholars propose a similar base for OFr. *avuec* and *poruec.* Following the vowel *a,* Gallo-Romance may either drop *c* or change it to yod: *ecce-hac >* Occ. *sa* or *sai,* OFr. *ça* or *çai; ĭllac >* Occ., OFr. *la* or *lai.*

362. Consonants in Secondary Final Position

Quite obviously, consonants enter into a secondary final position with particular frequency in the languages that are most prone to final-vowel loss: Rumanian, Catalan, Occitan and French. The problem is discussed in the following paragraphs mostly as it applies to those languages. It is important that proper attention be paid to the relative sound chronology, since consonants may have undergone certain changes when still intervocalic. It is not, in other words, the Latin consonant that becomes final, but an altered Romance sound. Another significant feature is the desonorization that affects consonants in final position. A word like *capu* must have undergone the change of *p* via *b* to *v* that is characteristic of the intervocalic position prior to the final-vowel loss, for it is only in this manner that the final *f* of OFr. *chief,* Fr. *chef* can be accounted for, since *f* represents a desonorization at the *v* stage. The consonants *r, l, m* and *n* are not affected by this change. The earliest Occitan texts provide graphical proof that intervocalic voicing must have preceded final-vowel loss. The *Boeci* uses voiced consonants in final position: *volg* (v. 45) < *vŏluit; dig* (v. 43) < *dīco; delcad* (v. 70) < *dēlĭcātu,* and similar spellings are regularly employed in the *Sainte Foi d'Agen: ciutad* (v. 65) < *cīvĭtāte; donad* (v. 70) < *dōnātu; mandad* (v. 72) < *mandātu; fog* (v. 374) < *fŏcu; cab* (v. 338) < *capu.*

The consonant that assumes final position is not necessarily intervocalic in Latin, but may also be postconsonantal: *lŭpu* vs. *campu.* Although, generally speaking, such clusters have been dealt with in the discussion of internal groups, it seems legitimate to rapidly survey them here in order to provide as full a picture as possible of the treatment of consonants in secondary final position.

363. Lat. *p, b, v*

It follows from the observations contained in the preceding paragraph that *capu* > Cat., Occ. *cap* and *lŭpu* > Cat. *llop,* Occ. *lop* are not simply instances of the retention of *p* in secondary final position, but rather *p* is the outcome of a desonorization that sets in when the final vowel is dropped from the conjectural intermediate stage **cabu.* French, as already seen, takes the intervocalic treatment all the way to **cavu,* whereupon final *v* desonorizes to *f:* OFr. *chief* > *chef.* It is only in Rumanian, where no voicing occurs, that one can accurately talk of the retention of final *p:* Rm. *cap, lup.* In secondary final position, *b* and *v* are vocalized to *u̯* in Catalan: *dēbet* > *deu; bĭbit* > *beu; *plŏvet* > *plou; lĕve* > *lleu; mŏvet* > *mou,* and Occitan shows the same evolution: *dēbet* > *deu; trabe* > *trau; scrībit* > *escriu; nave* > *nau; clāve* > *clau; brĕve* > *breu.* There are no examples of *b* and *v* in this position in Rumanian, since these consonants had dropped in intervocalic position. In French, *p, b* and *v* all merge into *v* when still intervocalic, and the uniform outcome is *f* obtained through desonorization following the loss of the final vowel: *ape* > OFr. *ef; trabe* > OFr. *tref; nĭve* > OFr. *neif, noif; bŏve* > OFr. *buef* > *bœuf.*

The preposition *apu(d)* gives *ab* in Occitan, with the voiced outcome traceable to syntactic phonetics. In French, final *f* may drop from pronunciation in some words: *clave* > *clef* > *clé.* This change is mostly caused by the flexional *s,* since *v* regularly drops before a consonant: *claves* > *cles* and hence, by analogy, a new singular *clé.* The difference between the two forms is maintained in *bŏve* > OFr. *buef,* Fr. *bœuf* vs. *bŏves* > OFr. *bues,* Fr. *bœufs* and **ŏvu* > OFr. *uef,* Fr. *œuf* vs. **ŏvos* > OFr. *ues,* Fr. *œufs.* If a velar vowel follows, the labial consonant combines with it in French to yield the semi-vowel *u̯: clavu* > *clou;* Frk. **blawu* > OFr. *blou* (Fr. *bleu* may be *picard*).

In postconsonantal position, Catalan and Occitan keep *p*: *campu* > *camp; col(a)phu* > *colp,* and *b* is desonorized to *p* in Occitan: *ŏrbu* > *orp; *corbu* > *corp.* Voiced final occlusives do not occur in Catalan (B. Moll §131), and *orb* is nothing more than a Latinizing graph for *orp.* Final *v* is desonorized to *f: salvu* > Occ. *salf; sĕrvu* > Cat., Occ. *serf.* French drops *p* from pronunciation, but retains it graphically: *campu* > *champ; colaphu* > OFr. *colp* > *coup.* P regularly falls when followed by a flexional *s,* and this development is then extended analogically to the absolute final position: *campos* > OFr. *chans; col(a)phos* > OFr. *cous.* French desonorizes *v* to *f: cĕrvu* > *cerf,* and *b* to *p: ŏrbu* > OFr. *orp; *corbu* > OFr. *corp.* There are no occurrences in Modern French of the unvoicing of final *b,* since *orp* is not continued, while *corp* has been replaced by the diminutive formation *corbeau.* Rumanian retains the postconsonantal *b: ŏrbu* > *orb; tŭrbo* > *turb; *cŏrbu* > *corb.* The replacement of Lat. *corvu* by **corbu* finds support in Fr. *corbeau.*

364. Lat. *t, d*

In Catalan and Occitan, *t* voices intervocalically, then unvoices upon becoming final: *nĕpōte* > Cat., Occ. *nebot; prātu* > Cat. *prat; partītu* > Cat., Occ. *partit,* while separate treatments are noted for the primitive *d* which, upon becoming final, vocalizes to *u̯* in Catalan: *hērēde* > *ereu; cadit* > *cau; rīdet* > *riu; pĕde* > *peu.* The wau is absorbed when a *u* precedes as in *nūdu* > *nuu* > *nu,* and no vocalization takes place where *d* had fallen early: *fīde* > *fe; mĕrcēde* > *mercè* (B. Moll §130; Fouché: *Phonétique historique,* p. 130; Badía Margarit §100, V). *D* mostly drops in Occitan: *crūdu* > *cru; fīde* > *fe; mĕrcēde* > *merce; crēdit* > *cre.* It is difficult to see how Occitan can keep final *t* and final *d* separate, and a certain fluctuation does, indeed, exist as regards the treatment of -*d*. *Crūdu* is continued both as *cru* and *crut*, *nōdu* as *no* and *not*, while no variant is documented for *nūdu* > *nut*. *Nĭdu* gives *ni* and *nit* as well as a form *nis*, which follows from a difference in the chronological process, intervocalic *d* having changed to a voiced *s* (§266) prior to the loss of the final vowel. Lat. *nōdu* similarly yields a variant *nos*. In French both *t* and *d* drop: *cantātu* > OFr. *chantet* > *chanté; nātu* > OFr. *net* > *né; nūdu* > OFr. *nut* > *nu; pĕde* > OFr. *piet* > *pied; nĭdu* > *nid; nōdu* > *nœud* (the *d* of *pied, nid* and *nœud* is purely graphical). It remains unclear whether the final *t* graph in Old French represents an occlusive, or whether it had moved to an interdental fricative pronunciation. Rumanian keeps the dentals in secondary final position: *mūtu* > *mut; crūdu* > *crud; nōdu* > *nod*.

In postconsonantal position, Rumanian likewise keeps both dentals unchanged: *factu* > *fapt; ŏcto* > *opt; cal(i)du* > *cald*, while Occitan merges them into *t*: *mŭltu* > *molt, mout; cĕrtu* > *cert; cal(i)du* > *calt, caut; tarde* > *tart*. If, however, the preceding consonant is *n*, the resulting -*nt* and -*nd* combinations are reduced to a stable *n*: *fŏnte* > *fon; talentu* > *talen; mŏnte* > *mon; tantu* > *tan; quando* > *can; mŭndu* > *mon; prĕhĕndo* > *prēndo* > *pren*, but an *nt* graph is not uncommon: *talent, tant, grant*, etc. *Can* as the regular outcome of *canto* is flanked by a variant *cant*, which owes its *t* to an analogy with the rest of the paradigm (*cantas, canta, cantam*, etc). The difference between the Occitan and Catalan developments is mostly of a purely graphical nature. A separation between *t* and *d* is maintained in Catalan in spelling only, while a voiceless pronunciation prevails throughout: *mŭltu* > *molt; cĕrtu* > *cert; tarde* > *tard; *frĭgĭdu* > *fred*. Final *nt* and final *nd* merge in *nt*, which is mostly pronounced *n*: *sĕntit* > *sent; cantando* > *cantant*. The dental has dropped in *grande* > *gran*. French has *t*: *sŏrte* > *sort; vĭr(i)de* > *vert*, with cases of *d* representing nothing more than a learned graph: *grande* > OFr. *grant* > *grand; *frĭgĭdu* > OFr. *freit, froit* > *froid; cal(i)du* > OFr. *chalt, chaut* > *chaud*.

365. Lat. Velar *k, g*

In secondary final position the velar *k* is kept in Rumanian: *jŏcu* > *joc; fŏcu* > *foc*, and *g* is similarly retained: *fagu* > *fag; jŭgu* > *jog; rŏgo* > *rog*. In Catalan the velar *k* first sonorizes, then unvoices as the final vowel drops: *fŏcu* > *foc; caecu* > *cec; amīcu* > *amic; lŏcu* > *lloc*. Cases involving velar *g* are very rare, my only example showing loss of the occlusive while still intervocalic: *jŭgu* > *jou*. In Occitan, the velar *k* behaves as in Catalan: *foc, cec, amic, loc*, while final *g* desonorizes: *Hūgo* > *Uc; *trago* > *trac*. In French the velar *k* mostly drops if the final *u* is retained: *fŏcu* > OFr. *fou*

> *feu: caecu* > OFr. *cieu*, but where *k* becomes final, its development is difficult to sort out. There are cases of *i̯*: *lacu* > OFr. *lai; Camerācu* > *Cambrai*, and some believe *ami* < *amīcu* derived from an earlier **amii̯*. Retention of *k* is learned: *lacu* > *lac; pūblĭcu* > *public*. The velar *g* follows the same evolution as *k*, but examples are very scarce: *vagu* > OFr. *vai*.

Rumanian keeps both velar *k* and *g* in postconsonantal position: *pŏrcu* > *porc; lŏngu* > *lung*. On the surface, the same is true of Catalan, but *g* is merely learned spelling, while a voiceless pronunciation prevails (B. Moll §131): *pŏrcu* > *porc; *frĭscu* > *fresc; largu* > *llarg*. In postconsonantal position, velar *k* and *g* both evolve to *k* in Occitan: *conōsco* > *conosc; *blanku* > *blanc; arcu* > *arc; plango* > *planc; largu* > *larc; albergu* > *alberc*. In French, the final velar *k* and *g* likewise give *k*, but the *k* often drops from pronunciation: *pŏrcu* > *porc; arcu* > *arc; clērĭcu* > *clerc; bŭrgu* > OFr. *borc* > *bourg; lŏngu* > OFr. *lonc* > *long; sangue* > OFr. *sanc* > *sang*. The loss frequently occurs in interconsonantal position and spreads from there analogically. The *g* present in *bourg, long* and *sang* is merely learned spelling.

366. Lat. Palatal *k, g, i̯*

A secondary final position does not obtain for Rumanian, since final front vowels are retained. In Catalan the palatal *k* had become *dz* prior to the loss of the final vowel. When assuming final position, this affricate undergoes a vocalization to *u̯*: *lĭcet* > *lleu; vōce* > *vou* > *veu; Fēlīce* > *Feliu*. The palatal *g* is continued as *i̯* in Catalan: *lēge* > *llei*, and final *i̯* evolves to [*tš*]: *maju* > *maig*. In Occitan the palatal *k* assibilates to *dz* intervocalically, then unvoices to *ts*, spelled *tz*, upon becoming final: *lūce* > *lutz; pace* > *patz; crŭce* > *crotz; dĕce* > *detz*. The palatal *g* and *i̯* merge, the outcome being *i̯*: *lēge* > *lei; rēge* > *rei; maiu* > *mai;* VL **aio* > *ai*. In French the palatals *k* and *g* are likewise kept separate; *k* does not voice to *g*, but had reached a voiced affricate stage *dz* intervocalically before unvoicing in final position, releasing a yod in the process. The *ts* is later simplified to *s*: *vōce* > *voiz; crŭce* > *croiz*. The palatal *g* merges with *i̯* just as in Occitan: *lēge* > OFr. *lei* > *loi; rēge* > OFr. *rei* > *roi; maiu* > *mai*, with the difference that the yod is absorbed into the *ei* diphthong in *lei, rei* whereas, in Occitan, it helps form the diphthong.

367. Lat. *s, r, l*

The *s* that becomes final is retained in Rumanian: *formōsu* > *frumos; rīsu* > *rǎs; ŭrsu* > *urs; passu* > *pas*. *S* moves via intervocalic voicing to desonorization in final position in Catalan: *casu* > *cas; hĕrbōsu* > *herbós*, and the postconsonantal *s* is kept: *falsu* > *fals*. Lat. *s* voices intervocalically both in Occitan and French and is then unvoiced in final position: *nasu* > Occ. *nas*, OFr. *nes*, Fr. *nez* (the *z* is an arbitrary spelling); *prĕhĕnsu* > VL *preso* > Occ. *pres*, Fr. *pris*; *-ōsu* > Occ. *-os*, Fr. *-eux*. The postconsonantal *s* remains unchanged: *falsu* > Occ. *fals*, *faus*, OFr. *fals*, *faus*, Fr. *faux*. *R* is generally kept in secondary final position: *rāru* > Rm. *rar*, OFr. *rer*; *carru* > Rm. *car*; *clāru* > Rm. *chiar*, Cat., Occ. *clar*, Fr. *clair*; *flōre* > Cat., Occ. *flor*, Fr. *fleur*. *L* is not treated as final in Rumanian; words such as Lat. *mĕl* and *sal* had received a paragogical *e* (§157), allowing for intervocalic treatment of *l*: *miere*, *sare* (§270), and even cases such as *caelu* > *cer* and *dŏlu* > *dor* show that intervocalic rhotacism precedes final-vowel loss in Rumanian. Double *l*, on the other hand, simplifies to *l* in final position: *caballu* > *cal*; *vĭtĕllu* > *viţel*; *mĭsĕllu* > *mişel*. The opposite chronology is seen in Portuguese, where the *l* that becomes final is retained, contrasting with its elimination in intervocalic position: *male* > *mal*; *tāle* > *tal*; *mŏr- tāle* > *mortal*; *sōle* > *sol* vs. *fīlu* > *fio*; *palatiu* > *paço* (§270). Occitan and French usually keep final *l*: *male* > Occ., Fr. *mal*, although here there are cases of *l* remaining silent in French: *cūlu* > *cul*, obtained analogically from the plural OFr. *cus* < *cūlos* (§371), as well as of vocalization as a poetic license or a dialectal feature in Occitan: *-āle* > *-au*. This rare form is encountered in rhyme-position only.

368. Lat. *m*, *n*

   In Romance final position *m* and *n* are both retained in Rumanian: *hŏmo* > *om*; *pōmu* > *pom*; *ŭlmu* > *ulm*; *bŏnu* > *bun*; *cŏrnu* > *corn*. Catalan keeps final *m*: *lūme* > *llum*; *fĭrmu* > *ferm*, whereas the *n* generally drops in this position: *planu* > *plà*; *de mane* > *demà*; *mānu* > *mà*; *vīnu* > *vi*; *pāne* > *pa*. It is retained if postconsonantal: *cŏrnu* > *corn*; *diŭrnu* > *jorn*, and it is kept proclitically in *ūnu* > *un*. In Portuguese *n* does not keep its consonantal value, but serves in the formation of nasal vowels and diphthongs: *bŏnu* > *bom*; *bĕne* > *bem* (§180). Occitan keeps *m*: *nōme* > *nom*; *hŏmo* > *om*; *lūme* > *lum*, while *n* becomes unstable: *bŏnu* > *bon̦*; *ūnu* > *un̦*; *bĕne* > *ben̦*; *ratiōne* > *razon̦* (§153). In French these consonants disappear after having nasalized the preceding vowel: *nom*, *on*, *bon*, *un* (§179). The post- consonantal nasal is retained in Occitan: *fĭrmu* > *ferm*; *ŭlmu* > *olm*; *carne* > *carn*; *diŭrnu* > *jorn*; *ĭnfĕrnu* > *enfern*, and the same is true of Old French: *vĕrme* > *verm*; *carne* > *charn*; *diŭrnu* > *jorn*. Later, however, the nasal drops; this occurs phonologically where the nasal finds itself in the weak interconsonantal position before a flexional *s*: *vermes* > Fr. *vers*; *carnes* > OFr. *charz*; *diŭrnos* > OFr. *jorz*, and it is extended analogically from there to the singular: *ver, chair, jour.* Such forms are rare in the South: *jor, enfer.*

369. Lat. *n', l'*

If a palatal *n* becomes final, it is retained in Catalan and Occitan: *ba(l)neu* > Cat. *bany,* Occ. *banh; lŏnge* > Cat. *lluny,* Occ. *luenh,* while French resolves it as *in,* with *n* subsequently nasalizing the diphthong: *ba(l)neu* > *bain; lŏnge* > *loin.* In Spanish the palatal *l* is depalatalized if it comes into final position: *pĕlle* > *piel; ĭlle* > *él; mīlle* > *mil;* cf. *val* vs. *valle,* and *n'* becomes *n: dŏmnu* > *don* vs. *dueño* (Menéndez Pidal §63.2.D). Catalan retains the palatal *l* in final position: *castĕllu* > *castell; pĕlle* > *pell; caballu* > *cavall,* while French shows the usual reduction to yod: *trapāliu* > *travail.*

370. Secondary Final Consonants in Spanish

Voicing of *t* to *d* occurs intervocalically prior to final-vowel loss, and *d,* representing a fricative pronunciation, is kept in most instances: *aetāte* > *edad;* VL *parēte* > *pared; līte* > *lid; rēte* > *red,* although medieval scribal practice often made use of *t,* representing the desonorization of *d* in final position. There are also occurrences of the loss of *d: fĭde* > OSp. *fed, fet* > *fe; pĕde* > *pied* > *pie.* The consonants *n, l, r* and *s* are retained: *pāne* > *pan; ratiōne* > *razón; sāle* > *sal; māre* > *mar;* CL *mēnse* > VL *mese* > *mes.* The palatal *k* and the *ki* and the *ti* clusters all evolve to *z,* which was originally voiced in intervocalic position, but which later desonorized upon becoming final: *pace* > *paz; vōce* > *voz; solaciu* > *solaz; prĕtiu* > *prez.* Medieval Spanish admitted certain consonant clusters in final position, which have since become internal again through the restoration of the fallen final vowel: *pŏnte* > *puent; mŏnte* > *mont; cŏmĭte* > *cuend; fŏrte* > *fuert; nŏcte* > *noch; lacte* > *lech.* The modern forms are *puente, monte, conde, fuerte, noche* and *leche;* for details on the restoration of the final vowel, see §206.

371. Pronunciation of Final Consonants in French

Most final consonants drop from pronunciation in the thirteenth century. In Old French, final *s* becomes *ts,* spelled *z,* if preceded by a dental or a palatal: *latus* > OFr. *lez; cantātis* > *chantez; ad-sātis* > *assez; nūdos* > *nuz; pŭgnos* > *poinz; annos* > *anz; diŭrnos* > *jorz; genŭcŭlos* > *genouz.* In the thirteenth century, *ts* is reduced to *s,* but some words retain a learned spelling. Final *s,* whether primitive or obtained from *ts,* eventually drops from pronunciation. *R* is usually kept: *fier, cher,* but it is not pronounced in the -*er* infinitive marker and in the -*ier* suffix: *parler, chevalier.* It had also dropped from pronunciation in the -*eur* suffix: *vendeur, danseur,* and the ensuing [ø] pronunciation allowed for the formation of feminine forms in -*euse*: *vendeuse, danseuse,* based on an analogy with -*eux,* -*euse*: *heureux—heureuse. R* was eventually restored here. *L* may remain silent following *u* [y] and *i*: *cul, fusil,* this by analogy with the plural where *l* regularly disappears following these vowels (§282). It is pronounced elsewhere: *cheval, miel* and also in *avril,* perhaps because this word has no plural form. Final *f* is kept: *bœuf, œuf,* but fluctuations are noted for the word *cerf. K* drops from pronunciation following a nasal: **blanku > blanc.* The pronunciation of the numeral *six* may offer a fairly accurate picture of the principles governing the pronunciation of final consonants in the medieval period: [*sis*] when the numeral stands alone, [*si*] before a consonant and [*siz*] before a vowel.

Syntactic Phonetics

372. Proclitics

Words are not isolated in the sentence, but form part of a context in which not all segments command the same importance. Words such as articles and adjectival (or reduced) possessives are proclitics. Receiving no independent stress, they are continued in weakened form, and the same fate may befall certain prepositions and adverbs. Articles are subject to an aphaeretic reduction in their evolution: *(il)la flore >* Fr. *la fleur,* and the adjectival possessives are likewise shortened: *s(u)a matre >* Fr. *sa mère.* In both instances, the vowel *a* receives the same treatment as pretonic *a* (cf. *lavare >* Fr. *laver; sapēre >* Fr. *savoir),* the article and noun combination being felt as a single unit, with the accent falling on the noun.

Some words may be either weak or tonic in the sentence. The Latin negation *nōn* is continued as a tonic *non* and a weak *ne* in French, *quĭd* is the source of both *quoi* and *que,* and similar alternations are encountered in the realm of personal pronouns: *moi* and *me < mē.* In the development of *fŏris* to OFr. *fors* and Fr. *hors,* retention of *o* is indicative of the proclitic status of the word, since *o* would have diphthongized if stressed (§151). A diphthongized *fuers* is a very rare variant, while *fuori* represents the normal evolution in Italian. Old Spanish shows occurrences of a stressed *cuemo* as a variant of *como < VL quomo < CL quomodo,* and Old French has both a weak *car* and a strong *quer* as reflexes of *quāre* (§152).

Being unstressed, the preposition *de* contains a weak *e,* which is continued as *i* in Italian and [ə] in French, paralleling the fate of pretonic *e* in these languages (§185). The syntagma *de Roma* evolves to It. *di Roma* and Fr. *de Rome,* with the preposition reflecting the same outcome as the pretonic *de-* in *declāro* > It. *dichiaro* and *dēbēre* > Fr. *devoir.* The Portuguese definite-article forms *o, os* and *a, as* lost their initial consonant in contexts such as *de lo, de los* and *a lo, a los,* where *l* has not evolved as initial, having come to be considered intervocalic in these close-knit structures (§270), and the French preposition plus article contractions arose in a similar manner, with *a l(e)* evolving to *au* before a noun beginning with a consonant (§282). To this may be added such variations in French as *bel* vs. *beau, vieil* vs. *vieux* and *fol* vs. *fou.* Fr. *les amis,* though written as two separate words, constitutes a single utterance, one *mot phonétique.* As a result, the *s* of *les* is not treated as final, but as intervocalic as seen from the voicing and the linking (§268).

The adaptation of one sound to another across a word boundary mostly takes the form of a partial assimilation. The pronunciation of the final *s* of the plural definite article in Portuguese varies according to the phonological environment: [š] before a voiceless consonant *(os pais)* and [ž] before a voiced consonant *(os bois)* or before a vowel *(as adegas).* For the pronunciation of Fr. *six,* see §371. The syntagma *in pāce* evolves to *em patz* in Occitan, with the dental *n* replaced by a bilabial *m* because of the contact with another labial. The preposition *en* may also develop an anteconsonantal variant *e* in Occitan: *e Roma.* Some conjunctions and prepositions have developed specific antevocalic forms as an anti-hiatus measure: Italian has *e—ed* from Lat. *et,* Occitan *e—ez,* and Lat. *aut* is continued as *o* and *od* in Italian, while Occitan has *o* and *oz* (§359). While Spanish has generalized the forms *y (= i)* and *o* for these conjunctions, it changes them to *e* and *u* to avoid the encounter of identical vowels as in: *aguja e hilo* and *siete u ocho.* The Latin preposition *ad* is reduced to *a.* While this may represent a development affecting final *d* in general: *apud* > **apu; quĭd* > Fr. *quoi* (§361), it seems likely that the elimination of *d* may have had its beginnings in the anteconsonantal position. In Occitan, *ad* has evolved into an antevocalic *az,* reflecting the regular change in the language of intervocalic *d* to a voiced *s* (§266), and Occitan similarly has *quez* from an earlier *qued* < *quĭd* (Appel §52). The variants *am* and *amb* of the Occitan preposition *ab* < *apu(d)* flow from considerations of syntactic phonetics, and the same holds true of *ab* itself, since the presence of a voiced oral occlusive in final position would otherwise remain unexplained (§362). Prosthetic vowels have survived in Italian only in a few prepositional locutions and after *non,* where the *s* + consonant cluster would have been preceded immediately by a consonant: *per istrada, per iscritto, in iscuola, non ispostare* (Rohlfs

§187). The distribution of forms with and without a prosthetic vowel in the tenth-century Old French text *La Vie de Saint Alexis: out esposede* (v. 48) vs. *la spouse* (v. 21), is likewise a result of syntactic phonetics; the prosthetic vowel persists if the preceding word ends in a consonant, it has no *raison d'être* if a vowel precedes.

373. Instability of Initial Consonants

It is beyond any doubt the blurring of word boundaries that constitutes the most striking aspect of the workings of syntactic phonetics. In Spanish the instability of the word-initial consonant is of significant proportions, resulting in a fricative pronunciation of the voiced occlusives and of the voiced labiodental *v* whenever the preceding word ends in a vowel: *la bandera, la dama, la guerra, la vida.* In popular speech one may even encounter *la ocena* for *la docena,* with *d* dropping intervocalically (§266). Catalan changes an initial voiced occlusive to the corresponding fricative if the preceding word ends in a vowel: *la boca, una dona* (B. Moll §238). Word-initial consonants are mostly stable elsewhere, but the *gorgia toscana,* the aspiration characteristic of certain Tuscan dialects, offers an instance of their instability on Italian soil: *la hasa* for *la casa, la thela* for *la tela,* with *h* marking an aspirated pronunciation (Rohlfs §196; Lausberg §577). The instability of initial consonants is above all a prominent feature of the *logudorese* dialect of Sardinian: *ĭpsu tĕmpus > su d̵empus* vs. **ĭpsos tĕmpos > sos tempos; ĭpsu fĭlu > su vilu* vs. *ĭpsos fĭlos > sos fĭlos.* Lausberg (§581) even ventures to speculate that the unstable initial may at one point have been a prominent ingredient in the consonantal make-up of the western Romance languages. This far-reaching conclusion is somewhat hastily inferred from the mysterious Fr. *fois* from Lat. *vĭce* which, like Holthausen before him (see §225), he interprets as having resulted from a very unlikely assimilation process, involving the desonorization of *v* in such combinations as **duas fedzes, *seis fedzes* vs. retention in **una vedze.* In Fr. *svelte, s* does not cause the unvoicing of *v* to *f,* but rather *s* voices because of the direct contact with *v,* and *Strasbourg* is not pronounced with *sp;* quite to the contrary, the *b* remains voiced and tends to sonorize the preceding *s.*

SELECT BIBLIOGRAPHY

ROMANCE

Agard, F.B. *A Course in Romance Linguistics.* Georgetown University Press, 2 vols., 1984.

Alonso, Amado. "La subagrupación románica del catalán." *RFE, 13* (1926), 1-38, 225-261.

Alvar, M. *Los nuevos atlas lingüísticos de la Romania.* Granada, 1960.

Auerbach, Erich. *Introduction aux études de philologie romane.* Frankfurt, 1949. English translation, New York, 1961; Italian translation, Torino, 1965.

Bahner, W. *Kontinuität und Diskontinuität in der Herausbildung der romanischen Sprachwissenschaft.* Berlin: Akademie, 1983.

Baldinger, Kurt. *La formación de los dominios lingüísticos en la península ibérica.* 2nd ed., Madrid: Gredos, 1972. Spanish translation of *Die Herausbildung der Sprachräume auf der Pyrenäenhalbinsel.* Berlin, 1958.

———. "La position du gascon entre la Galloromania et l'Ibéroromania." *RLiR, 22* (1958), 241-292.

Bartoli, M. *Das Dalmatische.* Vienna, 1906.

Bec, Pierre. *Manuel pratique de philologie romane.* 2 vols., Paris: Picard, 1970-1971.

Bourciez, Edouard. *Eléments de linguistique romane.* 4th ed., Paris: Klincksieck, 1956.

Clédat, L. *Manuel de phonétique et morphologie romanes.* Paris, 1925.

Coseriu, E. *La geografía lingüística.* Montevideo, 1956.

———. *Sincronía, diacronía e historia. El problema del cambio lingüístico.* Montevideo, 1958.

Dahmen, W., Holtus, G., Kramer, J. & Metzeltin, M., eds. *Latein und Romanisch.* Tübingen: Narr, 1987.

Dauzat, A. *La géographie linguistique.* Paris, 1922.

Diez, Friedrich. *Grammatik der romanischen Sprachen.* 5th ed., Bonn: E. Weber, 1882.

Elcock, W.D. *The Romance Languages.* London: Faber & Faber, 1960.

Gamillscheg, E. *Die Sprachgeographie und ihre Ergebnisse für die allgemeine Sprachwissenschaft.* Bielefeld-Leipzig, 1928.

———. *Romania germanica. Sprach- und Siedlungsgeschichte der Germanen auf dem Boden des alten Römerreiches.* 3 vols., Berlin: Walter de Gruyter, 1935.

Gröber, Gustav. "Die romanischen Sprachen. Ihre Einteilung und äussere Geschichte," *Grundriss der romanischen Philologie,* 2nd ed., Strasbourg, 1904-1906, 535-563.

————. *Grundriss der romanischen Philologie.* 2 vols., Strasbourg: Trübner, 1888-1906.

Guarnerio, P.E. *Fonologia romanza.* Milano, 1918.

Hadlich, Roger L. *The Phonological History of Vegliote.* Chapel Hill: University of North Carolina Press, 1965.

Hall, Robert A. *External History of the Romance Languages.* New York-London-Amsterdam: Elsevier, 1974.

————. *Proto-Romance Phonology.* New York: American Elsevier, 1976.

————. "The Reconstruction of Proto-Romance," *Language, 26* (1950), 6-27.

Harris, Martin and Nigel Vincent, eds. *The Romance Languages.* New York: Oxford University Press, 1988ff.

Holtus, Günter, Michael Metzeltin and Christian Schmitt, eds. *Lexicon der romanistischen Linguistik,* 7 vols., Tübingen: Niemeyer, 1988.

Hope, T.E. *Lexical Borrowing in the Romance Languages.* 2 vols., Oxford: Blackwell, 1971.

Hubschmid, J. "Hispano-Baskisches." *BF, 14* (1953), 1-26.

Iordan, Iorgu. *Introducere în studiul limbilor romanice.* Iaşi 1932. German translation by W. Bahner. *Einführung in die Geschichte und Methoden der romanischen Sprachwissenschaft.* Berlin, 1962.

———— and John Orr. *An Introduction to Romance Linguistics.* London: Methuen, 1937.

————, John Orr and Rebecca Posner. *An Introduction to Romance Linguistics.* Berkeley and Los Angeles: University of California Press, and Oxford: Blackwell, 1970.

———— and Maria Manoliu. *Manual de lingüística románica.* Revised ed. by Manuel Alvar, 2 vols., Madrid: Gredos, 1972.

Izzo, Herbert. *Tuscan and Etruscan. The Problem of Linguistic Substratum Influence in Central Italy.* Toronto: University of Toronto Press, 1972.

Jaberg, K. *Aspects géographiques du langage.* Paris, 1936.

————. and J. Jud. *Der Sprachatlas als Forschungsinstrument.* Halle, 1928.

Jungemann, Fredrick H. *La teoría del sustrato y los dialectos hispano-romances y gascones.* Madrid: Gredos, 1955.

Kontzi, R., ed. *Substrate und Superstrate in den romanischen Sprachen.* Darmstadt: Wissenschaftliche Buchgesellschaft, 1982.

Kuhn, A. *Romanische Philologie. Erster Teil: Die romanischen Sprachen* Berne: Francke, 1951.

Lausberg, Heinrich. *Romanische Sprachwissenschaft*. Berlin: W. de Gruyter, Sammlung Göschen, 1956. 2nd ed., 1963. Spanish translation, Madrid, 1965; Italian translation, Milano: Feltrinelli, 1971.

Malkiel, Yakov. "The Classification of Romance Languages." *RPh, 31* (1978), 467-500.

———. *Studies in the Reconstruction of Hispano-Latin Word Families*. Berkeley-Los Angeles, 1954.

Mańczak, W. *La classification des langues romanes*. Krakov: Universitas, 1991.

Meier, Harri. *Beiträge zur sprachlichen Gliederung der Pyrenäenhalbinsel*. Hamburg, 1930.

———. *Die Entstehung der romanischen Sprachen und Nationen*. Frankfurt, 1941.

Menéndez Pidal, R. *Toponimia prerrománica hispana*. Madrid, 1952.

Meyer-Lübke, W. *Einführung in das Studium der romanischen Sprachwissenschaft*. 3rd ed., Heidelberg, 1920. Spanish translation by A. Castro, Madrid, 1926.

———. *Grammatik der romanischen Sprachen*. 4 vols., Leipzig, 1890-1902. French translation by A. and G. Doutrepont. *Grammaire des langues romanes*. Paris: H. Welter, 1900-1906.

Millardet, G. *Linguistique et dialectologie romanes*. Montpellier-Paris, 1923.

Monteverdi, A. *Manuale di avviamento agli studi romanzi. Le lingue romanze*. Milano, 1952.

Navarro Tomás, T. *Atlas lingüístico de la Península Ibérica*. Madrid, 1962.

Niederehe, H.-J. & Schlieben-Lange, B. *Die Frühgeschichte der romanischen Philologie von Dante bis Diez*. Tübingen: Niemeyer, 1987.

Posner, R. *The Romance Languages*. Cambridge, University Press, 1996.

Posner, R. and J.N. Green, eds. *Trends in Romance Linguistics and Philology*. 4 vols., The Hague: Mouton, 1980-1982.

Pottier, Bernard. *Introduction à l'étude de la philologie hispanique*. 2 vols., Bordeaux, 1957-1958; 2nd ed., Paris: Payot, 1960.

Rohlfs, Gerhard. *Die lexikalische Differenzierung der romanischen Sprachen. Versuch einer romanischen Sprachgeographie*. München: 1954. Spanish translation by Manuel Alvar. *La diferenciación léxica de las lenguas románicas*. Madrid, 1960.

———. *Estudios sobre el léxico románico*. Revised ed. by Manuel Alvar, Madrid: Gredos, 1979.

————. *Le gascon. Etudes de philologie pyrénéenne.* Halle, 1935; 2nd ed., Tübingen-Pau, 1970.

————. *Manual de filología hispánica. Guia bibliográfica, crítica y metódica.* Bogotá, 1957.

————. *Romanische Philologie.* 2 vols., Heidelberg: Winter, 1950, 1952; 2nd ed., 1966.

————. *Romanische Sprachgeographie.* München: Beck, 1971.

————. *Studien zur romanischen Namenkunde.* München, 1956.

Schürr, Friedrich. «La diphtongaison romane». *RLiR, 20* (1956), 107-144; 161-248.

Straka, G. "La dislocation linguistique de la Romania et la formation des langues romanes à la lumière de la chronologie relative des changements phonétiques." *RLiR, 20* (1956), 249-267.

Tagliavini, Carlo. *Le origini delle lingue neolatine.* 4th ed., Bologna: Pàtron, 1964; 5th ed., 1969.

Thurneysen, R. *Kelto-romanisches.* Halle, 1884.

Vàrvaro, Alberto. *Storia, problemi e metodi della linguistica romanza.* Napoli: Liguori, 1968.

Vidos, B.E. *Manual de lingüística románica.* Madrid: Aguilar, 1963. Spanish translation by F. de B. Moll of the 1956 original Dutch version.

Wartburg, W. von. *Die Ausgliederung der romanischen Sprachräume.* Berne: Francke, 1950.

————. *Entstehung der romanischen Völker.* Halle, 1939. French translation. *Les origines des peuples romans.* Paris, 1941.

Zauner, A. *Romanische Sprachwissenschaft.* 2 vols., Berlin-Leipzig, 1921, 1926.

LATIN

Altheim, F. *Geschichte der lateinischen Sprache.* Frankfurt, 1951.

Baehrens, W.A. *Sprachlicher Kommentar zur vulgärlateinischen Appendix Probi.* Halle, 1922.

Battisti, C. *Avviamento allo studio del latino volgare.* Bari, 1949.

Blaise, A. *Manuel du latin chrétien.* Strasbourg, 1955.

Bonnet, Max. *Le latin de Grégoire de Tours.* Paris, 1890.

Brüch, J. *Der Einfluss der germanischen Sprachen auf das Vulgärlatein.* Heidelberg, 1913.

Buck, C.D. *A Grammar of Oscan and Umbrian.* 2nd ed., Boston, 1928.

Carnoy, A. *Le latin d'Espagne d'après les inscriptions.* Bruxelles, 1906.

Coseriu, E. *El llamado «latín vulgar» y las primeras diferenciaciones romances.* Montevideo, 1954.

Devoto, G. *Storia della lingua di Roma.* Bologna, 1940.

Díaz y Díaz, Manuel C. *Antología del latín vulgar.* 2nd ed., Madrid, 1962.

Ernout, A. *Aspects du vocabulaire latin.* Paris, 1954.

————. *Les éléments dialectaux du vocabulaire latin.* Paris, 1909.

————. *Morphologie historique du latin.* Paris: Klincksieck, 1927.

Goetzke, Karl. *Tabellen und Übungen zum Vulgärlatein.* Tübingen, 1946; 2nd ed., 1947.

Grandgent, C.H. *An Introduction to Vulgar Latin.* Boston, 1907. Spanish translation by Francisco de B. Moll, 3rd ed., Madrid, 1963.

Haadsma, R.A. and J. Nuchelmans. *Précis de latin vulgaire, suivie d'une anthologie annotée.* Groningen, 1963.

Leumann, M., J. Hofmann and A. Szantyr. *Lateinische Grammatik.* 2 vols., München: Beck, 1972-1977.

Lindsay, W.M. *The Latin Language.* Oxford, 1894.

Löfstedt, Einar. *Late Latin.* Oslo: Aschehoug, 1959.

————. *Philologischer Kommentar zur Peregrinatio Aetheriae.* Uppsala, 1911.

Maurer, Th.H. *Gramática do latim vulgar.* Rio de Janeiro, 1959.

Meillet, A. *Esquisse d'une histoire de la langue latine.* 5th ed., Paris, 1948.

Meyer-Lübke, W. «Die lateinische Sprache in den romanischen Ländern». *Gröbers Grundriss der romanischen Philologie,* vol. I, 2nd ed., pp. 451-497.

Mihaescu, M. *La langue latine dans le sud-est de l'Europe.* Paris: Les Belles Lettres, 1978.

Mohrmann, C. *Etudes sur le latin des chrétiens.* 3 vols., Roma, 1961-1965.

Muller, H.F. *A Chronology of Vulgar Latin.* Beiheft 78, ZRPh. Halle-Saale, 1929.

———— and P. Taylor. *A Chrestomathy of Vulgar Latin.* New York, 1932.

Niedermann, Max. *Précis de phonétique historique du latin.* 4th ed., Paris, 1959.

Palmer, L.R. *The Latin Language.* London: Faber & Faber, 1955.

Pirson, J. *La langue des inscriptions latines de la Gaule.* Bruxelles, 1901.

Pisani, V. *Grammatica latina storica e comparata.* Torino, 1948.

————. *Storia della lingua latina.* Torino, 1962.

Reichenkron, Günter. *Historische latein-altromanische Grammatik.* Wiesbaden, 1965.

Rohlfs, Gerhard. *Sermo vulgaris latinus.* Halle-Saale, 1951.

Rönssch, Hermann. *Itala und Vulgata.* 1st ed., 1869; 2nd ed., 1875 and München, 1965.

Schmeck, H. *Aufgaben und Methoden der modernen vulgärlateinischen Forschung.* Heidelberg, 1955.

Schuchardt, H. *Vokalismus des Vulgärlateins.* Leipzig, 1866-1868.

Silva Neto, Serafim da. *Fontes do latim vulgar.* Rio de Janeiro, 1938; 3rd ed., 1956.

————. *História do latim vulgar.* Rio de Janeiro, 1957.

Slotty, F. *Vulgärlateinisches Übungsbuch.* Berlin, 1960.

Sofer, J. *Zur Problematik des Vulgärlateins.* Vienna, 1963.

Sommer, F. *Handbuch der lateinischen Laut- und Formenlehre.* Heidelberg, 1914.

Väänänen, V. *Introduction au latin vulgaire.* 1st ed., Paris: Klincksieck, 1963; 2nd ed., 1967.

————. *Le latin vulgaire des inscriptions pompéiennes.* 2nd ed., Berlin, 1959.

RUMANIAN

Bahner, Werner. *Die lexikalischen Besonderheiten des Frühromanischen in Südosteuropa.* Berlin: Akademie Verlag, 1970.

Candrea-Hecht, J.A. *Les éléments latins de la langue roumaine: le consonantisme.* Paris, 1902.

Densusianu, O. *Histoire de la langue roumaine.* 2 vols., Paris, 1901, 1938.

Du Nay, André. *The Early History of the Rumanian Language.* Lake Bluff, Ill.: Jupiter Press, 1977.

Graur, A. *La langue roumaine. Esquisse historique.* Bucureşti, 1963.

————. *La romanité du roumain.* Bucureşti, 1965. English translation *The Romance Character of Roumanian.* Bucureşti, 1967.

Guillermou, A. *Manuel de langue roumaine.* Paris: Klincksieck, 1953.

Iordan, Iorgu. *Le lexique de la langue roumaine.* Bucureşti, 1964.

———— and V. Robu. *Limbă română contemporană.* Bucureşti, 1987.

Lombard, A. *La langue roumaine. Une présentation.* Paris: Klincksieck, 1974.

————. *Le verbe roumain. Etude morphologique.* Lund, 1954-1955.

Nandriş, Octave. *Phonétique historique du roumain.* Paris: Klincksieck, 1963.

Pop, S. *Grammaire roumaine.* Berne, 1947.

————. *La dialectologie.* 2 vols., Louvain, 1950.

———— and E. Petrovici. *Atlasul linguistic român.* 8 vols., Cluj-Sibiu-Bucureşti, 1938-1966.

Puşcariu, S. *Limbă română*, Bucureşti, 1940. German translation by H. Kuen. *Die rumänische Sprache*. Leipzig, 1943.

Rosetti, Alexandru. *Brève histoire de la langue roumaine des origines à nos jours*. The Hague: Mouton, 1973.

————. *Istoria limbii române*. 2 vols., Bucureşti, 1938. German translation *Geschichte der rumänischen Sprache*. Bucureşti, 1943.

Rothe, Wolfgang, *Einführung in die historische Laut- und Formenlehre des Rumänischen*. Halle-Saale, 1957.

Seiver, G.O. *Introduction to Roumanian*. New York, 1953.

Tiktin, H. *Rumänisches Elementarbuch*. Heidelberg, 1905.

ITALIAN

Battaglia, Salvatore. *La formazione dell' italiano*. Napoli, 1967.

Bertoni, G. *Italia dialettale*. Milano, 1916.

David, R. *Über die Syntax des Italienischen im Trecento*. Genève, 1887.

De Mauro, T. *Storia linguistica dell' Italia unita*. Bari, 1963.

Devoto, G. *Profilo di storia linguistica italiana*. 3rd ed., Firenze, 1960.

Grandgent, C.H. *From Latin to Italian*. Cambridge, Mass.: Harvard University Press, 1927.

Hall, Robert A. *Bibliografia della linguistica italiana*. 3 vols., Firenze, 1958.

Jaberg, K. and J. Jud. *Sprach- und Sachatlas Italiens und der Südschweiz*. AIS. Zofingen, 1928-1940.

Meyer-Lübke, W. *Italienische Grammatik*. Leipzig, 1890.

Migliorini, B. *Lingua Contemporanea*. Firenze, 1939.

————. *Storia della lingua italiana*. 3rd ed., Firenze: Sansoni, 1961. English translation and adaptation by Migliorini, B. and T.G. Griffith. The Italian Language. 2nd ed., London: Faber & Faber, 1984.

Muljačič, Z. *Fonologia della lingua italiana*. Bologna: Il Mulino, 1972.

————. *Introduzione allo studio della lingua italiana*. 2nd ed., Torino: Einaudi, 1982.

Pei, M. *The Italian Language*. New York, 1941.

Regula, M. and J. Jernej. *Grammatica italiana descrittiva*. Berne and München: Francke, 1965.

Rohlfs, Gerhard. *Historische Grammatik der italienischen Sprache und ihrer Mundarten*. 3 vols., Berne: Francke, 1949. Italian translation. *Grammatica storica della lingua italiana e dei suoi dialetti*. 3 vols., Torino: Einaudi, 1966-1969.

Schiaffini, A. *Momenti di storia della lingua italiana.* 2nd ed., Rome, 1953.

———. *Testi fiorentini del Dugento e dei primi del Trecento.* Firenze, 1926.

Schürr, Friedrich. *La classificazione dei dialetti italiani.* Leipzig, 1938.

Tekavčič, P. *Grammatica storica della lingua italiana.* 2nd ed., 3 vols., Bologna: Il Mulino, 1980.

Wiese, B. *Altitalienisches Elementarbuch.* Heidelberg, 1928.

SPANISH

Alarcos Llorach, E. *Fonología española.* 4th ed., Madrid: Gredos, 1968.

Alonso, Martín. *Evolución sintáctica del español.* Madrid: Aguilar, 1962.

Alvar, Manuel. *El dialecto aragonés.* Madrid, 1953.

——— and Bernard Pottier. *Morfología histórica del español.* Madrid: Gredos, 1983.

Baist, G. «Die spanische Sprache». *Gröbers Grundriss*, I, 878-915.

Entwistle, W.J. *The Spanish Language.* London: Faber & Faber, 1936. Spanish translation. *Las lenguas de España: castellano, catalán, vasco y gallego-portugués.* Madrid: Itsmo, 1969.

Galmes de Fuentes, A. *Dialectología mozárabe.* Madrid: Gredos, 1983.

García de Diego, Vicente. *Carácteres fondamentales del dialecto aragonés.* Zaragoza, 1919.

———. *Gramática histórica española.* Madrid: Gredos, 1951.

———. *Manual de dialectología española.* Madrid, 1946.

Hanssen, F. *Gramática histórica de la lengua castellana.* Halle, 1913 and Buenos Aires, 1945.

———. *Spanische Grammatik auf historische Grundlage.* Halle, 1910.

Lapesa, R. *Historia de la lengua española.* 8th ed., Madrid: Gredos, 1980.

Lloyd, Paul M. *From Latin to Spanish.* Philadelphia: Memoirs of the American Philosophical Society, vol. 173, 1987.

Macpherson, I.R. *Spanish Phonology: Descriptive and Historical.* Manchester: Manchester University Press, 1975.

Menéndez Pidal, R. *Cantar de Mio Cid. Texto, gramática y vocabulario.* 3 vols., 4th ed., Madrid: Espasa-Calpe, 1964.

———. *El idioma español en sus primeros tiempos.* 3rd ed., Buenos Aires, 1945.

———. *Manual de gramática histórica española.* 9th ed., Madrid: Espasa-Calpe, 1952.

———. *Orígenes del español.* 7th ed., Madrid: Espasa-Calpe, 1972.

Metzeltin, M. *Altspanisches Elementarbuch. I. Das Altkastilische.* Heidelberg: Winter, 1979.

Neuvonen, E.K. *Los arabismos del español en el siglo XIII.* Helsinki, 1941.

Oliver Asín, Jaime. *Iniciación al estudio de la historia de la lengua española.* 3rd ed., Zaragoza, 1939.

Pellegrini, G.B. *Grammatica storica spagnola.* Bari, 1950.

Pottier, Bernard. *Introduction à l'étude de la linguistique de l'espagnol.* 2nd ed., Bordeaux, 1978.

Rohlfs, Gerhard. *Manual de filología hispánica.* Bogotá, 1957.

Sala, M. *Le judéo-espagnol.* The Hague: Mouton, 1976.

Spaulding, R.K. *How Spanish Grew.* Berkeley-Los Angeles, 1948.

Zamora Vicente, A. *Dialectología española.* 2nd ed., Madrid: Gredos, 1967.

Zauner, A. *Altspanisches Elementarbuch.* 2nd ed., Heidelberg, 1921.

PORTUGUESE

Câmara, J. Mattoso. *The Portuguese Language.* Translated by A.J. Naro, Chicago: University of Chicago Press, 1972.

Cintra, L.F.L. *Estudos de dialectologia portuguesa.* Lisbon: Sá da Costa, 1983.

Cornu, J. «Die portugiesische Sprache», *Gröbers Grundriss,* I, 913-1037.

Couceiro Freijomil, A. *El idioma gallego. História, gramática, literatura.* Barcelona, 1935.

Cunha, C. and L.F.L. Cintra. *Nova gramática do português contemporâneo.* Lisbon: Sá da Costa, 1984.

García de Diego, Vicente. *Elementos de gramática histórica gallega.* Burgos, 1906.

Huber, J. *Altportugiesisches Elementarbuch.* Heidelberg, 1933.

Leite de Vasconcellos, J. *Esquisse d'une dialectologie portugaise.* Paris-Lisboa, 1901.

————. *Lições de filologia portuguesa.* Lisboa, 1946.

Maia, Clarinda de Azevedo. *História do Galego-Português. Estado linguístico da Galiza e do Noroeste de Portugal desde o século XIII ao século XVI.* Coimbra, 1986.

Michaëlis de Vasconcelos, C. *Lições de filologia portuguesa.* Rio de Janeiro, 1966.

Nunes, J.J. *Compêndio de gramática histórica portuguesa.* 3rd ed., Lisbon, 1945.

Paiva Boléo, M. de. *Introdução ao estudo da filología portuguesa.* Lisbon, 1946.

Silva Dias, A. Epiphania da. *Syntaxe histórica portuguesa.* 5th ed., Lisbon, 1970.

Silva Neto, Serafim da. *História da língua portuguesa.* Rio de Janeiro, 1952; 2nd ed., 1970.

————. *Manual de filologia portuguesa.* Rio de Janeiro, 1957.

Silveira Bueno, F. da. *A formação histórica da língua portuguesa.* Rio de Janeiro, 1955.

Sten, H. *Les particularités de la langue portugaise.* Copenhagen, 1944.

Teyssier, Paul. *História da língua portuguesa.* Lisbon: Sá da Costa, 1982.

————. *Manuel de langue portugaise (Portugal-Brésil).* 2nd ed., Paris: Klincksieck, 1984.

Vázquez Cuesta, P. and M. Luz. *Gramática portuguesa.* 3rd ed., Madrid: Gredos, 1971. Portuguese translation. *Gramática da língua portuguesa.* Lisbon: Edições 70, 1980.

Viana, A.R. Gonçalves. *Estudos de fonética portuguesa.* Lisbon: Imprensa Nacional, 1973.

Williams, E.B. *From Latin to Portuguese.* 2nd ed., Philadelphia: University of Pennsylvania Press, 1962.

CATALAN

Alarcos Llorach, E. *Estudis de lingüística catalana.* Barcelona: Ariel, 1983.

Badía i Margarit, Antoni M. *Gramática catalana.* 2 vols., Madrid: Gredos, 1962.

————. *Gramática histórica catalana.* Barcelona: Noguer, 1951.

Colon, Germà. *El léxico catalán en la Romania.* Madrid: Gredos, 1976.

Corominas, J. *El que s'ha de saber de la llengua catalana.* Palma de Mallorca, 1954.

Fabra, Pompeu. *Gramàtica catalana.* 4th ed., Barcelona: Teide, 1968.

Fouché, P. *Essai de grammaire historique de la langue catalane.* Perpignan, 1918.

————. *Phonétique historique du roussillonnais.* Toulouse: Privat, 1924.

Gili, J. *Introductory Catalan Grammar.* 2nd ed., New York, 1952.

Griera, A. *Atlas lingüístic de Catalunya (ALC).* Barcelona, 1923ff.

————. *Dialectología catalana.* Barcelona, 1949.

————. *Gramàtica històrica del català antic.* Barcelona, 1931.

Meyer-Lübke, W. *Das Katalanische.* Heidelberg: C. Winter, 1925.

Moll y Casasnovas, F. de B. *Gramática histórica catalana.* Madrid: Gredos, 1952.

Morel-Fatio, A. and J. Saroihandy. *Das Catalanische. Gröber's Grundriss*, I, 1904-1906, 841-877.

Nadal, Josep M. and Modest Prats. *Historia de la llengua catalana.* Barcelona, 1983.

Veny, Joan. *Els parlars catalans. (Síntesi de dialectologia).* Mallorca, 1982.

OCCITAN

Alibert, Loïs. *Gramatica occitana ségon los parlars lengadocians.* 2nd ed., Montpellier, 1976.

Anglade, J. *Grammaire de l'ancien provençal ou ancienne langue d'oc.* Paris: Klincksieck, 1921.

Appel, Carl. *Provenzalische Lautlehre.* Leipzig: Reisland, 1918.

Bec, Pierre. *La langue occitane.* 2nd ed., Paris: Presses Universitaires de France, 1967.

————. *Manuel pratique d'occitan moderne.* Paris: Picard, 1973.

Crescini, V. *Manuale per l'avviamento agli studi provenzali.* Milano: Ulrico Hoepli, 1926.

Grafström, Å. *Etude sur la graphie des plus anciennes chartes languedociennes avec un essai d'interprétation phonétique.* Uppsala: Almquist, 1958.

————. *Etude sur la morphologie des plus anciennes chartes languedociennes.* Stockholm: Almquist, 1968.

Grandgent, C.H. *An Outline of the Phonology and Morphology of Old Provençal.* Boston: Heath, 1905.

Hamlin, F.R., P.T. Ricketts and J. Hathaway. *Introduction à l'étude de l'ancien provençal.* Genève: Droz, 1967.

Jensen, F. *The Old Provençal Noun and Adjective Declension.* Odense: Odense University Press, 1976.

————. *Provençal Philology and the Poetry of Guillaume of Poitiers.* Odense: Odense University Press, 1983.

————. *The Syntax of Medieval Occitan.* Tübingen: Niemeyer, 1986.

Loos, Th. *Die Nominalflexion im Provenzalischen.* Marburg, 1884.

Pellegrini, G.B. *Appunti di grammatica storica del provenzale.* 3rd ed., Pisa, 1962.

Roncaglia, A. *La lingua dei trovatori.* Roma: Ateneo, 1965.

Ronjat, Jules. *Grammaire istorique des parlers provençaux modernes.* 4 vols., Montpellier: Société des Langues Romanes, 1930-1941.

Schultz-Gora, O. *Altprovenzalisches Elementarbuch.* Heidelberg: C. Winter, 1906.

Smith, Nathaniel B. and Thomas G. Bergin. *An Old Provençal Primer.* New York: Garland, 1984.

FRENCH

Bloch, O. *Grammaire de l'ancien français.* 4th ed., Leipzig, 1932.

Bourciez, E. and J. *Phonétique française. Etude historique.* Paris: Klincksieck, 1967.

Brunot, Ferdinand. *Histoire de la langue française des origines à 1900.* Paris 1905ff.

———— and Ch. Bruneau. *Précis de grammaire historique de la langue française.* Paris: Masson, 1969.

Dauzat, A. *La toponymie française.* Paris, 1946.

Ewert, A. *The French Language.* 2nd ed., London, 1943.

Fouché, Pierre. *Morphologie historique du français. Le verbe.* 2nd ed., Paris: Klincksieck, 1967.

————. *Phonétique historique du français.* Paris, 1952.

Foulet, Lucien. *Petite syntaxe de l'ancien français.* 3rd ed., Paris: Champion, 1968.

Gamillscheg, E. *Historische französische Syntax.* Tübingen: Niemeyer, 1957.

Gilliéron, J. and E. Edmont. *Atlas linguistique de la France (ALF).* 1902-1910.

Gossen, C.-Th. *Grammaire de l'ancien picard.* Paris: Klincksieck, 1970.

Grevisse, M. *Le bon usage.* 4th ed., Paris-Gembloux: Duculot, 1949.

Ineichen, Gustav. *Kleine altfranzösische Grammatik. Laut- und Formenlehre.* Berlin, 1968. 2nd ed., Berlin, 1985.

Jensen, F. *Old French and Comparative Gallo-Romance Syntax.* Tübingen: Niemeyer, 1990.

Jordan, Leo. *Altfranzösisches Elementarbuch.* Bielefeld-Leipzig, 1923.

Meyer-Lübke, W. *Historische Grammatik der französischen Sprache.* Heidelberg, 1934.

Moignet, Gérard. *Grammaire de l'ancien français.* Paris: Klincksieck, 1976.

Nègre, E. *Les noms de lieux en France.* Paris, 1963.

Nyrop, Kr. *Grammaire historique de la langue française.* 6 vols., Copenhagen: Gyldendal, 1930.

Plattner, Ph. *Ausführliche Grammatik der französischen Sprache.* 5 vols., Karlsruhe-Freiburg, 1899-1908.

Pope, M.K. *From Latin to Modern French with Especial Consideration of Anglo-Norman. Phonology and Morphology.* Manchester: Manchester University Press, 1934; 2nd ed., 1952.

Raynaud de Lage, Guy. *Introduction à l'ancien français.* Edited by G. Hasenohr, Paris: Sedes, 1990.

Regula, M. *Précis de grammaire française sur une base historique et psychologique.* Reichenberg, 1936.

Rheinfelder, Hans. *Altfranzösische Grammatik.* 2 vols., München: Max Hüber Verlag, 1963, 1967.

Richter, Elise. *Beiträge zur Geschichte der Romanismen. I: Chronologische Phonetik des Französischen bis zum Ende des 8. Jahrhunderts.* Halle-Saale, 1934.

Rohlfs, Gerhard. *Vom Vulgärlatein zum Altfranzösischen.* Tübingen: Niemeyer, 1960.

Sandfeld, Kr. *Syntaxe du français contemporain.* 3 vols., Paris: Droz, 1936-1943.

Schwan, E. and D. Behrens. *Grammatik des Altfranzösischen.* 2nd ed., Leipzig, 1925; reprinted 1963.

Sneyders de Vogel, K. *Syntaxe historique du français.* 2nd ed., Groningue, 1927.

Suchier, Hermann, «Die französische und provenzalische Sprache und ihre Mundarten». *Gröbers Grundriss,* I, 712-840.

Tobler, Adolf. *Vermischte Beiträge zur französischen Grammatik.* 5 vols., Leipzig: Hirzel, 1906-1921.

Togeby, K. *Précis historique de grammaire française.* Copenhagen: Akademisk Forlag, 1974.

Voretzsch, C. *Einführung in das Studium der altfranzösischen Sprache.* 8th ed. revised by G. Rohlfs, Halle, 1955.

Wartburg, W. von. *Evolution et structure de la langue française.* 8th ed., Berne: Francke, 1967.

RHAETO-ROMANCE

Ascoli, G.I. *Saggi ladini.* Roma-Firenze-Torino: Loescher, 1873.

Francescato, G. *Dialettologia friulana.* Udine: Società Filologica Friulana, 1966.

Gamillscheg, E. «Zur Entstehungsgeschichte des Alpenromanisches». *RF,* 61 (1948), 267-299.

Gartner, Th. *Handbuch der rätoromanischen Sprache und Literatur.* Halle: Niemeyer, 1910.

———. *Rätoromanische Grammatik.* Heilbronn: Henniger, 1883.

Gauchat, L. and J. Jeanjaquet. *Bibliographie linguistique de la Suisse Romande*. Neuchâtel, 1912, 1920.

Iliescu, M. *Le friulan*. The Hague: Mouton, 1972.

Nay, S. *Lehrbuch der rätoromanischen Sprache*. 3rd ed., Disentis: Lia Rumantscha, 1965.

Rohlfs, Gerhard. *Rätoromanisch*. München: Beck, 1975.

Schürr, R. «Die Alpenromanen». *Vox Rom., 20* (1963), 100-126.

SARDINIAN

Blasco-Ferrer, E. *La lingua sarda contemporanea*. Cagliari: Edizioni della Torre, 1986.

———. *Storia linguistica della Sardegna*. Tübingen: Niemeyer, 1984.

Campus, G. *Fonetica del dialetto logudorese*. Torino, 1901.

Hoffmann, G. *Die logudoresische und campidanesische Mundart*. Marburg, 1885.

Hubschmid, J. *Sardische Studien*. Berne, 1951.

Sanna, A. *Introduzione agli studi di linguistica sarda*. Cagliari, 1957.

Wagner, M.L. *Das ländliche Leben Sardiniens im Spiegel der Sprache*. Heidelberg, 1921.

———. «Die festländisch-italienischen sprachlichen Einflüsse in Sardinien». *AR, 16* (1932), 135-148.

———. «Flessione nominale e verbale del sardo antico e moderno». *ID, 14* (1938), 93-170 and *15* (1939), 1-110.

———. *Historische Lautlehre des Sardischen*. Halle: Niemeyer, 1941. Italian translation. Cagliari, 1984.

———. *Historische Wortbildungslehre des Sardischen*. Berne, 1952.

———. *La lingua sarda. Storia, spirito e forma*. Berne: Francke, 1951.

ETYMOLOGY, SEMANTICS, GENERAL WORKS

Bachmann, Armin. *Zur psychologischen Theorie des sprachlichen Bedeutungswandels*. München, 1935.

Baldinger, Kurt. «L'étymologie hier et aujourd'hui». *Cahiers de l'Association internationale des Etudes françaises*, 11 (1959), 233-264.

———. *Die Semasiologie. Versuch eines Überblicks*. Berlin, 1957.

Bechtoldt, Heinrich. «Der französische Wortschatz im Sinnbezirk des Verstandes». *RF, 49* (1935), 21-180.

Benveniste, Emile. «Problèmes sémantiques de la reconstruction». *Word, 10* (1954), 251-264.

Bertoldi, V. *L'arte dell' etimologia*. Napoli, 1952.

Bréal, M. *Essai de sémantique. Science des significations.* 5th ed., Paris, 1921.

Brunot, F. *La pensée et la langue.* 3rd ed., Paris, 1936.

Carnap, R. *Introduction to Semantics.* Cambridge, Mass., 1942.

Carnoy, A. *La science du mot. Traité de sémantique.* Louvain, 1927.

Casares, J. *Introducción a la lexicografía moderna.* Madrid, 1950.

Coseriu, E. *La creación metafórica en el lenguaje.* Montevideo, 1956.

Darmesteter, A. *La vie des mots étudiée dans leurs significations.* Paris, 1887.

Deroy, L. *L'emprunt linguistique.* Paris, 1956.

Gamillscheg, E. *Französische Bedeutungslehre.* Tübingen: Max Niemeyer Verlag, 1951.

Guiraud, P. *La sémantique.* Paris, 1955.

———. *L'étymologie.* Paris, 1964.

Hatzfeld, Helmut. *Leitfaden der vergleichenden Bedeutungslehre.* 2nd ed., München, 1928.

Huguet, E. *L'évolution du sens des mots depuis le XVIe siècle.* Paris, 1934.

———. *Mots disparus ou vieillis depuis le XVIe siècle.* Paris, 1935.

Jaberg, K. «Pejorative Bedeutungsentwicklung im Französischen». *ZRPh,* 25 (1901), 561-601; 27 (1903), 25-71; 29 (1905), 57-71.

Kronasser, H. *Handbuch der Semasiologie.* Heidelberg, 1952.

Malkiel, Yakov. *Etymology.* Cambridge University Press, 1993.

———. «Etymology and the Structure of Word Families». *Word, 10* (1954), 265-274.

Meier, H. «Zur Geschichte der romanischen Etymologie». *ASNS, 201* (1964), 81-109.

Meyer-Lübke, W. «Aufgaben der Wortforschung». *Germanisch-romanische Monatsschrift, 1,* 634-647.

Nyrop, Kr. *Grammaire historique de la langue française.* Vol. 4: *Sémantique.* Copenhagen, 1913.

Ogden, C.K. and I.A. Richards. *The Meaning of Meaning.* 4th ed., London, 1936.

Öhman, S. *Wortinhalt und Weltbild. Vergleichende und methodologische Studien zu Bedeutungslehre und Wortfeldtheorie.* Stockholm, 1951.

Pfister, Max. *Einführung in die romanische Etymologie.* Darmstadt, 1980.

Pisani, V. *Die Etymologie. Geschichte—Fragen—Methode.* München: Fink, 1975.

———. *L'etimologia.* 2nd ed., Brescia, 1967.

Sainéan, L. *Les sources indigènes de l'étymologie française.* Paris, 1925-1930

330   *A Comparative Study of Romance*

Schuchardt, H. «Zur Methodik der Wortgeschichte». *ZRPh, 27* (1903), 609-615; *28* (1904), 316-325.
Sperber, H. *Einführung in die Bedeutungslehre.* 2nd ed., Leipzig, 1930.
Thomas, Antoine. *Essais de philologie française. La sémantique et les lois intellectuelles du langage.* Paris, 1897.
Ullmann, Stephen. *Précis de sémantique française.* 2nd ed., Berne, 1959.
———. *Semantics. An Introduction to the Science of Meaning.* New York, 1962.
———. *The Principles of Semantics.* Oxford: Basil Blackwell, 1957. German translation. *Grundzüge der Semantik.* Berlin: Walter de Gruyter, 1967.
Wagner, M.L. «Betrachtungen über die Methodenfragen der Etymologie». *CN, 3,* 5-26.
Weinrich, U. *Languages in Contact. Findings and Problems.* New York, 1953.

ETYMOLOGICAL AND MEDIEVAL DICTIONARIES
Atzori, M.T. *Glossario di sardo antico.* Modena: *STEM*-Mucchi, 1975.
Battisti, C. and G. Alessio. *Dizionario etimologico italiano.* 5 vols., Firenze, 1950-1957.
Candrea, I.A. and O. Densusianu. *Dicţionarul etimologic al limbii române. I. Elementele latine.* Bucureşti, 1907-1914.
Cioranescu, A. *Diccionario etimológico rumano.* La Laguna, 1966.
Corominas, J. *Breve diccionario etimológico de la lengua castellana.* 1 vol., Madrid: Gredos, 1961.
———. *Diccionario crítico-etimológico de la lengua castellana.* 4 vols., Berne: Francke and Madrid: Gredos, 1954-1957.
———. *Diccionari etimologìc i complementari de la llengua catalana.* Barcelona: Curial/La Caixa, 1980ff.
——— and J.A. Pascual. *Diccionario crítico etimológico castellano e hispánico.* 6 vols., Madrid: Gredos, 1980-1986.
Dauzat, Albert. *Dictionnaire étymologique de la langue française.* Paris, 1938; 2nd ed., 1943.
———, J. Dubois and M. Mitterand. *Nouveau dictionnaire étymologique et historique.* Paris, 1964.
Devoto, G. *Avviamento alla etimologia italiana.* Firenze: Le Monnier, 1967.
Ernout, A. and A. Meillet. *Dictionnaire étymologique de la langue latine.* 4th ed., Paris, 1959.

Gamillscheg, E. *Etymologisches Wörterbuch der französischen Sprache*. Heidelberg, 1928.

García de Diego, Vicente. *Diccionario etimológico español e hispánico*. Madrid, 1955.

Godefroy, F. *Dictionnaire de l'ancienne langue française et de tous ses dialectes*. 10 vols., Paris, 1881-1902.

Greimas, A.J. *Dictionnaire de l'ancien français jusqu'au milieu du XVIe siècle*. Paris: Larousse, 1969.

Klein, E. *A Comprehensive Etymological Dictionary of the English Language*. Amsterdam-London-New York: Elsevier, 1966.

Levy, Emil. *Petit dictionnaire provençal-français.*Heidelberg: C. Winter, 1966.

————. *Provenzalisches Supplement-Wörterbuch*. 8 vols., Leipzig: Reisland, 1894-1924; 2nd ed., Hildesheim-New York, 1973.

Machado, J.P. *Dicionário etimológico da língua portuguesa*. 2 vols., Lisbon, 1953-1959; 2nd ed., Lisbon, 1967.

Meyer-Lübke, W. *Romanisches etymologisches Wörterbuch*. 3rd ed., Heidelberg: C. Winter, 1935.

Migliorini, B. and A. Duro. *Prontuario etimologico italiano*. Torino, 1950.

Nascentes, Antenor. *Dicionário etimológico da língua portuguêsa*. Rio de Janeiro, 1932.

Piel, J.M. *Miscelânea de etimologia portuguesa e galega*. Coimbra, 1953.

Prati, A. *Vocabolario etimologico italiano*. Milano, 1951.

Puşcariu, Sextil. *Etymologisches Wörterbuch der rumänischen Sprache. I. Lateinisches Element*. Heidelberg, 1905.

Raynouard, J.-F. *Lexique roman*. 6 vols., Paris, 1836-1844; 2nd ed., Heidelberg: C. Winter, 1927-1929.

Skeat, Walter W. *A Concise Etymological Dictionary of the English Language*. New York, 1980.

Tobler, A. and E. Lommatzsch. *Altfranzösisches Wörterbuch*. Berlin: Weidmann, 1915ff.

Wagner, M.L. *Dizionario etimologico sardo*. Heidelberg: Winter, 1960-1964.

Walde, A. and J.B. Hofmann. *Lateinisches etymologisches Wörterbuch*. 3rd ed., Heidelberg, 1938-1954.

Wartburg, W. von. *Französisches etymologisches Wörterbuch*. Bonn-Leipzig-Berlin-Basel, 1928ff.

———— and Otto Bloch. *Dictionnaire étymologique de la langue française*. 6th ed., Paris: Presses Universitaires de France, 1975.

Weekley, Ernest. *An Etymological Dictionary of Modern English.* New York: Dover, 1967.

WORD INDEX

avispa 84
avunculu 87
axe 311
axilla 311

baca 274
badiu 319, 320
balancia, *see bilancia*
balneare 324
balneu 48, 223, 324, 369
balsamu 215
baneare, *see balneare*
baneu, *see balneu*
barba 280
barbati 267
barbatu 188, 267
basiare 195, 322
basiat 322
basiu 166, 322
bassiare 323
bassu 323
battualia 220
battuere 140
battuo 140, 213, 220
bella 37, 342
bellatiore 316
bellos 175, 199, 336
bellum (noun) 342
bene 153, 178, 179, 180, 187,
    206, 223, 368
beneficiu 328
berbicarius 110
berbice 110
Bergomu 214
bestia 169, 318
bestiu 169
bestula 169
bibere 172, 292
bibit 363
bibliotheca 48

bilancia 191, 328
-bile 42, 214
bis 225
bistia, *see bestia*
blandu 247
blasphemare 126, 247, 304
blastimare 247
blatta 247
bona 180, 187, 270, 272
Bonifatiu 120
bonitate 206, 219
Bononia 217
bonu 153, 178, 180, 223, 272,
    368
bovariu 110
bove 46, 110, 150, 363
Bracala 217
bracas 49, 274
bracchia 328
bracchios 209
bracchiu 48, 209, 233, 244,
    328
brebis 264
breve 145, 172, 331, 363
bubalu 46, 265
bubulcu 265
bucca 37, 131, 150
bufalu, *see bubalu*
bullire 87
burgense 281
burgu 365
Burgundia 321
butticula 299

caballa 88
caballariu 174, 342
caballi 342
caballos 175
caballu 28, 152, 196, 207, 235,
    263, 342, 367, 369

cadere 266, 293, 297
cadit 266, 364
caeca 154, 274
caecas 154
caecos 154
caecu 105, 154, 365
caelos 175
caelu 148, 160, 172, 252, 270,
    367
calamellu 219
calce 175, 282
calcea 328
calceare 328
calceus 138
calcius 138
calda, *see calida*
caldaria 327
caldu, *see calidu*
calente 152, 190
calere 152
calice 282
calida 36, 152
calidu 213, 282, 364
callare 297
calore 268, 270
calorosu 268
calumniare 325
calvas sorices 37
calvu 282
camara 286
camba 125, 236
cambiare 331
cambiat 179
camera 48, 179, 214, 215, 235,
    286, 348
Cameracu 235, 365
camerata 198
caminu 49
camisia 49, 188, 322
camminu 49

campania 324
campsare 347
campu 178, 180, 283, 362, 363
cane 100, 171
canes 206
canonicu 324
cantai 210
cantando 364
cantant 353, 360
cantare 198, 283
cantas 209, 211, 212, 356, 357
cantat 179, 208, 359
cantatis 371
cantatore 219
cantatu 364
cantavi 166, 210
cantavit 155
cantione 317
canto 207, 364
canutu 187, 237
capere 141
capiam 330
capiat 330
capillos 175, 196
capillu 262, 270
capit 206
capitale 219, 306, 351
capitellu 306
capitiale 317
capitulu 300, 342
capra 100, 171, 235, 260, 289
caprae 357
capsa 166, 307
capsu 166
captivu 306
capu 171, 235, 262, 359, 362,
    363
caput 144, 171, 306, 359
cara (noun) 154, 269
carbonariu 219

carbone 188, 196
carcere 214, 217, 346
carne 177, 206, 261, 368
carnes 368
caro 41
caronia 41
caronis 41
carricare 100
carricatus 351
carru 49, 343, 367
carruca 49, 116, 274
caru 171
casa 87, 268
casas 209
caseu 322
Casparu 217
Cassia 323
castellanu 342
castellos 175
castellu 164, 173, 304, 369
castigare 277, 304
castigat 277
casu 367
catella 342
catena 160, 257
cathedra 135, 137, 293
Catiliacum 49
cattu 84, 235, 236
cauda 130, 155
causa 28, 155, 235, 261, 268
cavea 331
cella 342
cellariu 233
cena 233
censor 285
centu 160, 234
cepa 171
cera 149, 171, 252, 328
cerebellu 219
ceresea 233, 322

cereu 161, 327
cerevisia 49
certu 364
cervu 234, 363
cesor 285
christianu 250, 318
Christophoru 265
chronica 214
ciccu 234
cicer 234, 361
ciconia 275
cicuta 275
cilia 168
ciliu 168
cimice 234
cincta 167
cinere 171, 179, 269, 348
cingula 167, 194
cinquaginta 252
cinque, *see quinque*
circare 185, 260
citera 143
cithara 143, 217
civiles 206
civitate 264, 308, 351, 362
clamare 249, 271
clamat 249
claru 249, 367
Claudia 319
clausi 146
clausu 146
clave 249, 363
clavicula 260
clavu 363
clericu 365
Clodius 155
Cnaeus 47
coagulare 301
coagulat 253
cocens 333

porcellos 175
porcos 148, 151, 158, 207, 347
porcu 145, 148, 151, 158, 159,
 207, 365
porcu pisce 305
porta 87, 133, 135, 145, 151,
 281
portae 357
portare 187
porticu 209
Portu Cale 219
positu 213
posse 41
post 357
postu 213
posui 161, 205
potentia 317
potere 41, 189
potestate 257, 267
potione 195
potui 161, 162, 205
praebiter 172
praeceptu 306
praeda 145, 154, 172
praemiu 332
prandiu 321
prata 267
pratu 244, 267, 364
precare 246, 274
preco 172
prehendere 182
prehendo 364
prehenserunt 348
prehensione 193, 322
prehensit 206
prehensu 285, 367
prendere 182
prendo 364
prensa 154
prensu, *see presu*

presa, *see prensa*
presbyter 172
presione 193
presit 206
presu 285, 367
pretiare 316
pretiat 316
pretiu 148, 316, 370
primariu 327
primu tempus 184, 198
probare 263
profectu 163, 164, 265, 309
profundu 265
Provincia 264
proximu 311
psalmu 259
psalteriu 259
ptisana 259
publicu 365
pugnare 313
pugnos 371
pugnu 167, 313
pulcra 37
pulegiu 329
pulice 216, 236, 270, 282, 351
pullu 342
pulvere 124
punctu 167
punere 178
purgare 186
Puteoli 138
puteu 316, 319

quacola 299
quadernu 267
quadragesima 253, 293
quadraginta 293
quadratu 293
quadru 293
quaerere 252

zel 256

louer 99, 189, 274
louve 181, 296
luitier 165
lundi 198
lune 208, 232
lunsdi 156, 198
lutter 165
Lyon 49

mai 279, 366
main 224
maiour 279
maissele 311
maistre, *see maître*
maître 275
majeur 279
mal 367
mâle 302, 304
malheur 192
manatce 37
manger 126
mari 136
mars 317
marteau 124
marz, *see mars*
masle, *see mâle*
massue 317
Mathieu 210
maturité 105
maussade 306
mauvais 120, 265
me 372
méchant 120
medesme 247
meie 156
meis, *see mois*
meisson, *see moisson*
mêler 302
membrer 219
menace 37

mener 185
menu 185
menuise 316
menut 185
mer 100, 145, 146, 152, 170
mercresdi 156
mère 372
mescheant, *see méchant*
mesle 173
mesler, *see mêler*
meule 270
mëur, *see mûr*
meüreté 105
meurt 102
miel 148, 157, 371
mieldre 209
mien 354
miracle 299
mirent 104, 139
misdrent 104, 139, 348
mistrent 104, 139
moi 372
moie 156
moillier 138
moins 179
mois 285
moisson 323
moldre, *see moudre*
molt, *see mout*
mon 354
mont (< monte) 179
mont (= molt) 224
montagne 179, 198, 324
Montaigne 179
Montmartre 350
moraliser 319
mordre 350
mort 187
mortel 187
mosteile 126

mot (= molt) 224
mouche à miel 83
mouche-ep 84
mouchette 83
moudre 84, 348
mourir 102
mout 165, 224, 282
mouvoir 187, 189
moveir, *see mouvoir*
muele 270
muer 186, 190
mui 319
muid 319
mur 149, 354
mûr 105, 136, 188, 190

nafrer 108
nag(i)er 100, 192
naistre, *see naître*
naître 305, 346
Nantes 49
nation 106
naviger 192
naviguer 192
navré 108
navrer 108
ne 124, 355, 372
né 364
nèfle 173
negiee 147
negier, *see neiger*
neient 276
neif, *see noif*
neige 147
neiger 147
neiier, *see noiier*
neir, *see noir*
neis 147
nes (< nasu) 367
nes (< naves) 347

nesple 173
net (< natu) 364
net (< nitidu) 42
nettoyer 42
neuf 151
neuve 264
neveu 185
nevout 185
nez 367
ni 229
nid 229, 364
nièce 185, 317
nier 277
nit 229
niveau 260
nivel 260
Noël 192
noer (< nodare) 192
noer (< notare) 192
noeud 364
noif 147, 363
noiier (< negare) 277
noir 294
nom 355, 368
non 355, 372
nonque 337
norreture 219
nouer 192
nourriture 219
nous 356
nouvel 187
novel, *see nouvel*
noyer (< necare) 127, 274
nu 229, 364
nue 263
nuef 151
nueve 264
nuit 98, 162, 309
nus 282
nut 229, 364

vendeuse 371
venir 185
Venise 316
vent (< vendit) 328
vent (< ventu) 179
veoir, *see voir*
ver 368
verdoyer 42, 319
verg(i)er 174, 320
vergogne 321
verm 368
vers (< vermes) 368
vers (< versus) 281
vert 42, 147, 364
vertu 185
veuve 181, 340
veve, *see veuve*
viande 127, 190, 264
viaz 264
vicaire 84
vidhe 146, 267, 352
vie 146, 261, 267, 352
vieil 218, 300, 372
vieux 372
vigne 287, 324
villain 184
Villeneuve-les-Avignon 152
vin 145, 179, 180, 225
vingt 110, 205
vint, *see vingt*
virent 104
vivace 264
voeu 223
voie 156
voir 190, 266
voisin 192, 273
voiz 169, 366
voler 270

zèle 256

ARABIC
al-amir 53
al-banni 53
alhómbra 53
al-ka-di 53
al-kasr 53
al-máhzan 53
faqih 118
gabal-tarig 53
kasr 53
madina 53
rehén 53
sokkar 217
wadi-al-kabir 53

BASQUE
bake 233
-err 193
esku 193
ezkerr 50, 193
i-bai 50
márgin 237

ENGLISH
apostle 218, 300
aunt 260
blame 304
bush 313
castle 304
caught 306
chair 293
cold 152
court 182
feast 304
fold 225
guard 254
hundredfold 225
isle 304
level 260
male 304